FAIRY TAIL

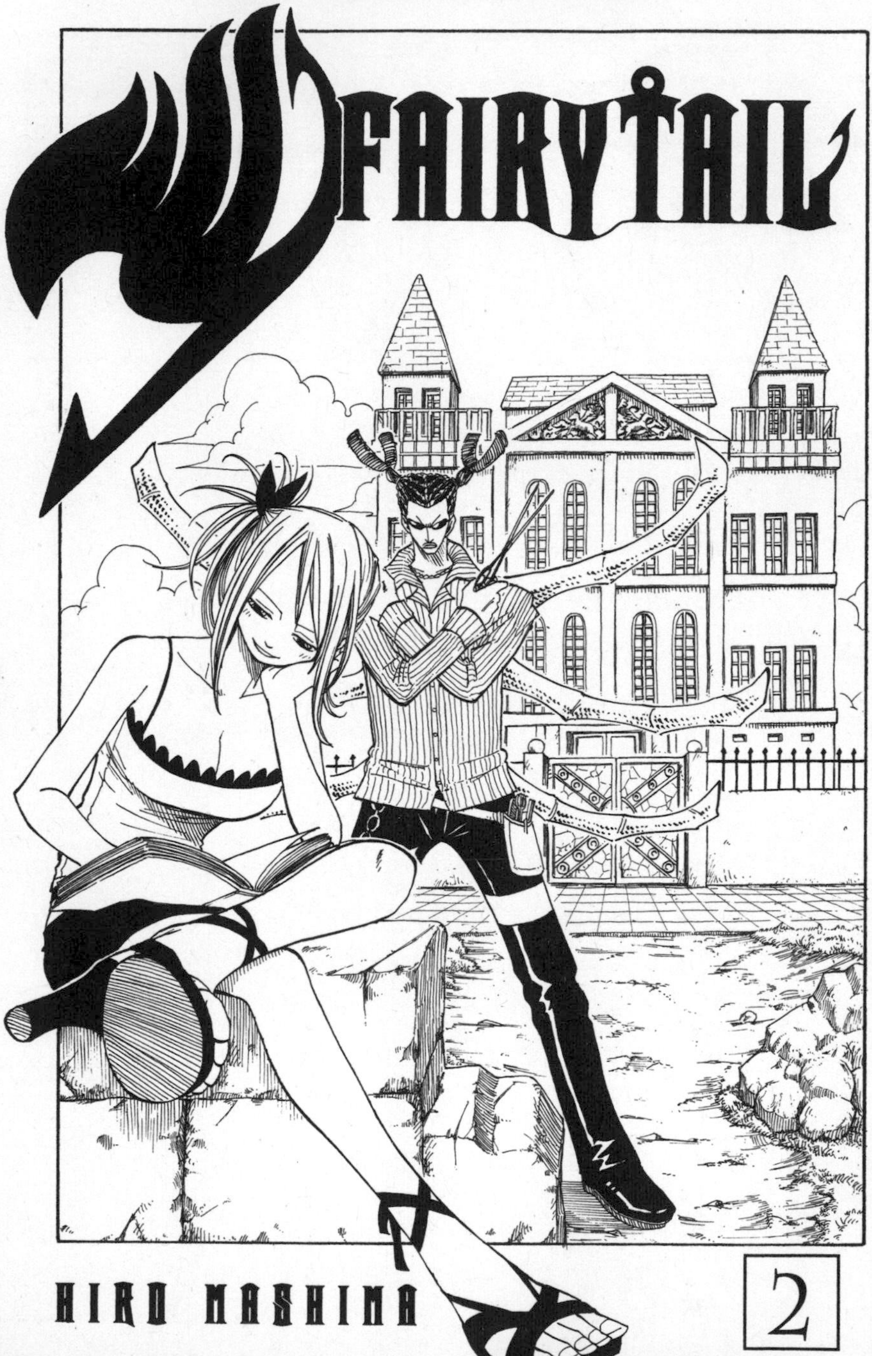

2

HIRO MASHIMA

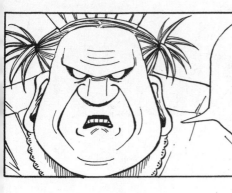

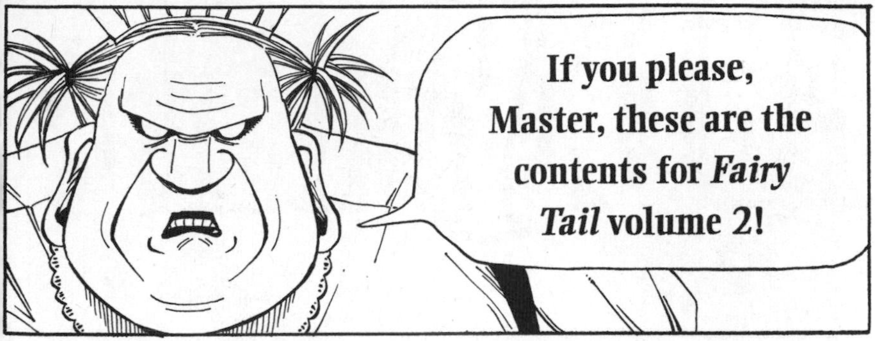

If you please, Master, these are the contents for *Fairy Tail* volume 2!

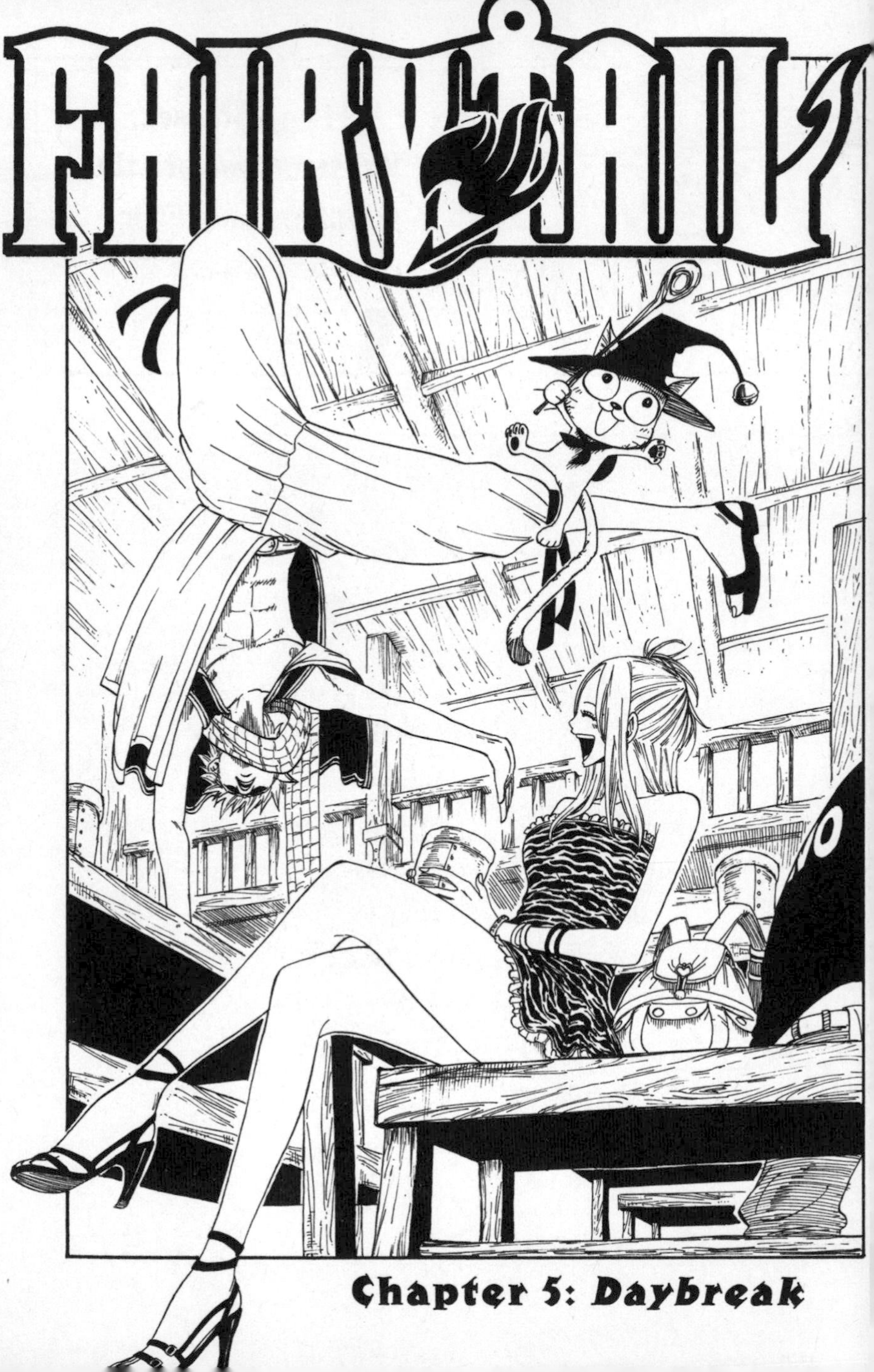
FAIRY TAIL

Chapter 5: *Daybreak*

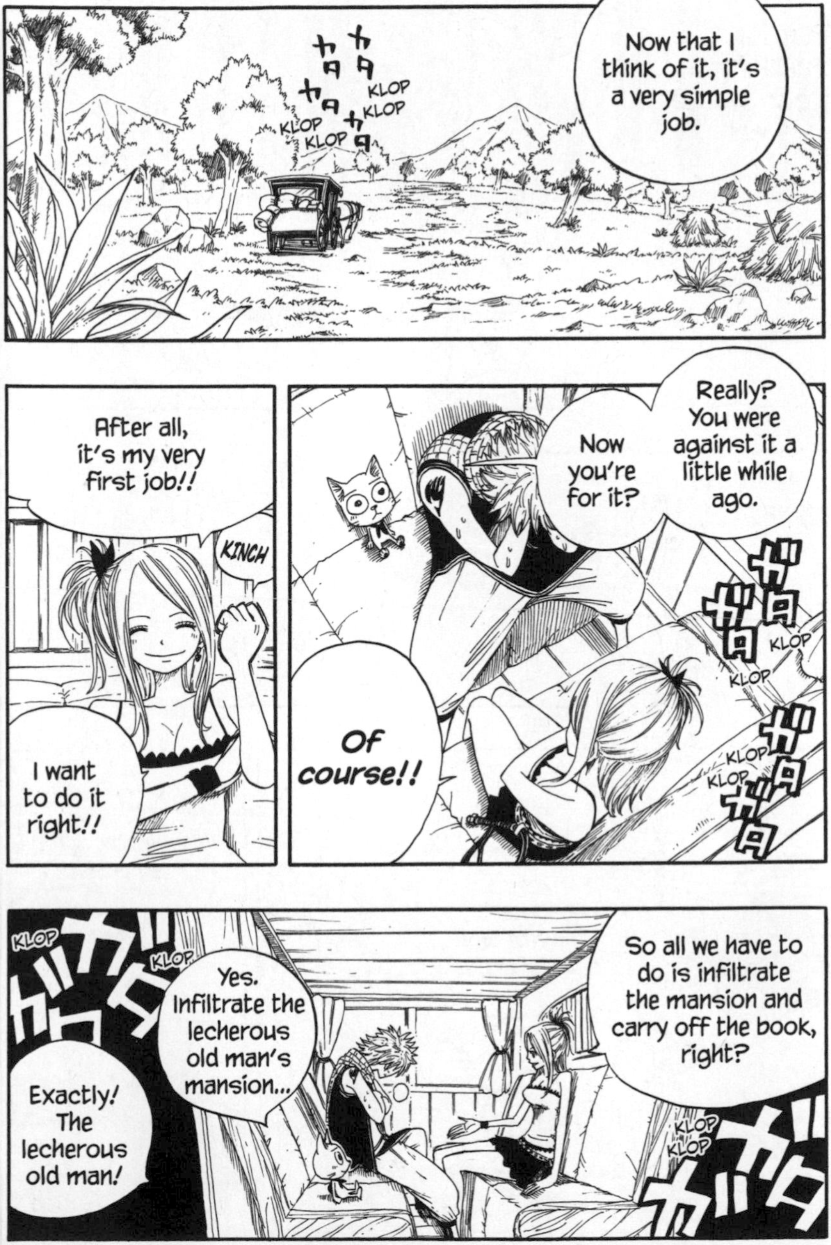
Now that I think of it, it's a very simple job.
KLOP KLOP
KLOP KLOP
Really? You were against it a little while ago.
Now you're for it?
KLOP
KLOP
KLOP
KLOP
Of course!!
After all, it's my very first job!!
KINCH
I want to do it right!!
So all we have to do is infiltrate the mansion and carry off the book, right?
KLOP KLOP
Yes. Infiltrate the lecherous old man's mansion...
KLOP
KLOP
Exactly! The lecherous old man!

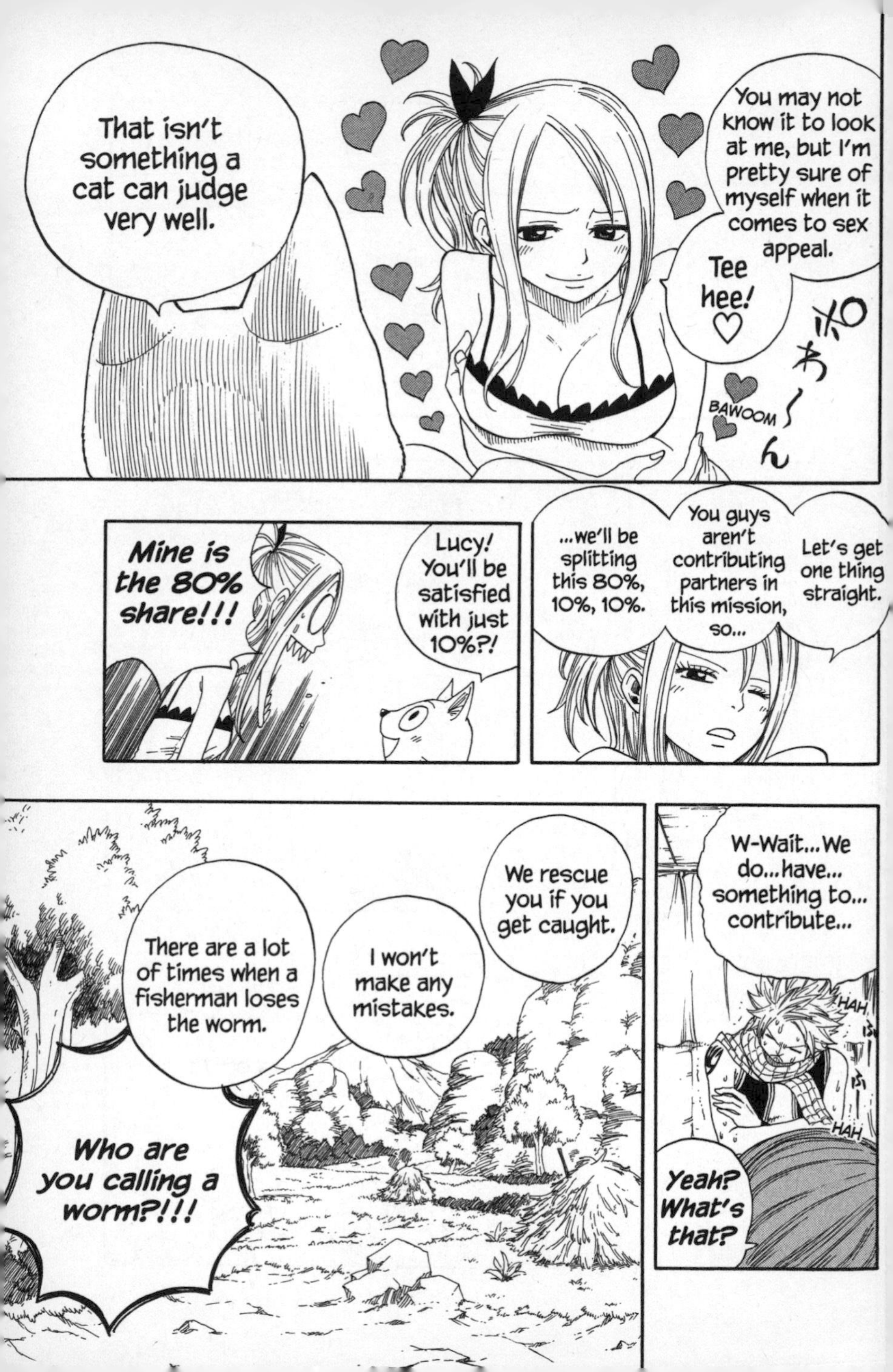
You may not know it to look at me, but I'm pretty sure of myself when it comes to sex appeal.
Tee hee! ♡
BAWOOM
That isn't something a cat can judge very well.
Let's get one thing straight.
You guys aren't contributing partners in this mission, so...
...we'll be splitting this 80%, 10%, 10%.
Lucy! You'll be satisfied with just 10%?!
Mine is the 80% share!!!
W-Wait...We do...have... something to... contribute...
HAH
HAH
Yeah? What's that?
We rescue you if you get caught.
I won't make any mistakes.
There are a lot of times when a fisherman loses the worm.
Who are you calling a worm?!!!

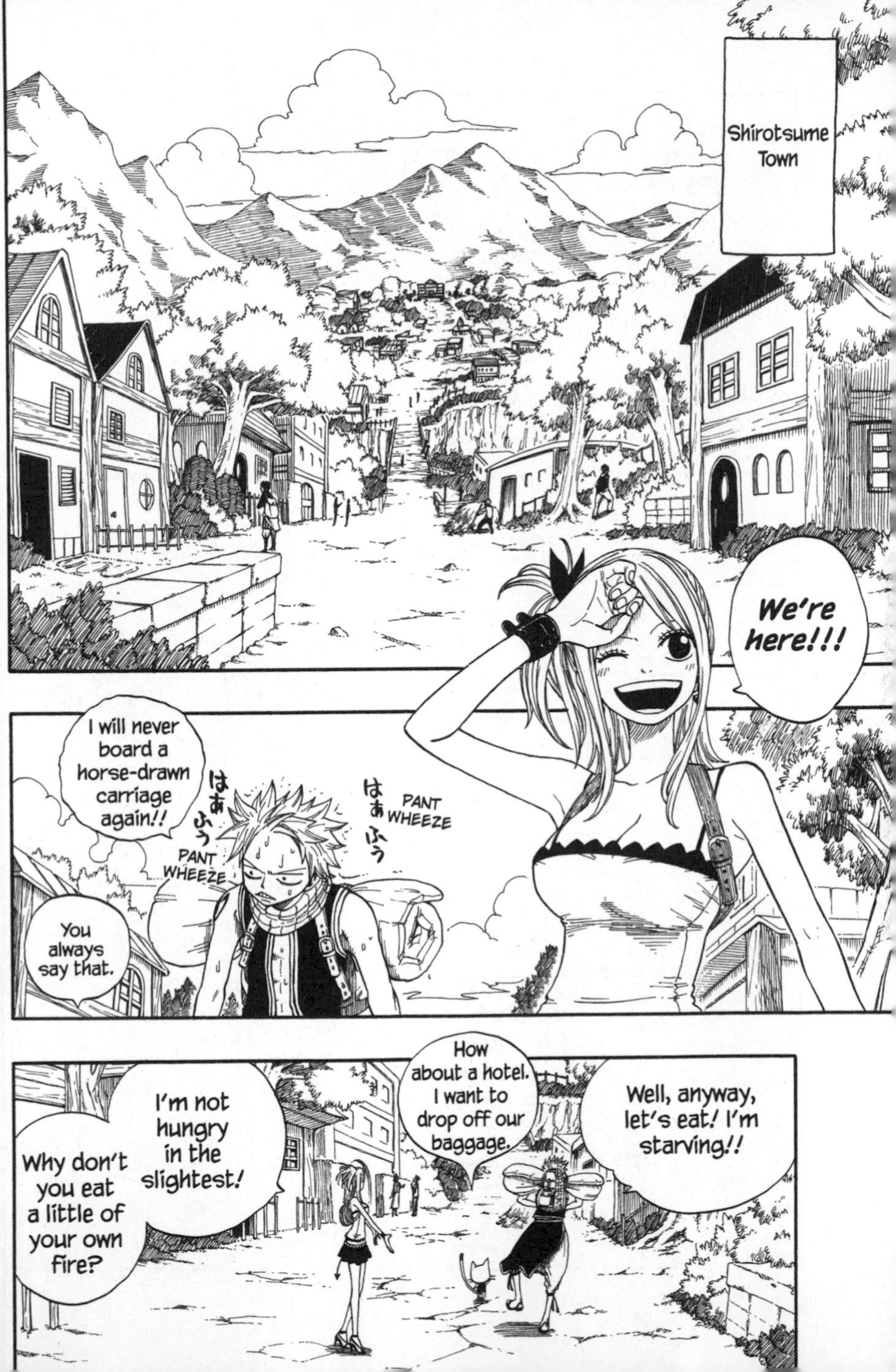

Shirotsume Town
We're here!!!
はあ ふう PANT WHEEZE
I will never board a horse-drawn carriage again!!
はあ ふう PANT WHEEZE
You always say that.
Well, anyway, let's eat! I'm starving!!
How about a hotel. I want to drop off our baggage.
I'm not hungry in the slightest!
Why don't you eat a little of your own fire?

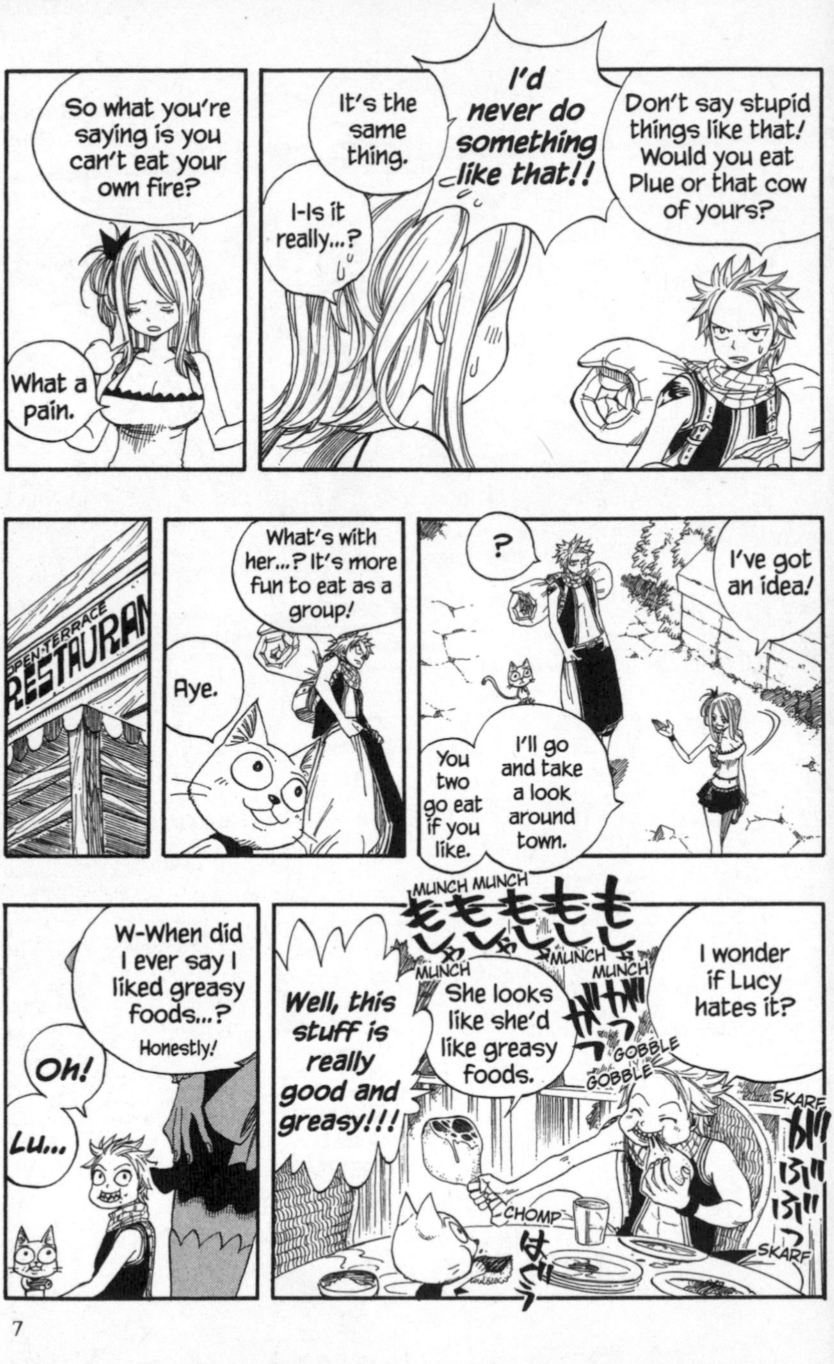
Don't say stupid things like that! Would you eat Plue or that cow of yours?
I'd never do something like that!!
It's the same thing.
I-Is it really...?
So what you're saying is you can't eat your own fire?
What a pain.
I've got an idea!
?
I'll go and take a look around town.
You two go eat if you like.
What's with her...? It's more fun to eat as a group!
Aye.
OPEN-TERRACE
RESTAURAN
I wonder if Lucy hates it?
MUNCH MUNCH
MUNCH
MUNCH
MUNCH
She looks like she'd like greasy foods.
Well, this stuff is really good and greasy!!!
GOBBLE
GOBBLE
SKARF
SKARF
CHOMP
W-When did I ever say I liked greasy foods...?
Honestly!
Oh!
Lu...

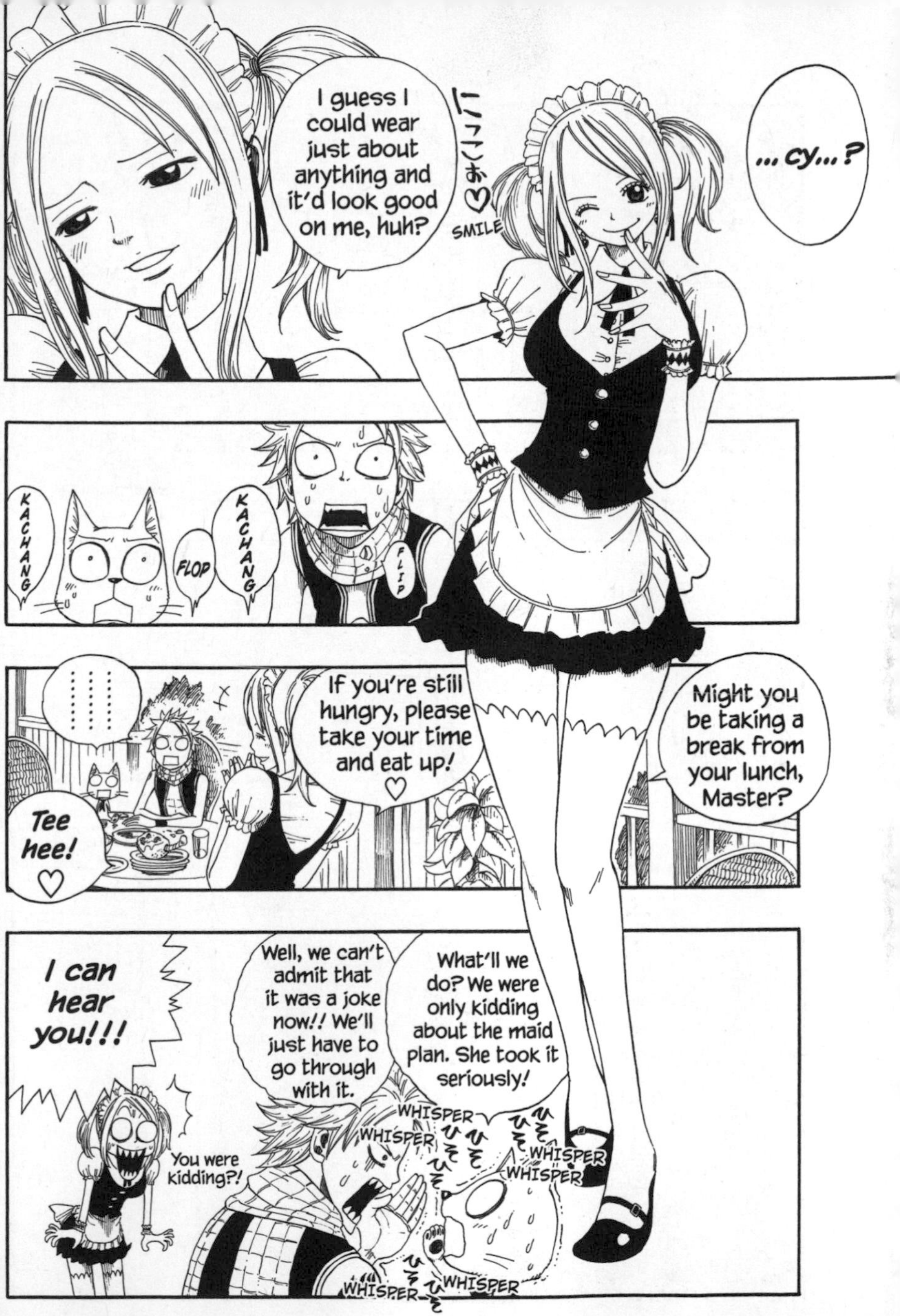

...cy...?
I guess I could wear just about anything and it'd look good on me, huh?
にっこぉ♡
SMILE
FLIP
KACHANG
FLOP
KACHANG
Might you be taking a break from your lunch, Master?
If you're still hungry, please take your time and eat up! ♡
......
Tee hee! ♡
What'll we do? We were only kidding about the maid plan. She took it seriously!
Well, we can't admit that it was a joke now!! We'll just have to go through with it.
WHISPER
WHISPER
WHISPER
WHISPER
WHISPER
WHISPER
I can hear you!!!
You were kidding?!

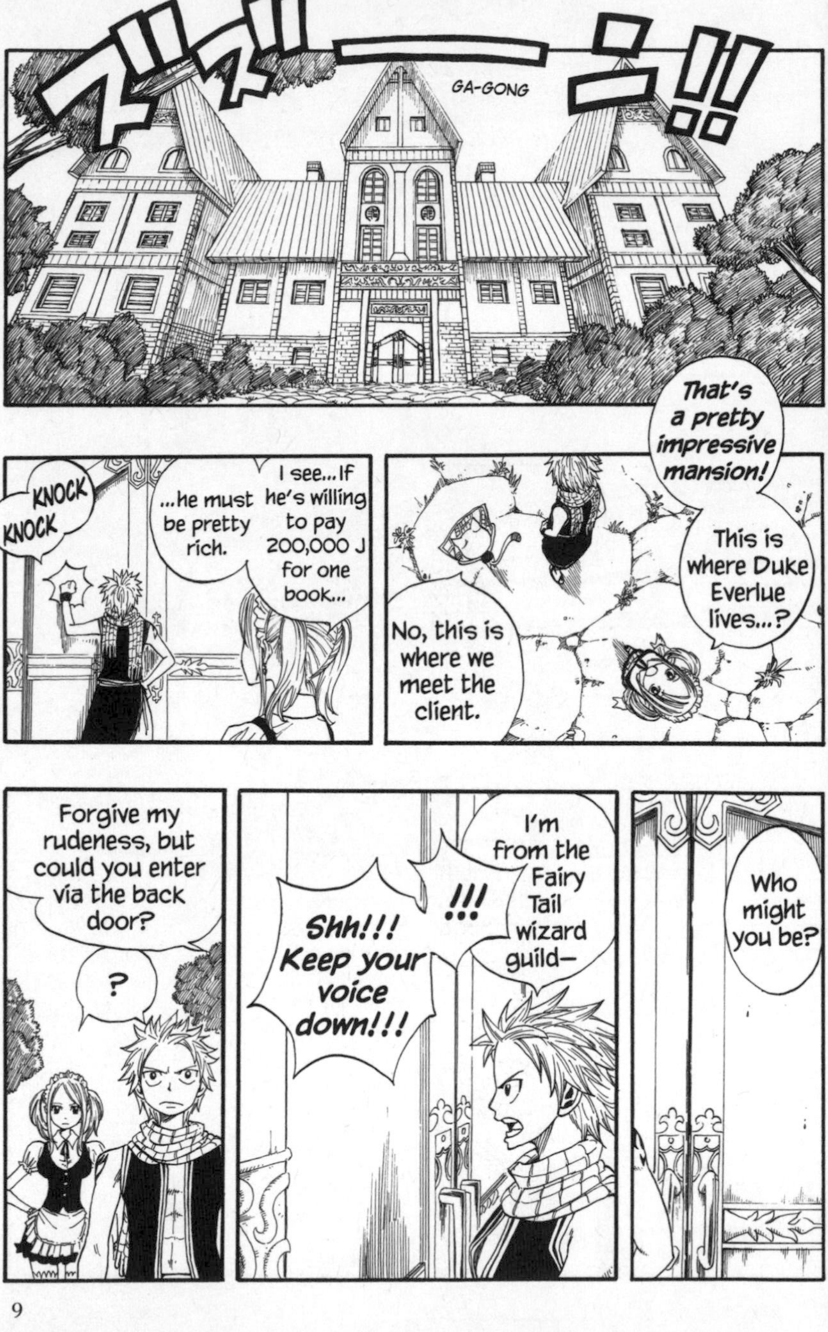
ズズーーン!!
GA-GONG
That's a pretty impressive mansion!
This is where Duke Everlue lives...?
No, this is where we meet the client.
I see...If he's willing to pay 200,000 J for one book...
...he must be pretty rich.
KNOCK KNOCK
Who might you be?
I'm from the Fairy Tail wizard guild–
!!!
Shh!!! Keep your voice down!!!
Forgive my rudeness, but could you enter via the back door?
?

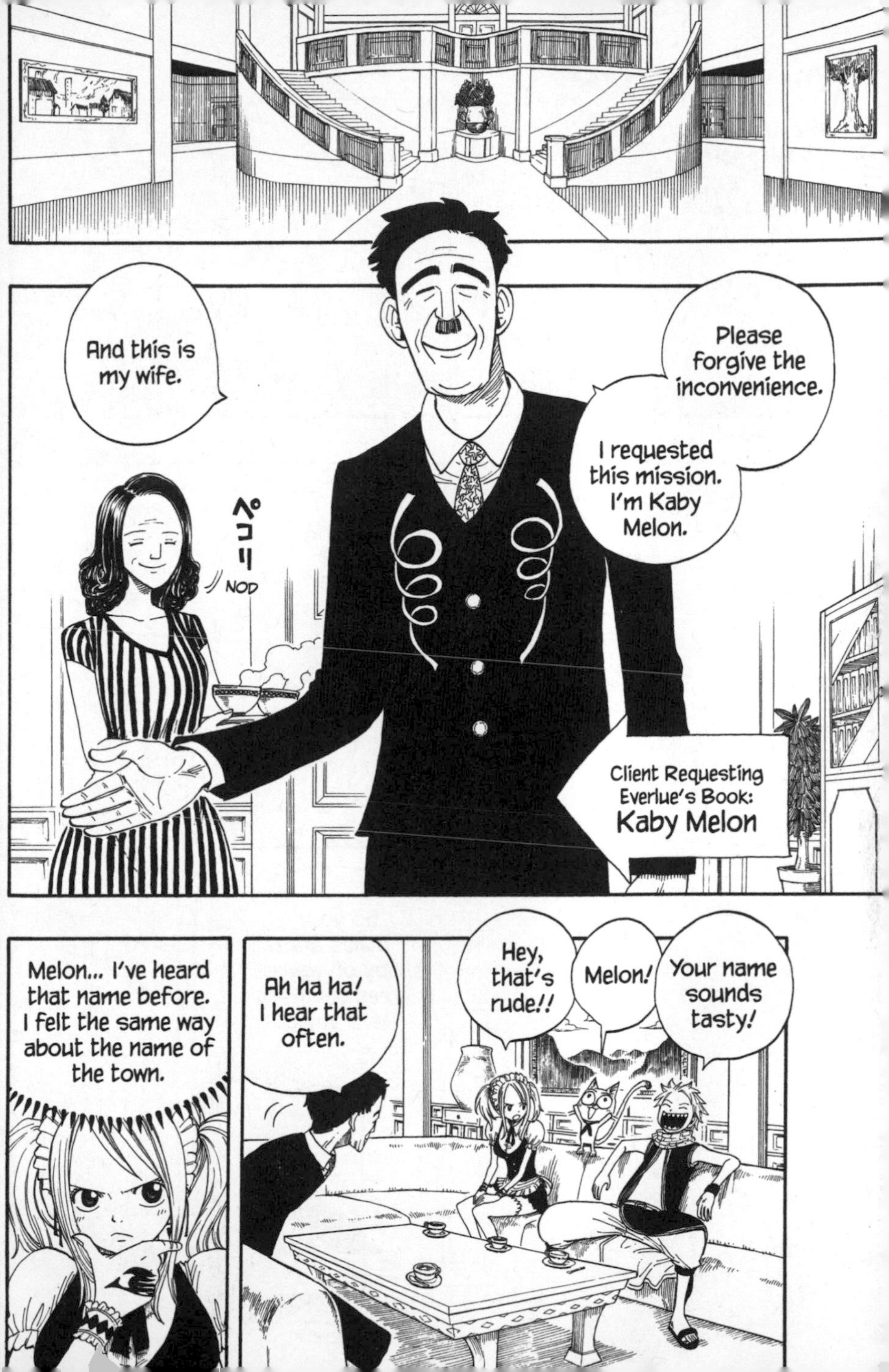
Please forgive the inconvenience.
I requested this mission. I'm Kaby Melon.
And this is my wife.
ペコリ
NOD
Client Requesting Everlue's Book: Kaby Melon
Your name sounds tasty!
Melon!
Hey, that's rude!!
Ah ha ha! I hear that often.
Melon... I've heard that name before. I felt the same way about the name of the town.

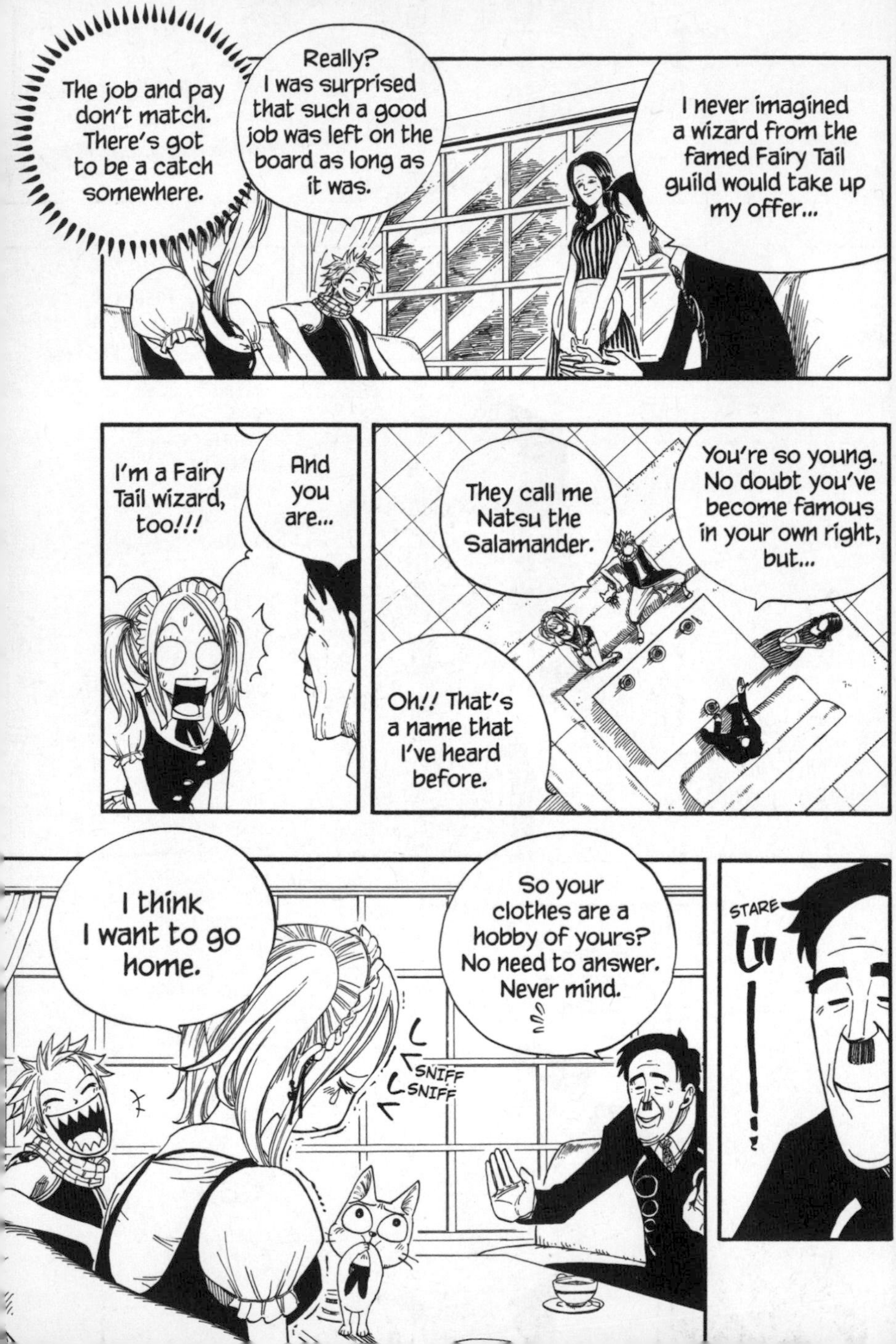
I never imagined a wizard from the famed Fairy Tail guild would take up my offer...
Really? I was surprised that such a good job was left on the board as long as it was.
The job and pay don't match. There's got to be a catch somewhere.
You're so young. No doubt you've become famous in your own right, but...
They call me Natsu the Salamander.
Oh!! That's a name that I've heard before.
And you are...
I'm a Fairy Tail wizard, too!!!
STARE
So your clothes are a hobby of yours? No need to answer. Never mind.
SNIFF
SNIFF
I think I want to go home.

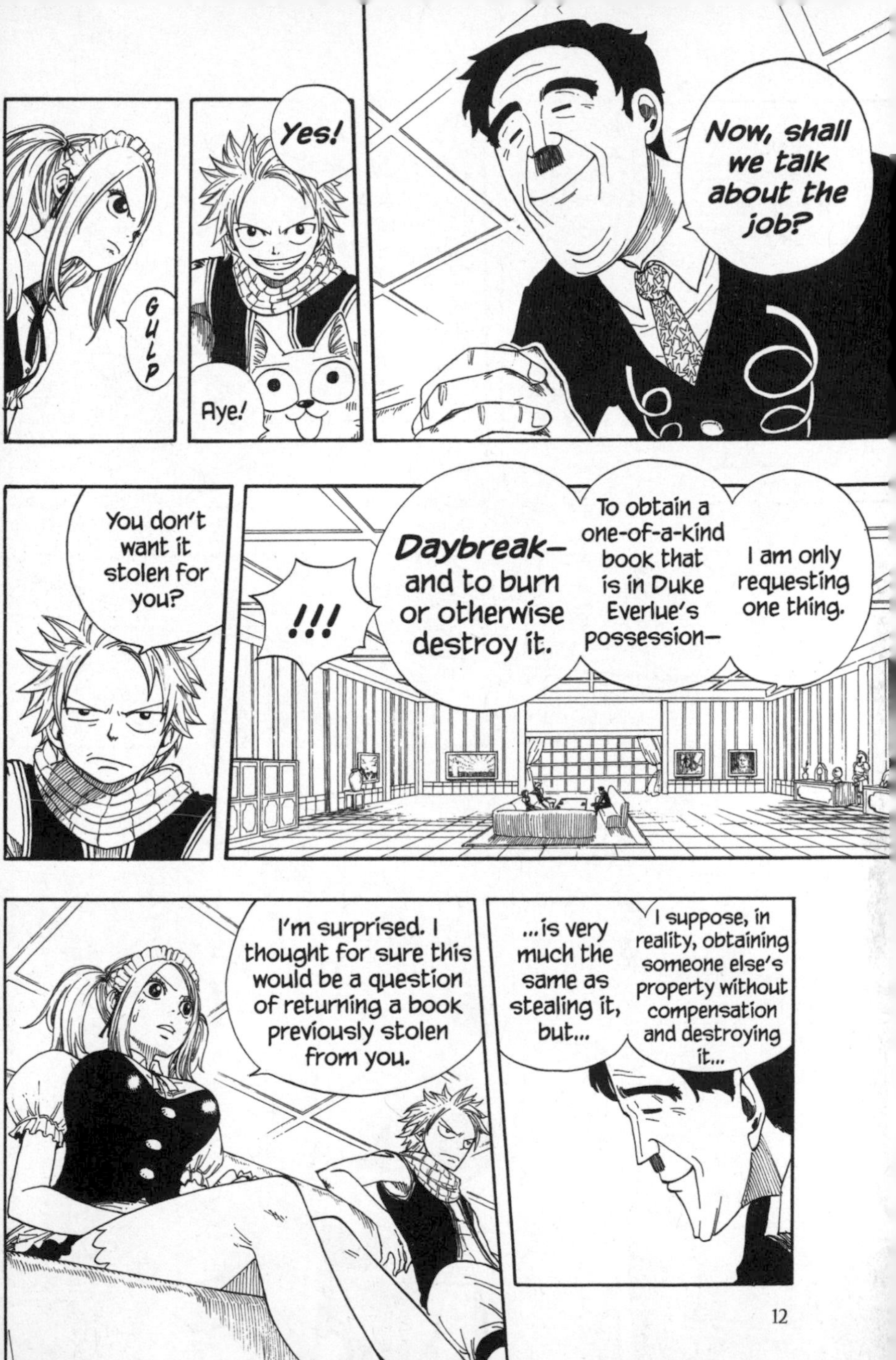
Now, shall we talk about the job?
Yes!
Aye!
GULP
I am only requesting one thing.
To obtain a one-of-a-kind book that is in Duke Everlue's possession—
Daybreak— and to burn or otherwise destroy it.
!!!
You don't want it stolen for you?
I suppose, in reality, obtaining someone else's property without compensation and destroying it...
...is very much the same as stealing it, but...
I'm surprised. I thought for sure this would be a question of returning a book previously stolen from you.

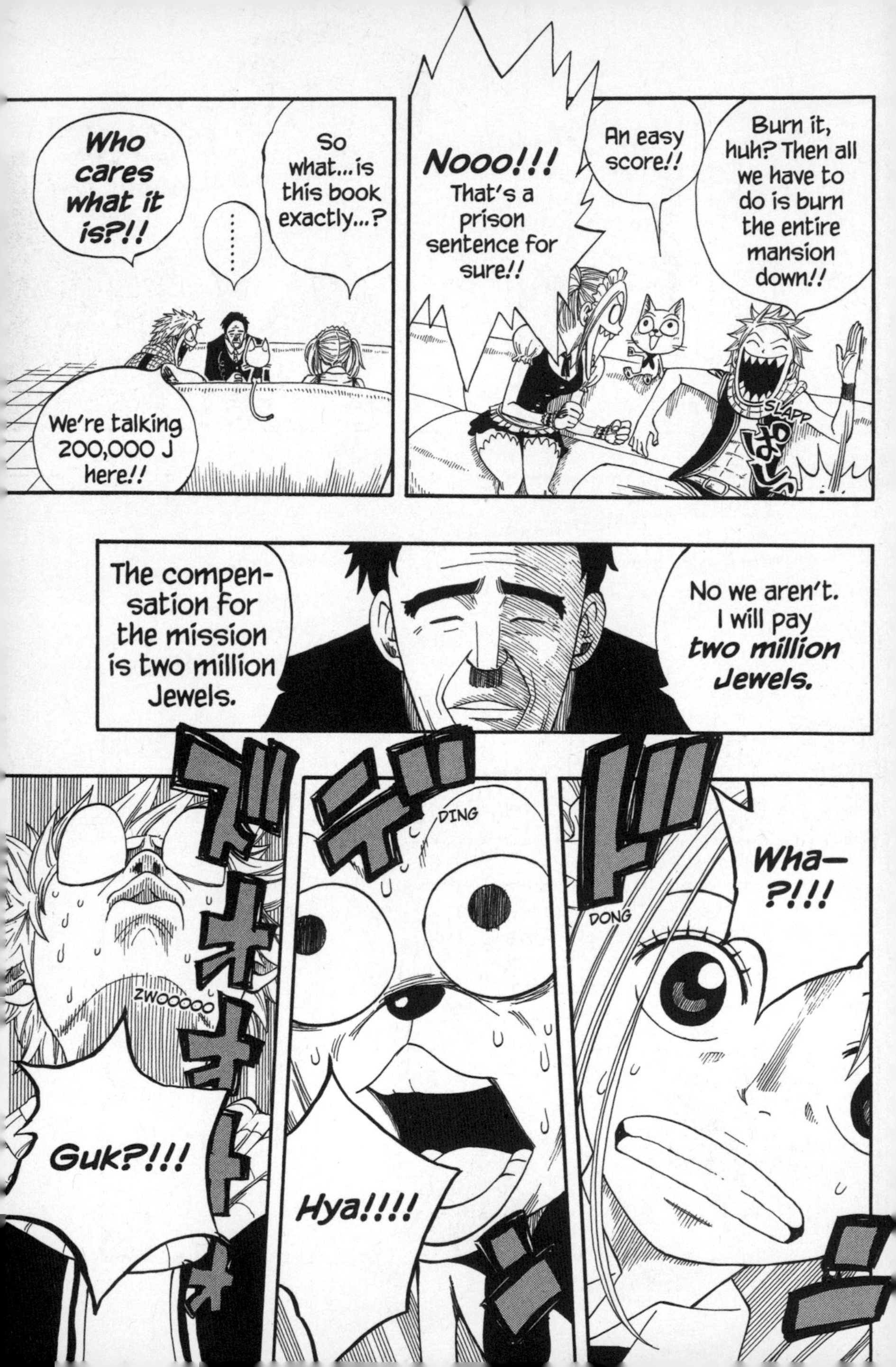
Burn it, huh? Then all we have to do is burn the entire mansion down!!
An easy score!!
SLAPP
Nooo!!! That's a prison sentence for sure!!
So what...is this book exactly...?
......
Who cares what it is?!!
We're talking 200,000 J here!!
No we aren't. I will pay two million Jewels.
The compensation for the mission is two million Jewels.
DONG
Wha—?!!!
DING
Hya!!!!
ZWOOOOO
Guk?!!!

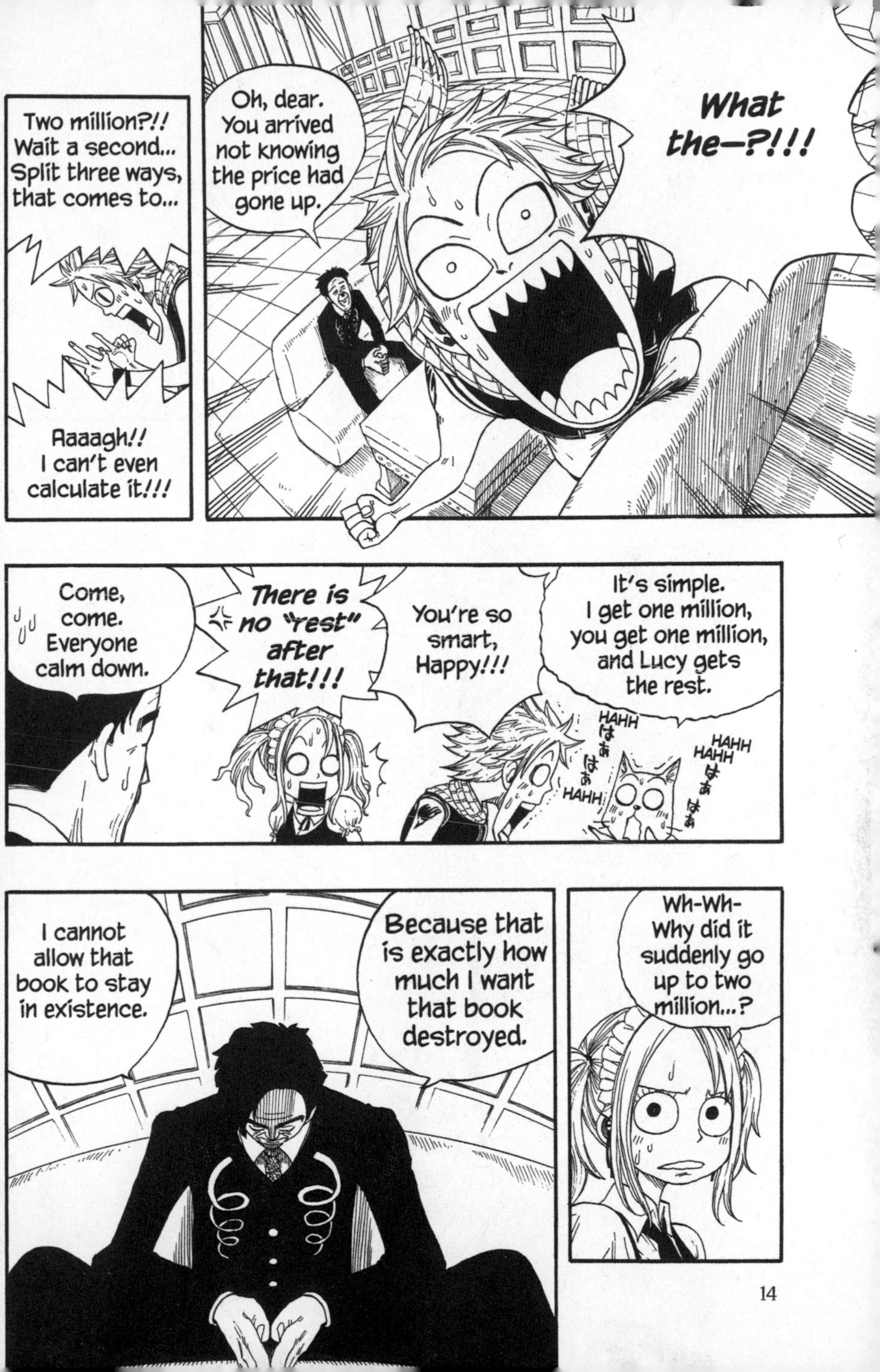

What the—?!!!
Oh, dear. You arrived not knowing the price had gone up.
Two million?!! Wait a second... Split three ways, that comes to...
Aaaagh!! I can't even calculate it!!!
It's simple. I get one million, you get one million, and Lucy gets the rest.
HAHH HAHH はあ はあ
HAHH はあ はあ HAHH
You're so smart, Happy!!!
There is no "rest" after that!!!
Come, come. Everyone calm down.
Wh-Wh- Why did it suddenly go up to two million...?
Because that is exactly how much I want that book destroyed.
I cannot allow that book to stay in existence.

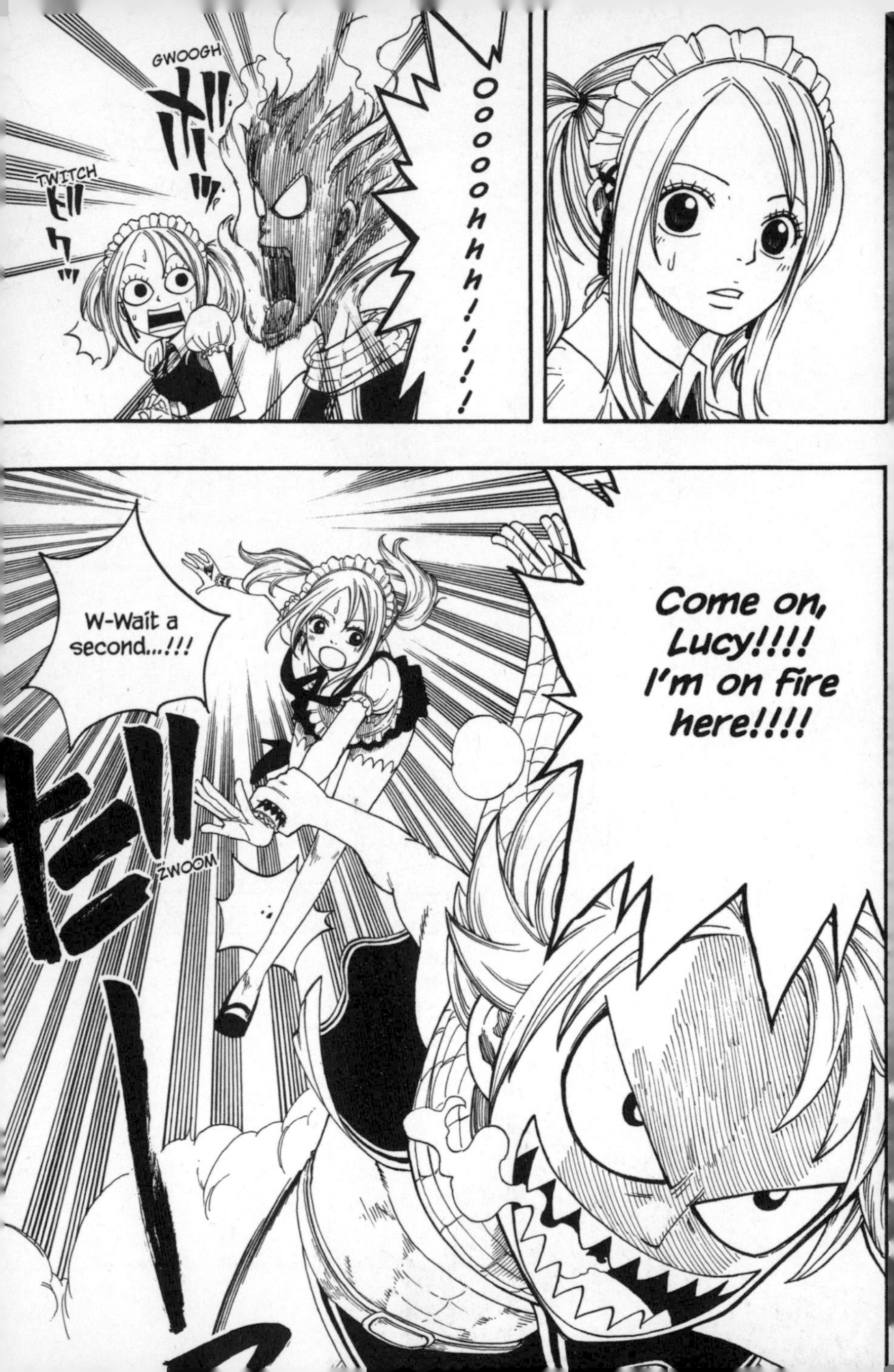
Ooooohhh!!!!
GWOOGH
TWITCH
Come on, Lucy!!!! I'm on fire here!!!!
W-Wait a second...!!!
ZWOOM

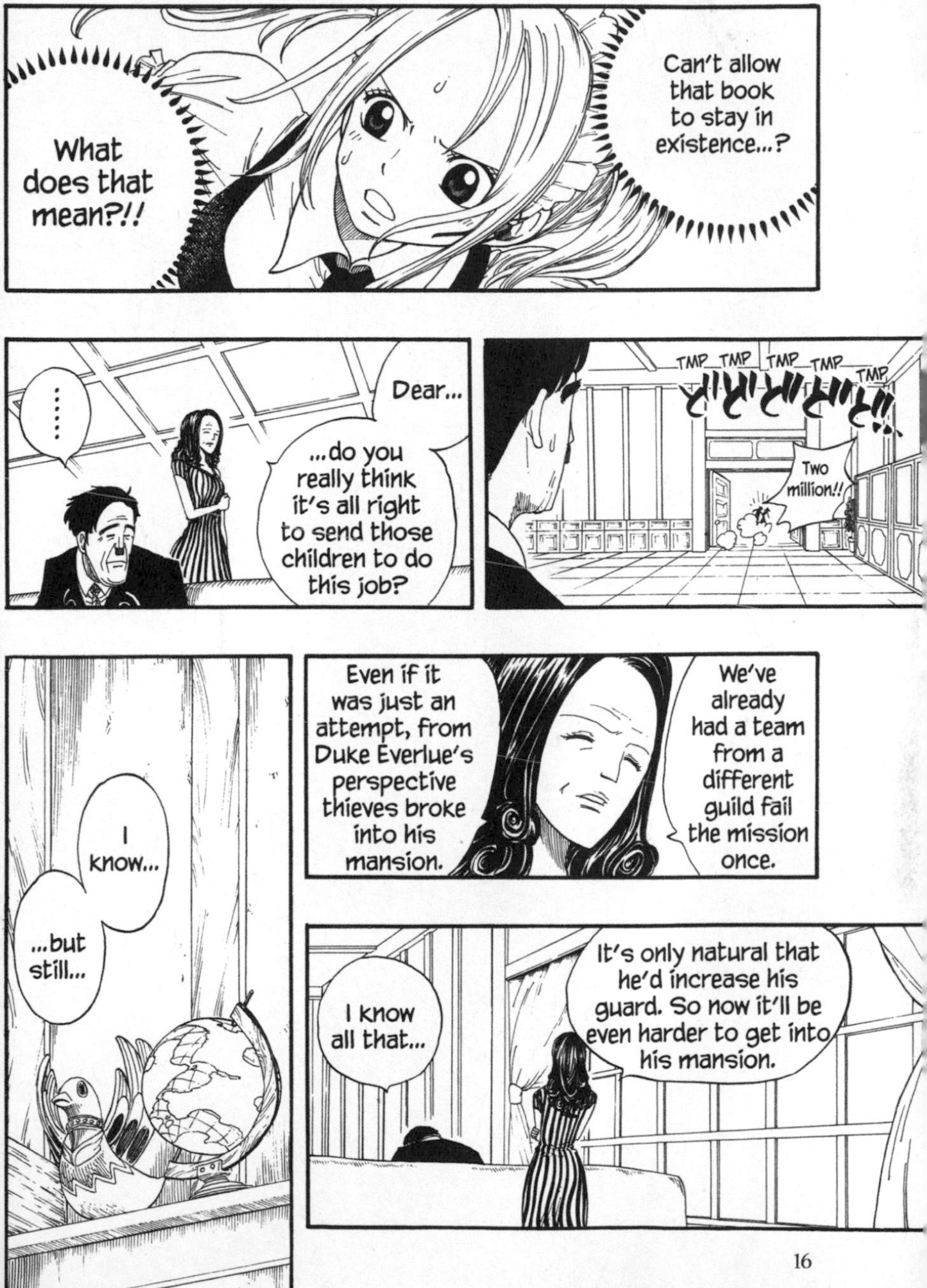
Can't allow that book to stay in existence...?
What does that mean?!!
TMP TMP TMP TMP TMP
Two million!!
Dear...
...do you really think it's all right to send those children to do this job?
......
We've already had a team from a different guild fail the mission once.
Even if it was just an attempt, from Duke Everlue's perspective thieves broke into his mansion.
It's only natural that he'd increase his guard. So now it'll be even harder to get into his mansion.
I know all that...
I know...
...but still...

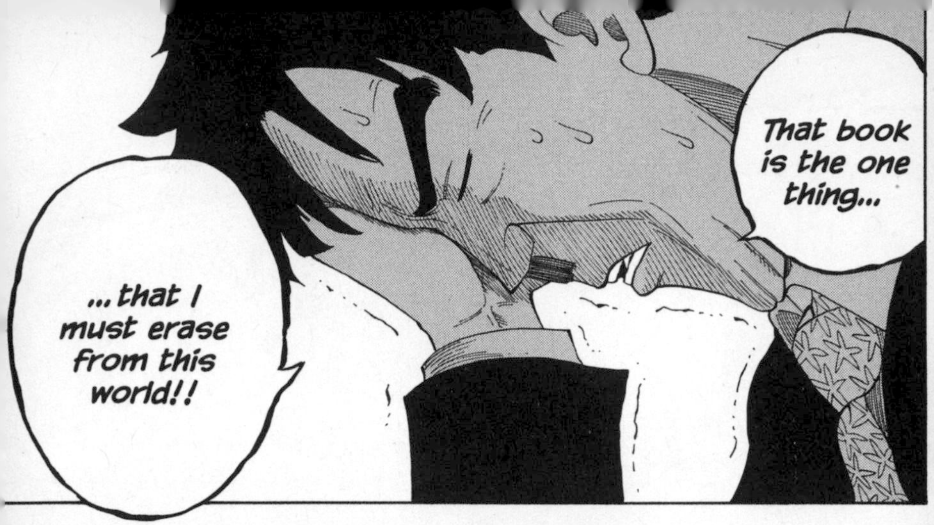
That book is the one thing...
...that I must erase from this world!!

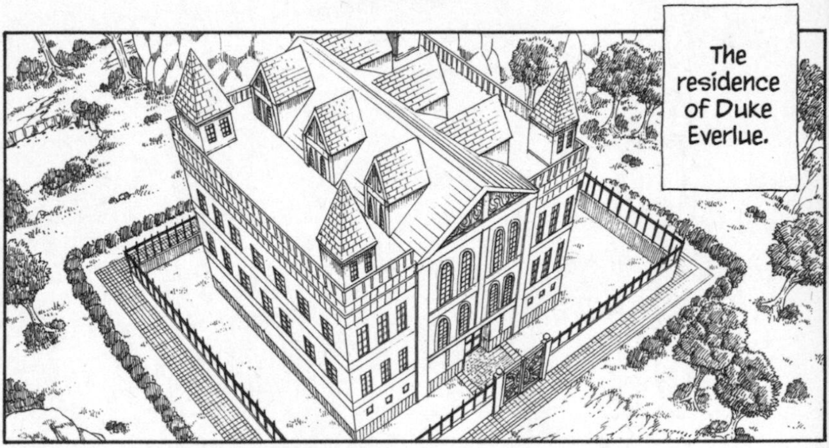
The residence of Duke Everlue.

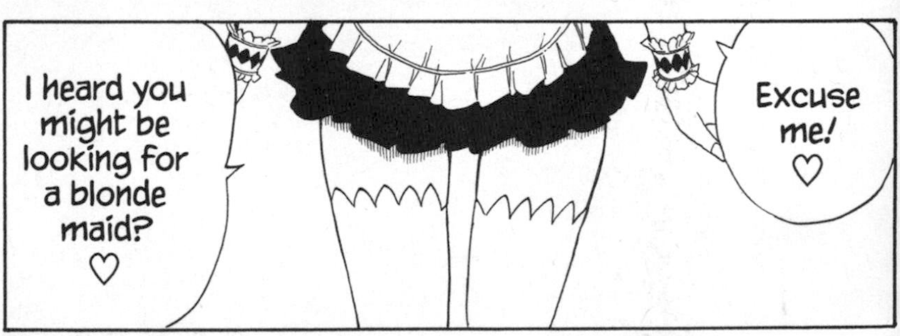
Excuse me! ♡
I heard you might be looking for a blonde maid? ♡

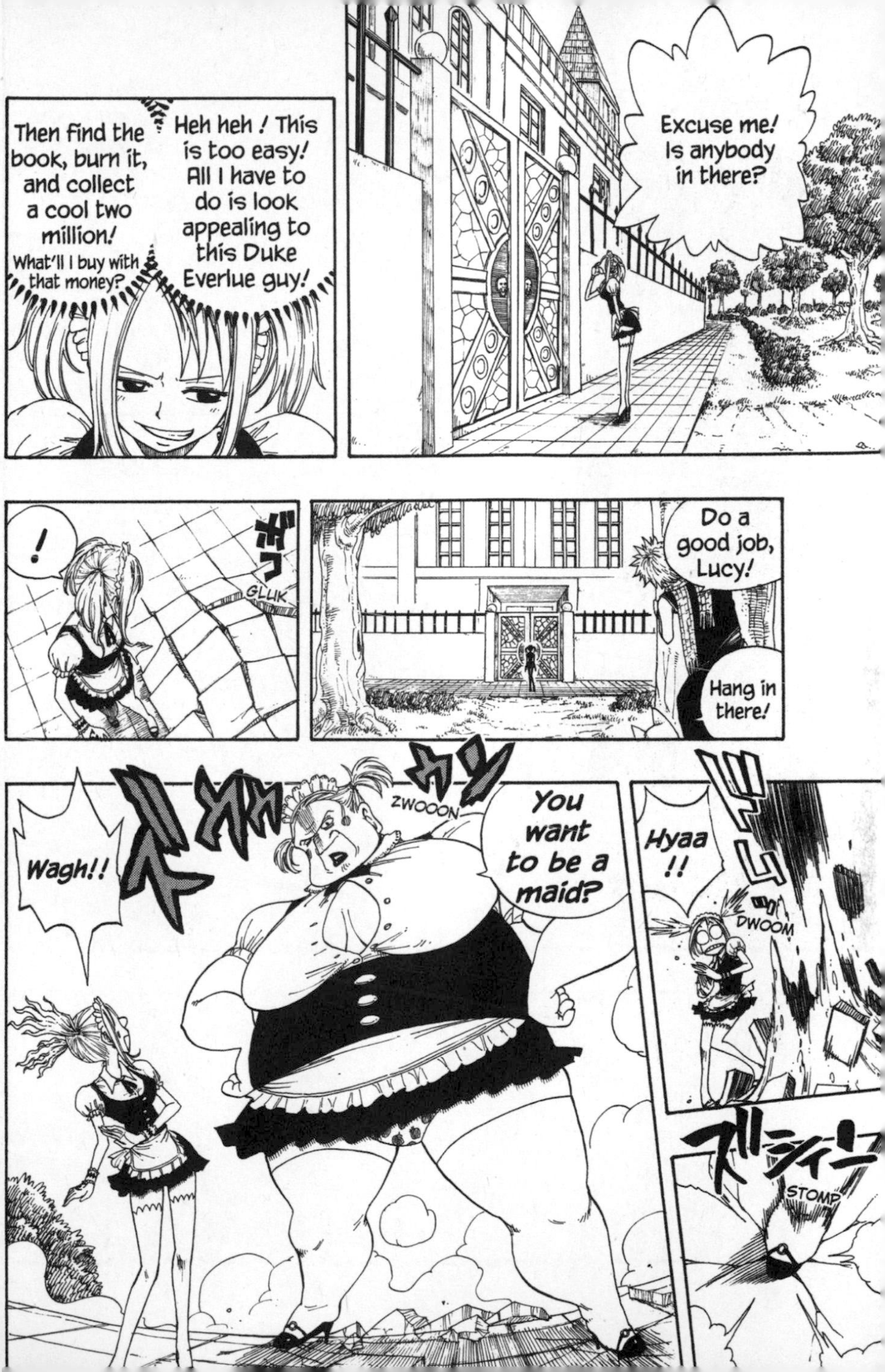

Excuse me! Is anybody in there?
Heh heh! This is too easy! All I have to do is look appealing to this Duke Everlue guy!
Then find the book, burn it, and collect a cool two million!
What'll I buy with that money?
Do a good job, Lucy!
Hang in there!
!
GLUK
Hyaa!!
DWOOM
STOMP
ZWOOON
You want to be a maid?
Wagh!!

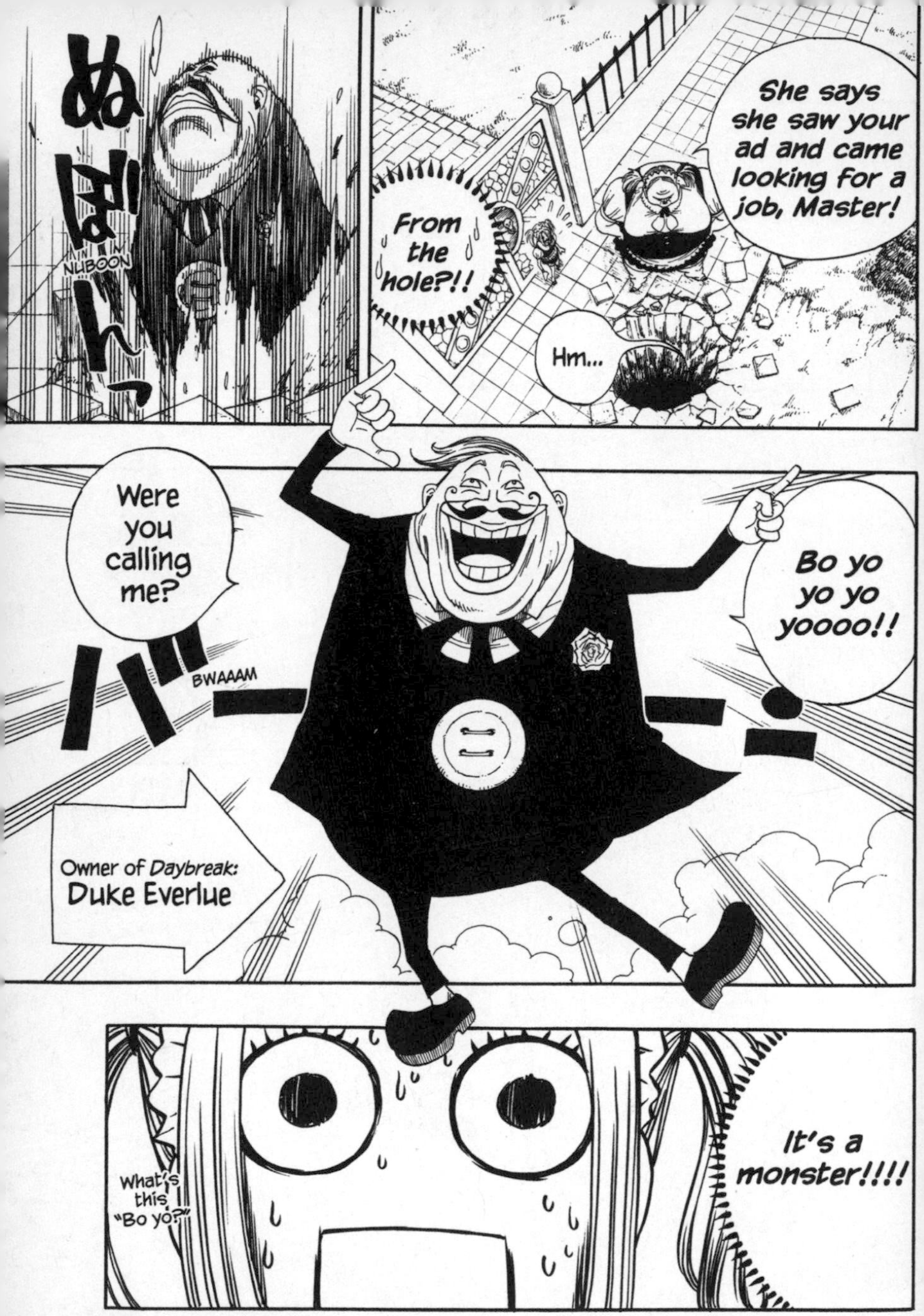
She says she saw your ad and came looking for a job, Master!
From the hole?!!
Hm...
ぬぼ〜ん
NUBOON
Bo yo yo yo yoooo!!
Were you calling me?
BWAAAM
Owner of *Daybreak*: Duke Everlue
It's a monster!!!!
What's this "Bo yo?"

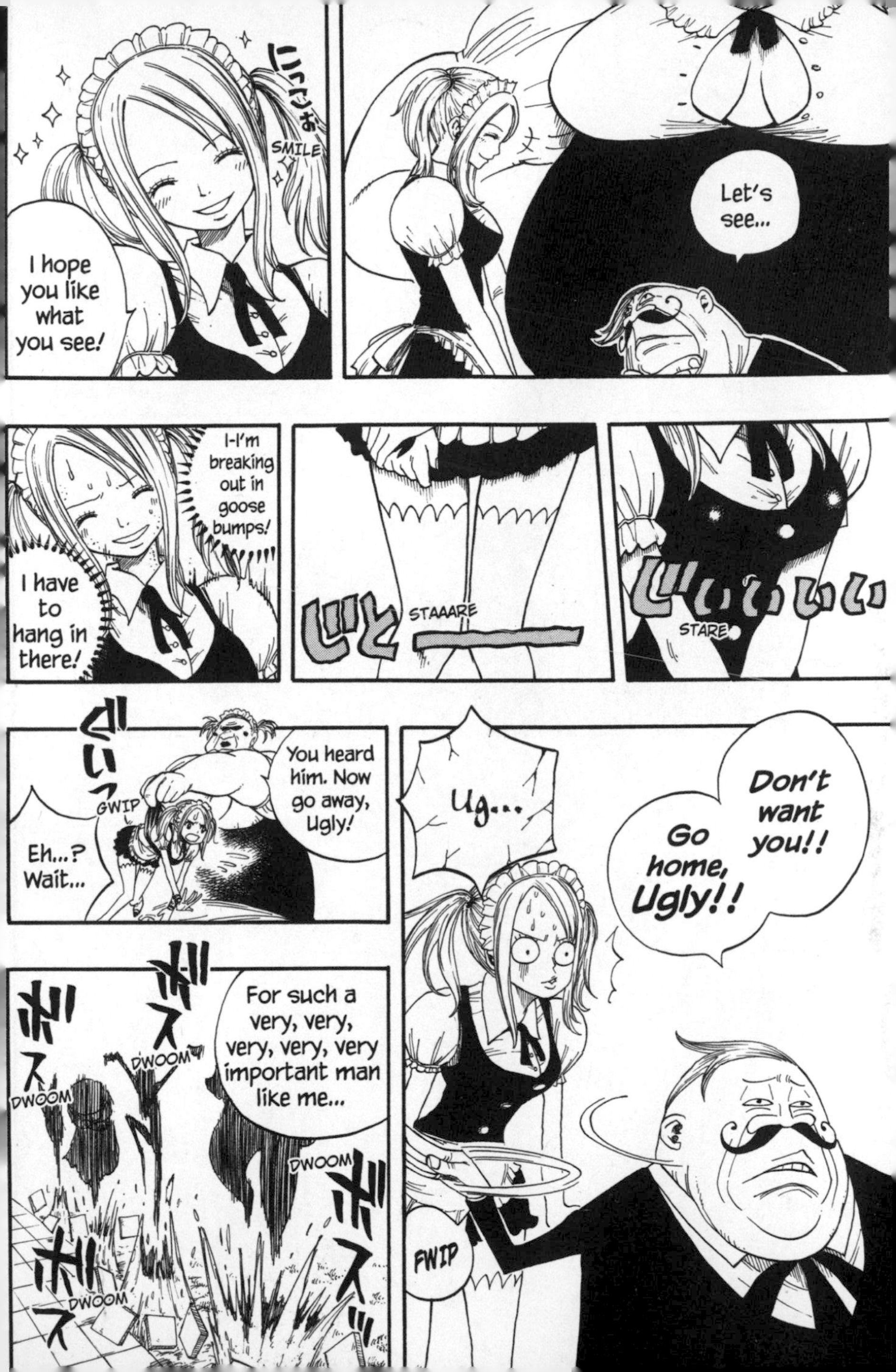
Let's see...
にっこぉ
SMILE
I hope you like what you see!
じぃぃぃぃ
STARE
じと
STAAARE
I-I'm breaking out in goose bumps!
I have to hang in there!
Don't want you!!
Go home, Ugly!!
Ug...
FWIP
You heard him. Now go away, Ugly!
ぐいっ
GWIP
Eh...? Wait...
ボス
DWOOM
For such a very, very, very, very, very important man like me...
ボス
DWOOM
ボスッ
DWOOM
ボス
DWOOM

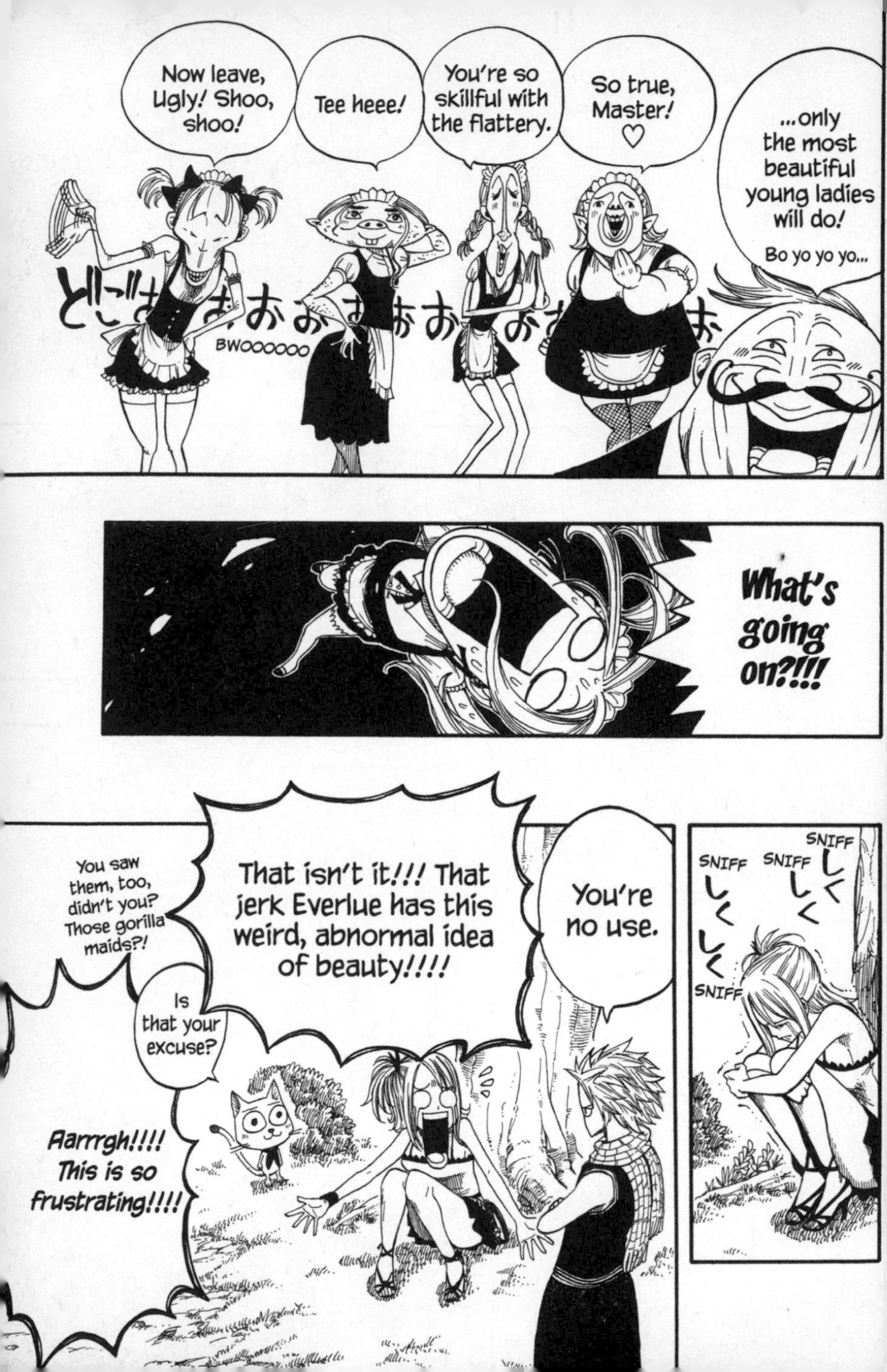
...only the most beautiful young ladies will do!
Bo yo yo yo...
So true, Master! ♡
You're so skillful with the flattery.
Tee heee!
Now leave, Ugly! Shoo, shoo!
BWOOOOOO
What's going on?!!!
SNIFF
SNIFF
SNIFF
SNIFF
You're no use.
That isn't it!!! That jerk Everlue has this weird, abnormal idea of beauty!!!!
You saw them, too, didn't you? Those gorilla maids?!
Is that your excuse?
Aarrrgh!!!! This is so frustrating!!!!

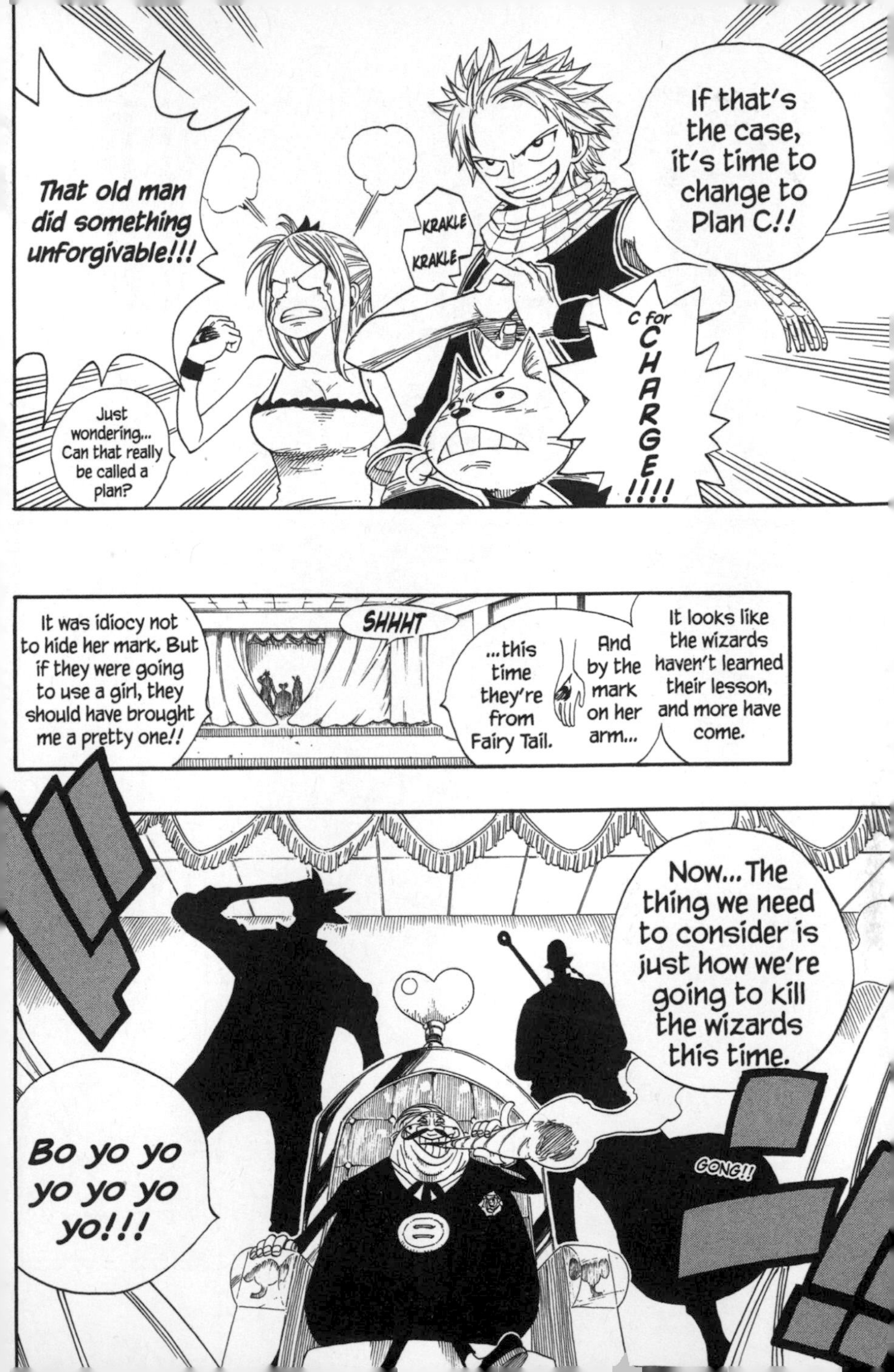
If that's the case, it's time to change to Plan C!!
C for CHARGE!!!!
KRAKLE
KRAKLE
That old man did something unforgivable!!!
Just wondering... Can that really be called a plan?
It looks like the wizards haven't learned their lesson, and more have come.
And by the mark on her arm...
...this time they're from Fairy Tail.
SHHHT
It was idiocy not to hide her mark. But if they were going to use a girl, they should have brought me a pretty one!!
Now... The thing we need to consider is just how we're going to kill the wizards this time.
GONG!!
Bo yo yo yo yo yo yo!!!

FAIRY TAIL

Chapter 6: Invade!! The Everlue Mansion

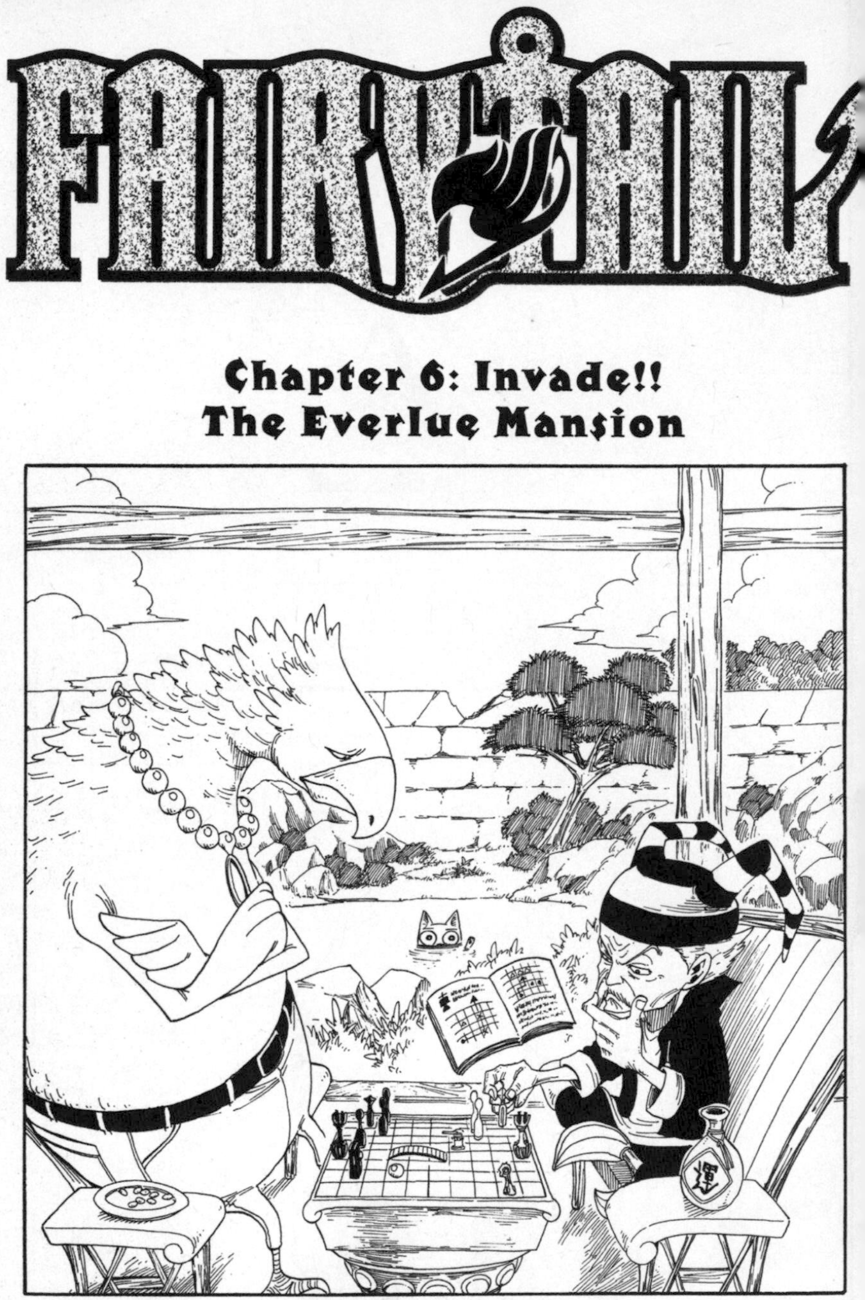

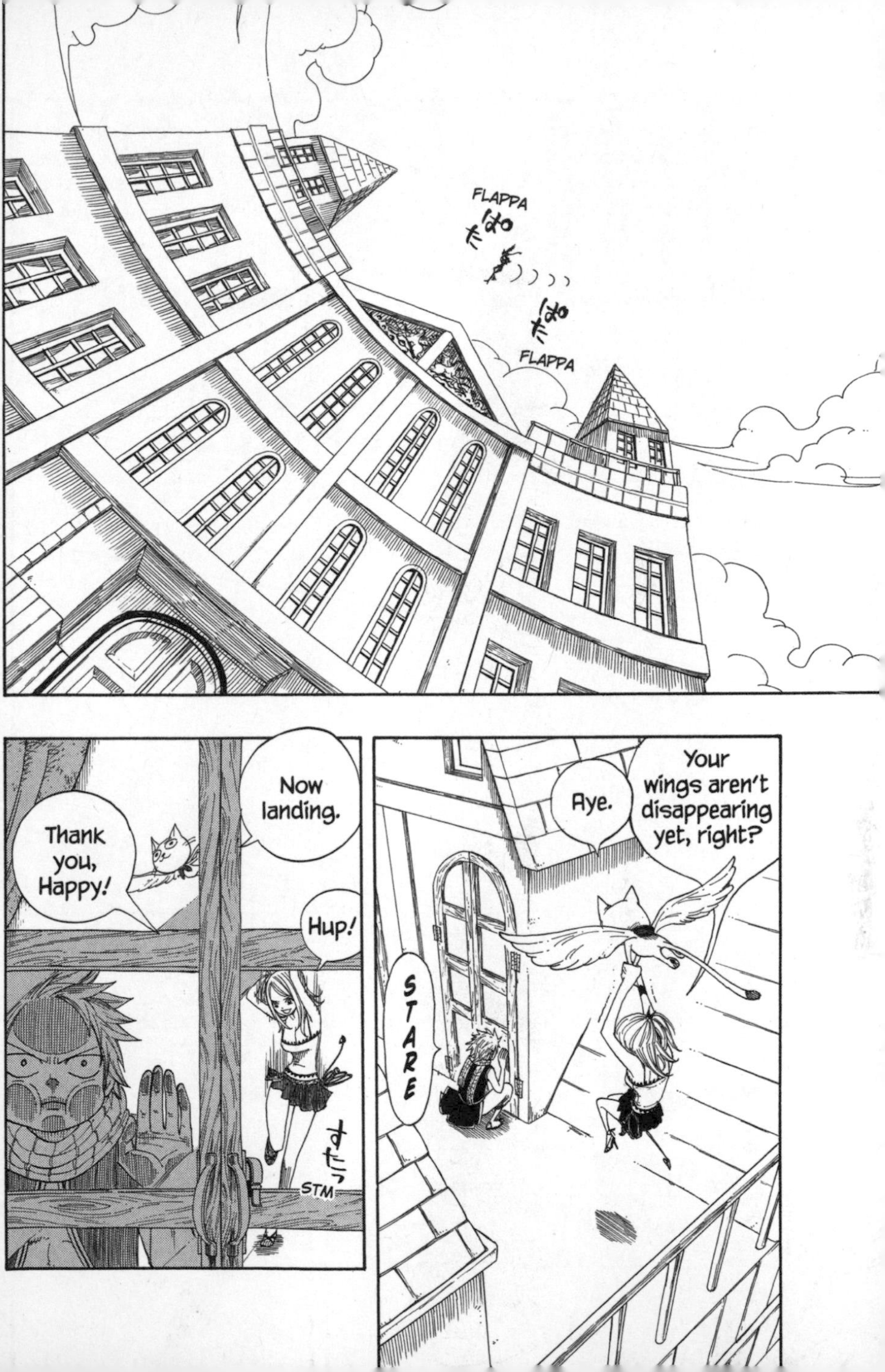
FLAPPA
FLAPPA
Your wings aren't disappearing yet, right?
Aye.
STARE
Now landing.
Thank you, Happy!
Hup!
STM

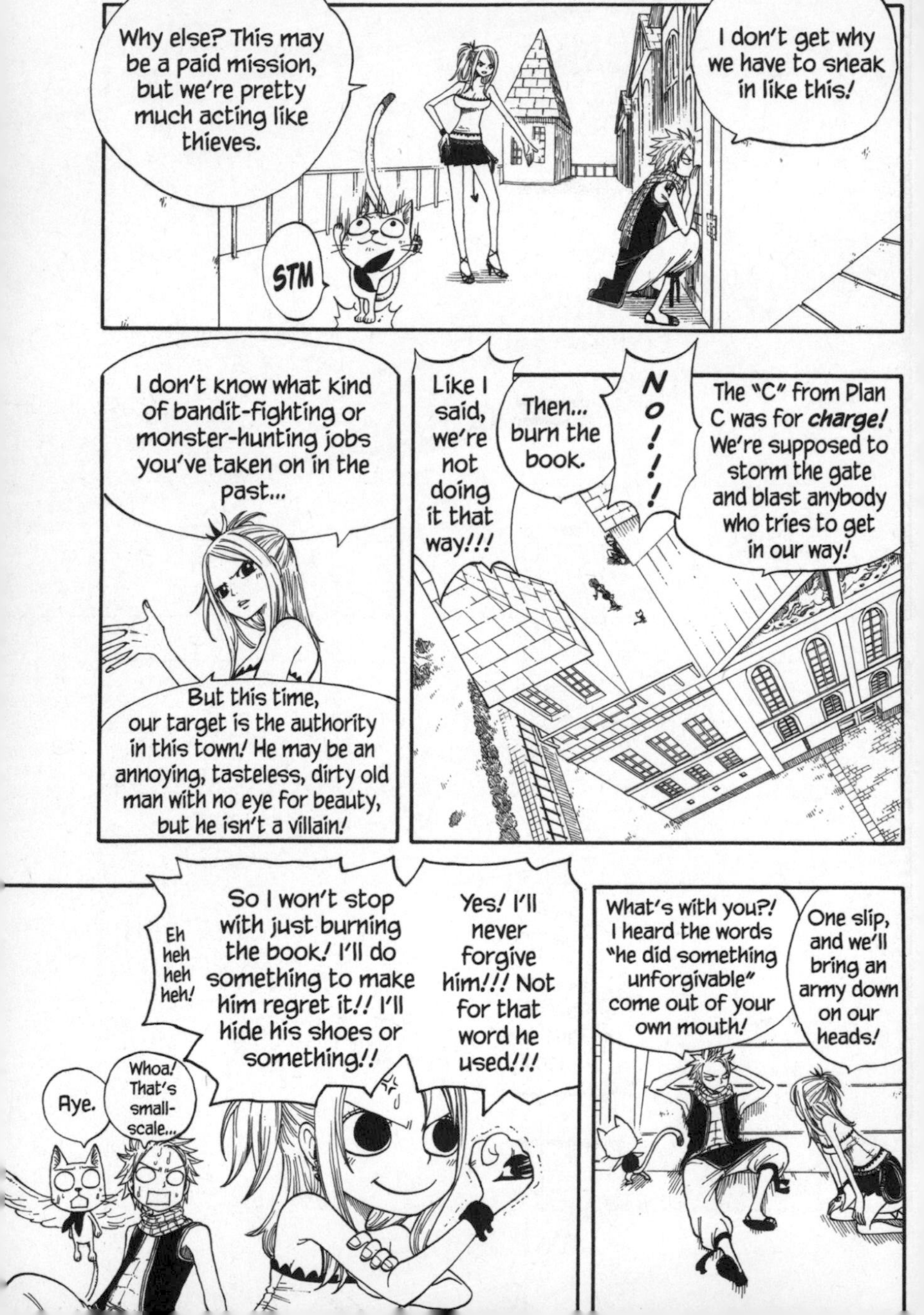
I don't get why we have to sneak in like this!
Why else? This may be a paid mission, but we're pretty much acting like thieves.
STM
The "C" from Plan C was for charge! We're supposed to storm the gate and blast anybody who tries to get in our way!
NO!!!!
Then... burn the book.
Like I said, we're not doing it that way!!!
I don't know what kind of bandit-fighting or monster-hunting jobs you've taken on in the past...
But this time, our target is the authority in this town! He may be an annoying, tasteless, dirty old man with no eye for beauty, but he isn't a villain!
One slip, and we'll bring an army down on our heads!
What's with you?! I heard the words "he did something unforgivable" come out of your own mouth!
Yes! I'll never forgive him!!! Not for that word he used!!!
So I won't stop with just burning the book! I'll do something to make him regret it!! I'll hide his shoes or something!!
Eh heh heh heh!
Whoa! That's small-scale...
Aye.

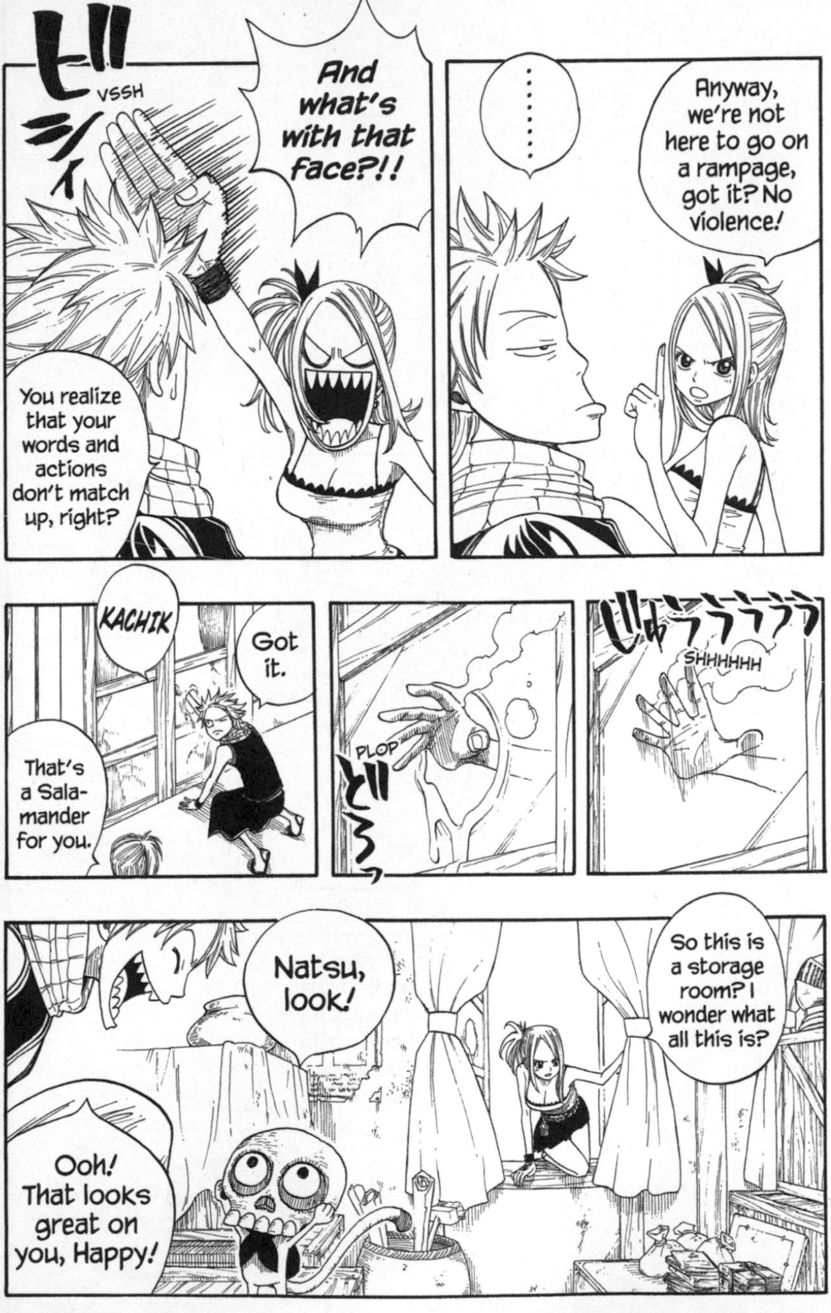
Anyway, we're not here to go on a rampage, got it? No violence!
. . . .
And what's with that face?!!
VSSH
You realize that your words and actions don't match up, right?
SHHHHHH
PLOP
Got it.
KACHIK
That's a Salamander for you.
So this is a storage room? I wonder what all this is?
Natsu, look!
Ooh! That looks great on you, Happy!

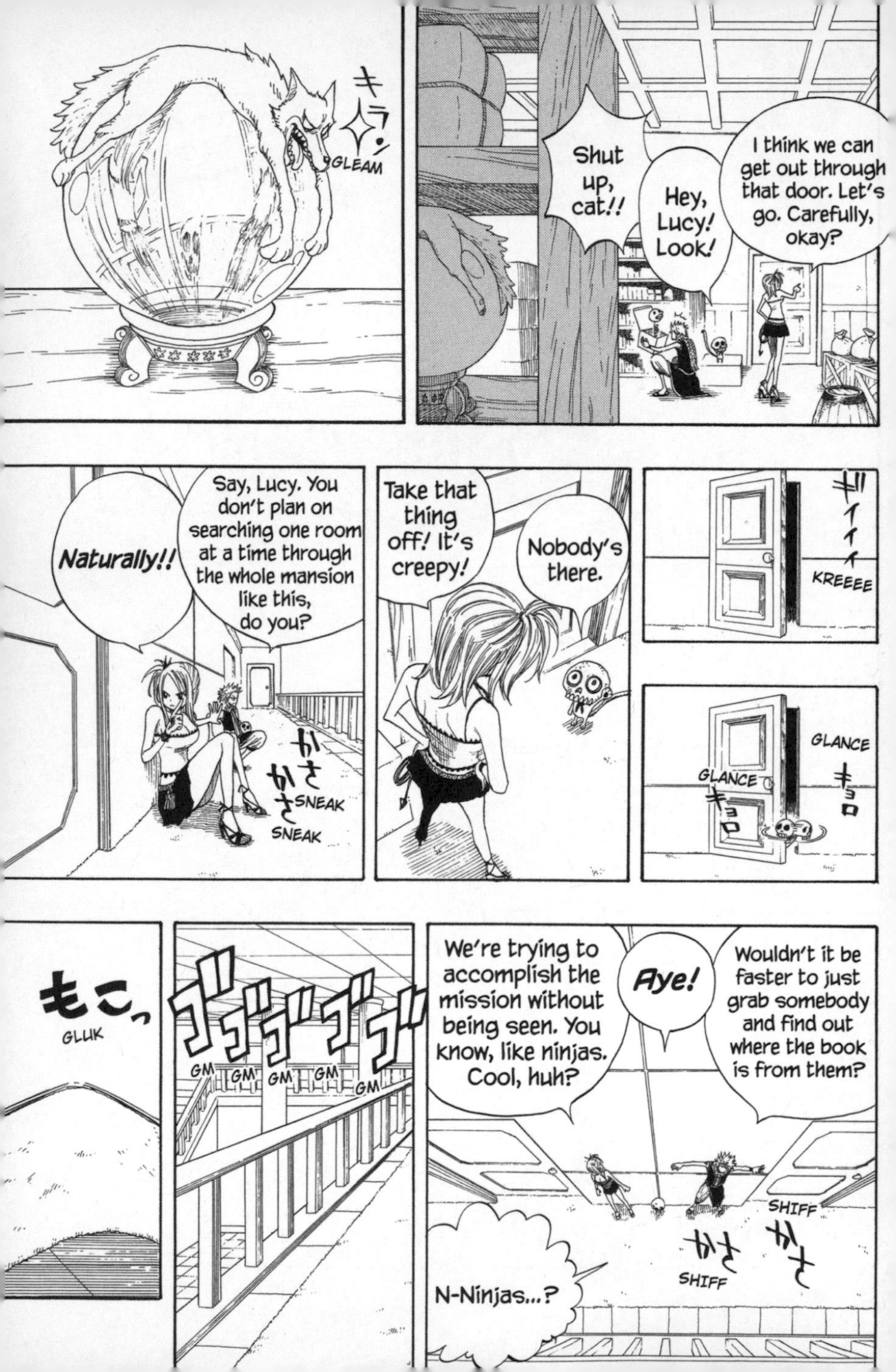

I think we can get out through that door. Let's go. Carefully, okay?
Hey, Lucy! Look!
Shut up, cat!!
キラン
GLEAM
ギィィィ
KREEEE
GLANCE
キョロ
GLANCE
キョロ
Nobody's there.
Take that thing off! It's creepy!
Say, Lucy. You don't plan on searching one room at a time through the whole mansion like this, do you?
Naturally!!
かさ
かさ
SNEAK
SNEAK
Wouldn't it be faster to just grab somebody and find out where the book is from them?
Aye!
We're trying to accomplish the mission without being seen. You know, like ninjas. Cool, huh?
SHIFF
かさ
かさ
SHIFF
N-Ninjas...?
GM GM GM GM GM
もこっ
GLUK

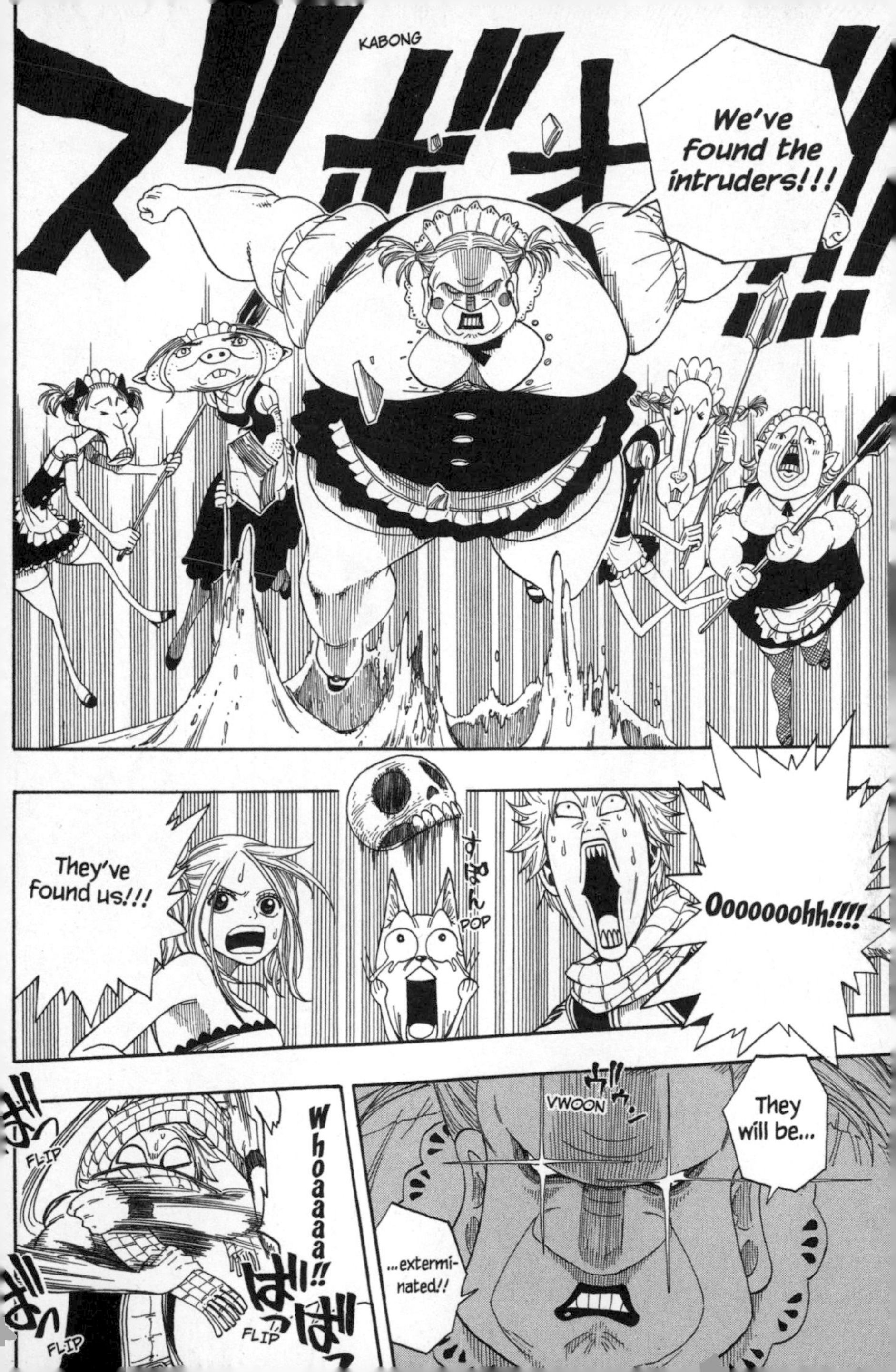
KABONG
We've found the intruders!!!
Ooooooohh!!!!
POP
They've found us!!!
VWOON
They will be...
...extermi-nated!!
Whoaaaaa!!
FLIP
FLIP
FLIP

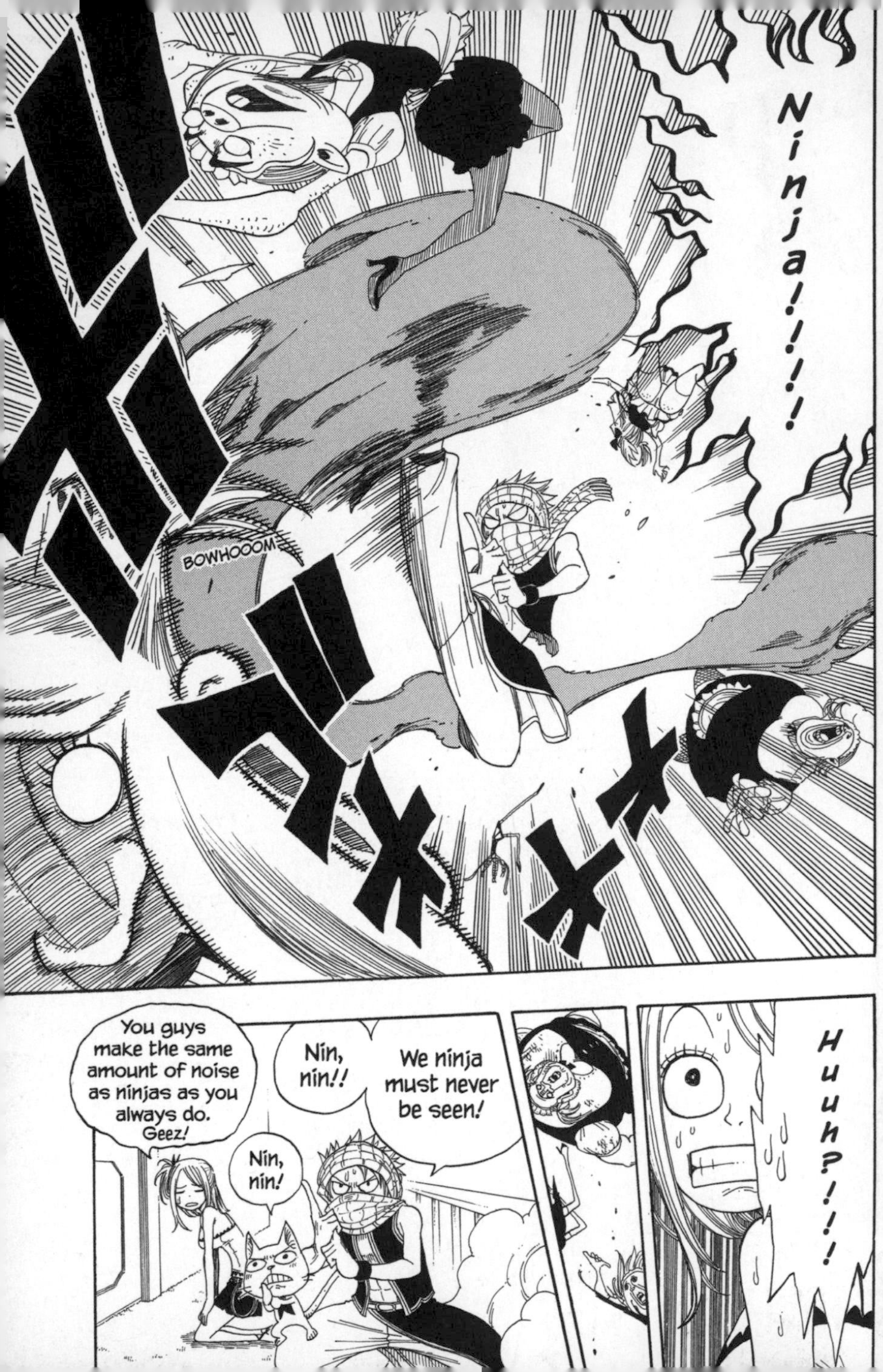
Ninja!!!!!
BOWHOOOM
Huuuh?!!!
We ninja must never be seen!
Nin, nin!!
You guys make the same amount of noise as ninjas as you always do. Geez!
Nin, nin!

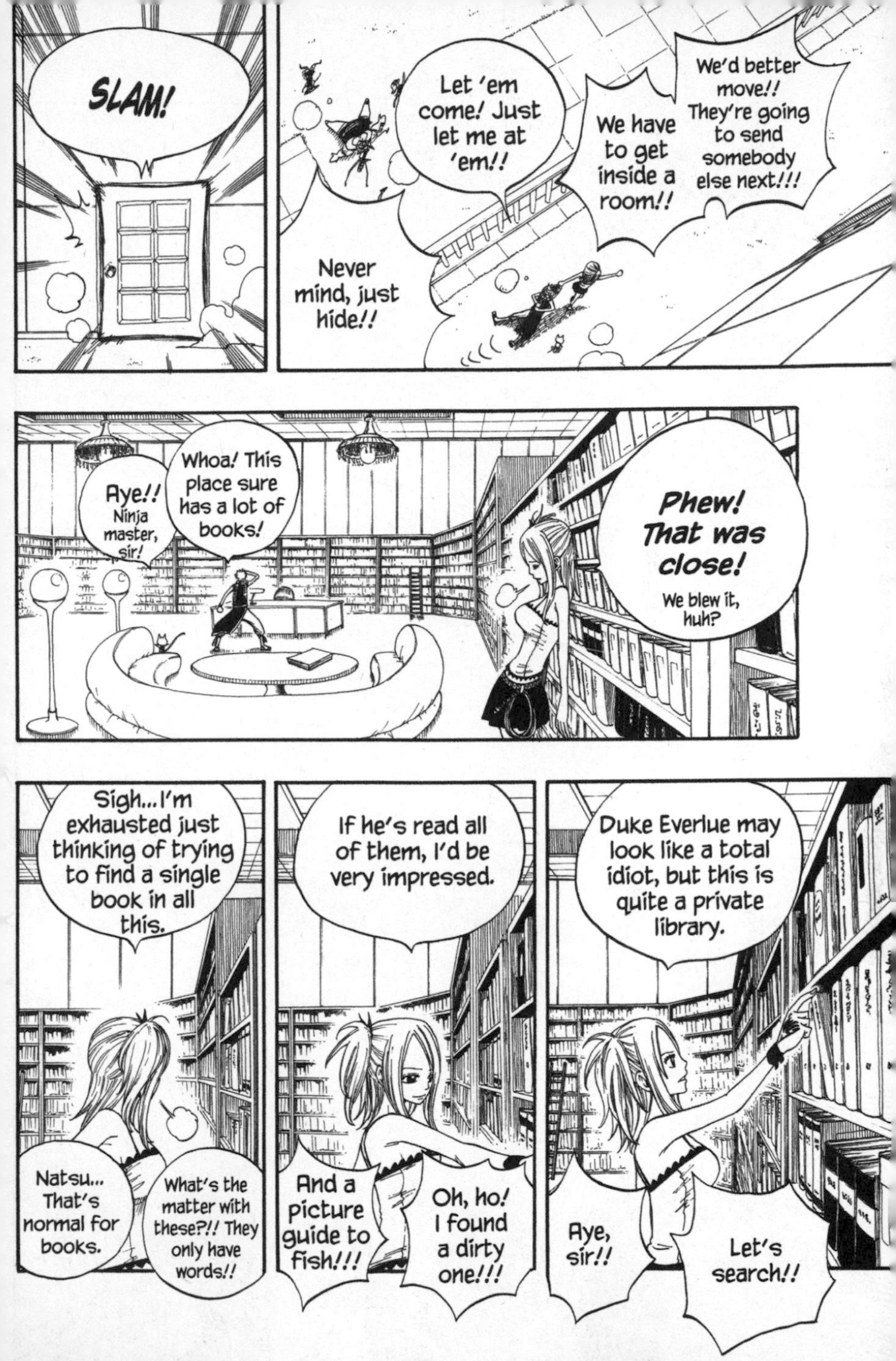
We'd better move!! They're going to send somebody else next!!!
We have to get inside a room!!
Let 'em come! Just let me at 'em!!
Never mind, just hide!!
SLAM!
Phew! That was close!
We blew it, huh?
Whoa! This place sure has a lot of books!
Aye!! Ninja master, sir!
Duke Everlue may look like a total idiot, but this is quite a private library.
Let's search!!
Aye, sir!!
If he's read all of them, I'd be very impressed.
Oh, ho! I found a dirty one!!!
And a picture guide to fish!!!
Sigh...I'm exhausted just thinking of trying to find a single book in all this.
What's the matter with these?!! They only have words!!
Natsu... That's normal for books.

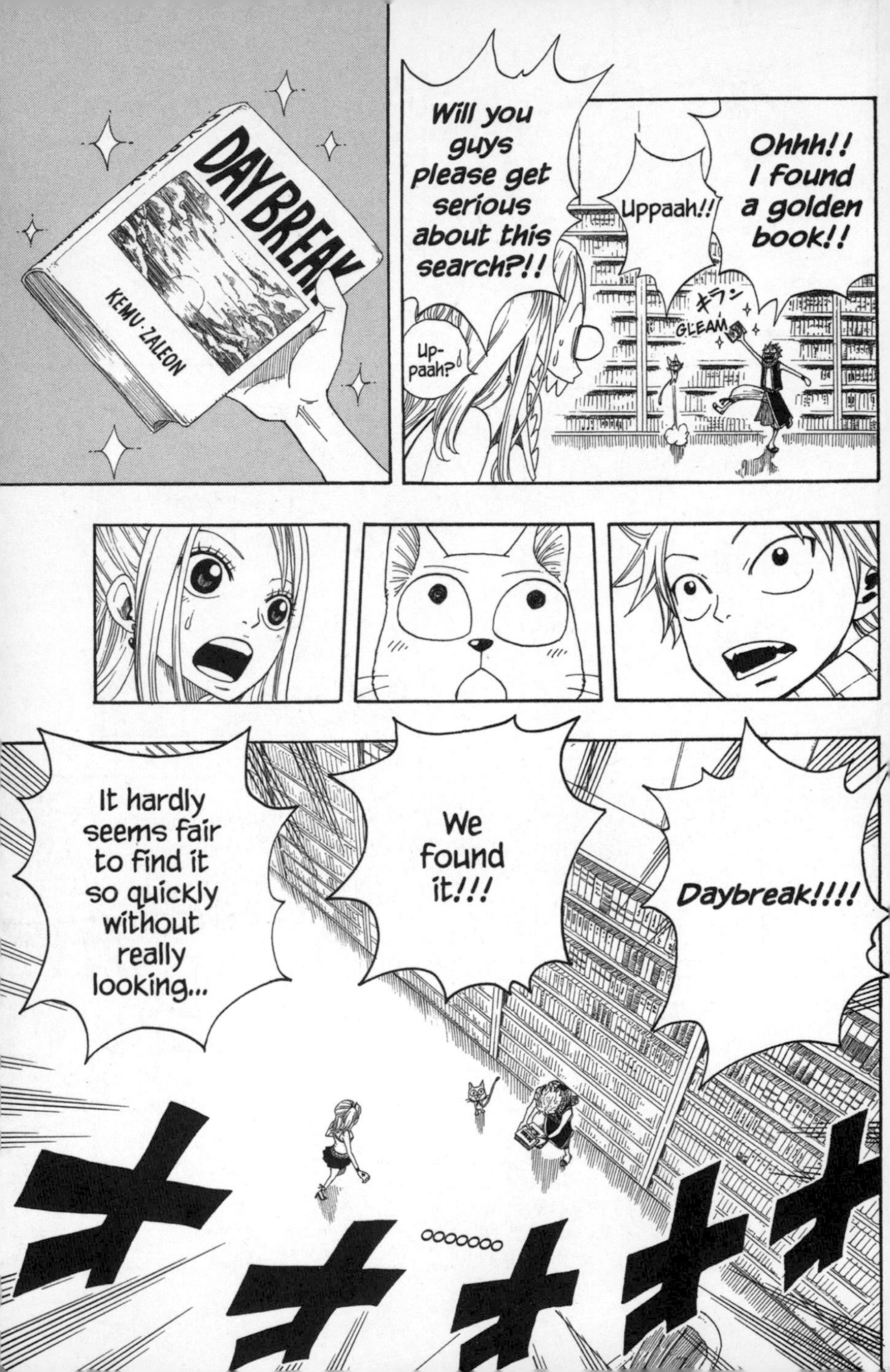
Ohhh!! I found a golden book!!
Uppaah!!
Will you guys please get serious about this search?!!
キラン
GLEAM
Up-paah?
DAYBREAK
KEMU·ZALEON
Daybreak!!!!
We found it!!!
It hardly seems fair to find it so quickly without really looking...
オオオオオ
ooooooo

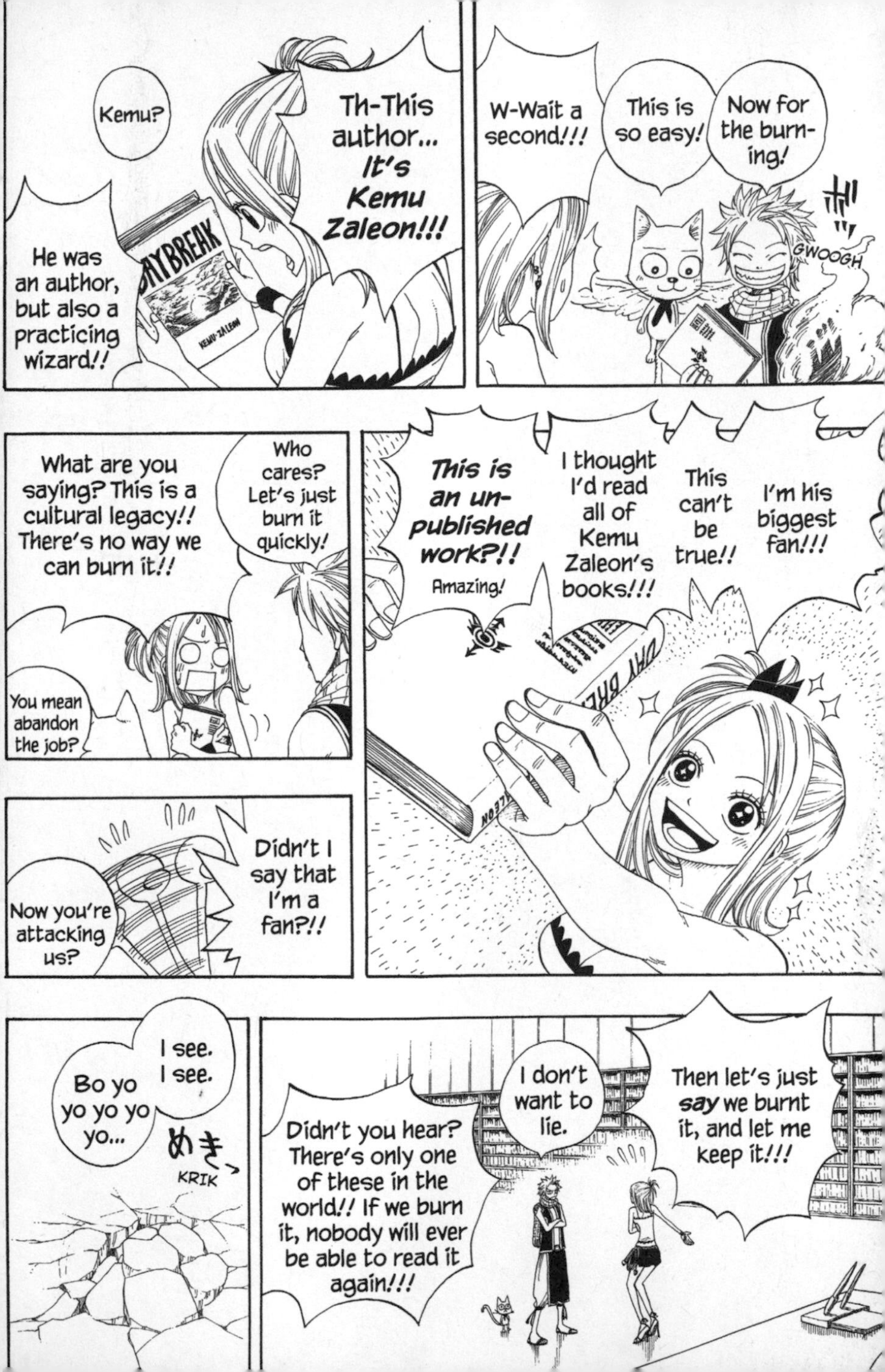

Now for the burn-ing!
This is so easy!
W-Wait a second!!!
GWOOGH
Th-This author... It's Kemu Zaleon!!!
Kemu?
DAYBREAK
KEMU ZALEON
He was an author, but also a practicing wizard!!
I'm his biggest fan!!!
This can't be true!!
I thought I'd read all of Kemu Zaleon's books!!!
This is an un-published work?!!
Amazing!
Who cares? Let's just burn it quickly!
What are you saying? This is a cultural legacy!! There's no way we can burn it!!
You mean abandon the job?
Didn't I say that I'm a fan?!!
Now you're attacking us?
Then let's just say we burnt it, and let me keep it!!!
I don't want to lie.
Didn't you hear? There's only one of these in the world!! If we burn it, nobody will ever be able to read it again!!!
I see. I see.
Bo yo yo yo yo...
めき
KRIK

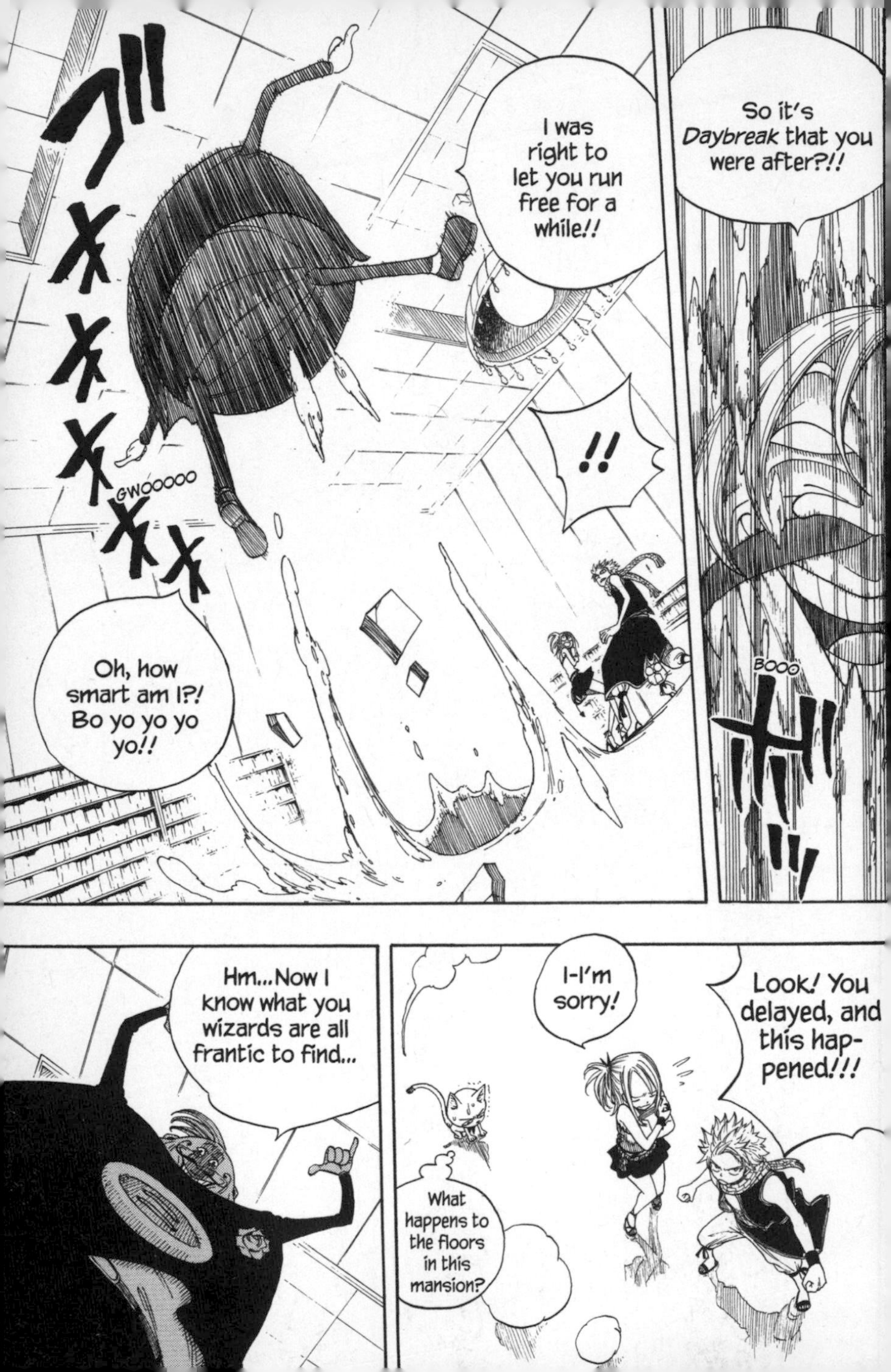
So it's *Daybreak* that you were after?!!
BOOO
I was right to let you run free for a while!!
!!
GWOOOOO
Oh, how smart am I?! Bo yo yo yo yo!!
Look! You delayed, and this hap-pened!!!
I-I'm sorry!
What happens to the floors in this mansion?
Hm...Now I know what you wizards are all frantic to find...

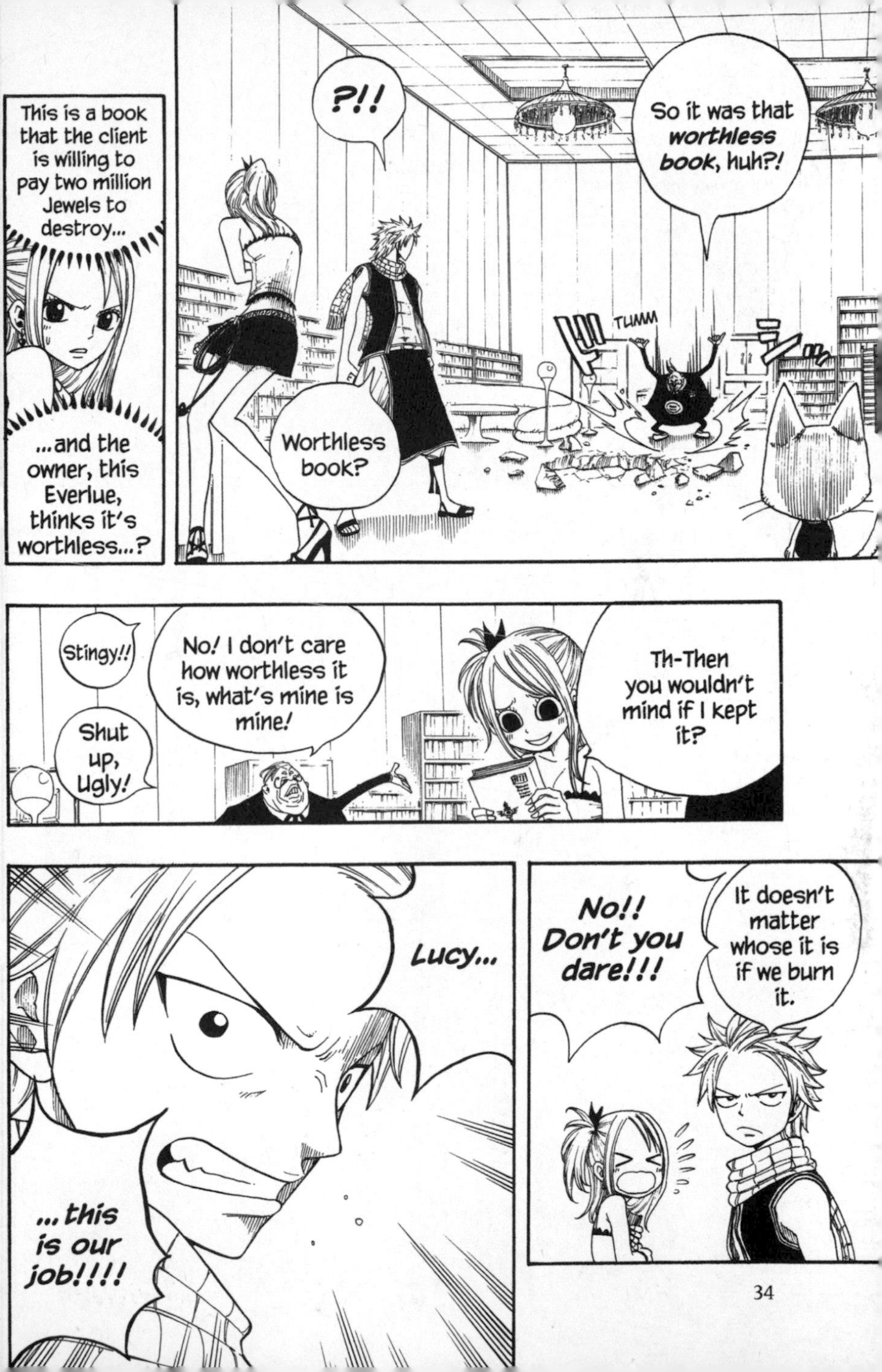

So it was that *worthless book*, huh?!
?!!
TUMM
Worthless book?
This is a book that the client is willing to pay two million Jewels to destroy...
...and the owner, this Everlue, thinks it's worthless...?
Th-Then you wouldn't mind if I kept it?
No! I don't care how worthless it is, what's mine is mine!
Stingy!!
Shut up, Ugly!
It doesn't matter whose it is if we burn it.
No!! Don't you dare!!!
Lucy...
...this is our job!!!!

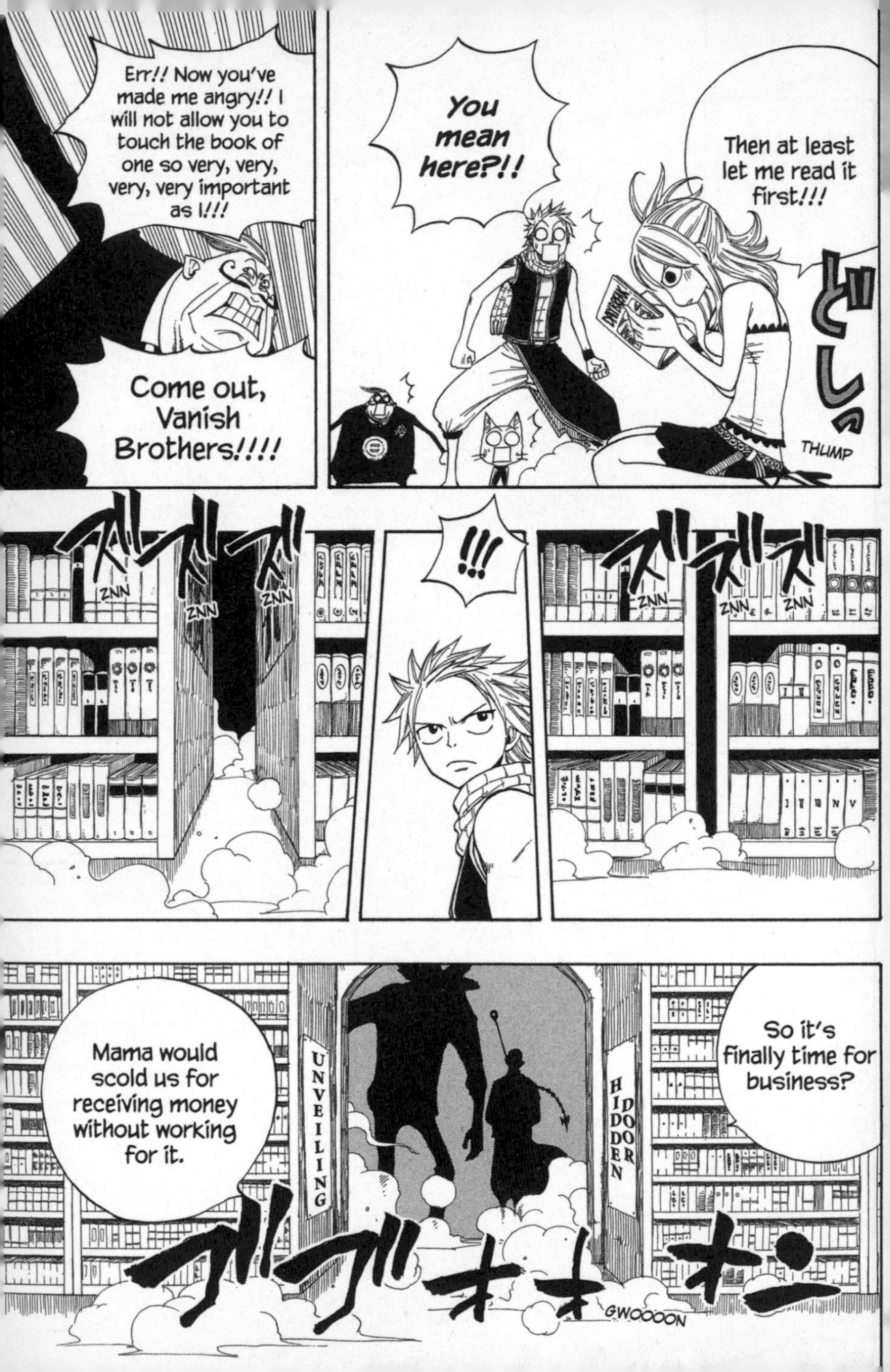

Then at least let me read it first!!!
どしっ
THUMP
You mean here?!!
Err!! Now you've made me angry!! I will not allow you to touch the book of one so very, very, very, very important as I!!!
Come out, Vanish Brothers!!!!
ZNN
ZNN
ZNN
!!!
ZNN
ZNN
ZNN
So it's finally time for business?
HIDDEN DOOR
UNVEILING
Mama would scold us for receiving money without working for it.
GWOOOON

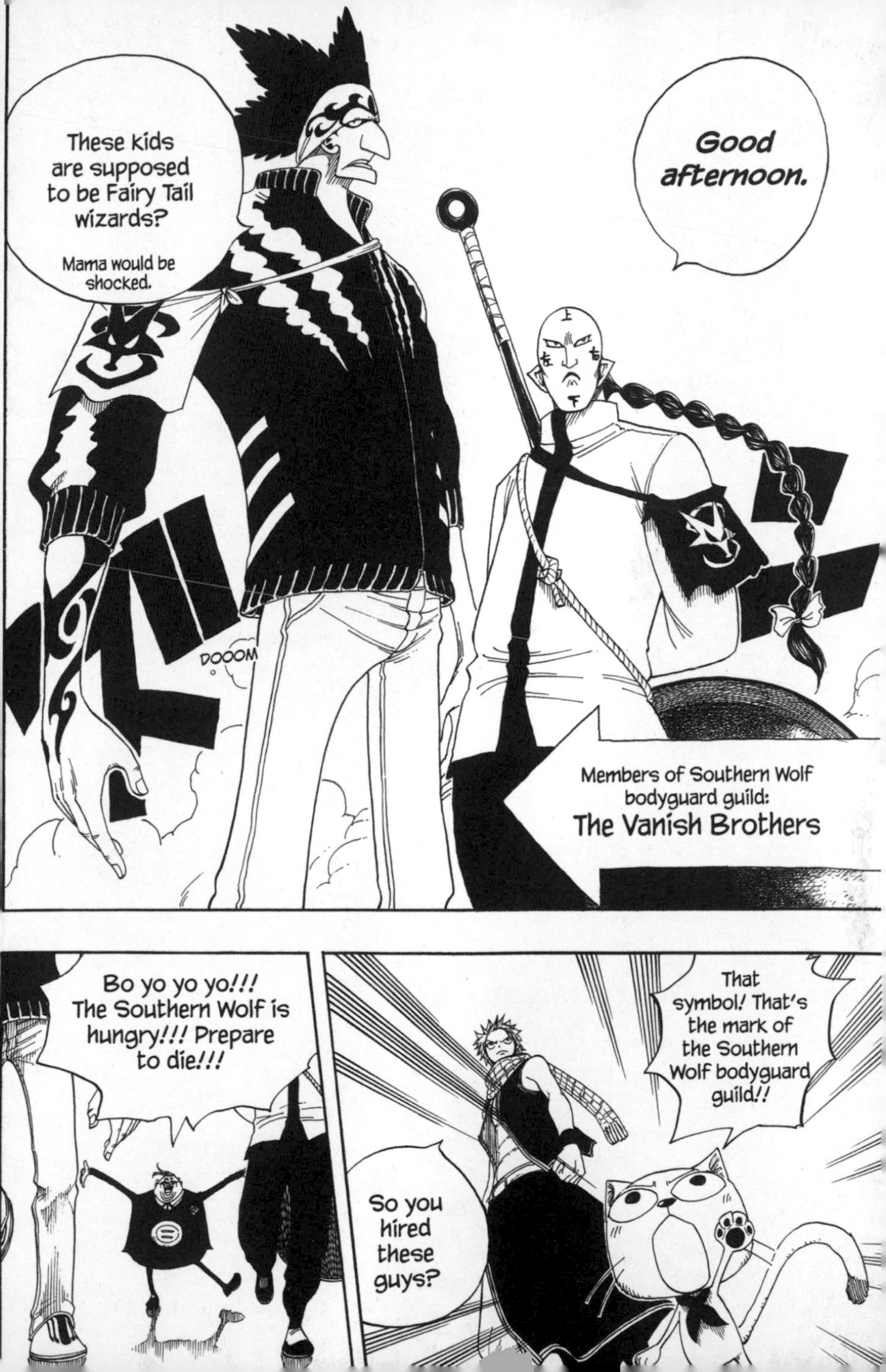
Good afternoon.
These kids are supposed to be Fairy Tail wizards?
Mama would be shocked.
DOOOM
Members of Southern Wolf bodyguard guild:
The Vanish Brothers
That symbol! That's the mark of the Southern Wolf bodyguard guild!!
So you hired these guys?
Bo yo yo yo!!! The Southern Wolf is hungry!!! Prepare to die!!!

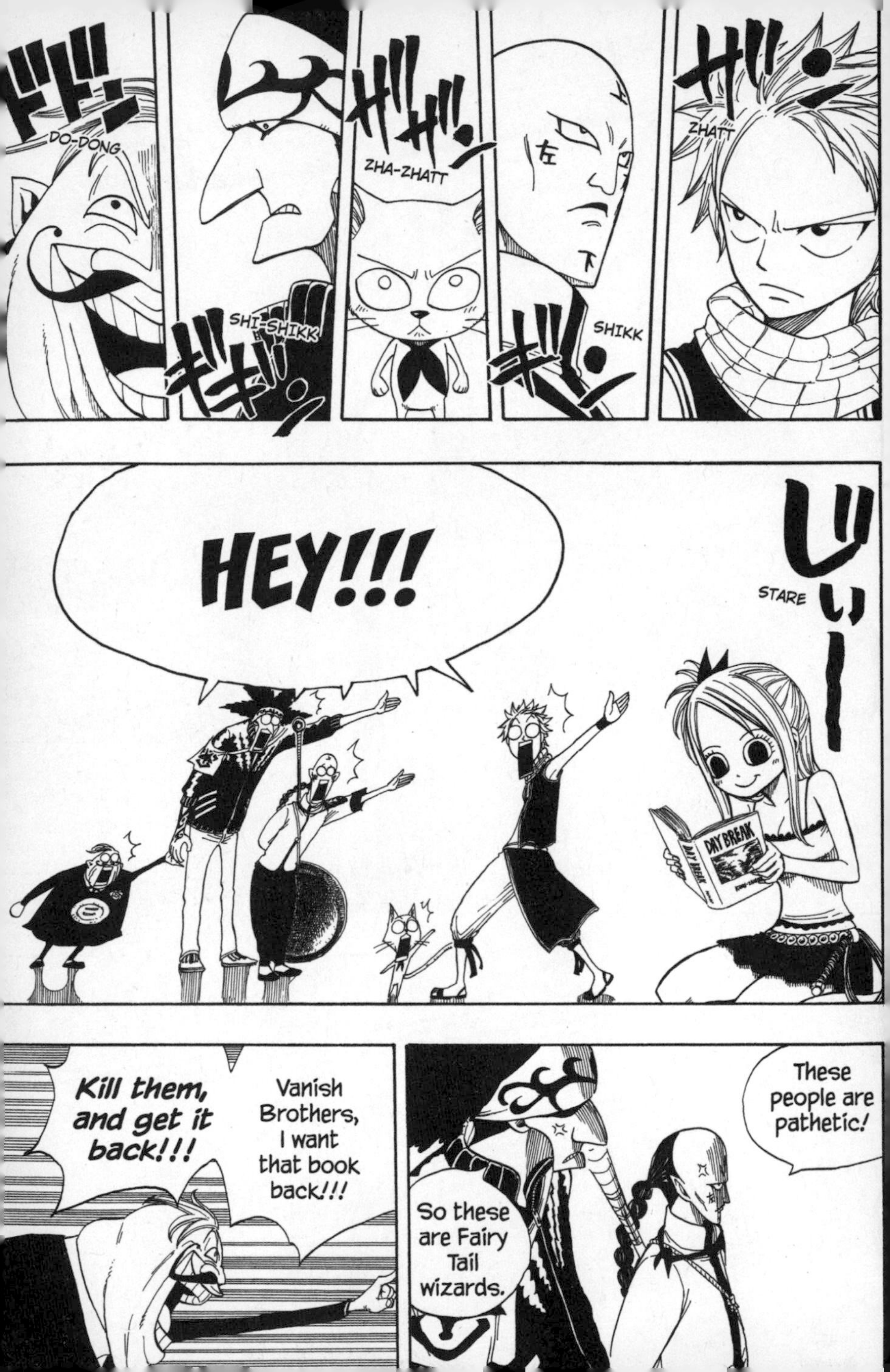
ZHATT
SHIKK
ZHA-ZHATT
SHI-SHIKK
DO-DONG
STARE
HEY!!!
These people are pathetic!
So these are Fairy Tail wizards.
Vanish Brothers, I want that book back!!!
Kill them, and get it back!!!

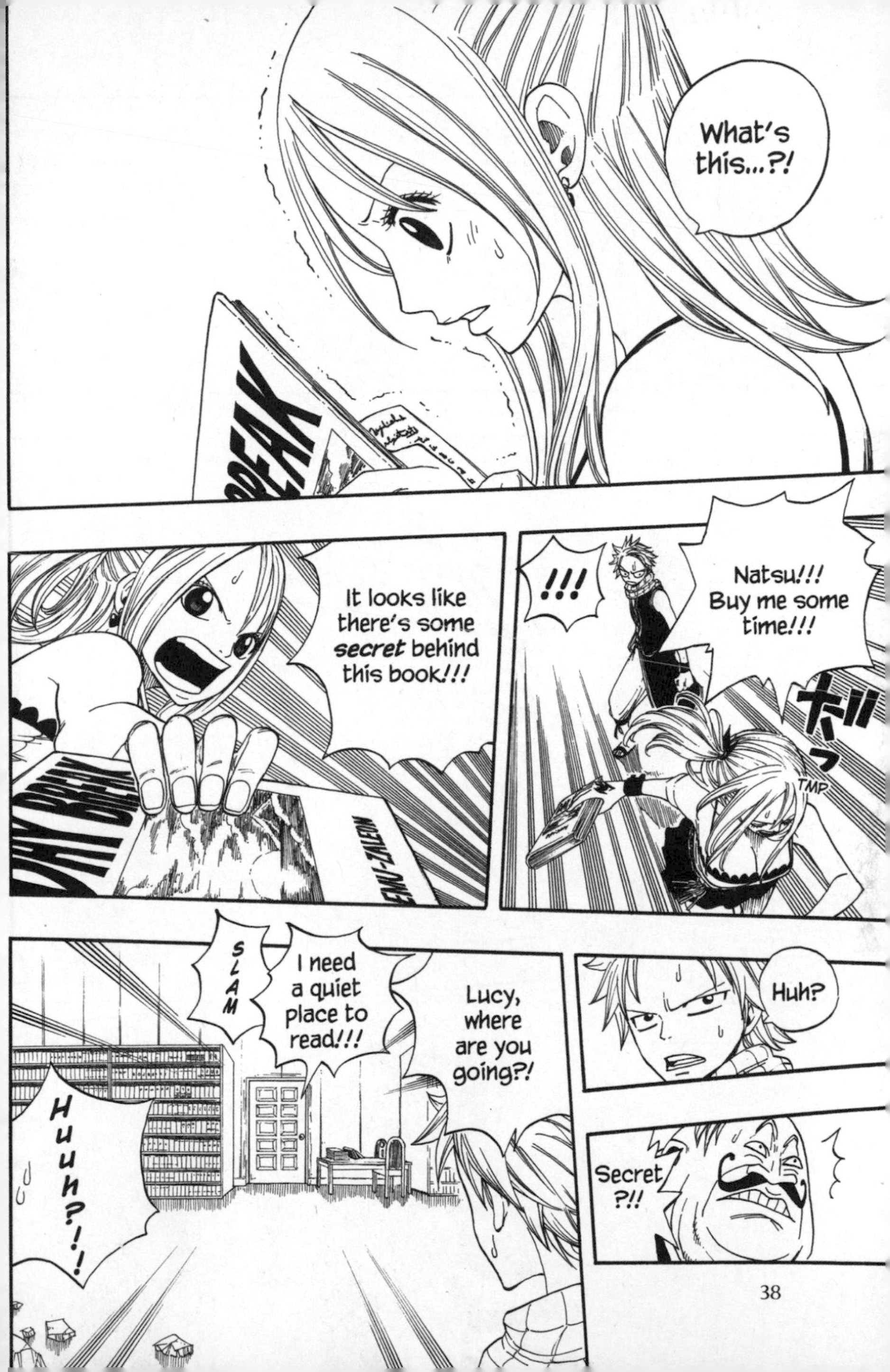
What's this...?!
!!!
Natsu!!! Buy me some time!!!
TMP
It looks like there's some *secret* behind this book!!!
Huh?
Secret?!!
Lucy, where are you going?!
I need a quiet place to read!!!
SLAM
Huuuh?!!

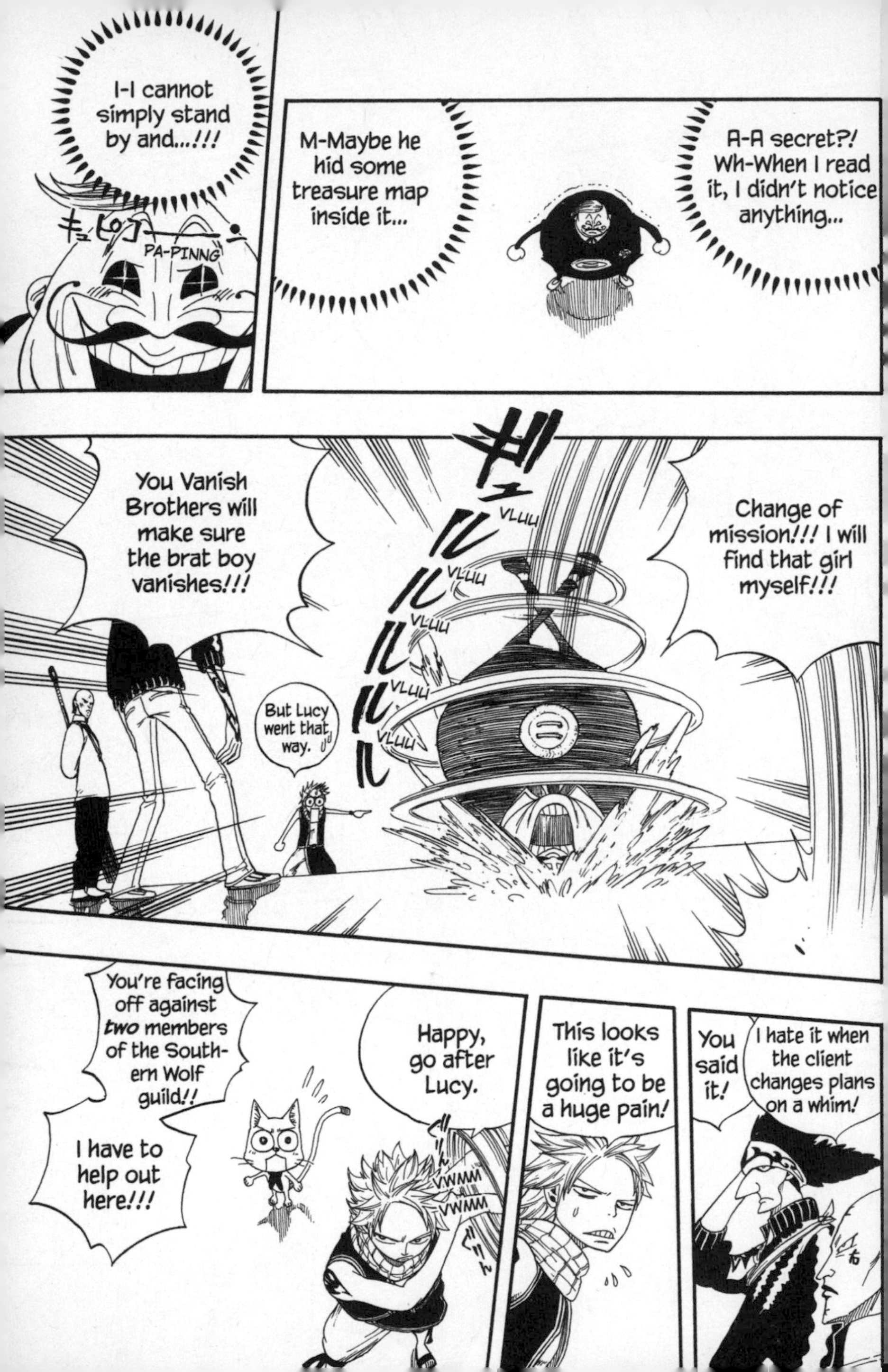

A-A secret?! Wh-When I read it, I didn't notice anything...
M-Maybe he hid some treasure map inside it...
I-I cannot simply stand by and...!!!
PA-PINNG
Change of mission!!! I will find that girl myself!!!
VLUU VLUU VLUU VLUU VLUU
You Vanish Brothers will make sure the brat boy vanishes!!!
But Lucy went that way.
I hate it when the client changes plans on a whim!
You said it!
This looks like it's going to be a huge pain!
Happy, go after Lucy.
VWMM VWMM
You're facing off against *two* members of the Southern Wolf guild!!
I have to help out here!!!

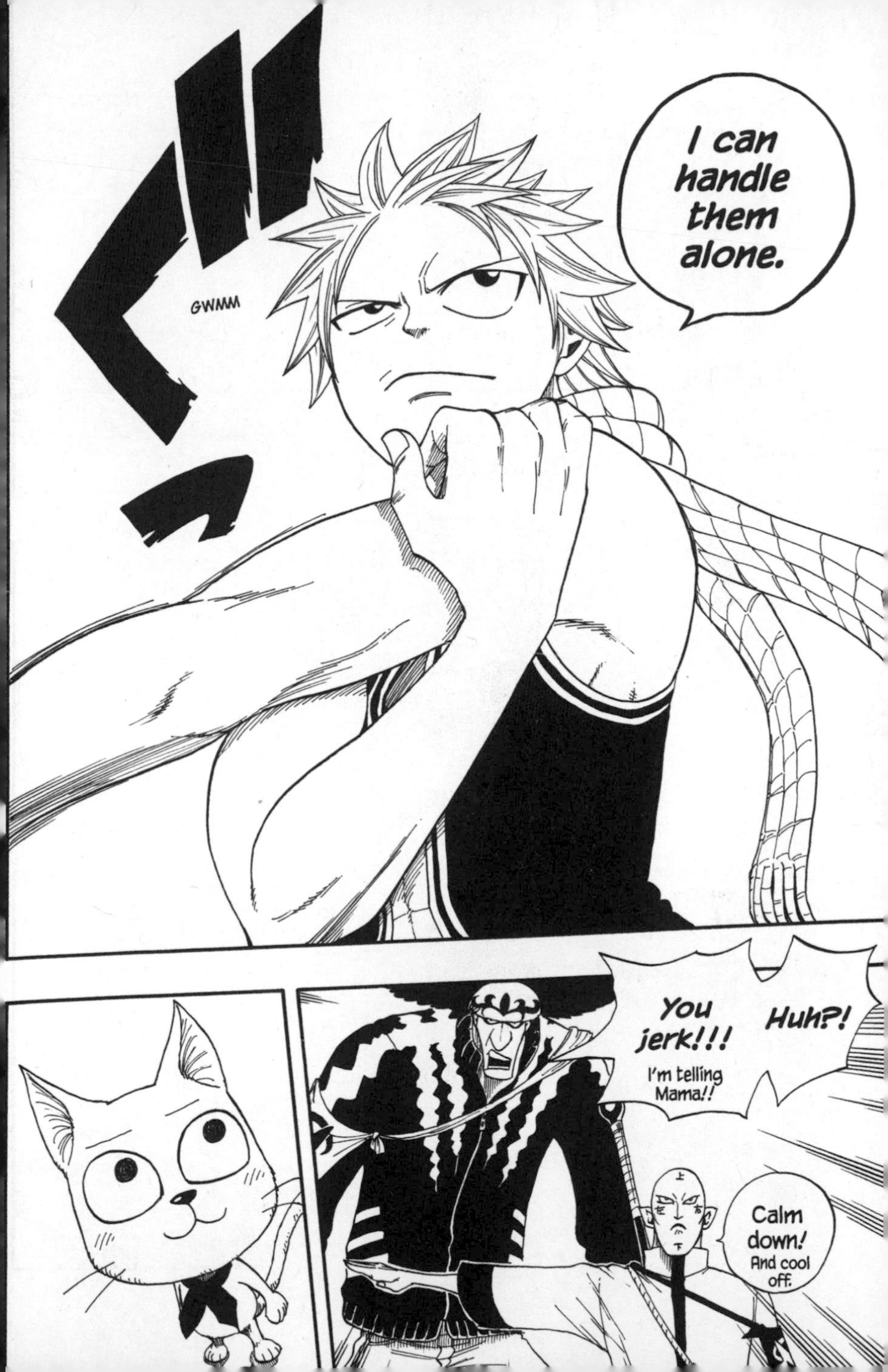
I can handle them alone.
GWMM
Huh?!
You jerk!!!
I'm telling Mama!!
Calm down! And cool off.

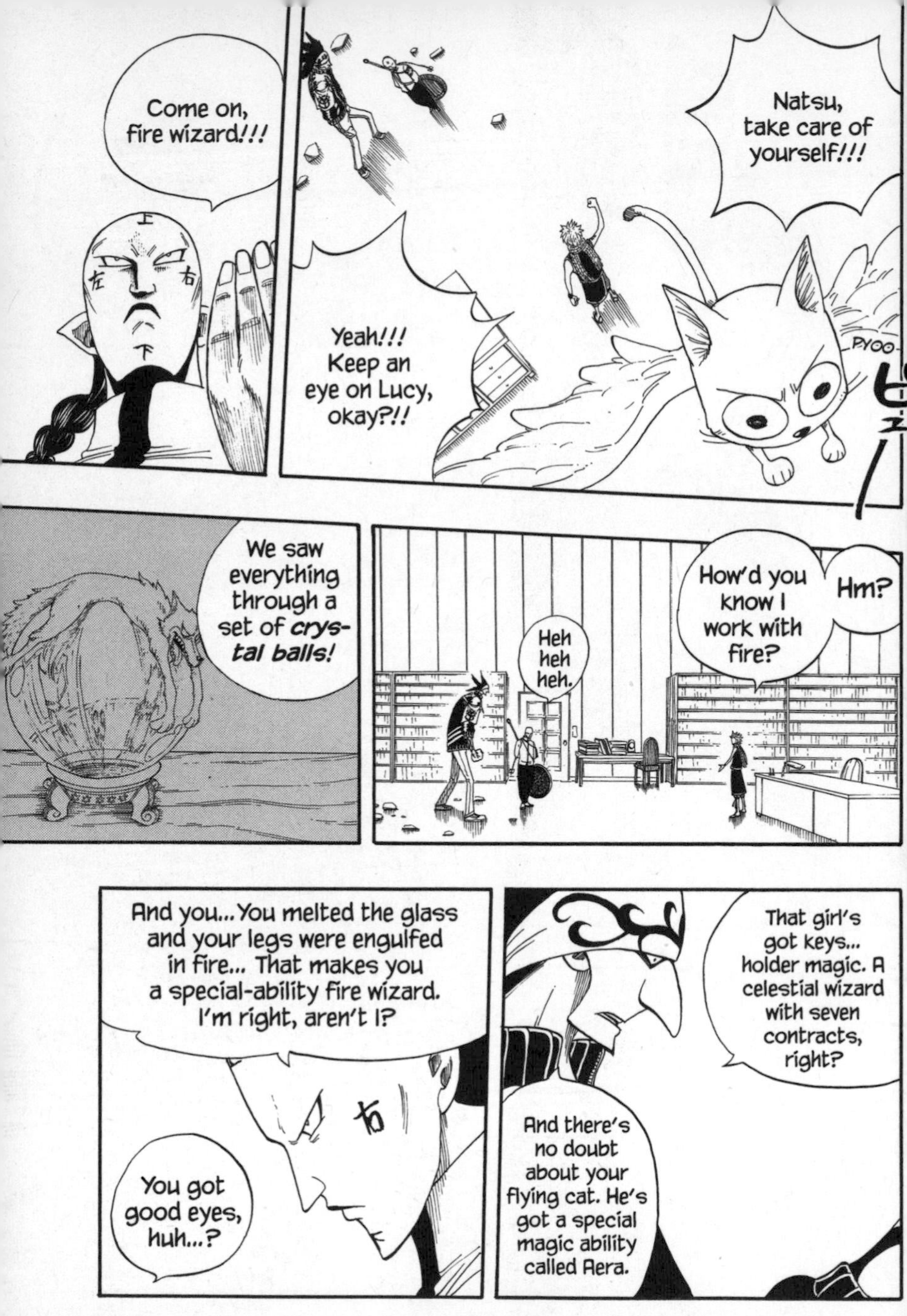
Natsu, take care of yourself!!!
Yeah!!! Keep an eye on Lucy, okay?!!
PYOO
ピュー
Come on, fire wizard!!!
Hm?
How'd you know I work with fire?
Heh heh heh.
We saw everything through a set of *crystal balls!*
That girl's got keys... holder magic. A celestial wizard with seven contracts, right?
And there's no doubt about your flying cat. He's got a special magic ability called Aera.
And you... You melted the glass and your legs were engulfed in fire... That makes you a special-ability fire wizard. I'm right, aren't I?
You got good eyes, huh...?

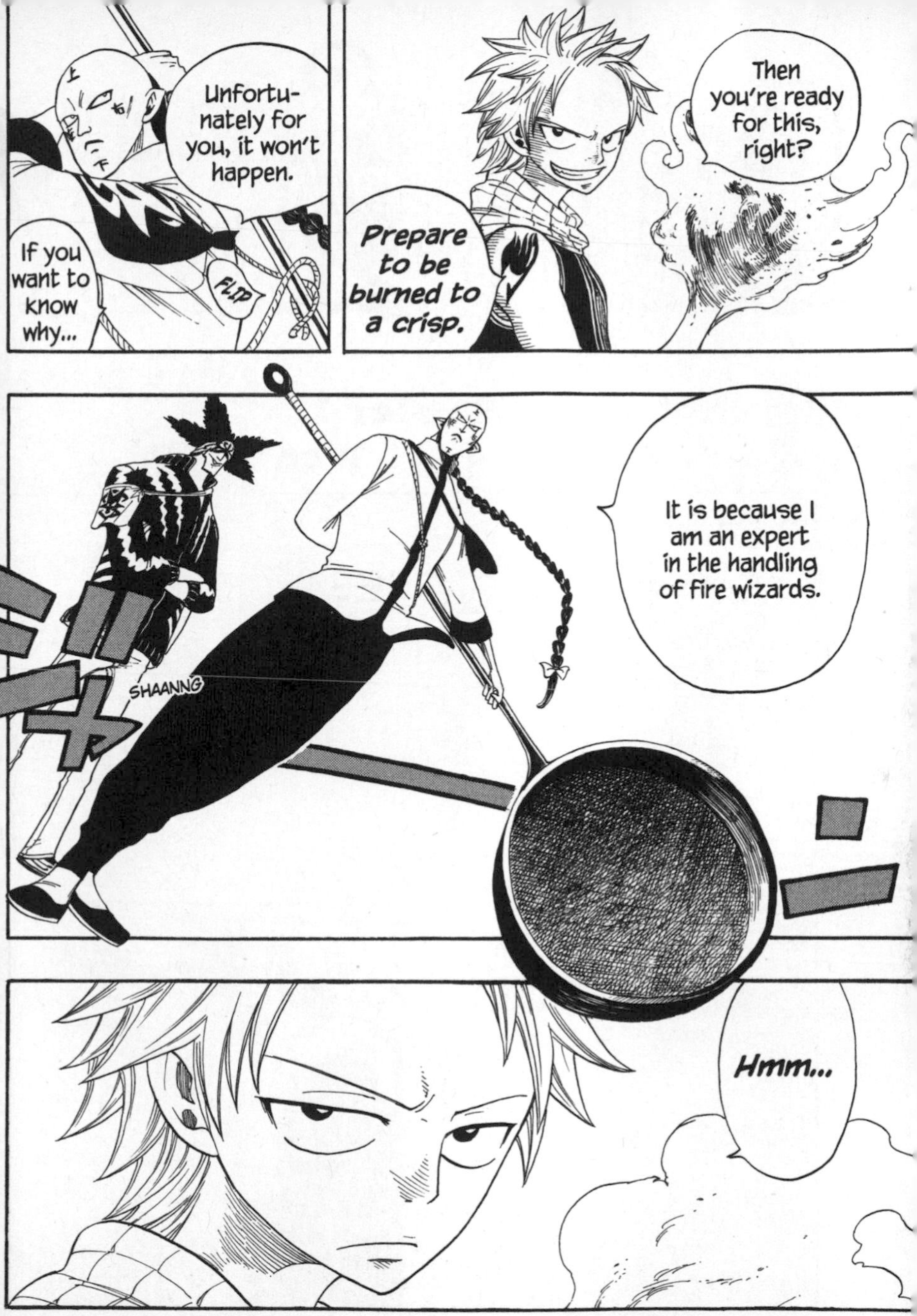
Then you're ready for this, right?
Prepare to be burned to a crisp.
Unfortu-nately for you, it won't happen.
FLIP
If you want to know why...
It is because I am an expert in the handling of fire wizards.
SHAANNG
Hmm...

FAIRY TAIL

Chapter 7: The Wizard's Weakness

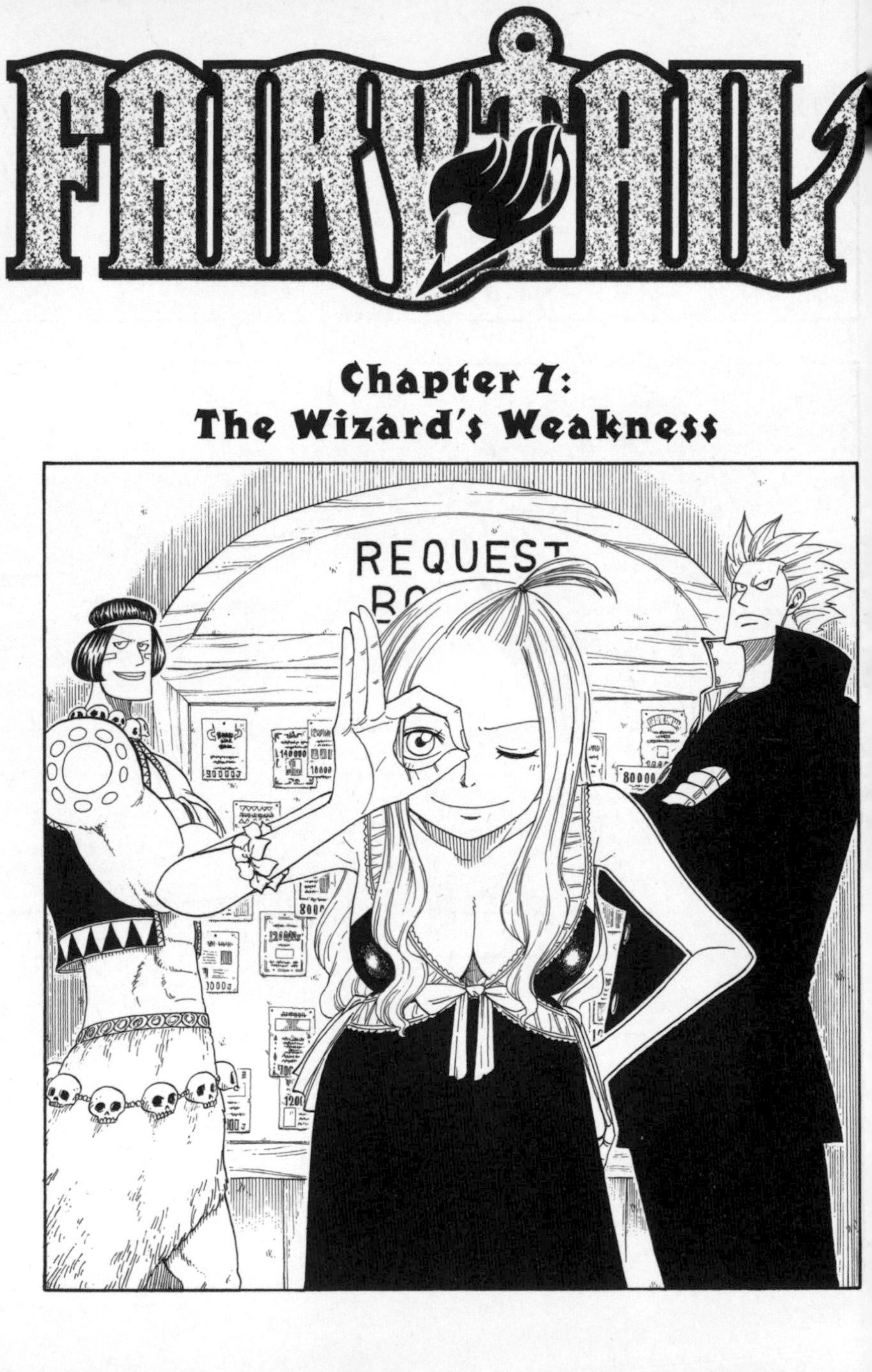
REQUEST

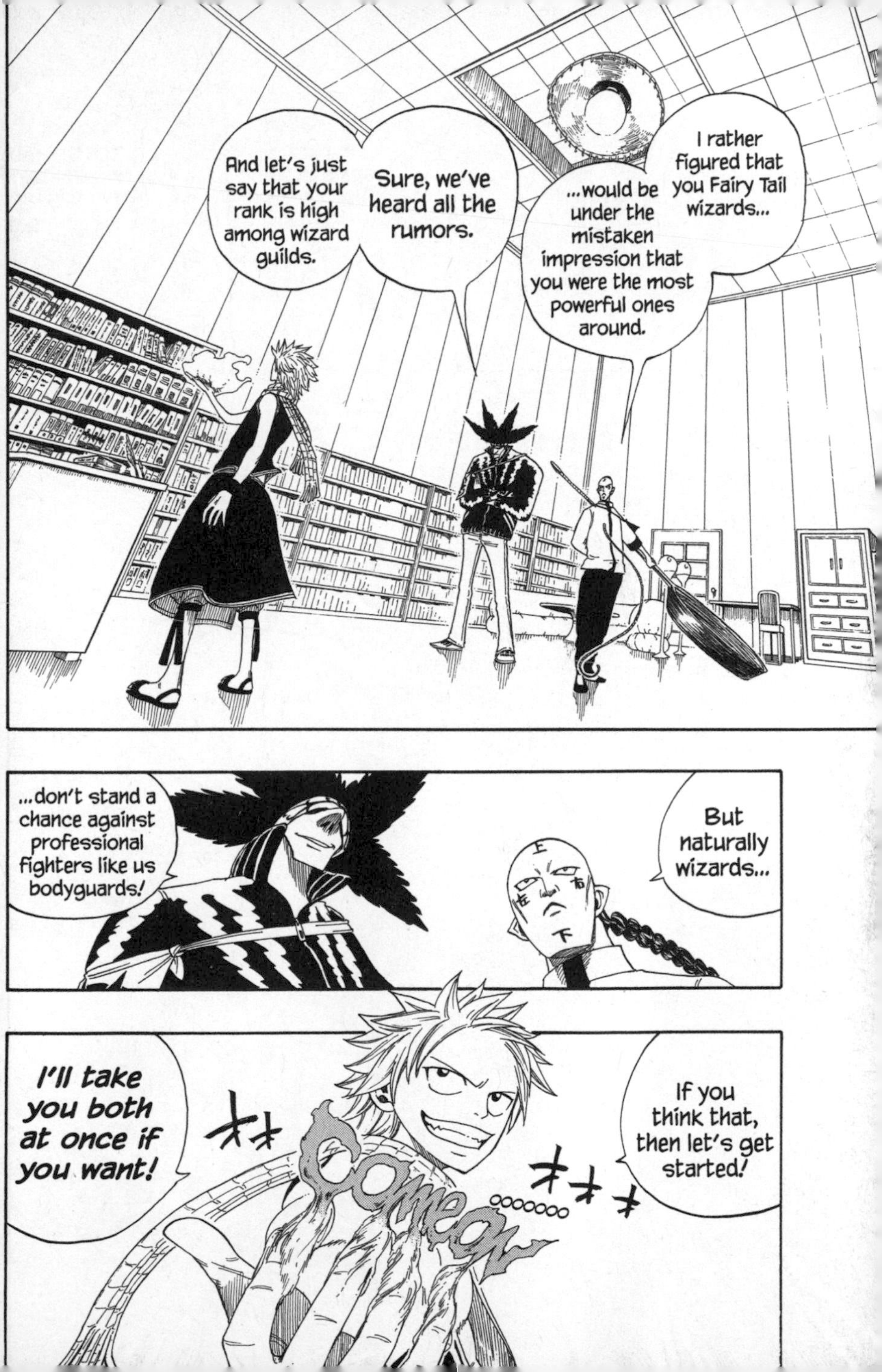
I rather figured that you Fairy Tail wizards...
...would be under the mistaken impression that you were the most powerful ones around.
Sure, we've heard all the rumors.
And let's just say that your rank is high among wizard guilds.
But naturally wizards...
...don't stand a chance against professional fighters like us bodyguards!
If you think that, then let's get started!
I'll take you both at once if you want!

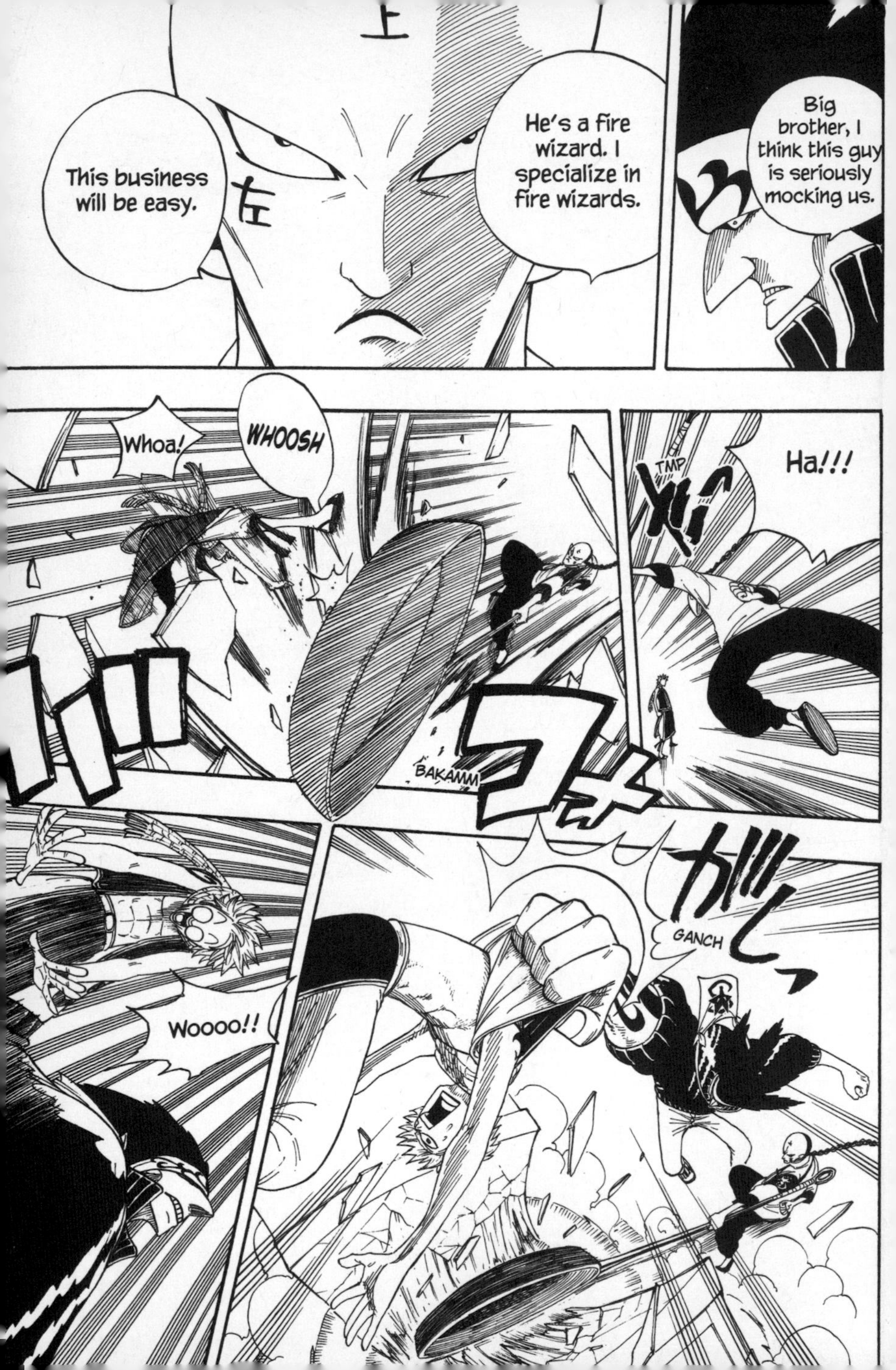
Big brother, I think this guy is seriously mocking us.
He's a fire wizard. I specialize in fire wizards.
This business will be easy.
TMP
Ha!!!
WHOOSH
Whoa!
BAKAMM
GANCH
Woooo!!

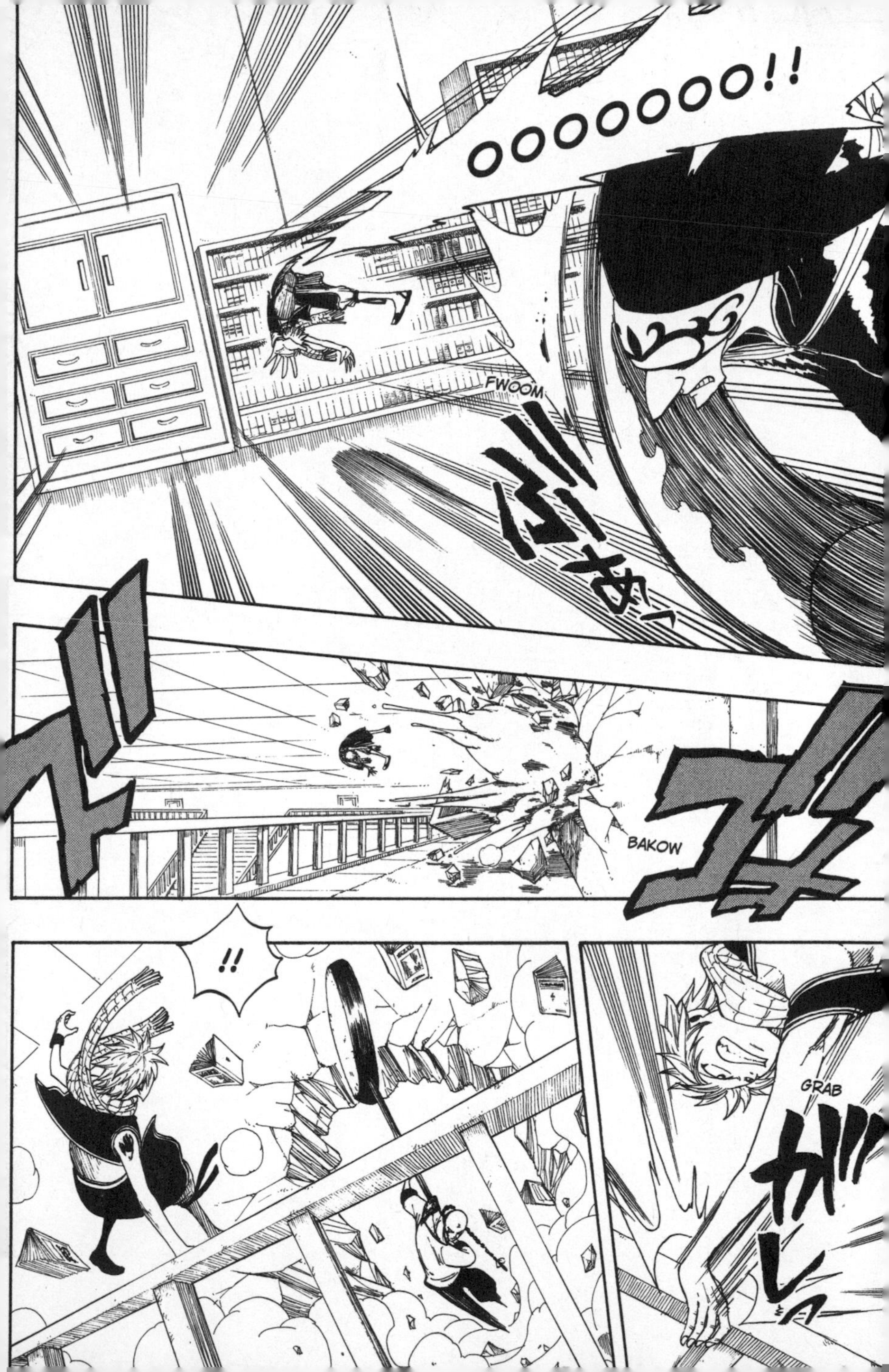
OOOOOOOO!!
FWOOM
BAKOW
GRAB
!!

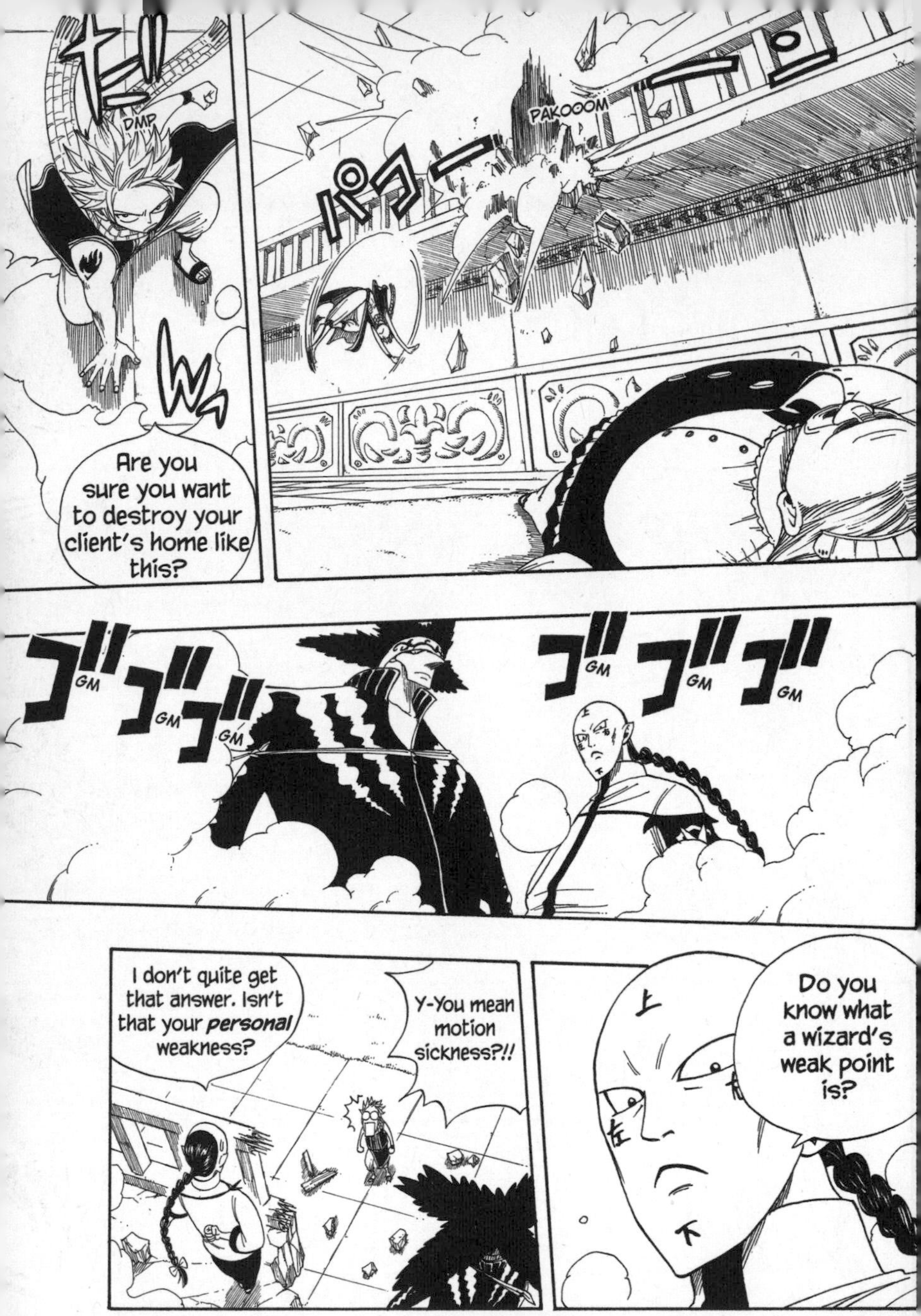
PAKOOOM
DMP
Are you sure you want to destroy your client's home like this?
GM GM GM
GM GM GM
Do you know what a wizard's weak point is?
Y-You mean motion sickness?!!
I don't quite get that answer. Isn't that your *personal* weakness?

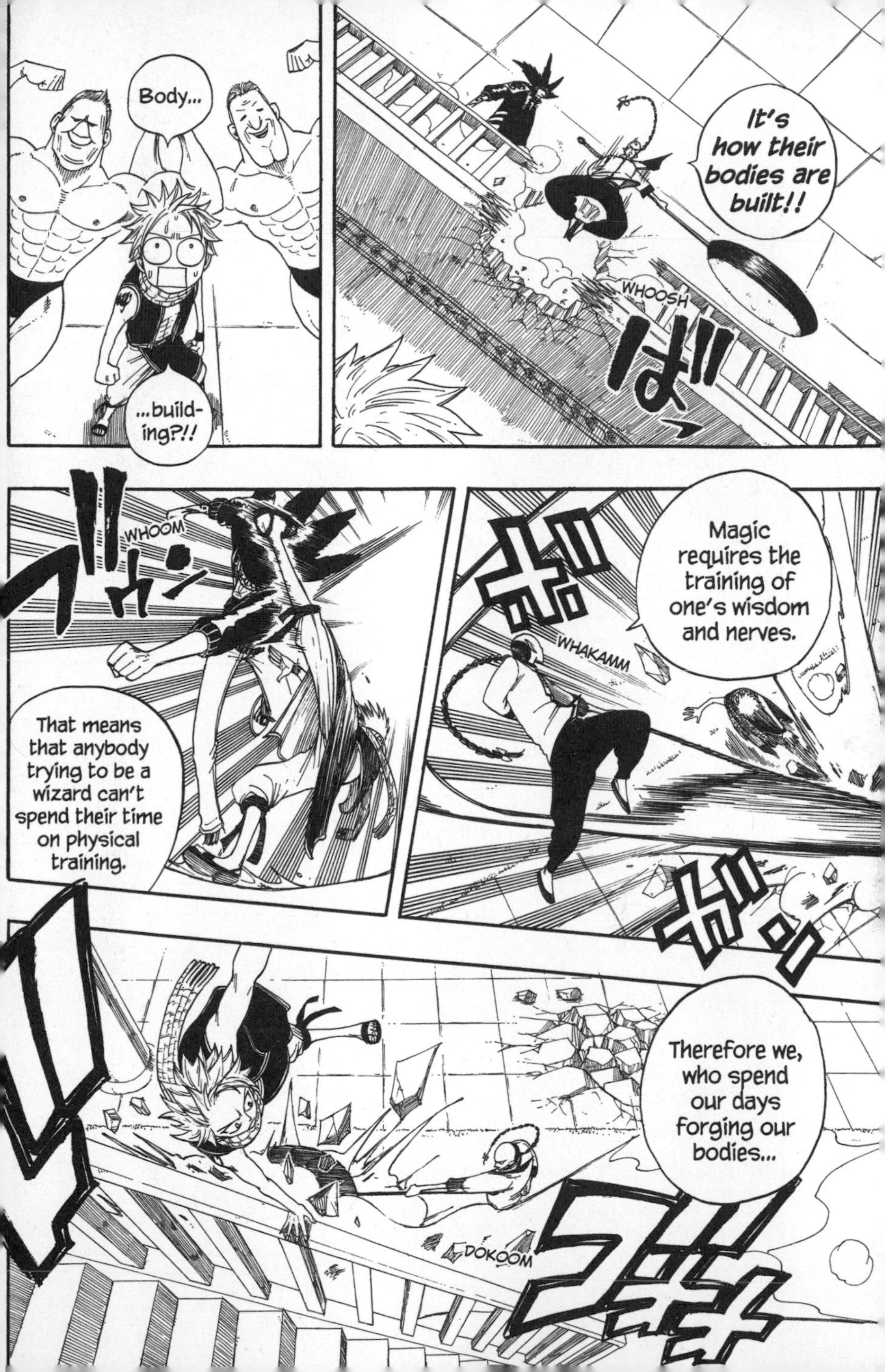
It's how their bodies are built!!
WHOOSH
Body...
...building?!!
Magic requires the training of one's wisdom and nerves.
WHAKAMM
WHOOM
That means that anybody trying to be a wizard can't spend their time on physical training.
Therefore we, who spend our days forging our bodies...
DOKOOM

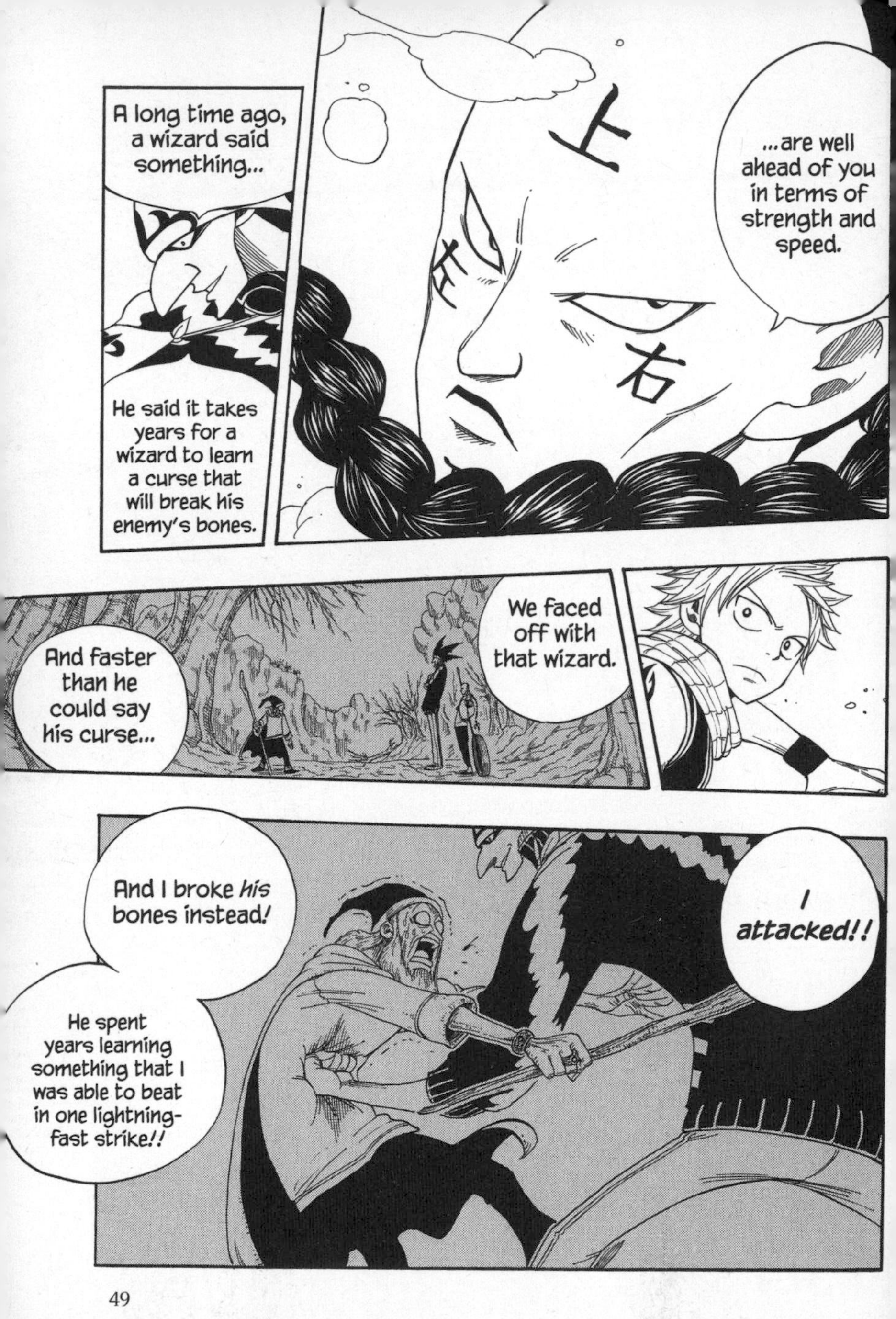
...are well ahead of you in terms of strength and speed.
A long time ago, a wizard said something...
He said it takes years for a wizard to learn a curse that will break his enemy's bones.
We faced off with that wizard.
And faster than he could say his curse...
I attacked!!
And I broke *his* bones instead!
He spent years learning something that I was able to beat in one lightning-fast strike!!

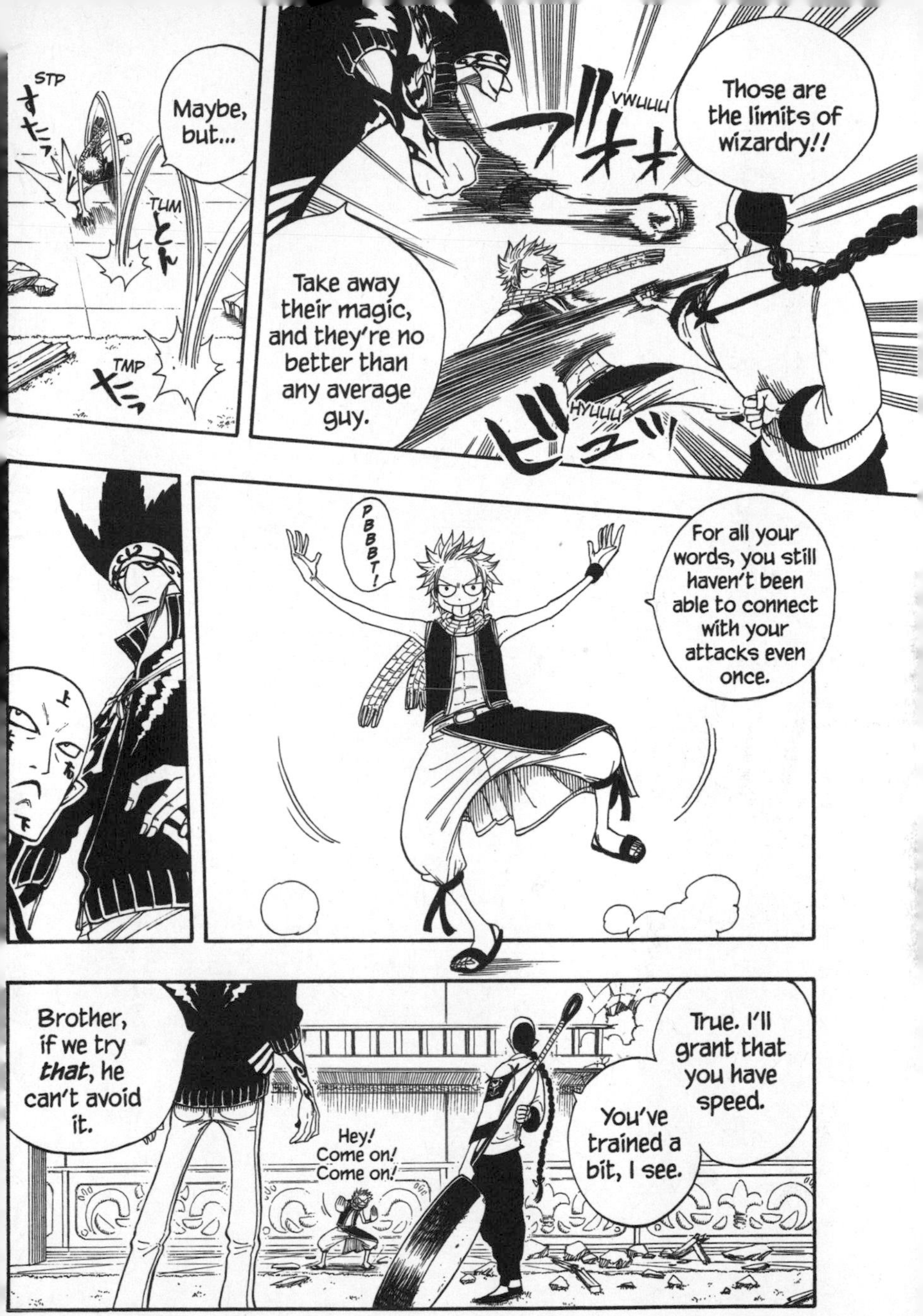
VWUUU
Those are the limits of wizardry!!
Take away their magic, and they're no better than any average guy.
HYUUU
Maybe, but...
STP
TUM
TMP
PBBBT!
For all your words, you still haven't been able to connect with your attacks even once.
True. I'll grant that you have speed.
You've trained a bit, I see.
Hey! Come on! Come on!
Brother, if we try *that*, he can't avoid it.

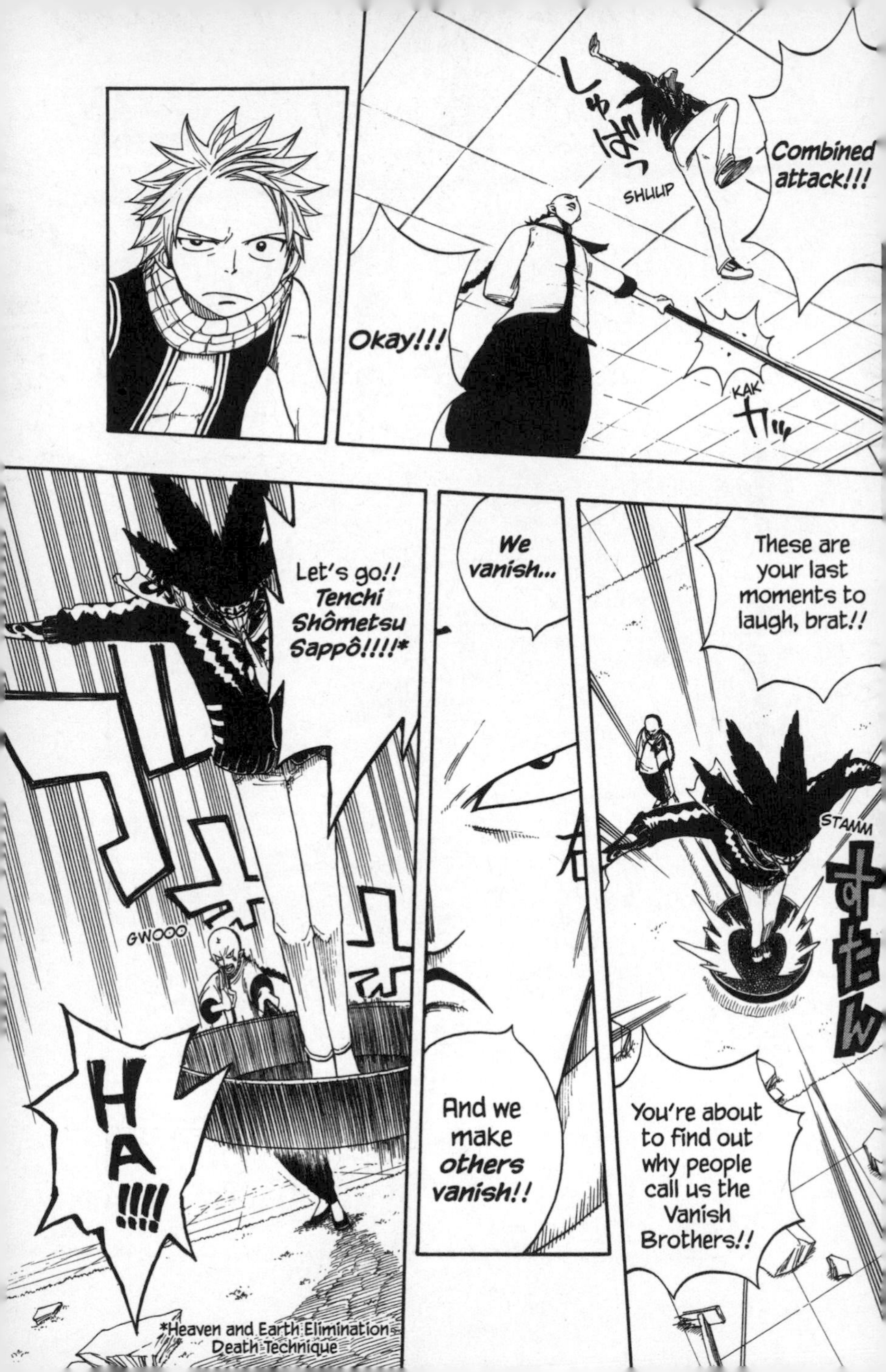
Combined attack!!!
しゅぼっ
SHUUP
Okay!!!
KAK
カッ
These are your last moments to laugh, brat!!
STAMM
すたん
You're about to find out why people call us the Vanish Brothers!!
We vanish...
And we make *others* vanish!!
Let's go!! *Tenchi Shômetsu Sappô!!!!**
GWOOO
HA!!!!

*Heaven and Earth Elimination Death Technique

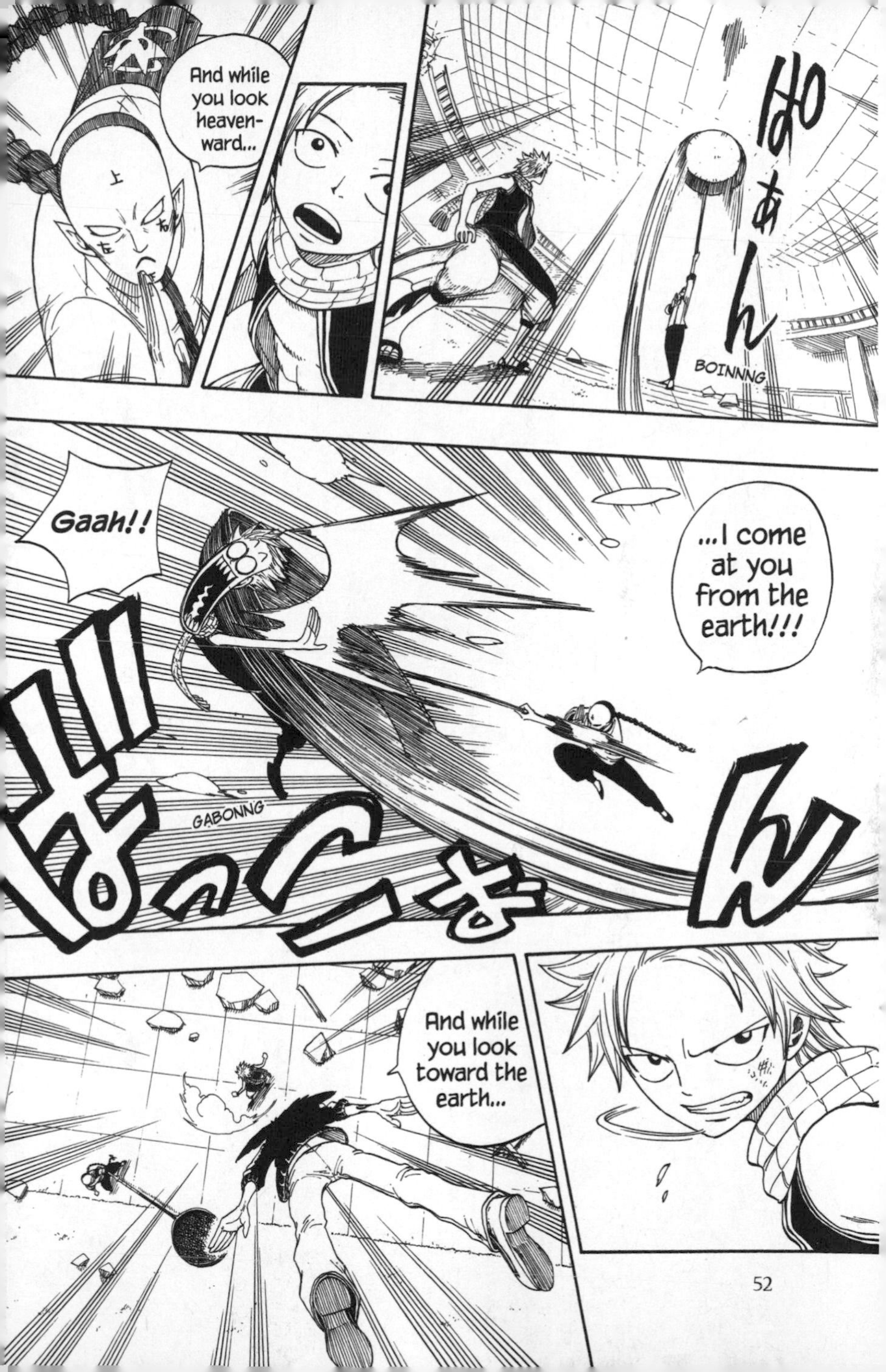
BOINNNG
And while you look heavenward...
...I come at you from the earth!!!
Gaah!!
GABONNG
And while you look toward the earth...

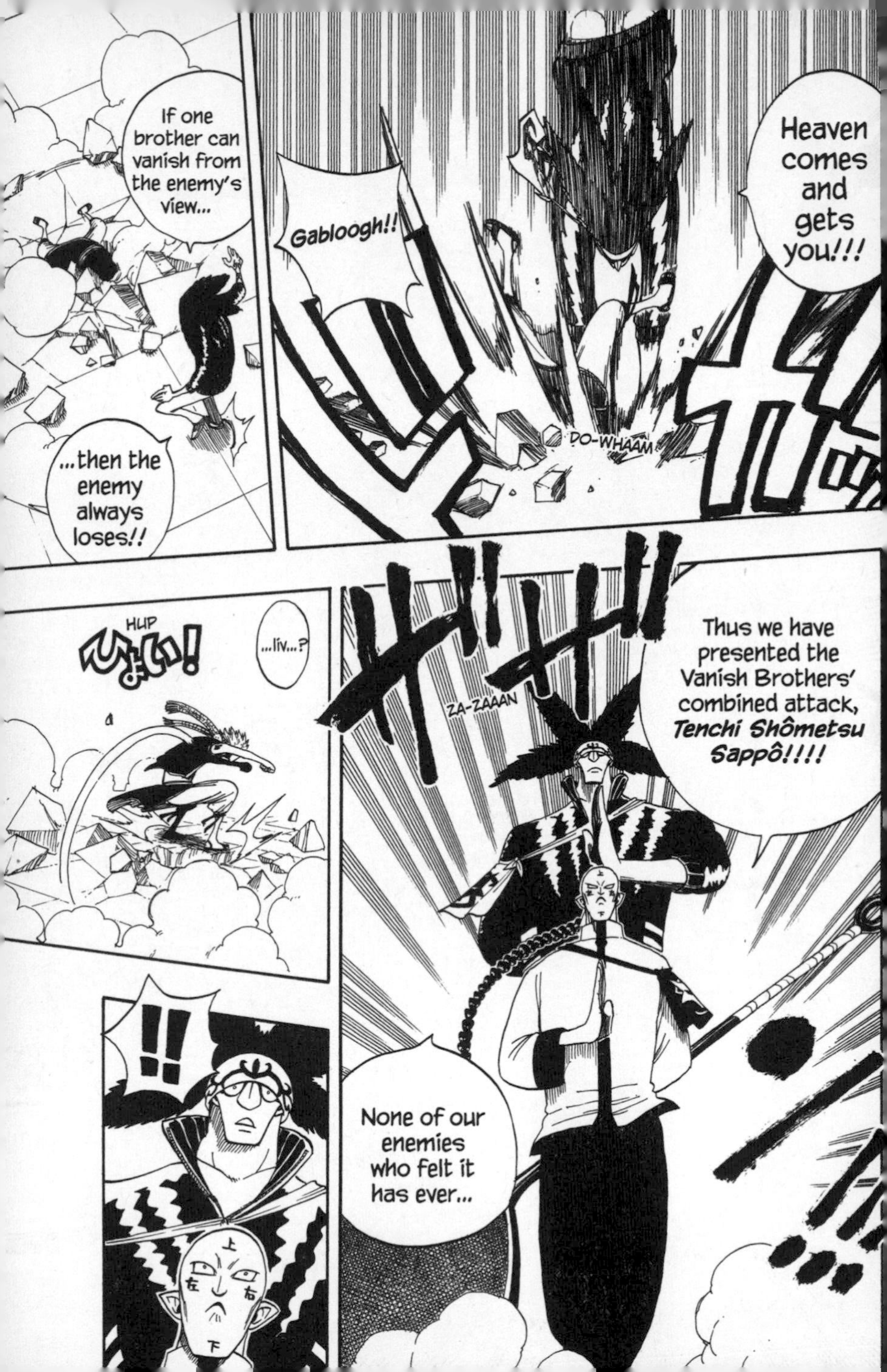

Heaven comes and gets you!!!
Gabloogh!!
DO-WHAAM
If one brother can vanish from the enemy's view...
...then the enemy always loses!!
ZA-ZAAAN
Thus we have presented the Vanish Brothers' combined attack, *Tenchi Shômetsu Sappô!!!!*
None of our enemies who felt it has ever...
HUP
...liv...?
!!

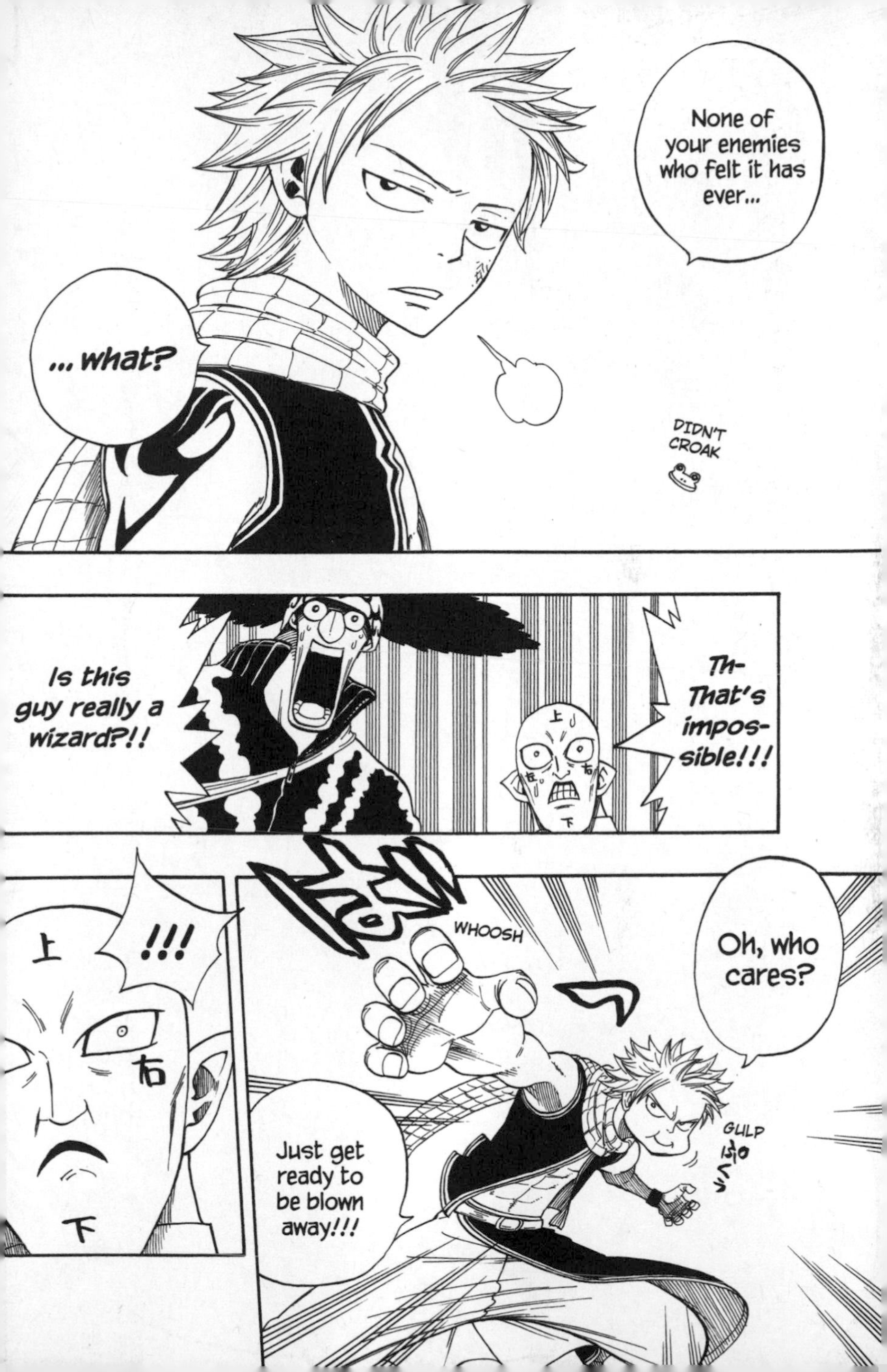
None of your enemies who felt it has ever...
...what?
DIDN'T CROAK
Th- That's impossible!!!
Is this guy really a wizard?!!
WHOOSH
Oh, who cares?
GULP
Just get ready to be blown away!!!
!!!

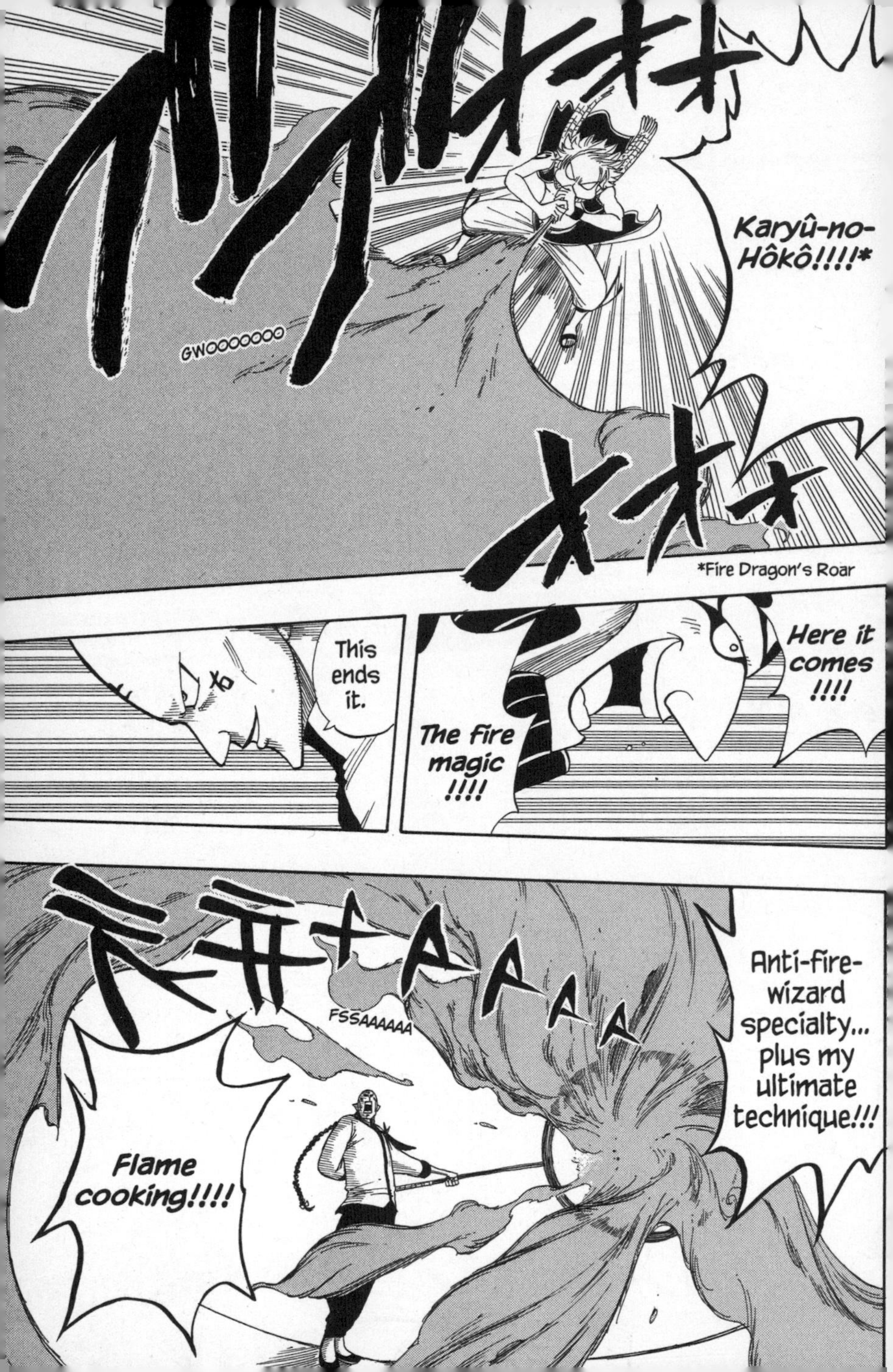
Karyû-no-Hôkô!!!!*
GWOOOOOOO
*Fire Dragon's Roar
Here it comes!!!!
The fire magic!!!!
This ends it.
Anti-fire-wizard specialty... plus my ultimate technique!!!
FSSAAAAAA
Flame cooking!!!!

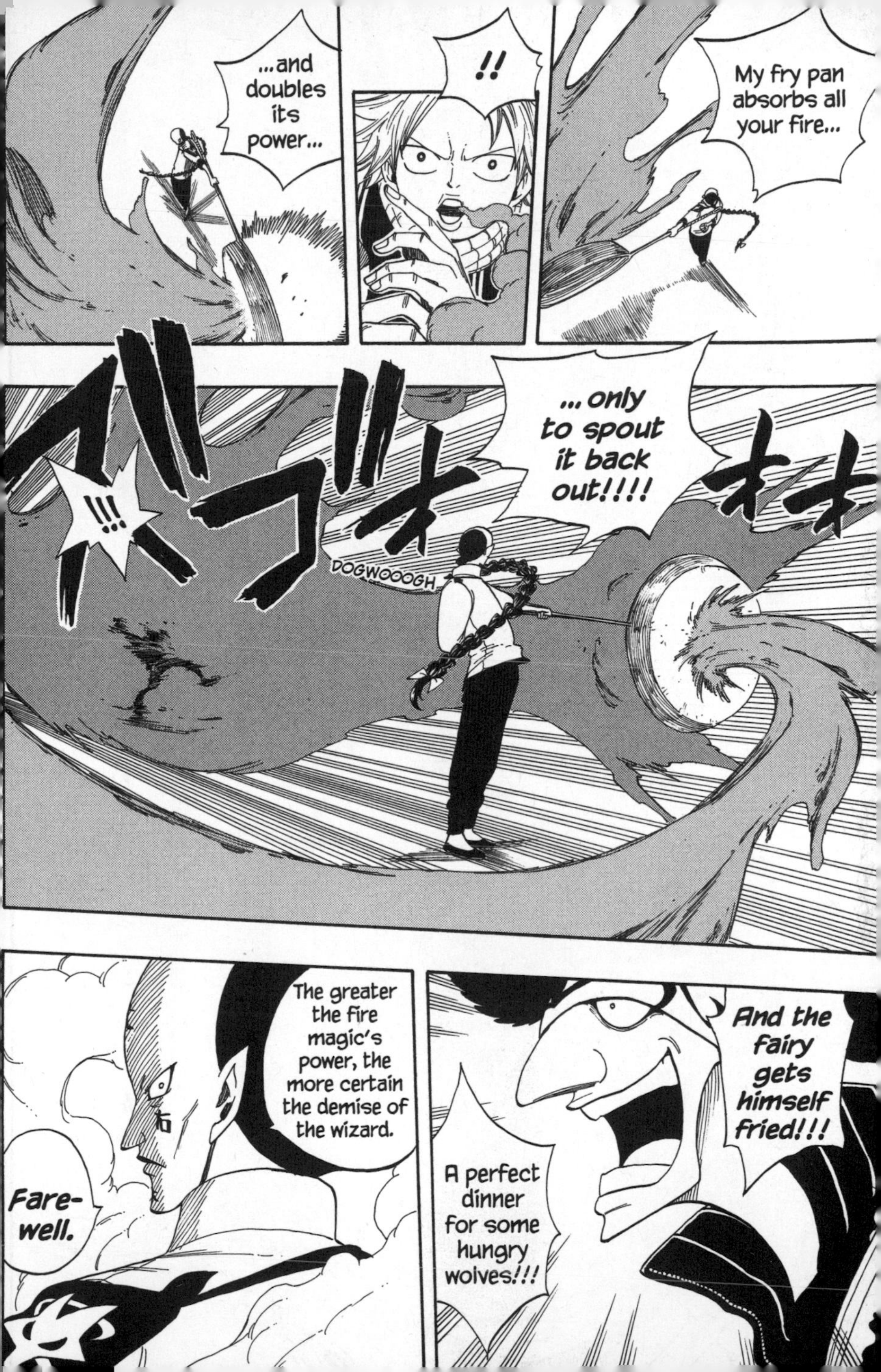
My fry pan absorbs all your fire...
!!
...and doubles its power...
...only to spout it back out!!!!
!!!
DOGWOOOGH
And the fairy gets himself fried!!!
A perfect dinner for some hungry wolves!!!
The greater the fire magic's power, the more certain the demise of the wizard.
Fare-well.

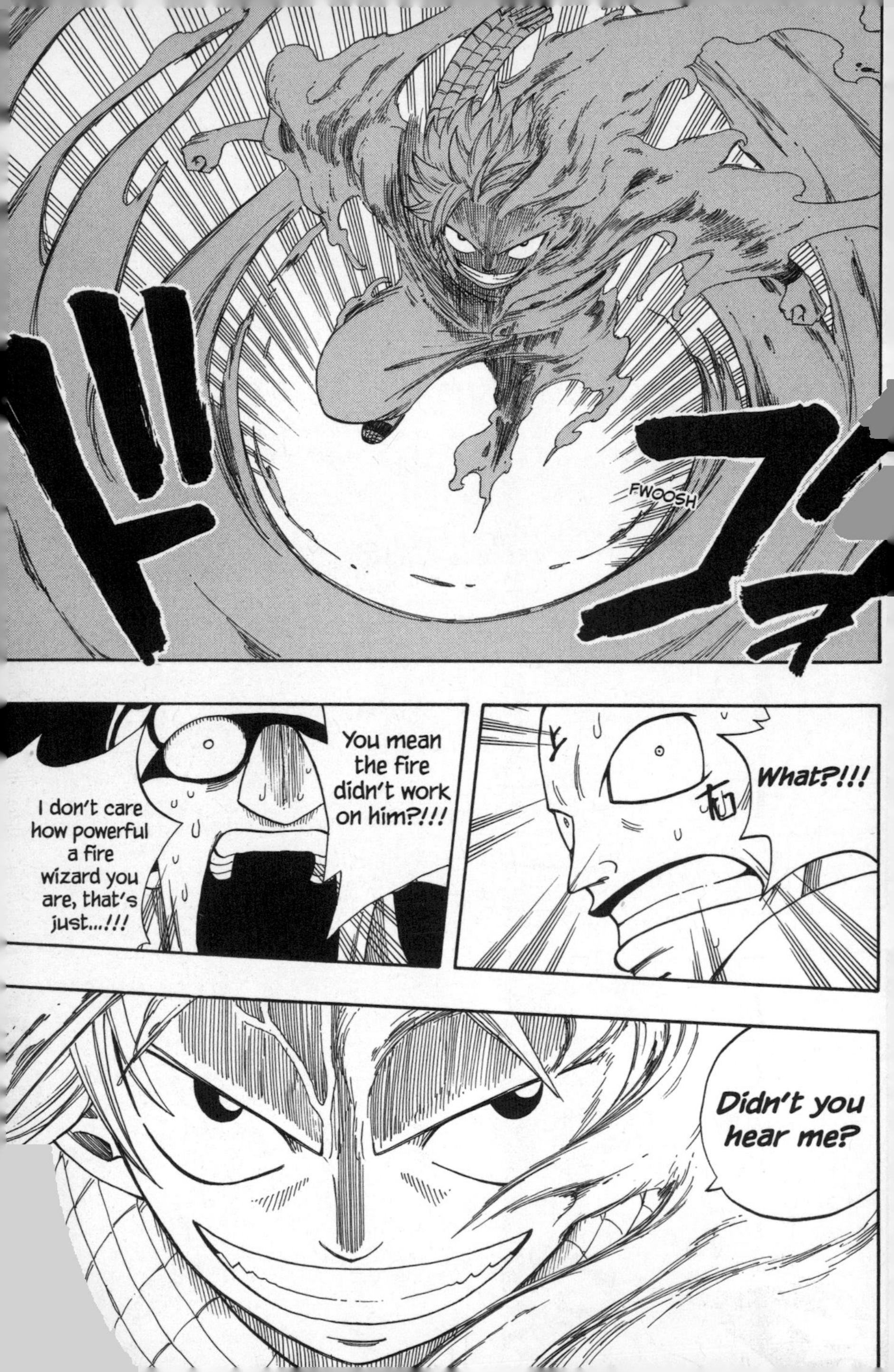
FWOOSH
What?!!!
You mean the fire didn't work on him?!!!
I don't care how powerful a fire wizard you are, that's just...!!!
Didn't you hear me?

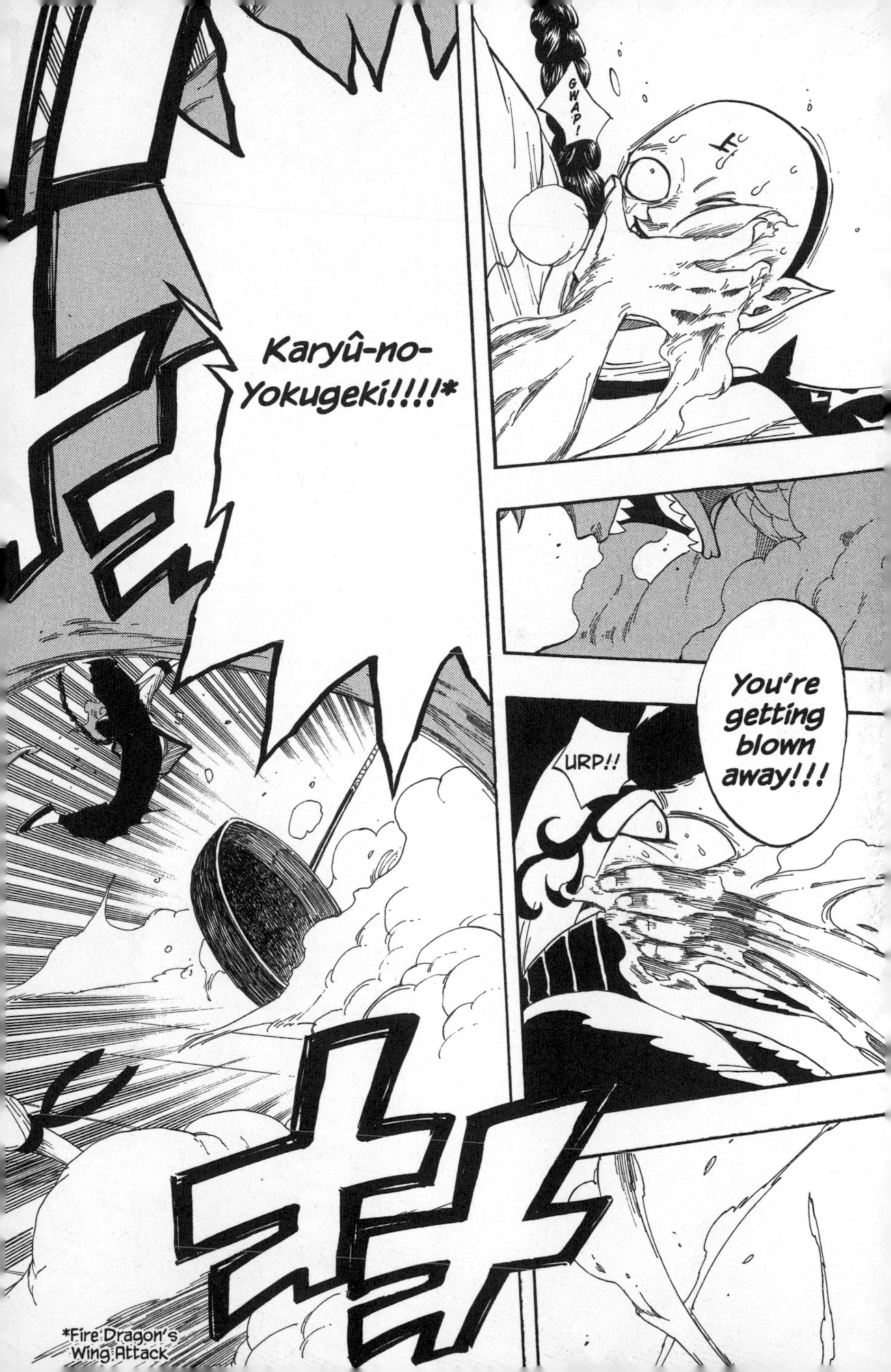
GWAP!
You're getting blown away!!!
URP!!
Karyû-no-Yokugeki!!!!*
*Fire Dragon's Wing Attack

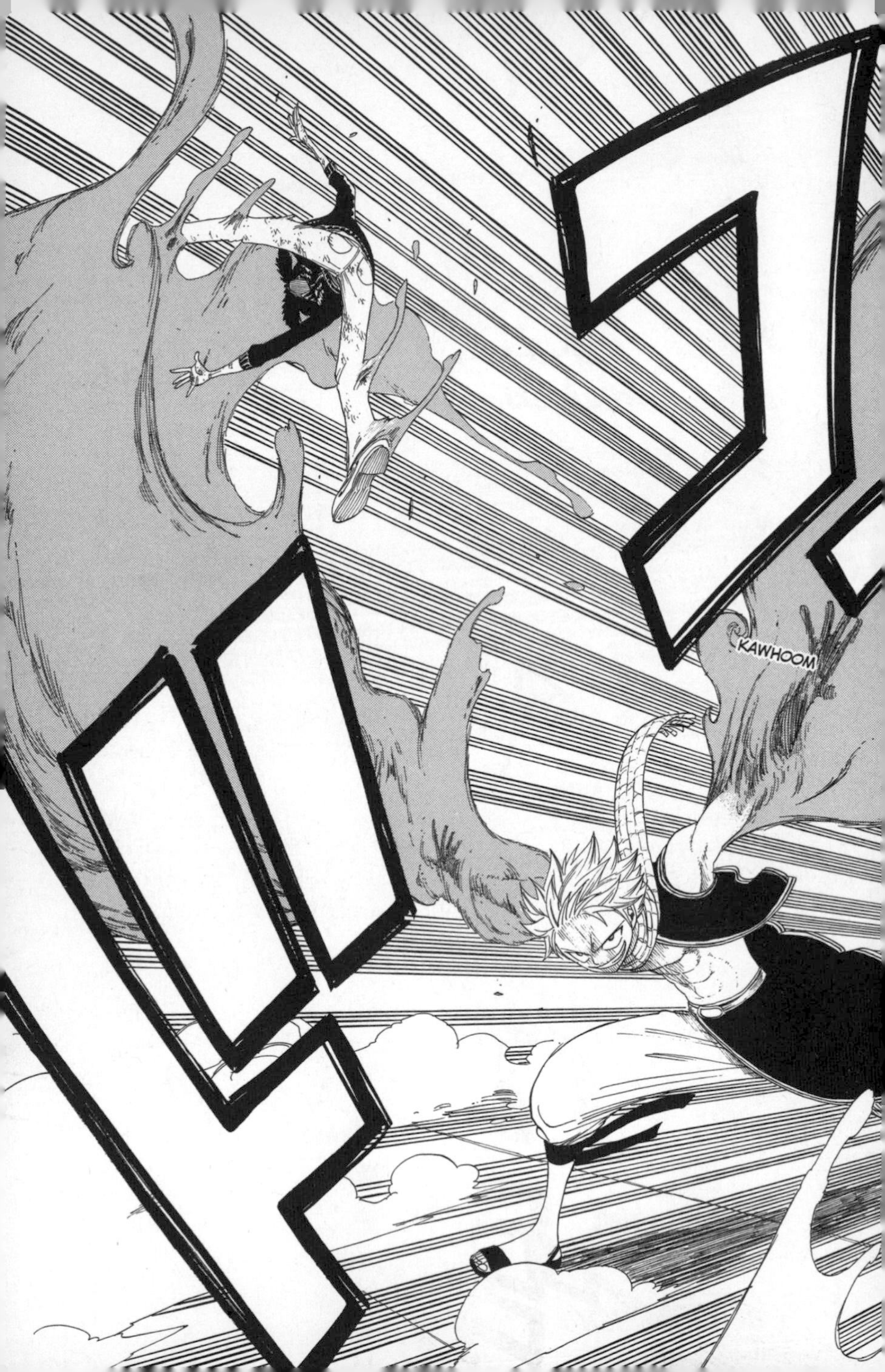
KAWHOOM

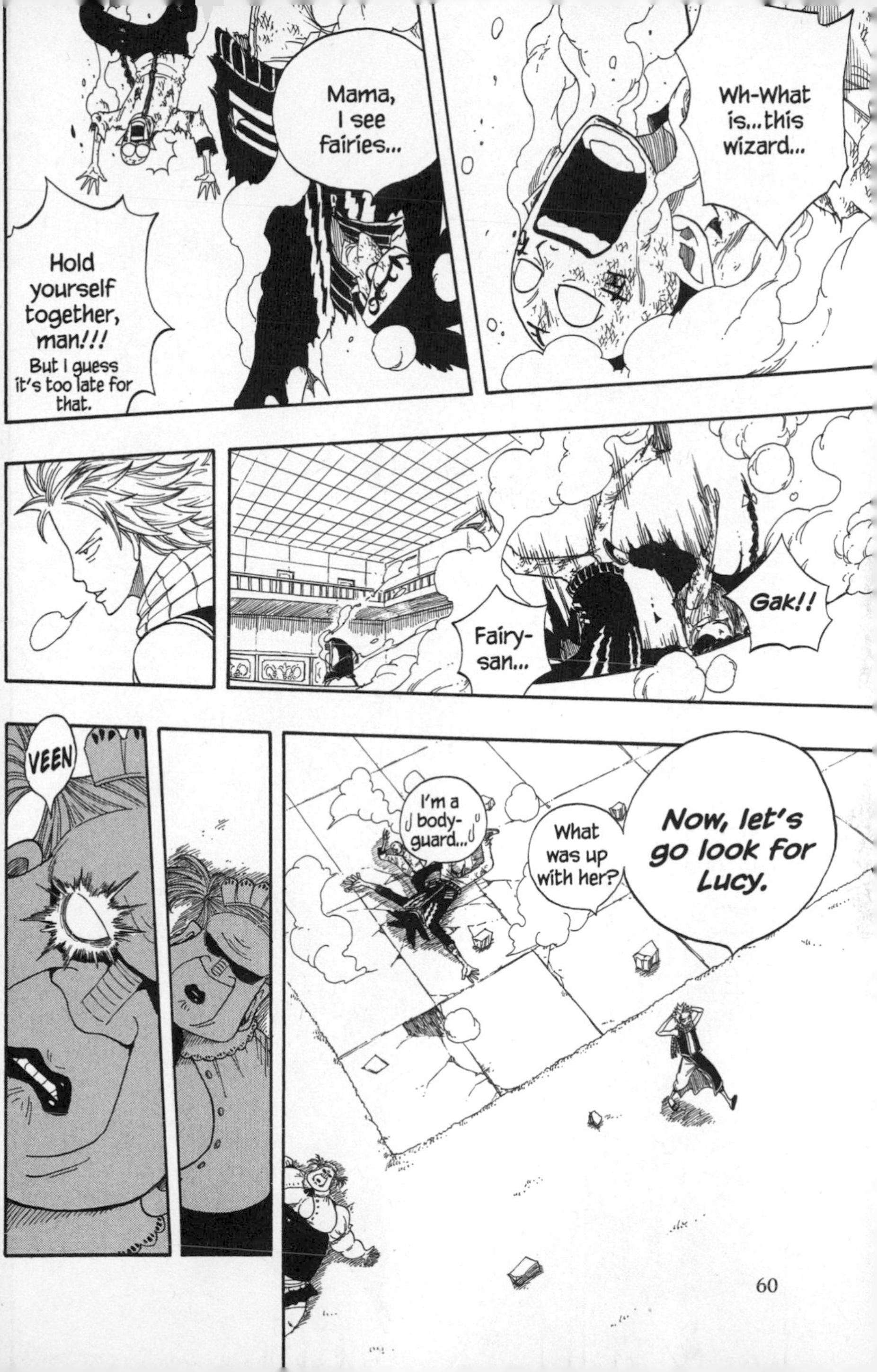
Wh-What is...this wizard...
Mama, I see fairies...
Hold yourself together, man!!!
But I guess it's too late for that.
Gak!!
Fairy-san...
Now, let's go look for Lucy.
What was up with her?
I'm a bodyguard...
VEEN

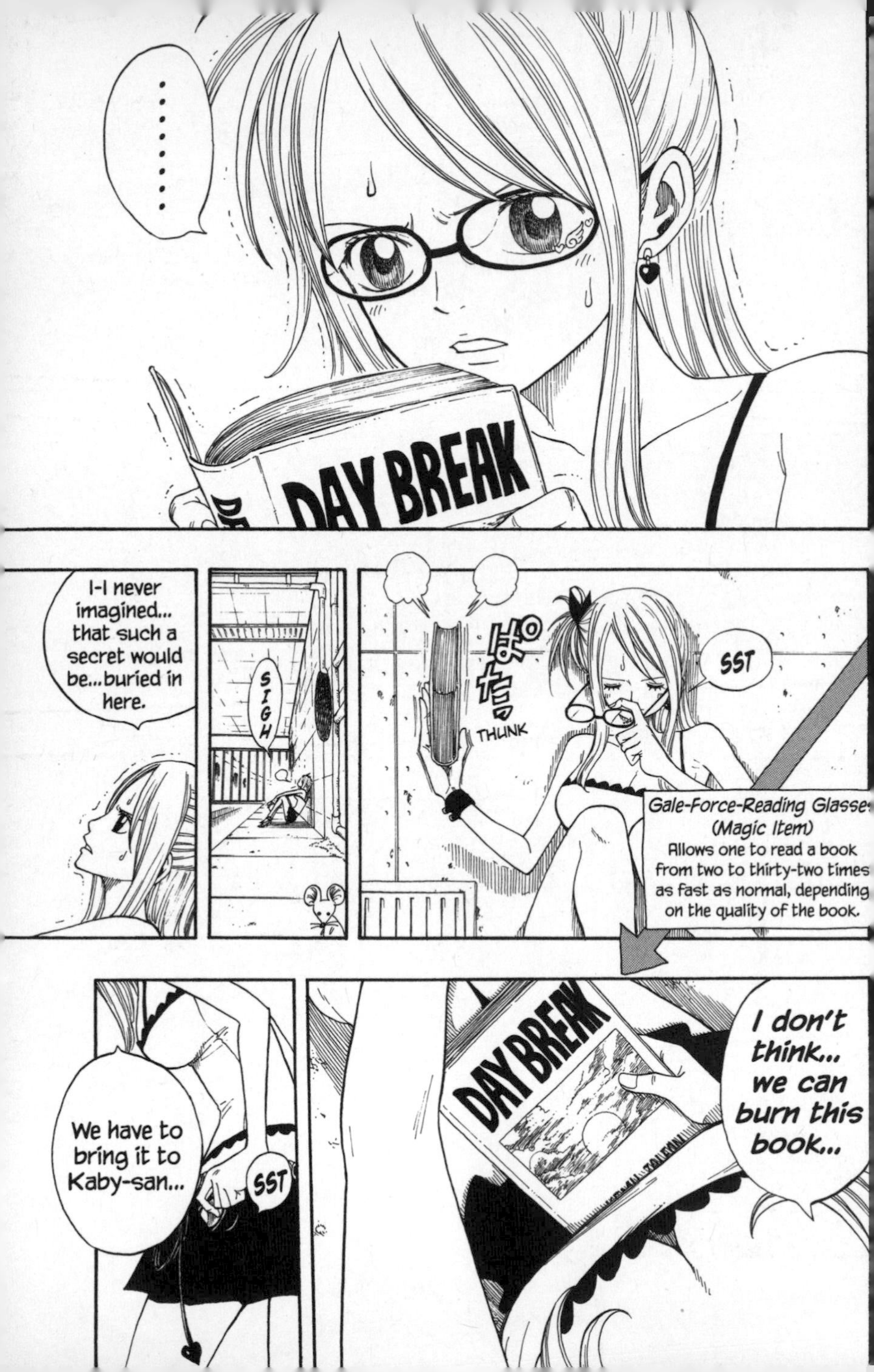
....
DAY BREAK
SST
THUNK
Gale-Force-Reading Glasses
(Magic Item)
Allows one to read a book from two to thirty-two times as fast as normal, depending on the quality of the book.
SIGH
I-I never imagined... that such a secret would be...buried in here.
I don't think... we can burn this book...
DAY BREAK
SST
We have to bring it to Kaby-san...

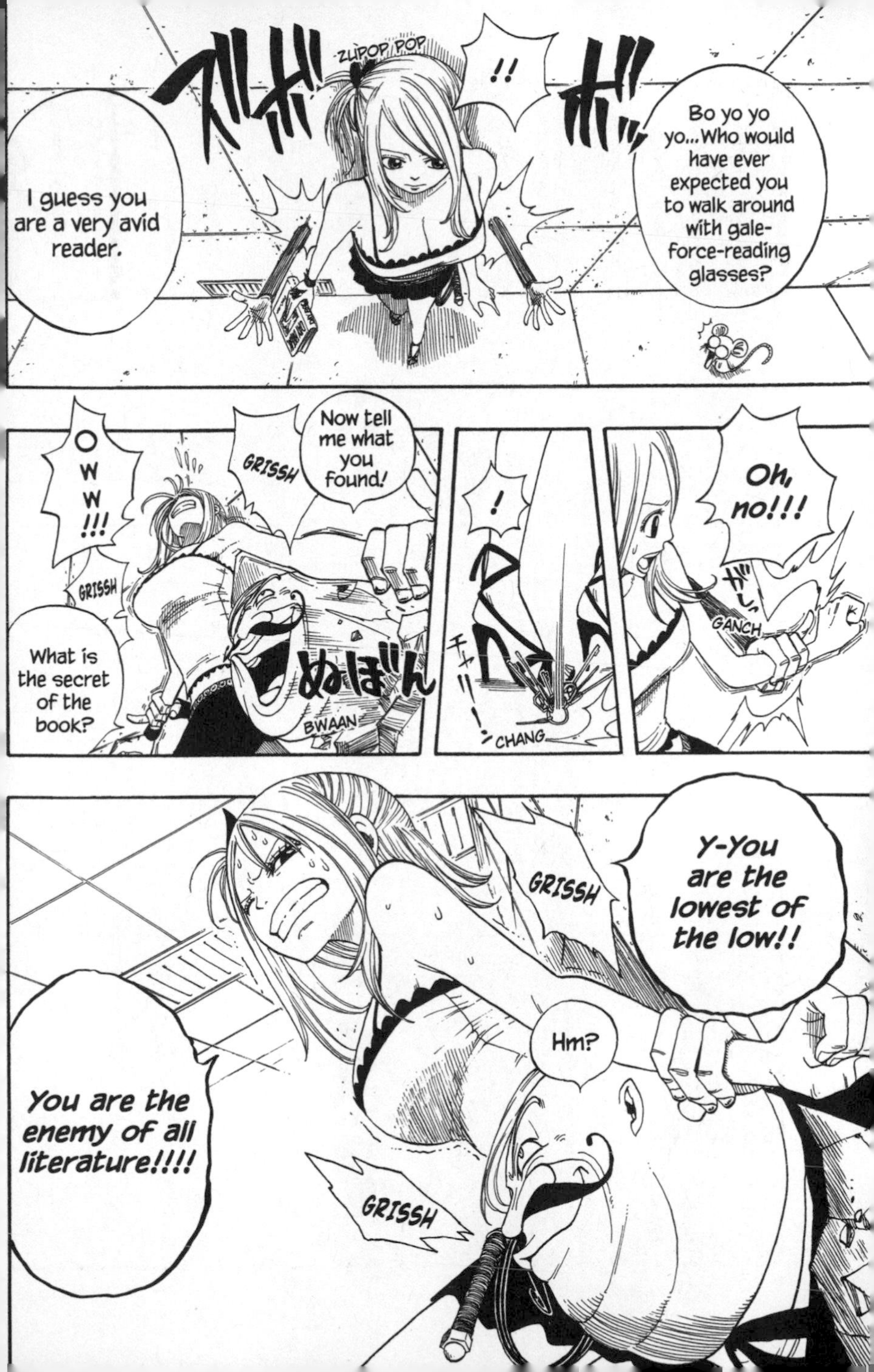
Bo yo yo yo...Who would have ever expected you to walk around with gale-force-reading glasses?
!!
ZUPOP POP
I guess you are a very avid reader.
Oh, no!!!
GANCH
!
CHANG
Now tell me what you found!
GRISSH
OWW!!!
GRISSH
What is the secret of the book?
BWAAN
Y-You are the lowest of the low!!
GRISSH
Hm?
You are the enemy of all literature!!!!
GRISSH

FAIRY TAIL

Chapter 8:
Lucy vs. Duke Everlue

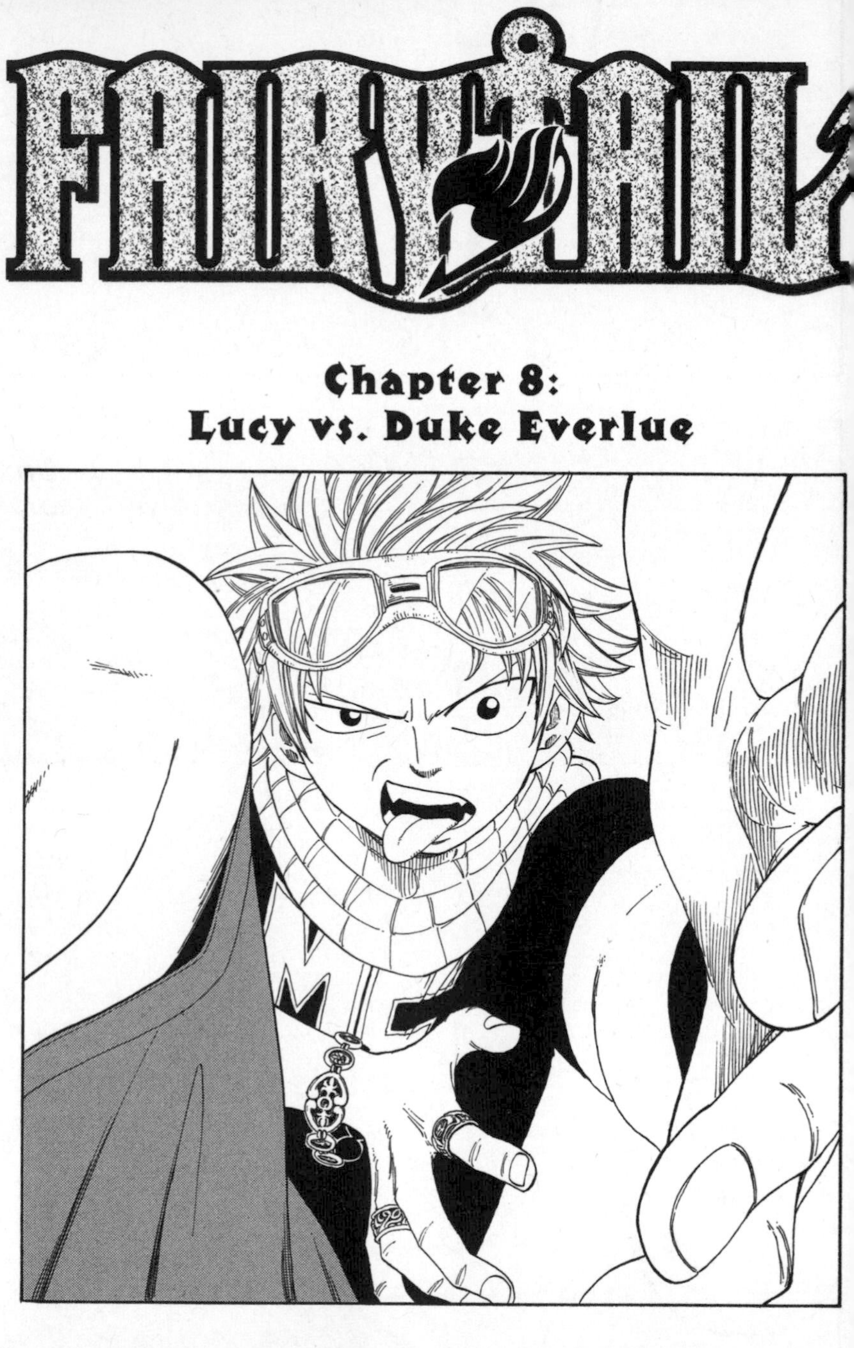

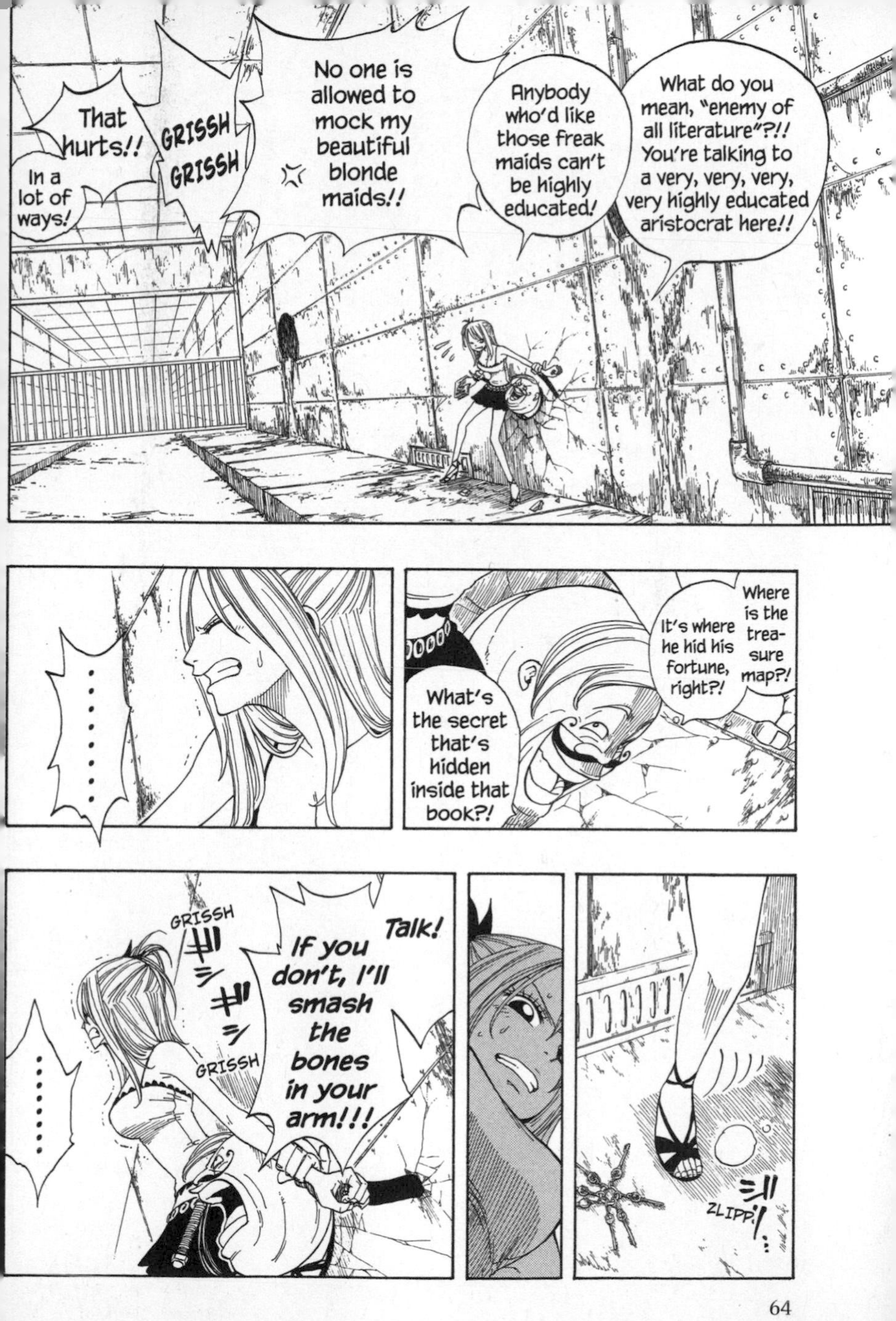
What do you mean, "enemy of all literature"?!! You're talking to a very, very, very, very highly educated aristocrat here!!
Anybody who'd like those freak maids can't be highly educated!
No one is allowed to mock my beautiful blonde maids!!
GRISSH GRISSH
That hurts!!
In a lot of ways!
Where is the treasure map?!
It's where he hid his fortune, right?!
What's the secret that's hidden inside that book?!
......!
ZLIPP!
Talk!
If you don't, I'll smash the bones in your arm!!!
GRISSH
GRISSH
......

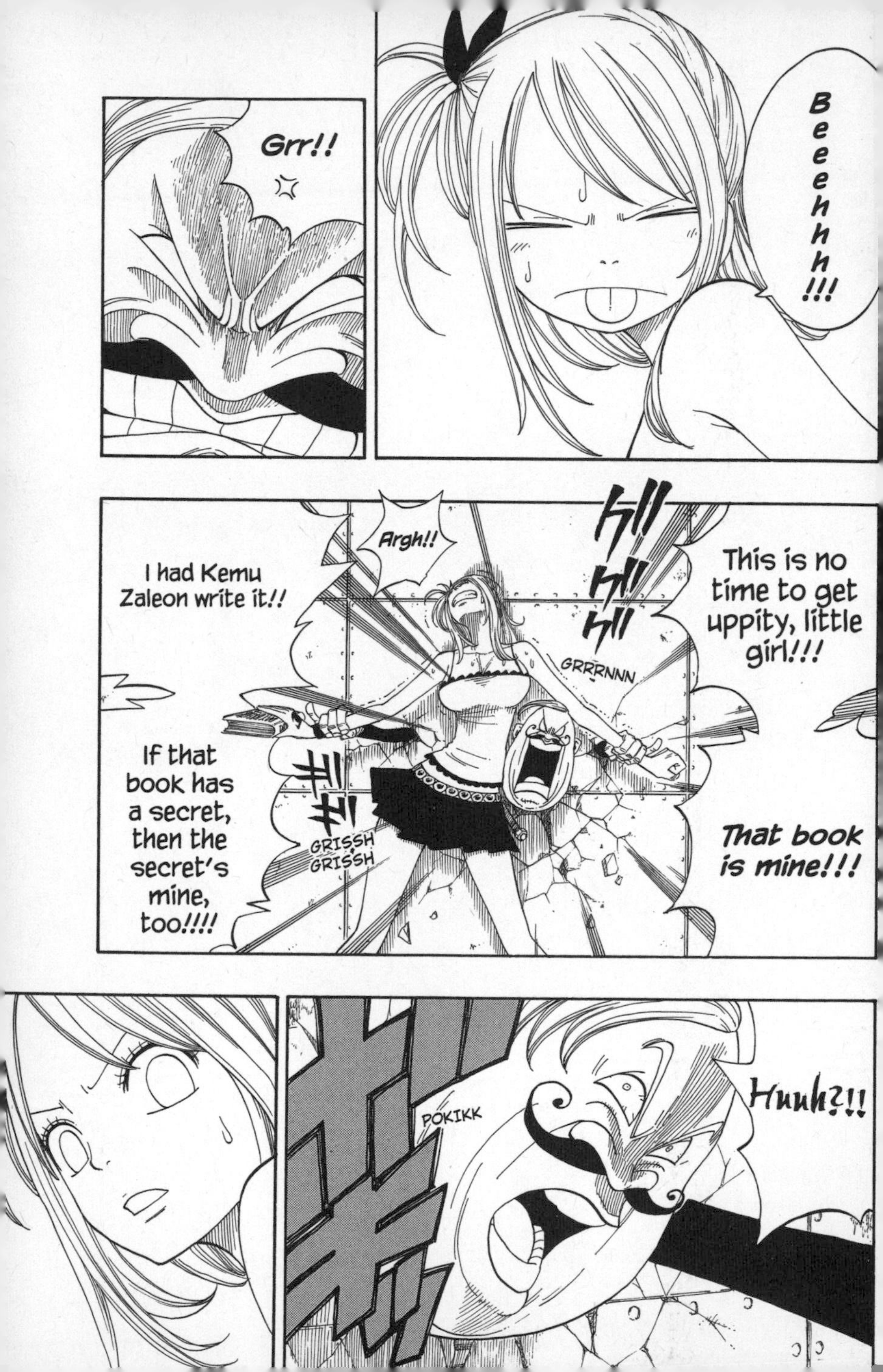
Beeeehhh!!!
Grr!!
This is no time to get uppity, little girl!!!
That book is mine!!!
GRRRNNN
Argh!!
I had Kemu Zaleon write it!!
If that book has a secret, then the secret's mine, too!!!!
GRISSH GRISSH
Huuh?!!
POKIKK

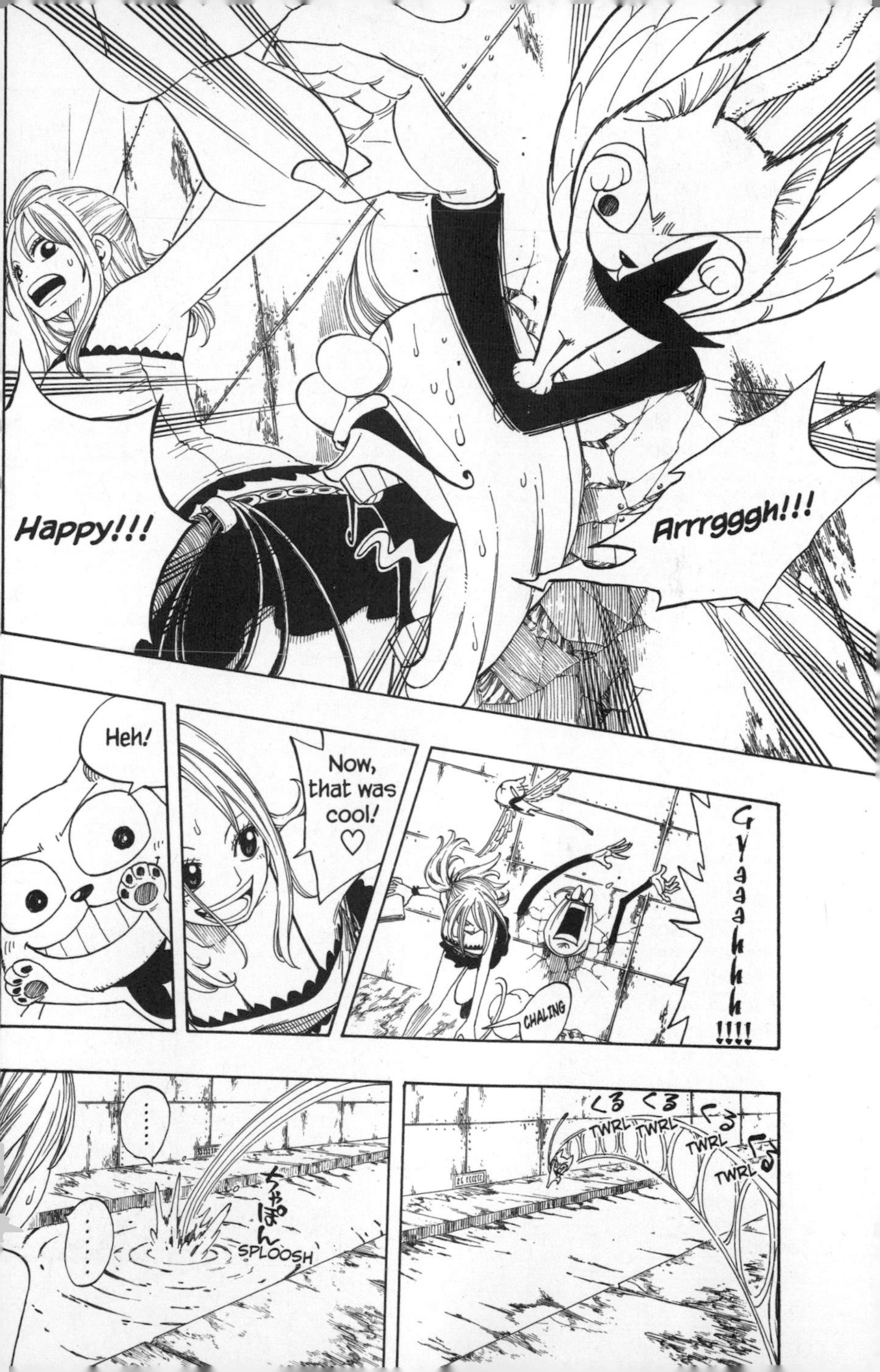
Arrrggh!!!
Happy!!!
Gyaaahhhh!!!!
CHALING
Now, that was cool! ♡
Heh!
くる くる
TWRL TWRL
くる
TWRL
くる
TWRL
......
ちゃぽん
SPLOOSH
......

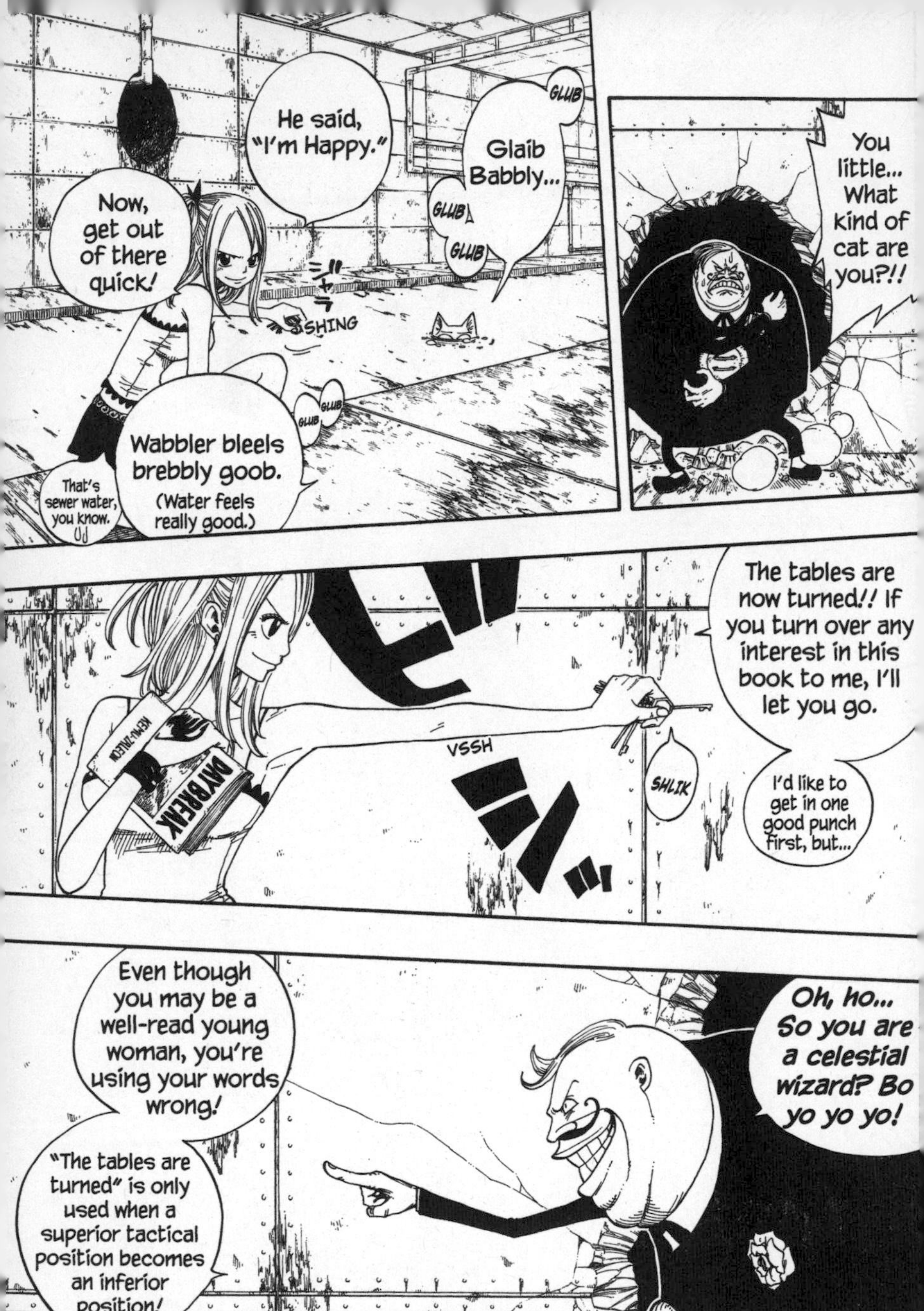
You little... What kind of cat are you?!!
GLUB
Glaib Babbly...
GLUB
GLUB
He said, "I'm Happy."
Now, get out of there quick!
SHING
GLUB
GLUB
Wabbler bleels brebbly goob.
(Water feels really good.)
That's sewer water, you know.
The tables are now turned!! If you turn over any interest in this book to me, I'll let you go.
I'd like to get in one good punch first, but...
SHLIK
VSSH
DAYBREAK
Oh, ho... So you are a celestial wizard? Bo yo yo yo!
Even though you may be a well-read young woman, you're using your words wrong!
"The tables are turned" is only used when a superior tactical position becomes an inferior position!

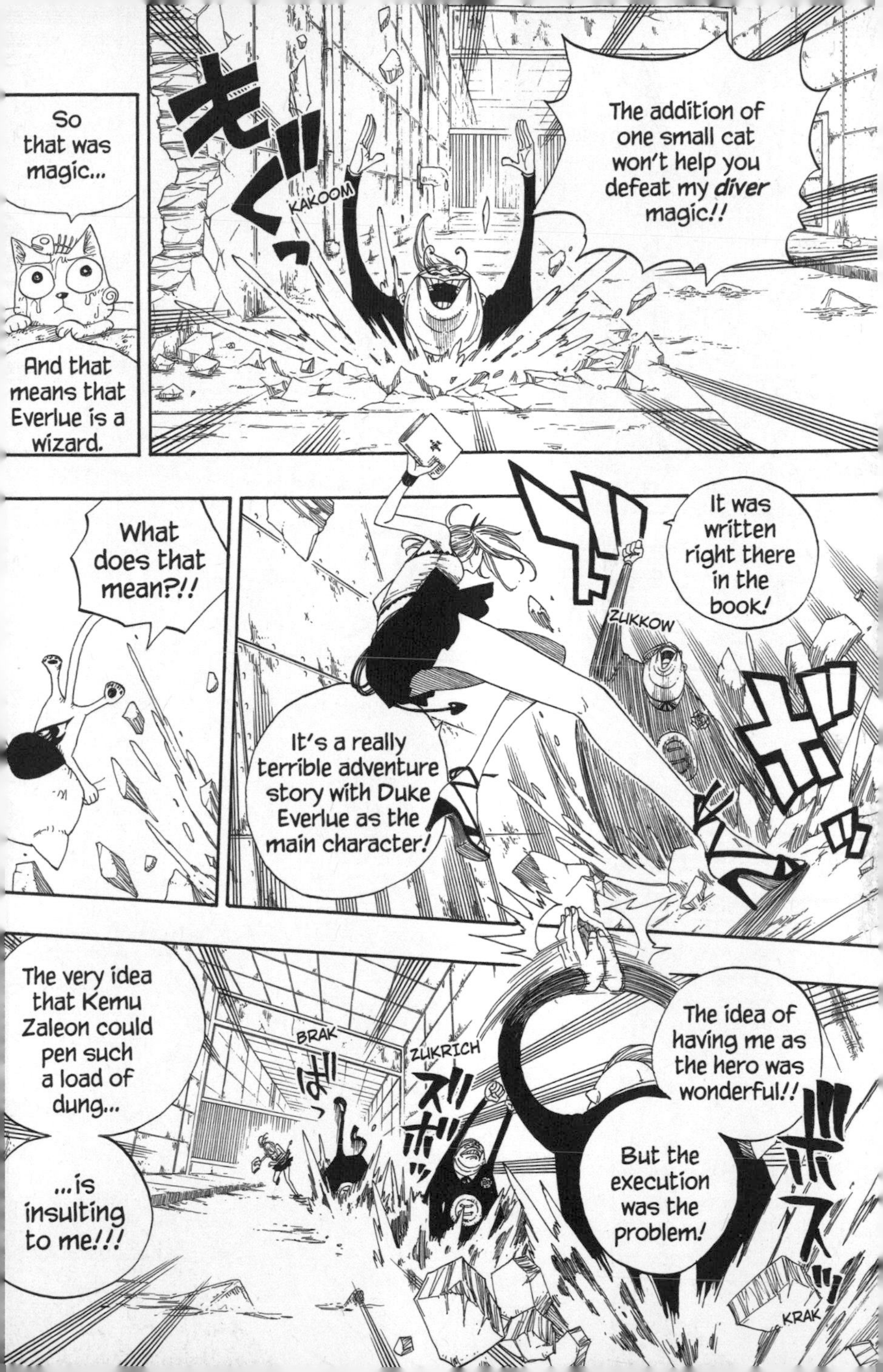

The addition of one small cat won't help you defeat my *diver* magic!!
KAKOOM
So that was magic...
And that means that Everlue is a wizard.
It was written right there in the book!
ZUKKOW
It's a really terrible adventure story with Duke Everlue as the main character!
What does that mean?!!
The idea of having me as the hero was wonderful!!
But the execution was the problem!
KRAK
ZUKRICH
BRAK
The very idea that Kemu Zaleon could pen such a load of dung...
...is insulting to me!!!

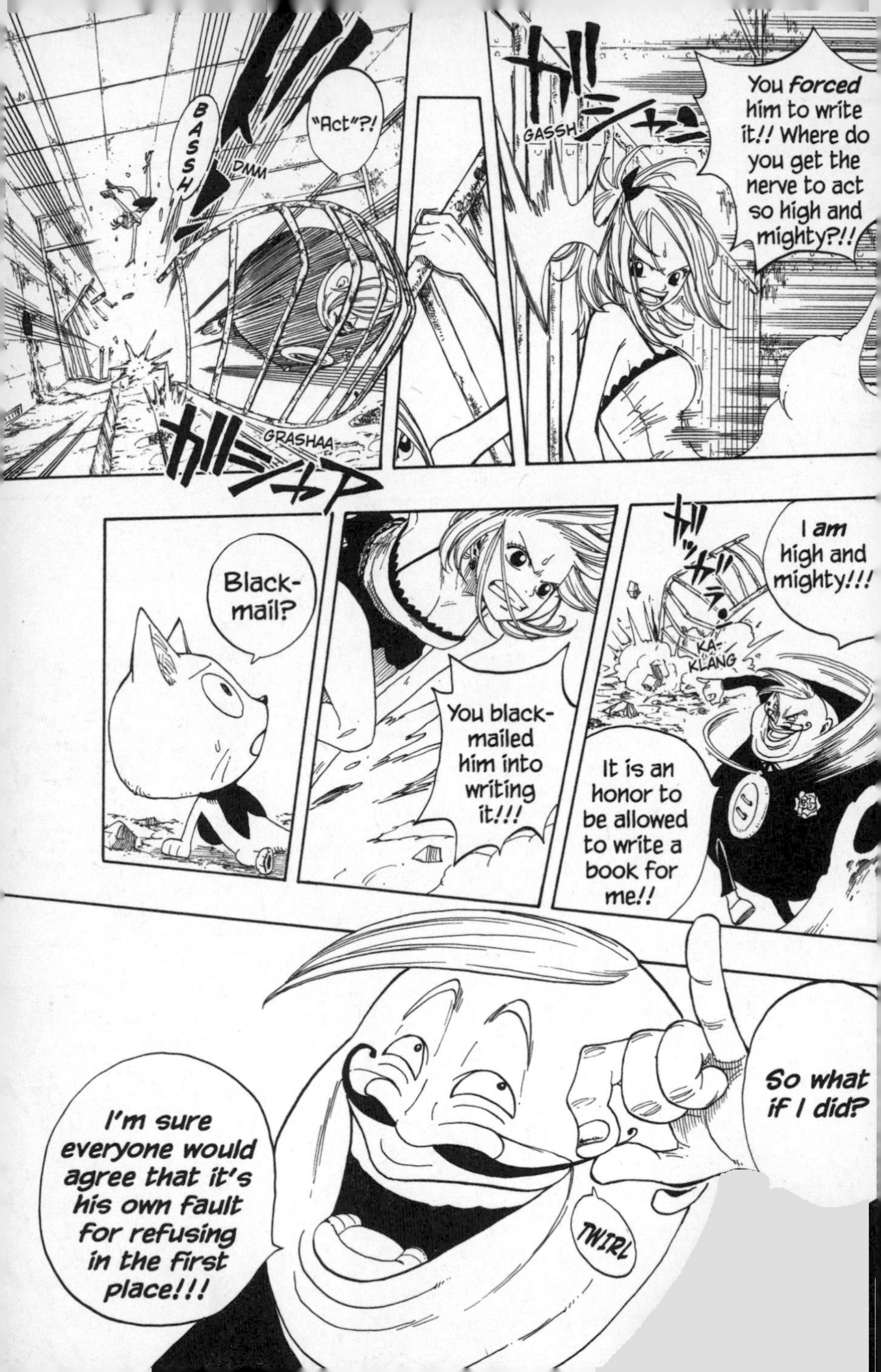

GASSH
You *forced* him to write it!! Where do you get the nerve to act so high and mighty?!!
"Act"?!
BASSH
DMM
GRASHAA
I *am* high and mighty!!!
KA-KLANG
It is an honor to be allowed to write a book for me!!
You black-mailed him into writing it!!!
Black-mail?
So what if I did?
TWIRL
I'm sure everyone would agree that it's his own fault for refusing in the first place!!!

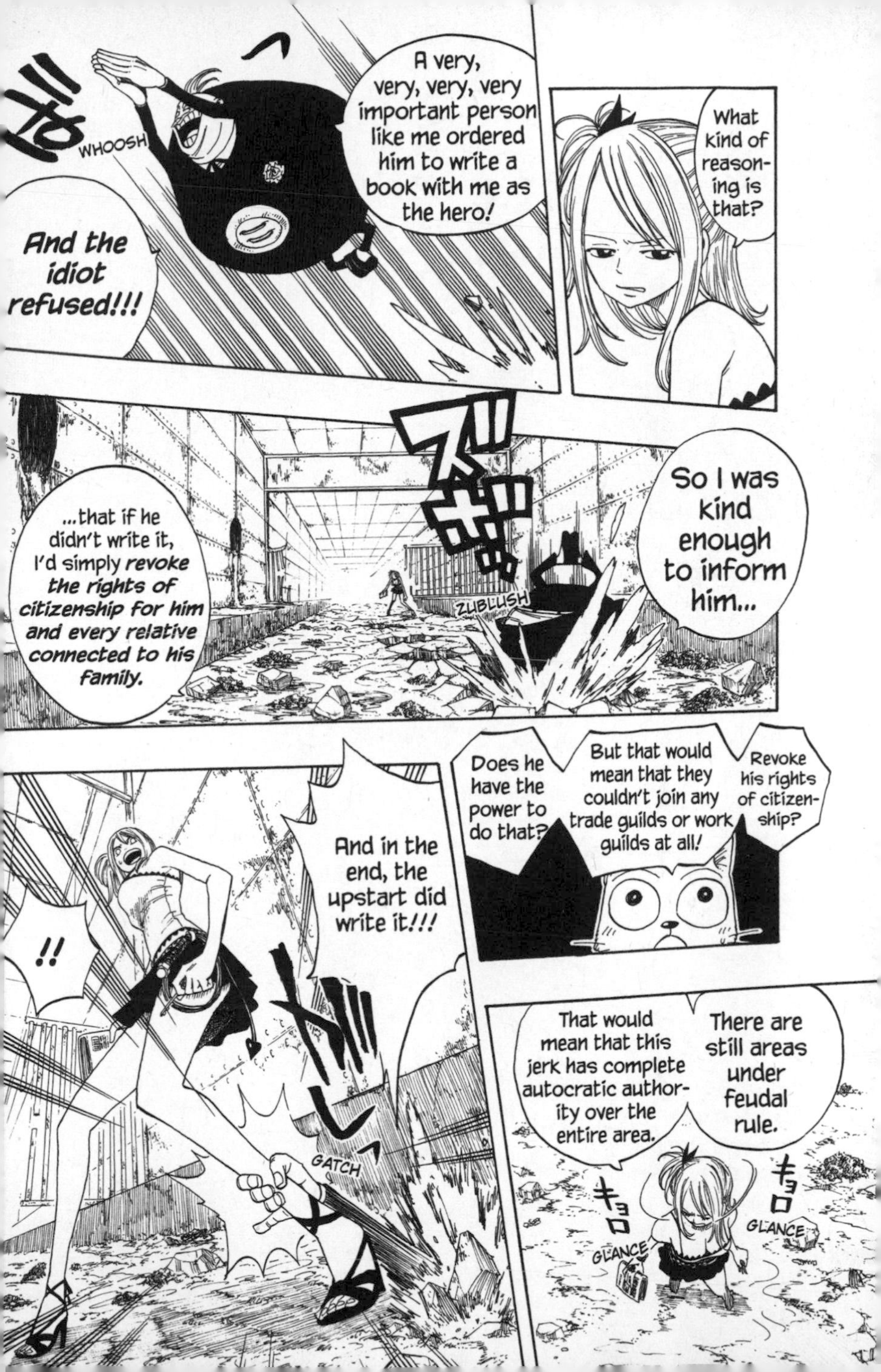

What kind of reasoning is that?
A very, very, very, very important person like me ordered him to write a book with me as the hero!
WHOOSH
And the idiot refused!!!
So I was kind enough to inform him...
ZUBLUSH
...that if he didn't write it, I'd simply *revoke the rights of citizenship for him and every relative connected to his family.*
Revoke his rights of citizenship?
But that would mean that they couldn't join any trade guilds or work guilds at all!
Does he have the power to do that?
There are still areas under feudal rule.
That would mean that this jerk has complete autocratic authority over the entire area.
GLANCE
GLANCE
And in the end, the upstart did write it!!!
!!
GATCH

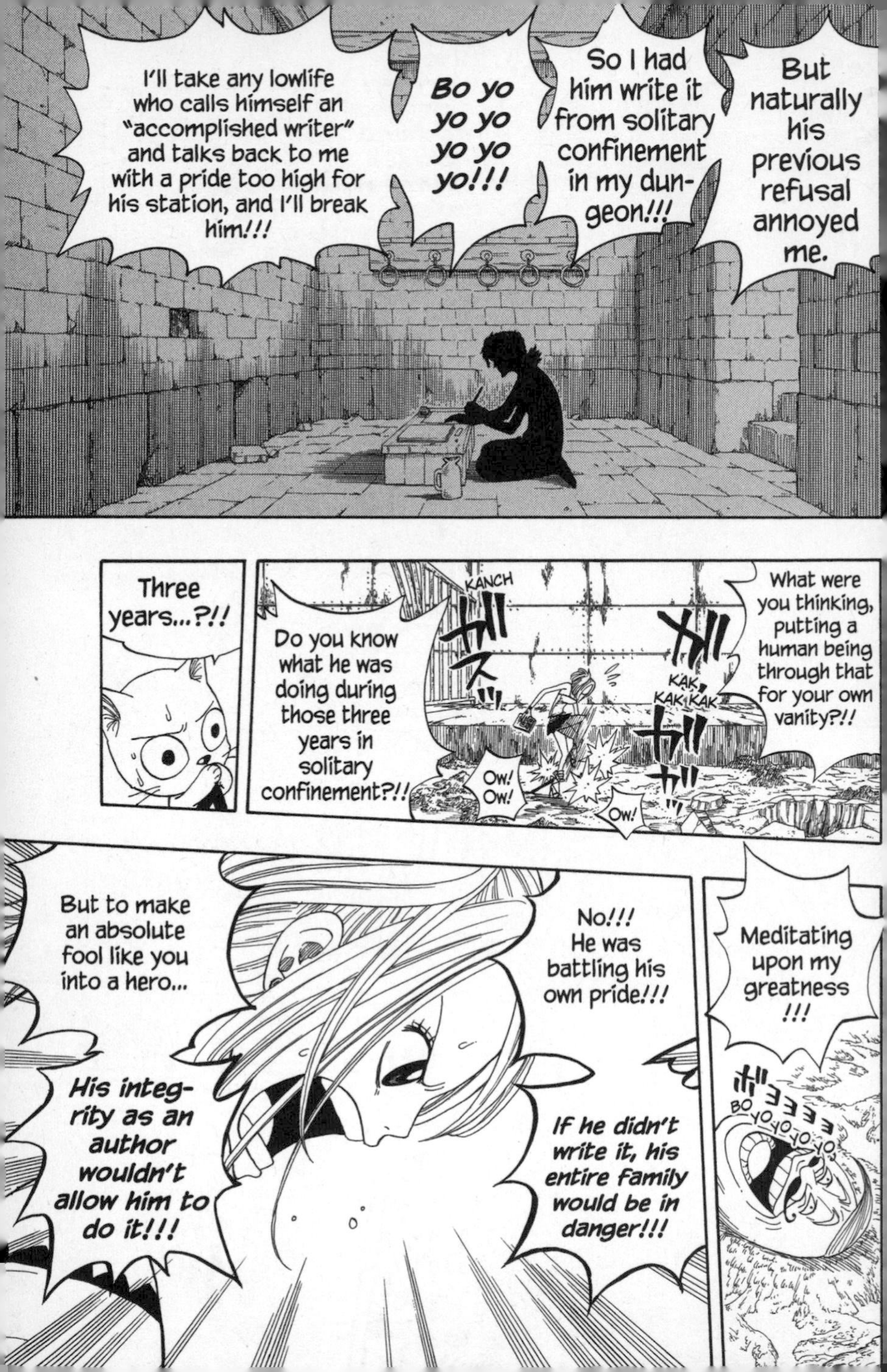
But naturally his previous refusal annoyed me.
So I had him write it from solitary confinement in my dungeon!!!
Bo yo yo yo yo yo yo!!!
I'll take any lowlife who calls himself an "accomplished writer" and talks back to me with a pride too high for his station, and I'll break him!!!
What were you thinking, putting a human being through that for your own vanity?!!
KAK, KAK KAK
KANCH
Ow! Ow!
Ow!
Do you know what he was doing during those three years in solitary confinement?!!
Three years...?!!
Meditating upon my greatness!!!
BO YO YO YO YO
No!!! He was battling his own pride!!!
If he didn't write it, his entire family would be in danger!!!
But to make an absolute fool like you into a hero...
His integrity as an author wouldn't allow him to do it!!!

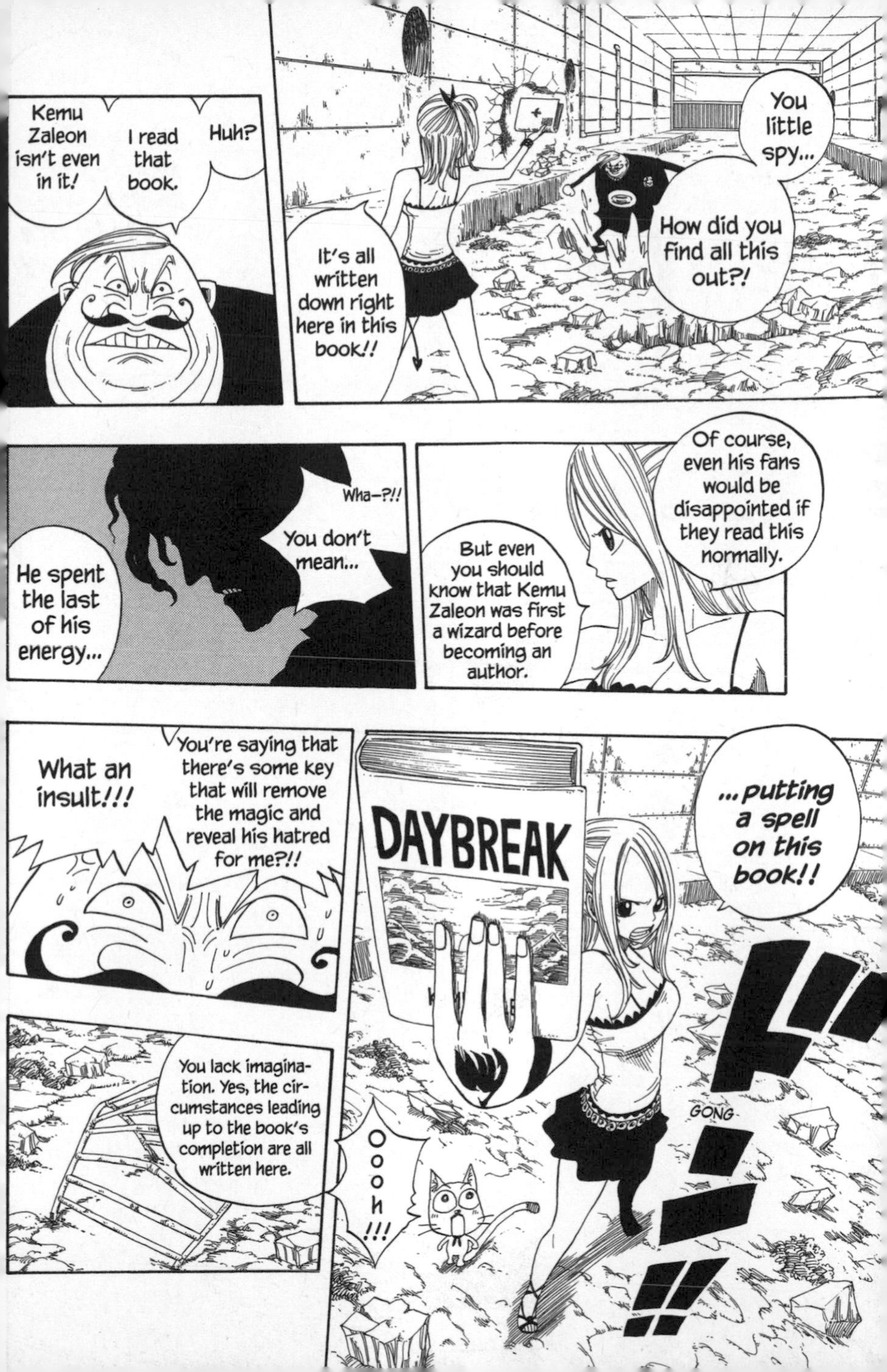
You little spy...
How did you find all this out?!
It's all written down right here in this book!!
Huh?
I read that book.
Kemu Zaleon isn't even in it!
Of course, even his fans would be disappointed if they read this normally.
But even you should know that Kemu Zaleon was first a wizard before becoming an author.
Wha–?!!
You don't mean...
He spent the last of his energy...
...putting a spell on this book!!
DAYBREAK
GONG
Oooh!!!
You're saying that there's some key that will remove the magic and reveal his hatred for me?!!
What an insult!!!
You lack imagination. Yes, the circumstances leading up to the book's completion are all written here.

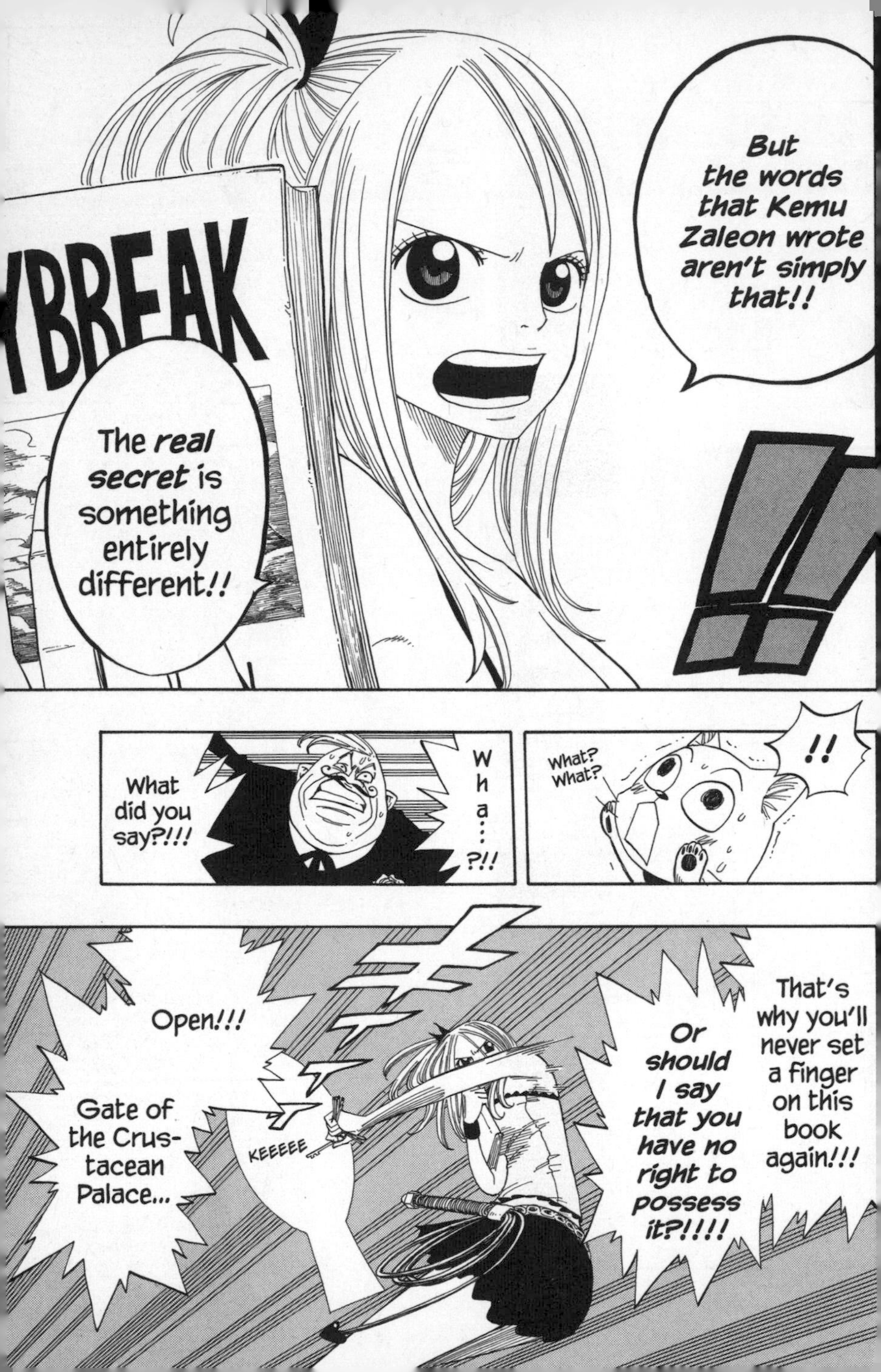
But the words that Kemu Zaleon wrote aren't simply that!!
The *real secret* is something entirely different!!
!!
What? What?
Wha...?!!
What did you say?!!!
That's why you'll never set a finger on this book again!!!
Or should I say that you have no right to possess it?!!!!
Open!!!
Gate of the Crus-tacean Palace...
KEEEEE

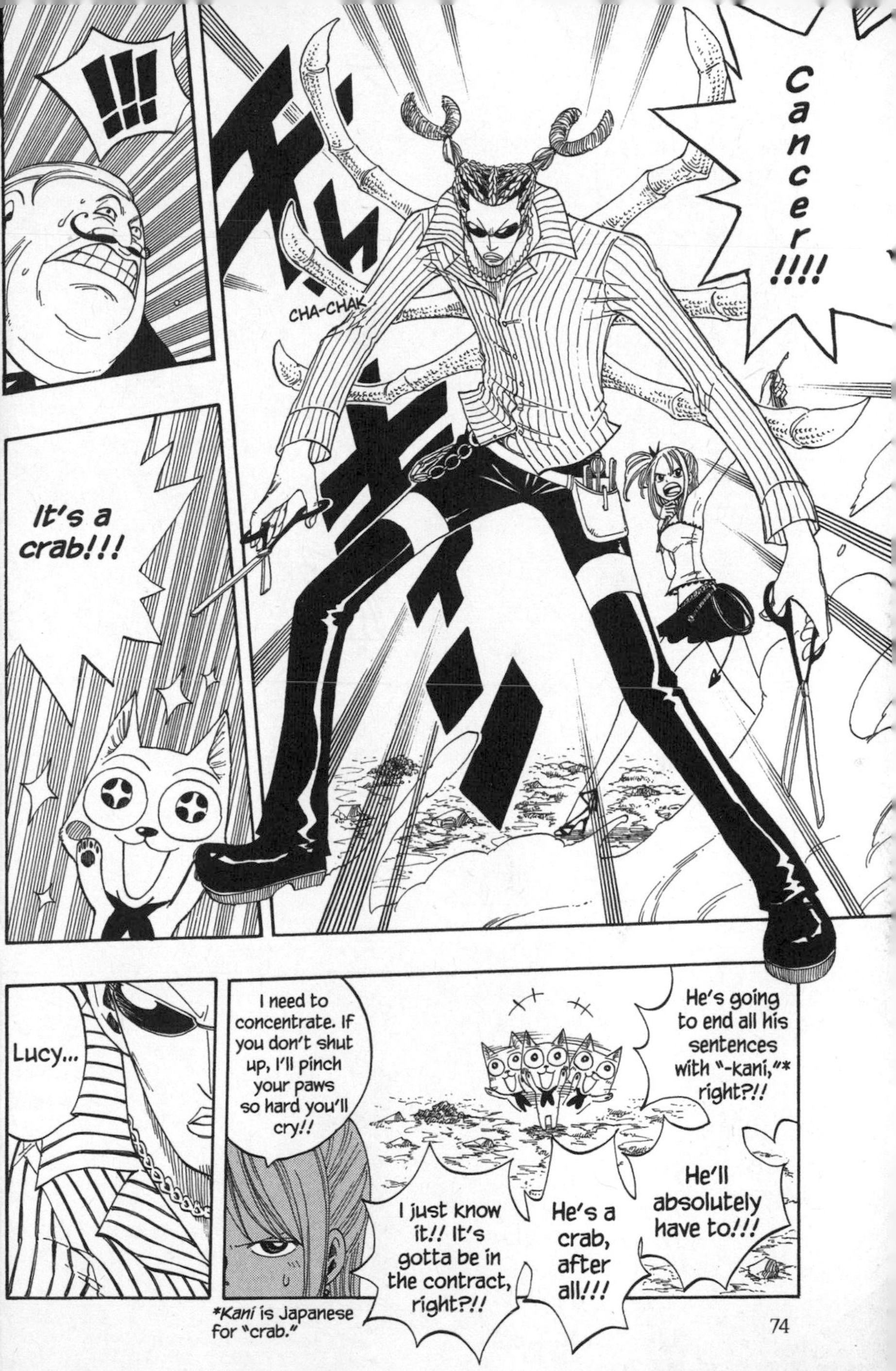
Cancer!!!!
CHA-CHAK
!!!
It's a crab!!!
He's going to end all his sentences with "-kani,"* right?!!
He'll absolutely have to!!!
He's a crab, after all!!!
I just know it!! It's gotta be in the contract, right?!!
I need to concentrate. If you don't shut up, I'll pinch your paws so hard you'll cry!!
Lucy...

**Kani* is Japanese for "crab."

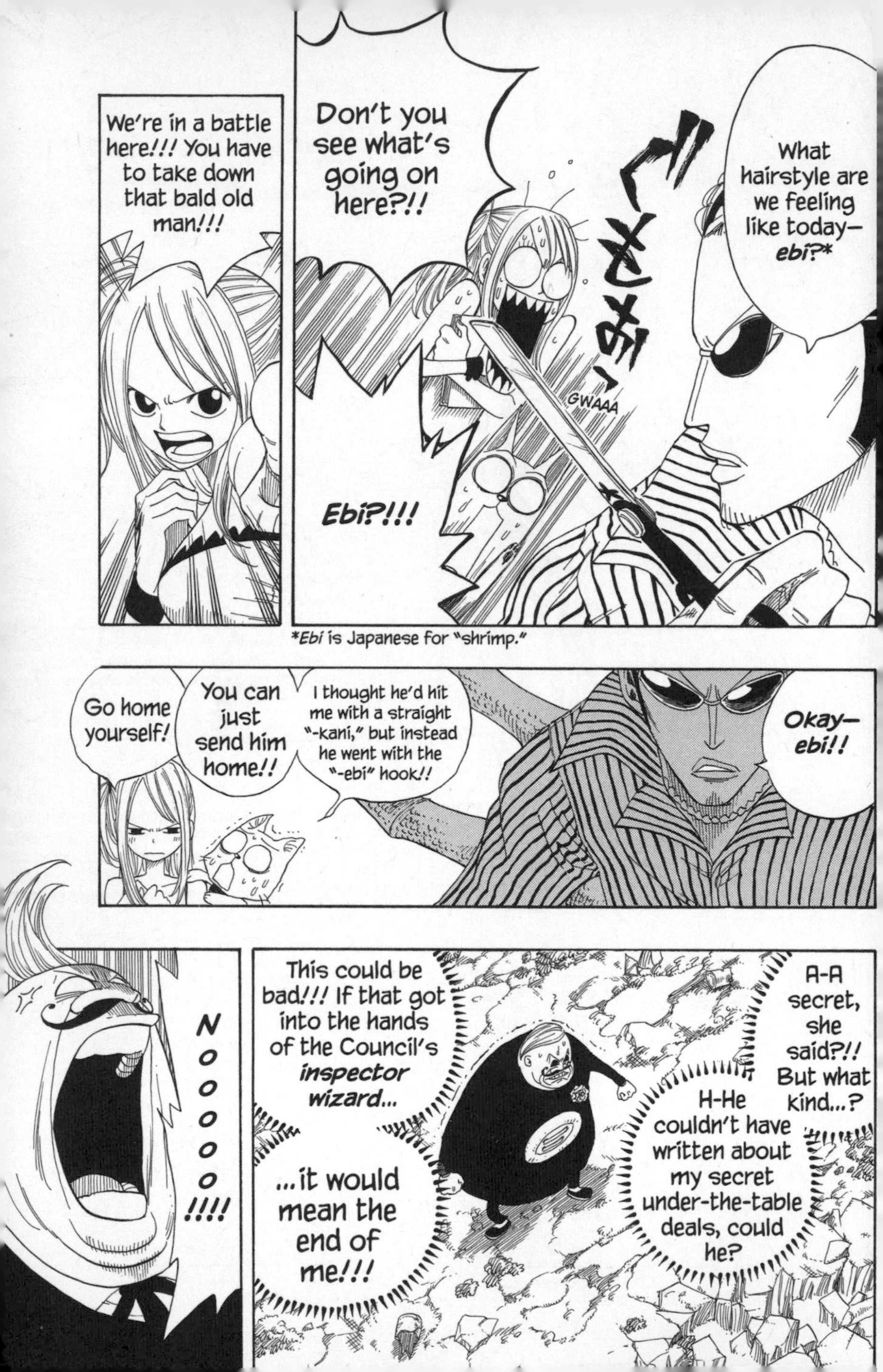
What hairstyle are we feeling like today—*ebi*?*
GWAAA
Don't you see what's going on here?!!
Ebi?!!!
We're in a battle here!!! You have to take down that bald old man!!!
Ebi is Japanese for "shrimp."
Okay—ebi!!
I thought he'd hit me with a straight "-kani," but instead he went with the "-ebi" hook!!
You can just send him home!!
Go home yourself!
A-A secret, she said?!! But what kind...?
H-He couldn't have written about my secret under-the-table deals, could he?
This could be bad!!! If that got into the hands of the Council's *inspector wizard*...
...it would mean the end of me!!!
NOOOOOO!!!!

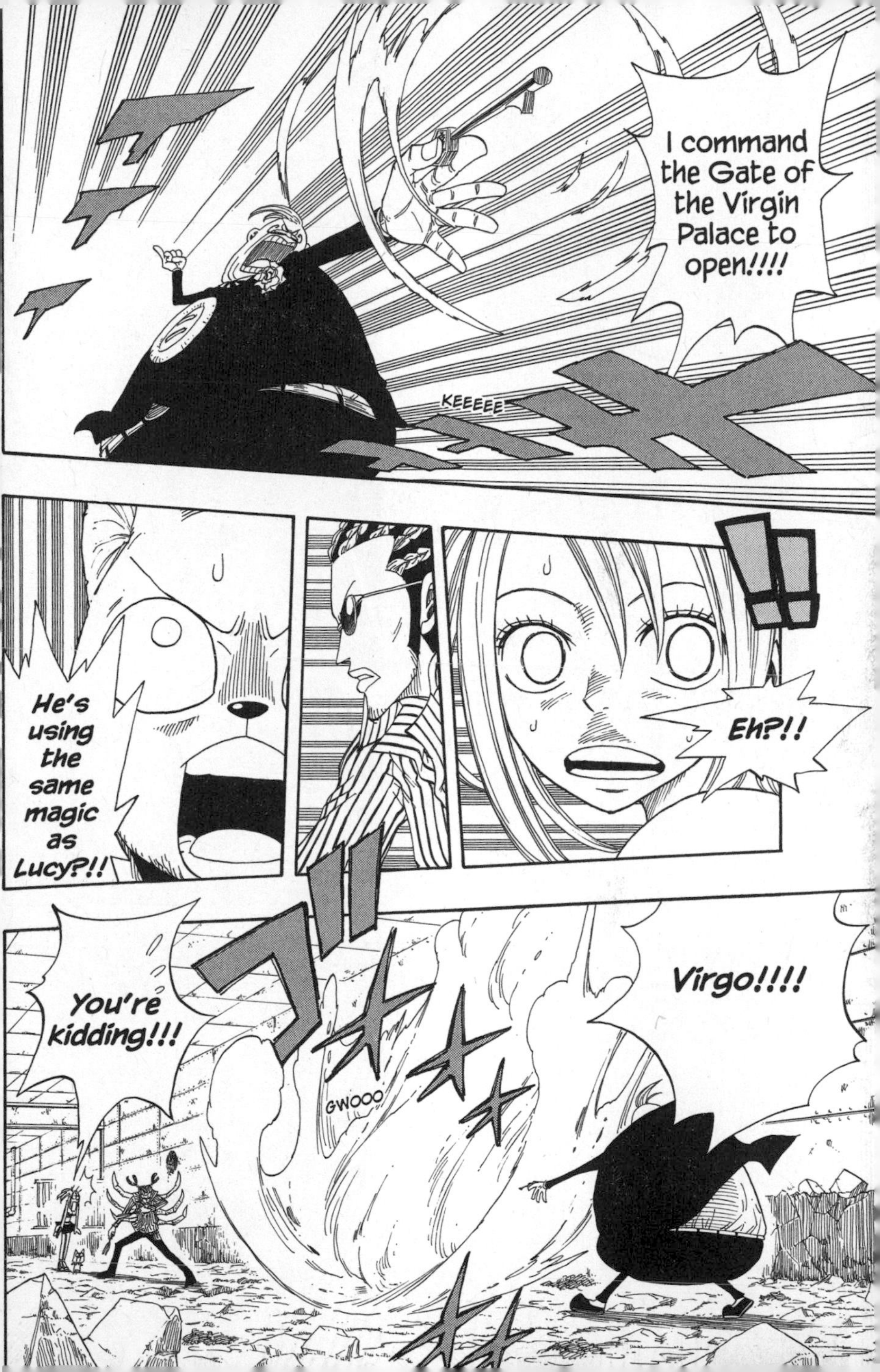
I command the Gate of the Virgin Palace to open!!!!
KEEEEE
Eh?!!
He's using the same magic as Lucy?!!
Virgo!!!!
You're kidding!!!
GWOOO

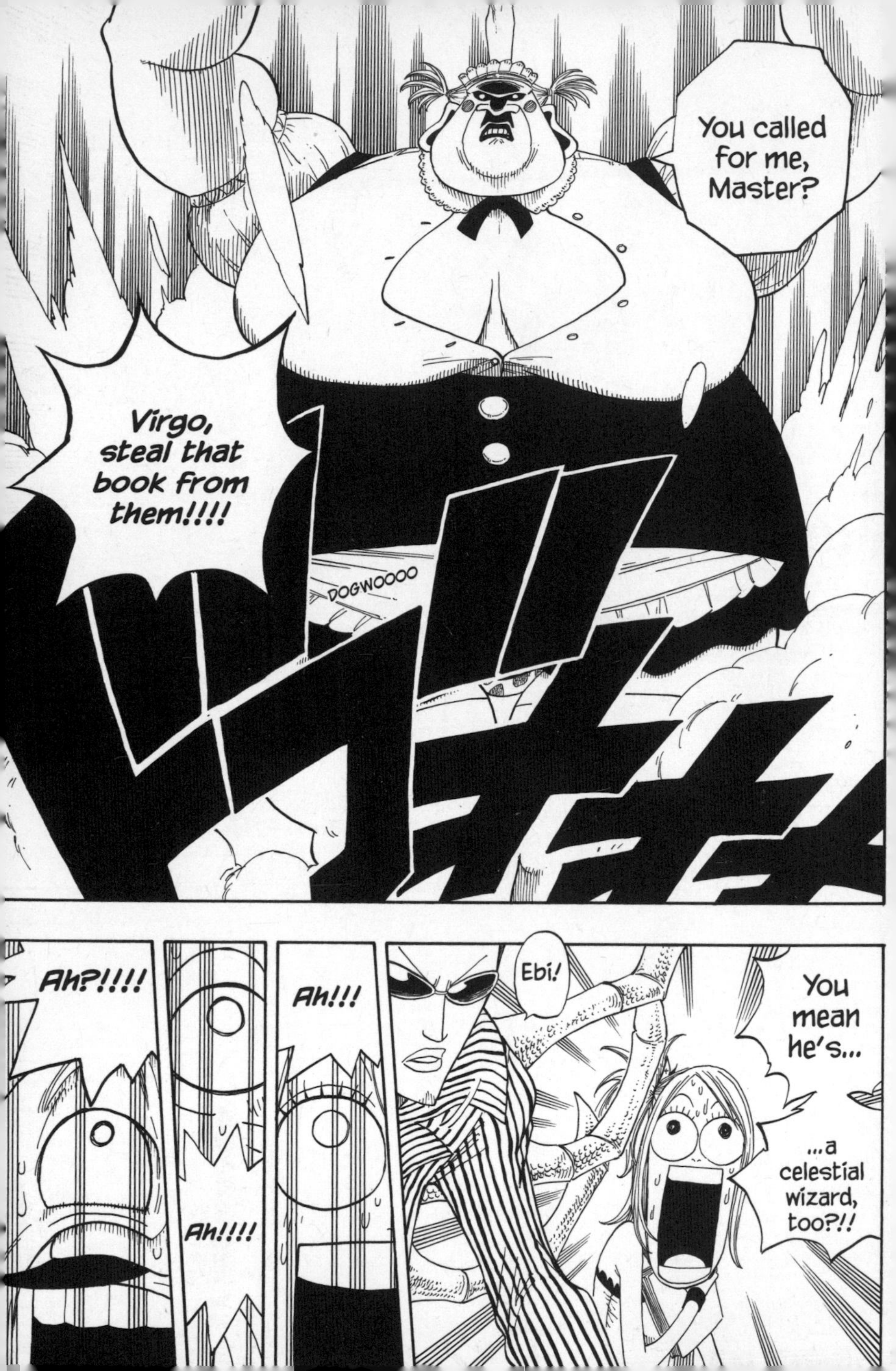
You called for me, Master?
Virgo, steal that book from them!!!!
DOGWOOOO
Ebi!
You mean he's...
...a celestial wizard, too?!!
Ah!!!
Ah!!!!
Ah?!!!!

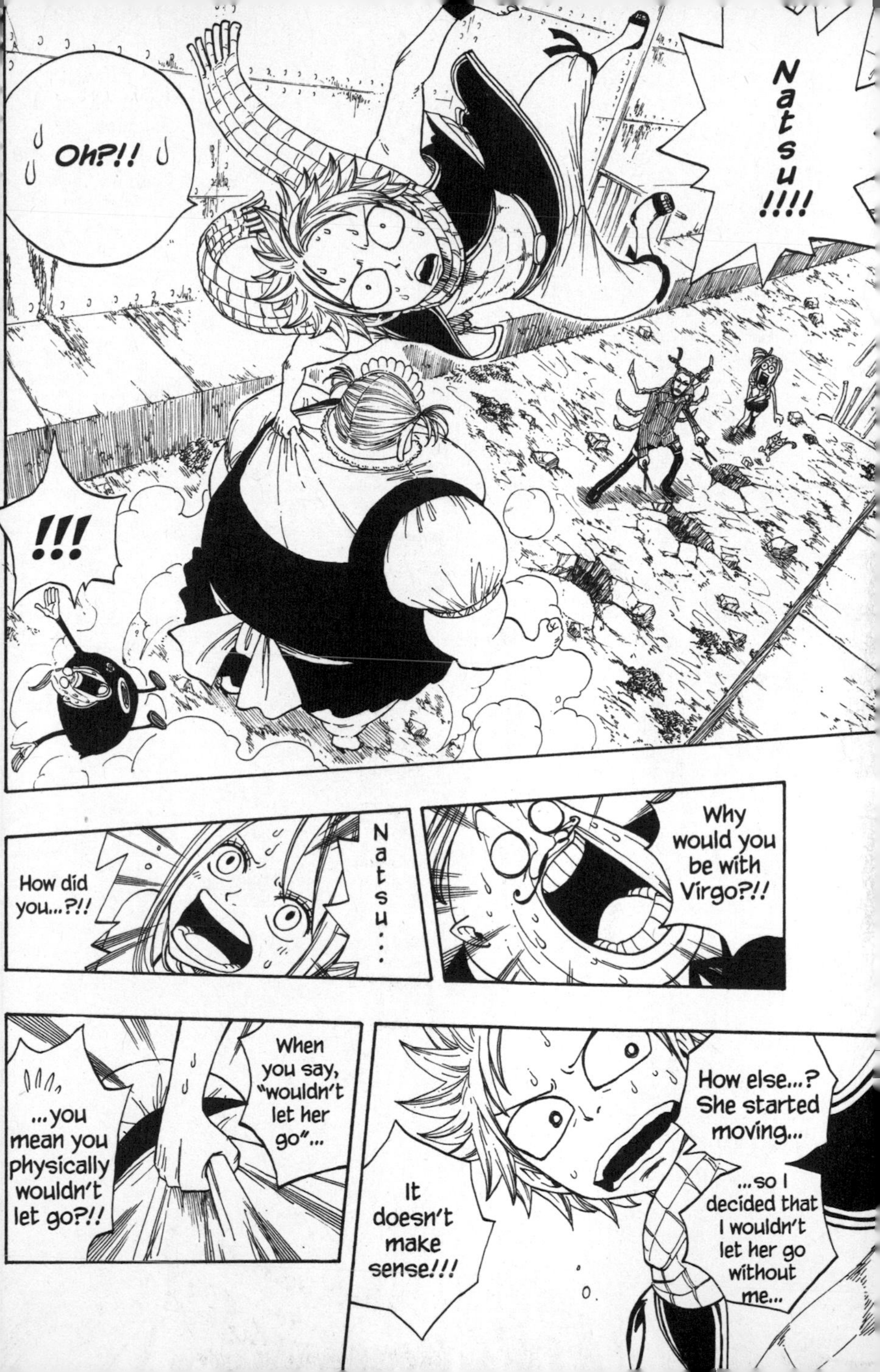
Natsu!!!!
Oh?!!
!!!
Why would you be with Virgo?!!
Natsu...
How did you...?!!
How else...? She started moving...
...so I decided that I wouldn't let her go without me...
It doesn't make sense!!!
When you say, "wouldn't let her go"...
...you mean you physically wouldn't let go?!!

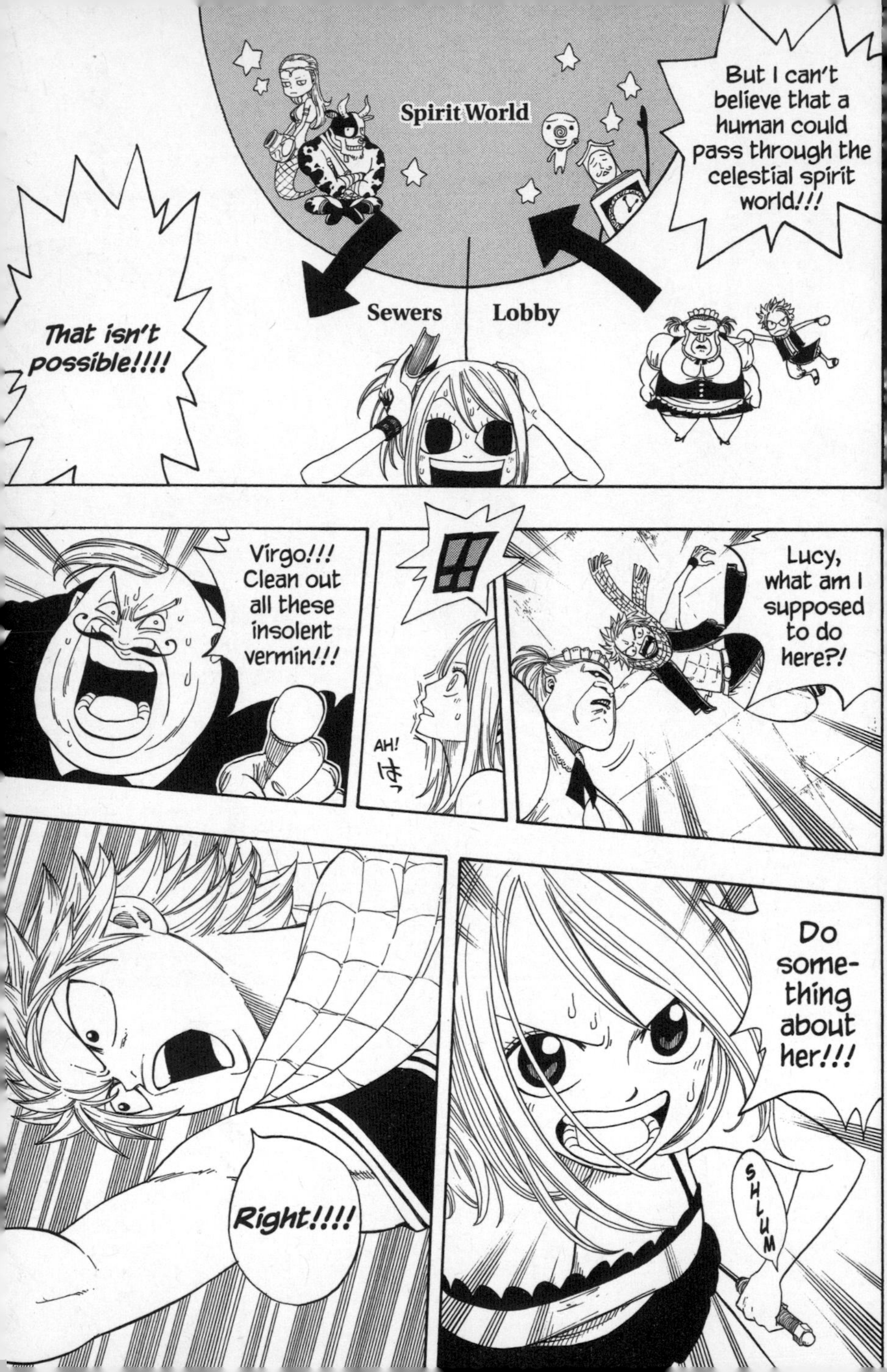
But I can't believe that a human could pass through the celestial spirit world!!!
Spirit World
Lobby
Sewers
That isn't possible!!!!
Lucy, what am I supposed to do here?!
AH!
はっ
Virgo!!! Clean out all these insolent vermin!!!
Do some-thing about her!!!
SHLUM
Right!!!!

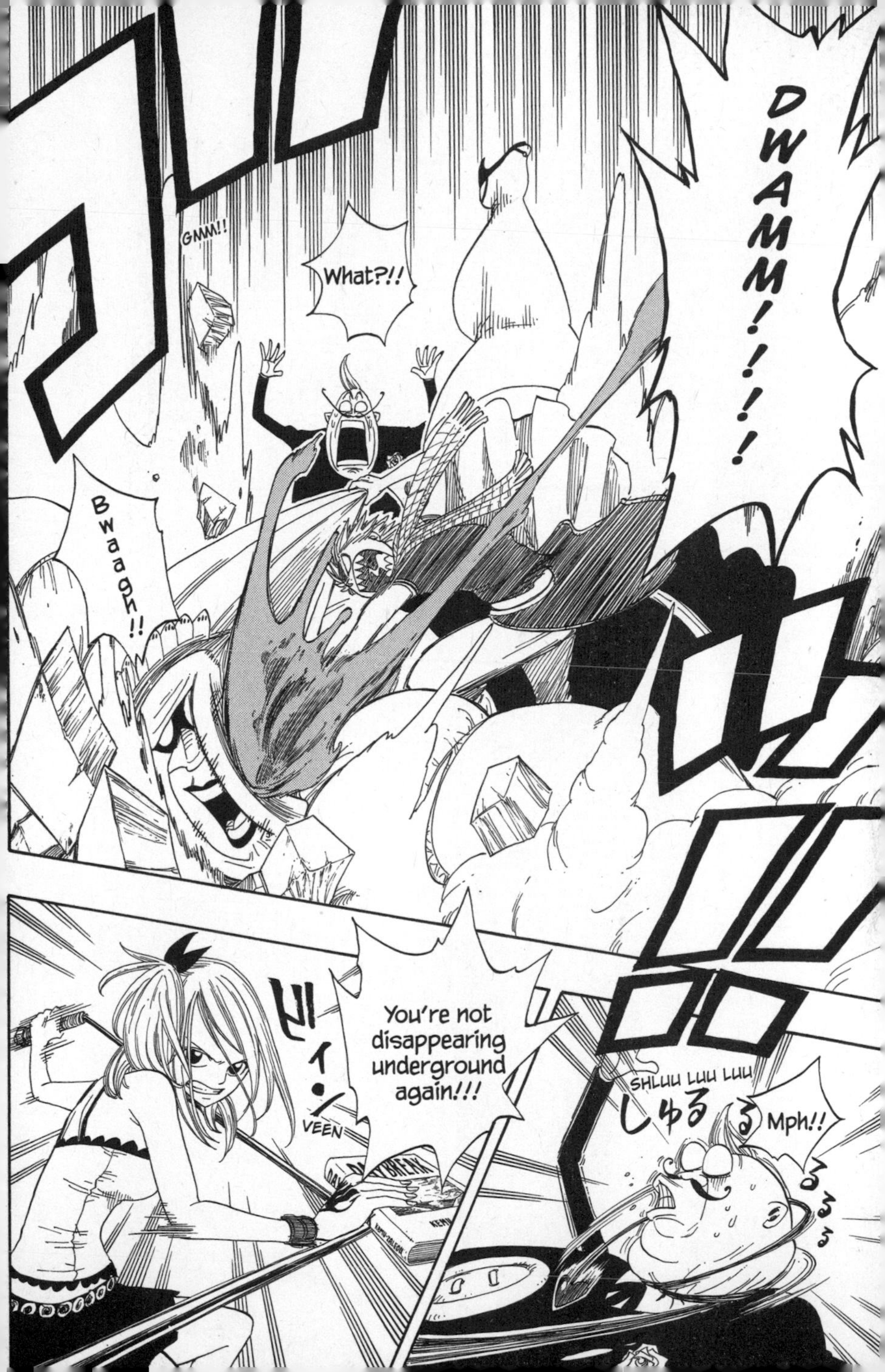
DWAMM!!!!!!
What?!!
GNN!!
Bwaagh!!
SHLUU LUU LUU
Mph!!
You're not disappearing underground again!!!
VEEN

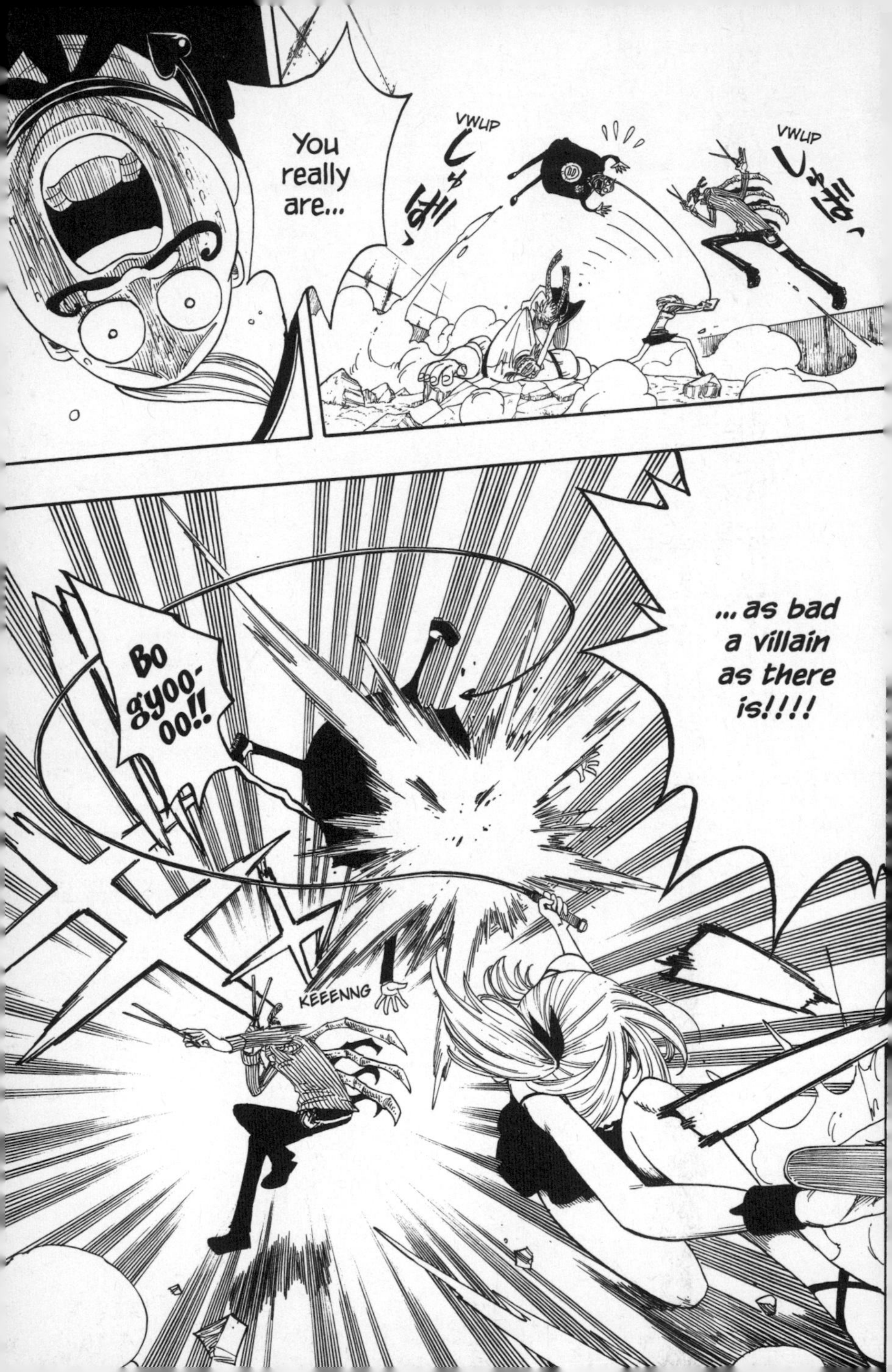
VWUP
VWUP
You really are...
...as bad a villain as there is!!!!
Bo gyoo-oo!!
KEEENNG

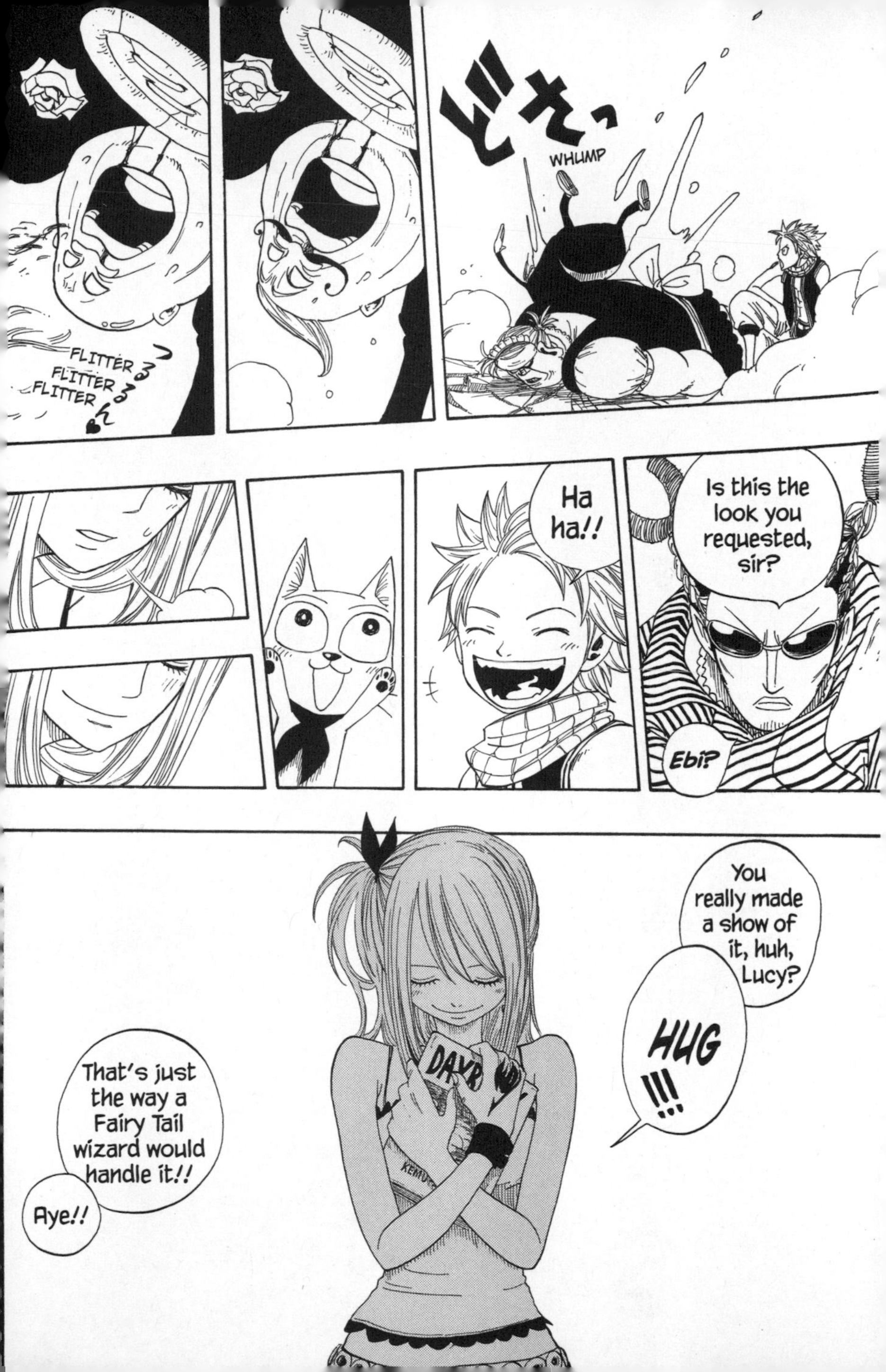

どさっ
WHUMP
FLITTER
FLITTER
FLITTER
Is this the look you requested, sir?
Ebi?
Ha ha!!
You really made a show of it, huh, Lucy?
HUG!!!
That's just the way a Fairy Tail wizard would handle it!!
Aye!!

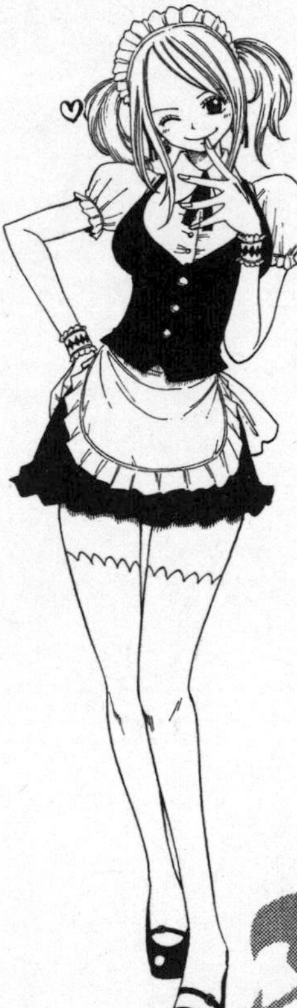

FAIRY TAIL

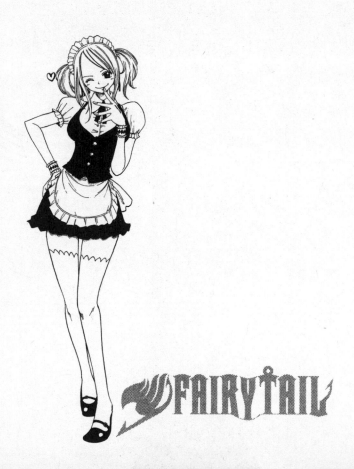

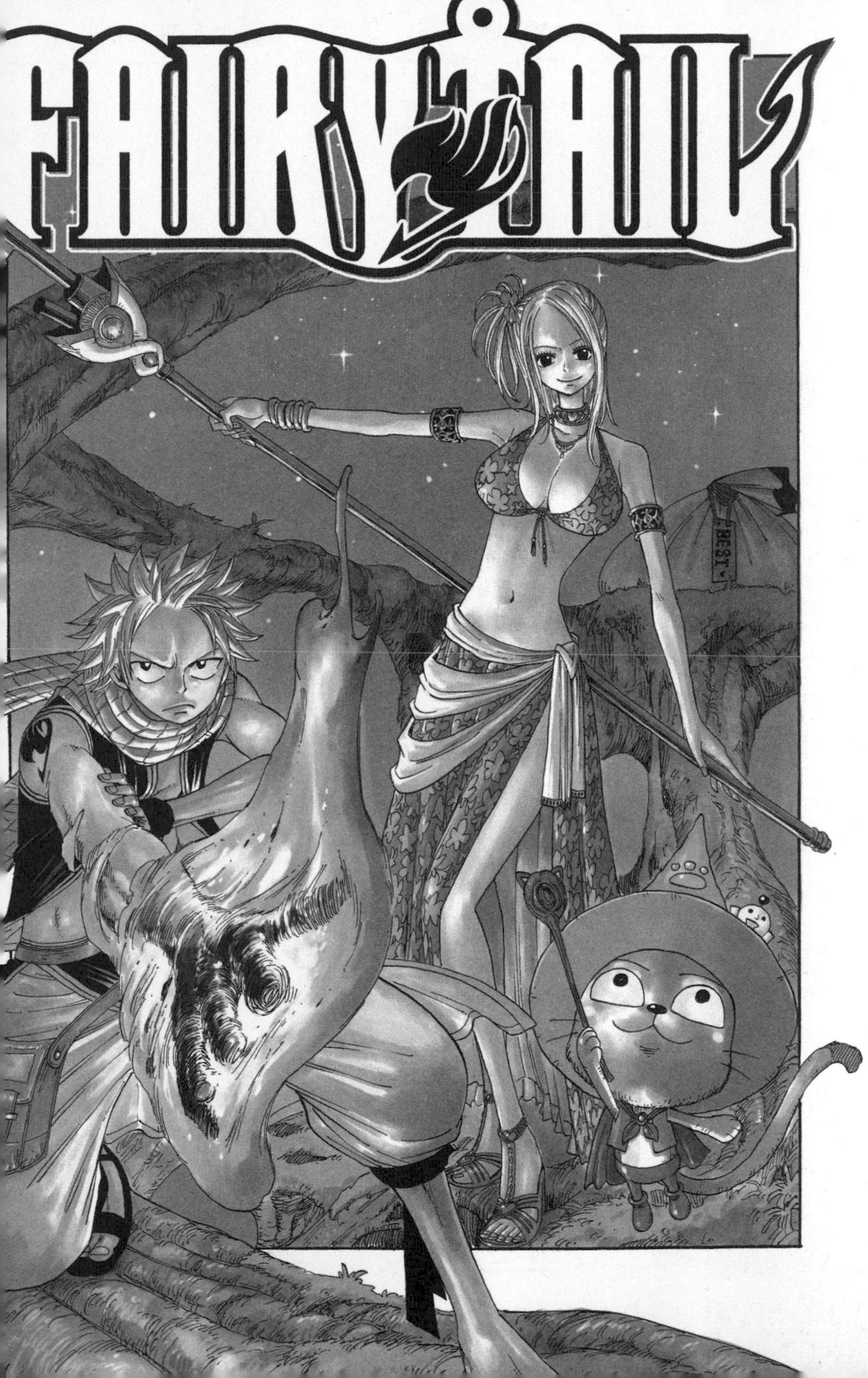
FAIRY TAIL

Chapter 9: Dear Kaby

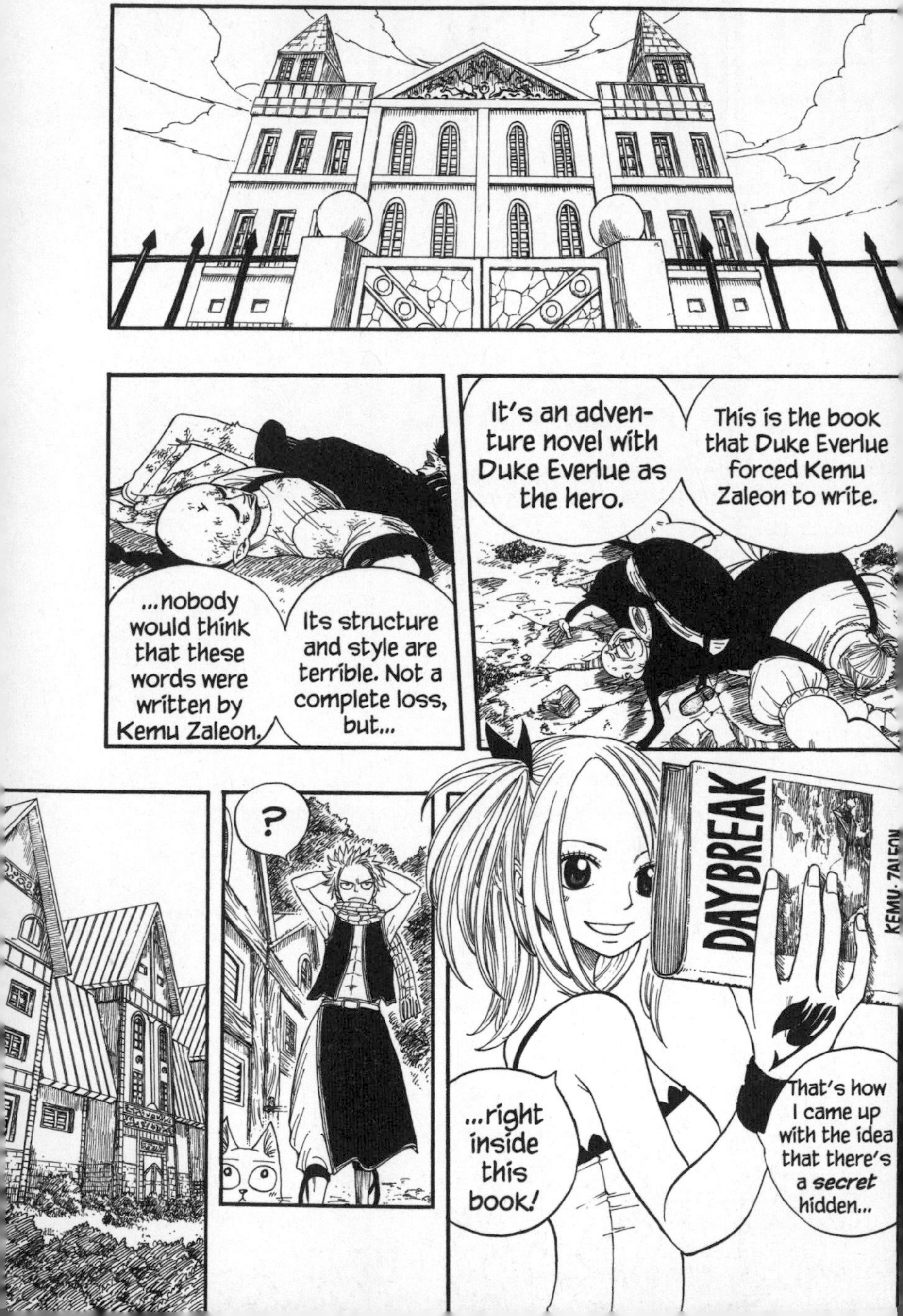
This is the book that Duke Everlue forced Kemu Zaleon to write.
It's an adven-ture novel with Duke Everlue as the hero.
Its structure and style are terrible. Not a complete loss, but...
...nobody would think that these words were written by Kemu Zaleon.
DAYBREAK
KEMU · ZALEON
That's how I came up with the idea that there's a *secret* hidden...
...right inside this book!
?

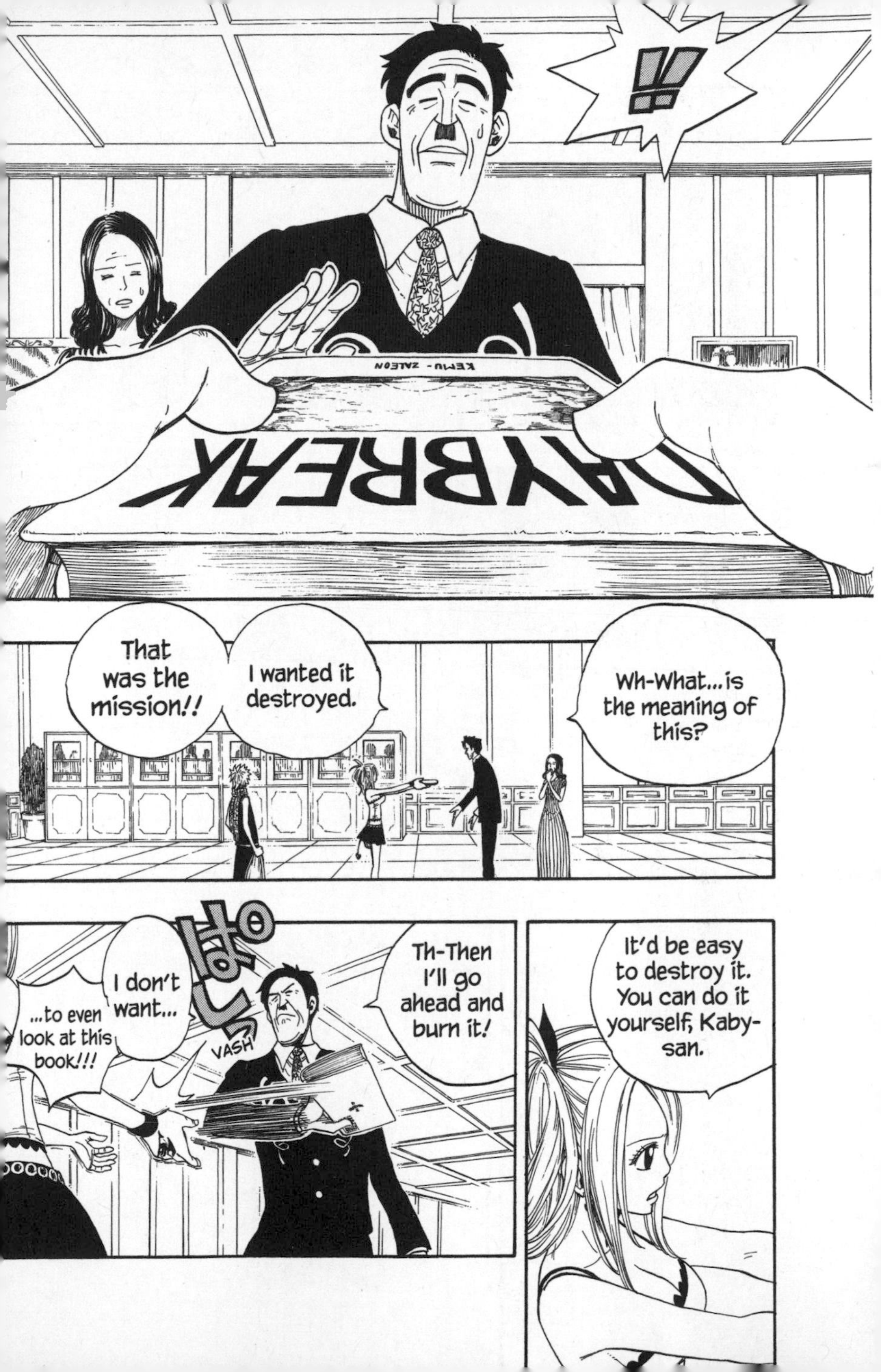
!!
KEMU - ZALEON
DAYBREAK
Wh-What...is the meaning of this?
I wanted it destroyed.
That was the mission!!
It'd be easy to destroy it. You can do it yourself, Kaby-san.
Th-Then I'll go ahead and burn it!
ぱしっ
VASH
I don't want...
...to even look at this book!!!

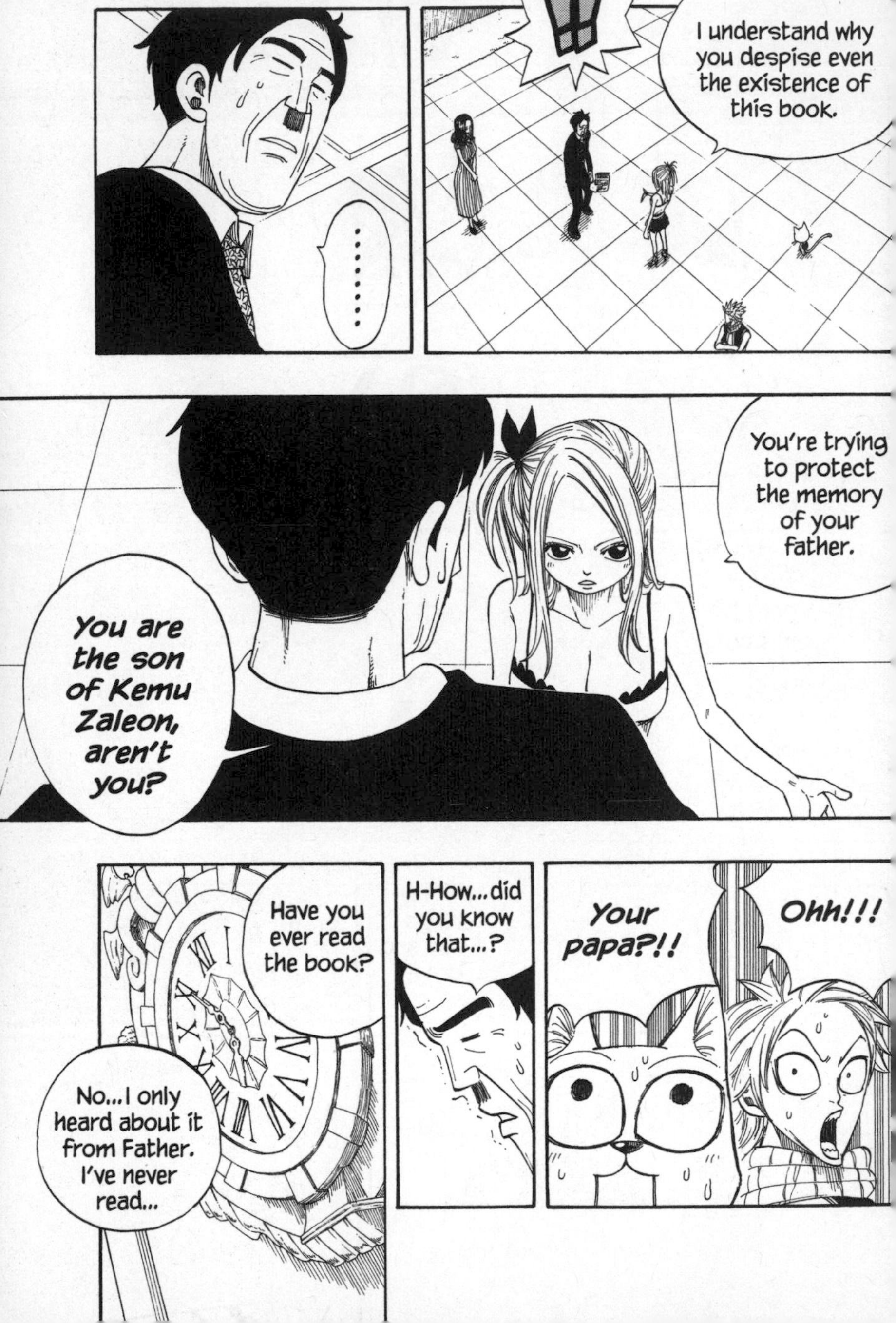
!!
I understand why you despise even the existence of this book.
......
You're trying to protect the memory of your father.
You are the son of Kemu Zaleon, aren't you?
Ohh!!!
Your papa?!!
H-How...did you know that...?
Have you ever read the book?
No...I only heard about it from Father. I've never read...

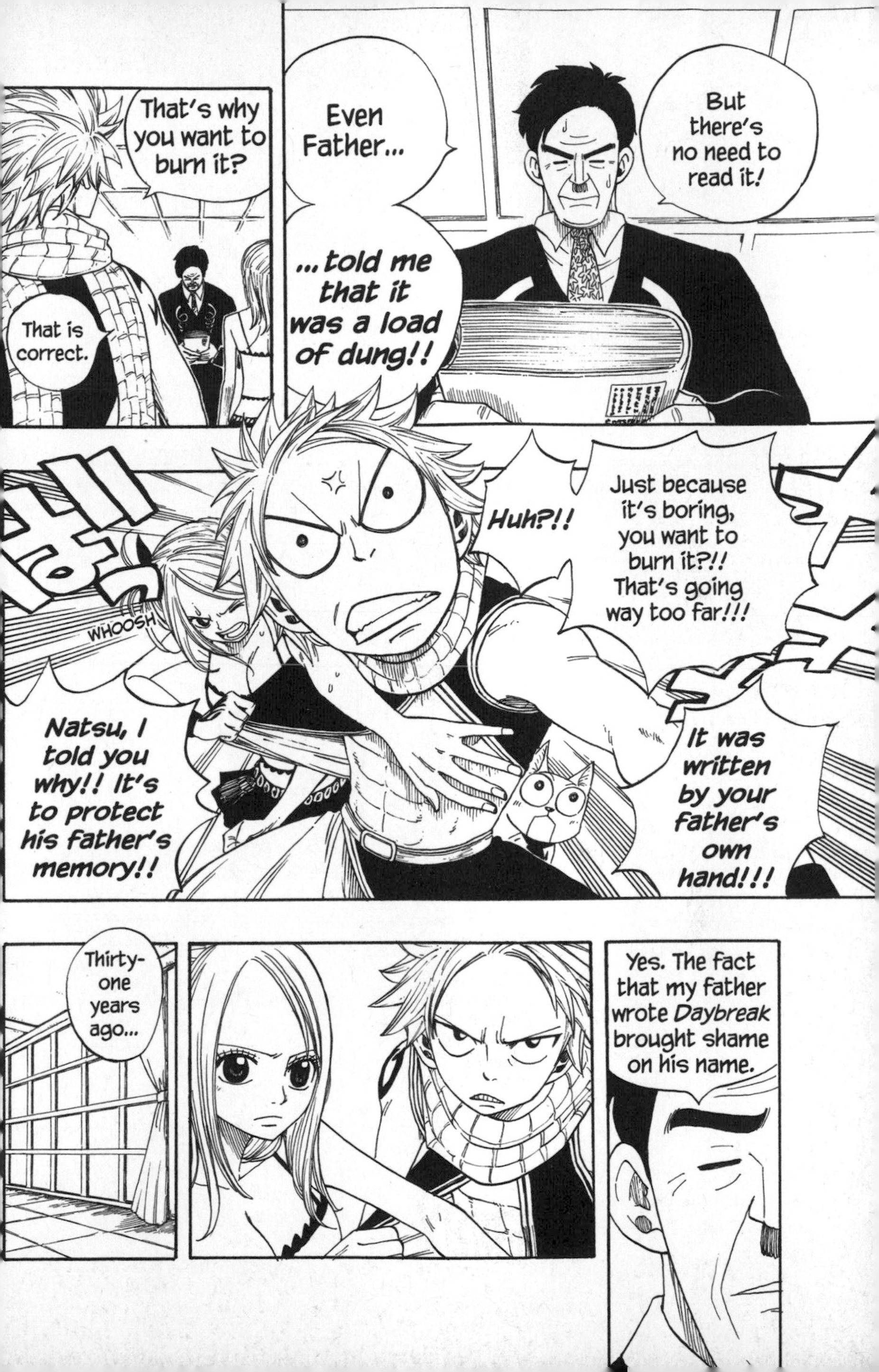
But there's no need to read it!
Even Father...
...told me that it was a load of dung!!
That's why you want to burn it?
That is correct.
Just because it's boring, you want to burn it?!! That's going way too far!!!
Huh?!!
It was written by your father's own hand!!!
Natsu, I told you why!! It's to protect his father's memory!!
WHOOSH
Yes. The fact that my father wrote *Daybreak* brought shame on his name.
Thirty-one years ago...

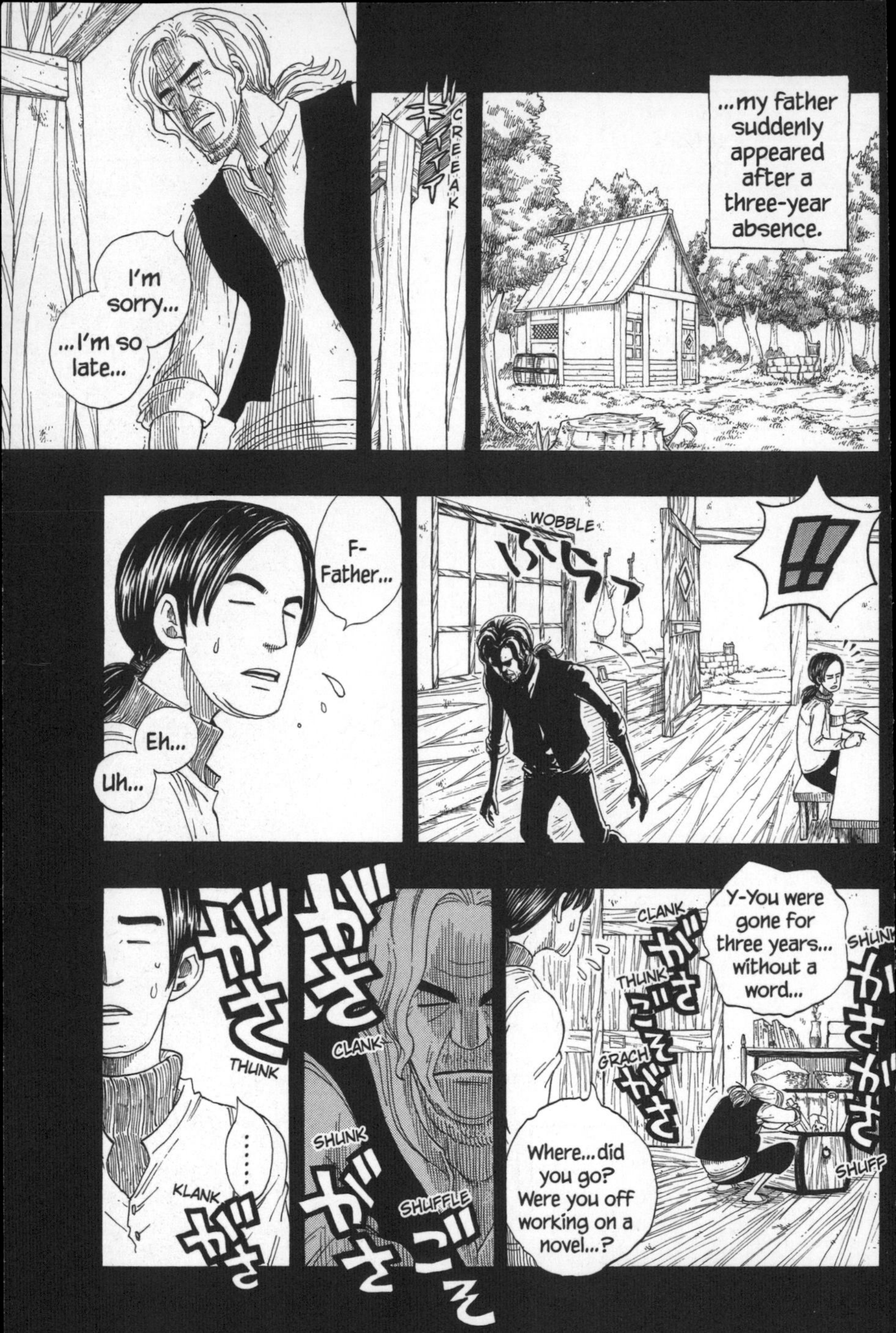
...my father suddenly appeared after a three-year absence.
CREEAK
キィィ
I'm sorry...
...I'm so late...
!!
WOBBLE
ふらっ
F- Father...
Eh...
Uh...
Y-You were gone for three years... without a word...
SHUNK
CLANK
THUNK
GRACH
SHUFF
Where...did you go? Were you off working on a novel...?
CLANK
SHUNK
SHUFFLE
THUNK
......
KLANK

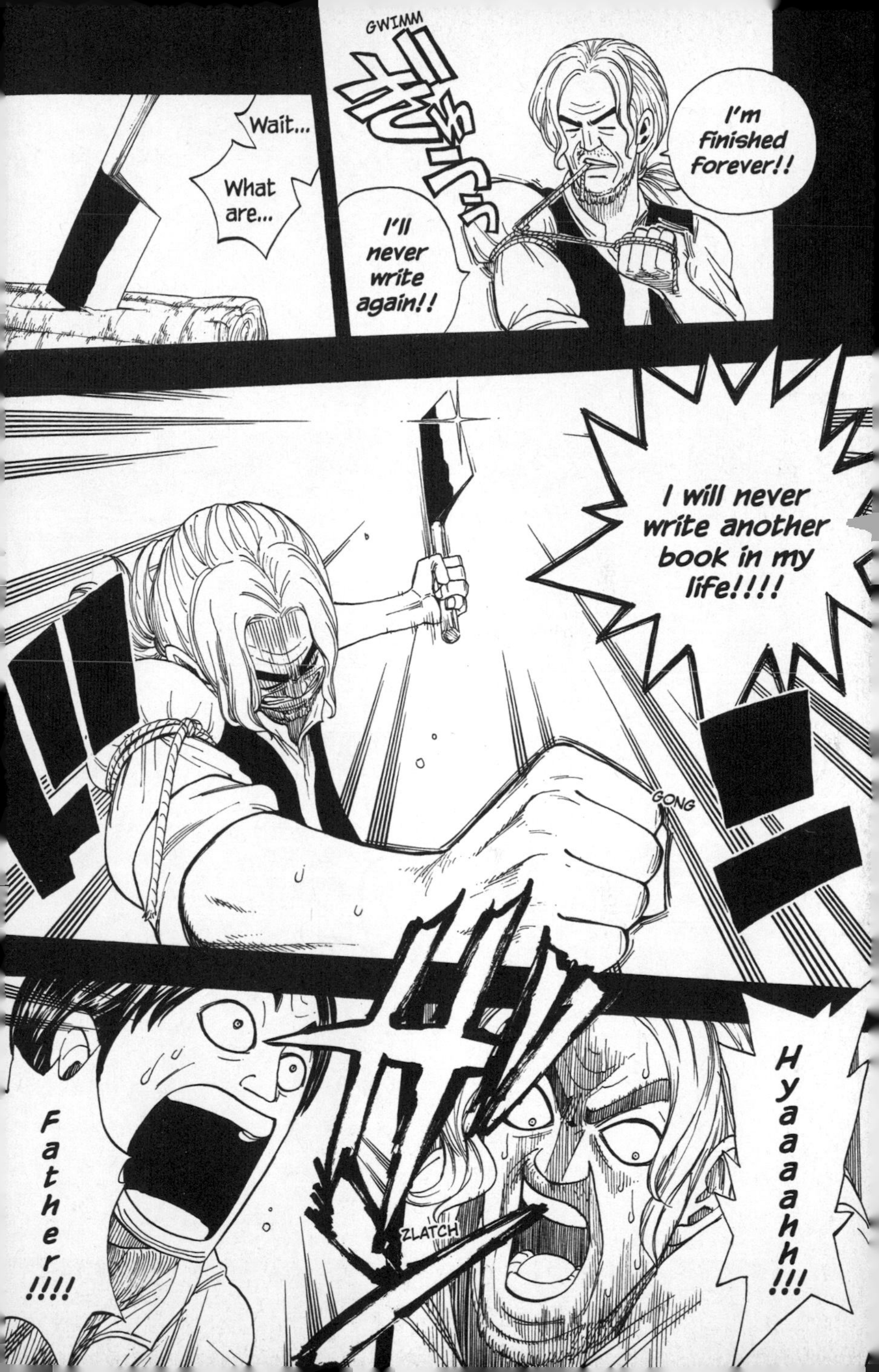
I'm finished forever!!
GWIMM
I'll never write again!!
Wait...
What are...
I will never write another book in my life!!!!
GONG
Hyaaaahh!!!
ZLATCH
Father!!!!

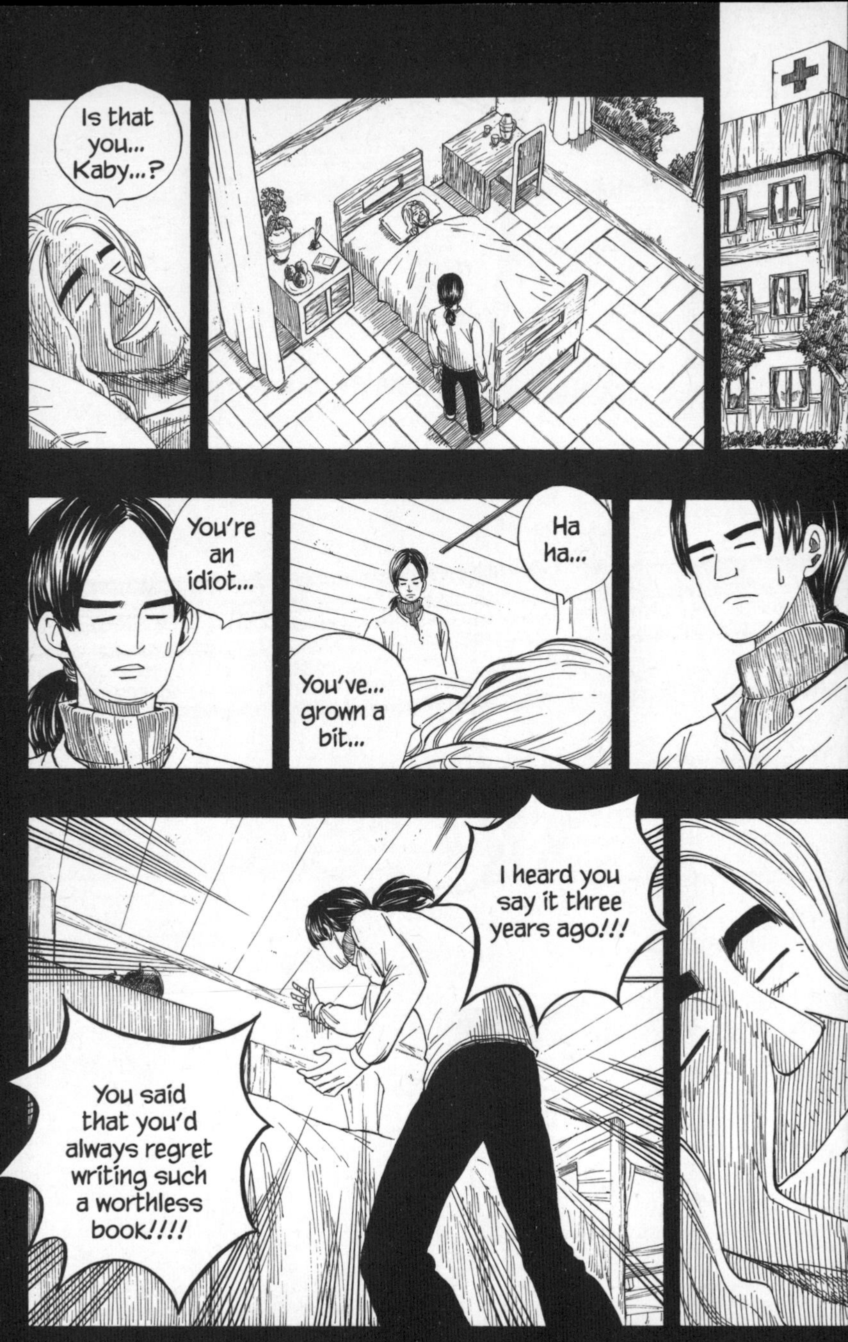
Is that you... Kaby...?
Ha ha...
You've... grown a bit...
You're an idiot...
I heard you say it three years ago!!!
You said that you'd always regret writing such a worthless book!!!!

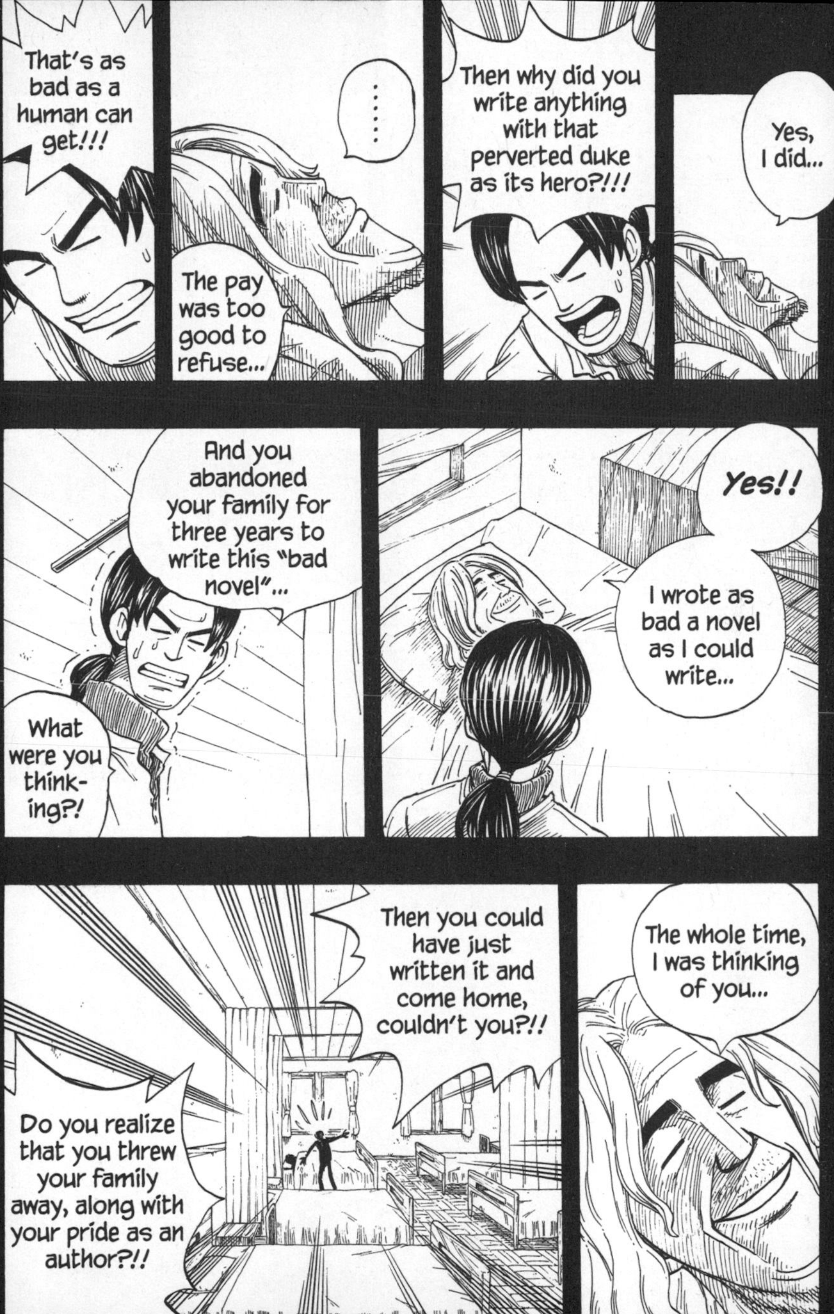

Yes, I did...
Then why did you write anything with that perverted duke as its hero?!!!
......
The pay was too good to refuse...
That's as bad as a human can get!!!
Yes!!
I wrote as bad a novel as I could write...
And you abandoned your family for three years to write this "bad novel"...
What were you thinking?!
The whole time, I was thinking of you...
Then you could have just written it and come home, couldn't you?!!
Do you realize that you threw your family away, along with your pride as an author?!!

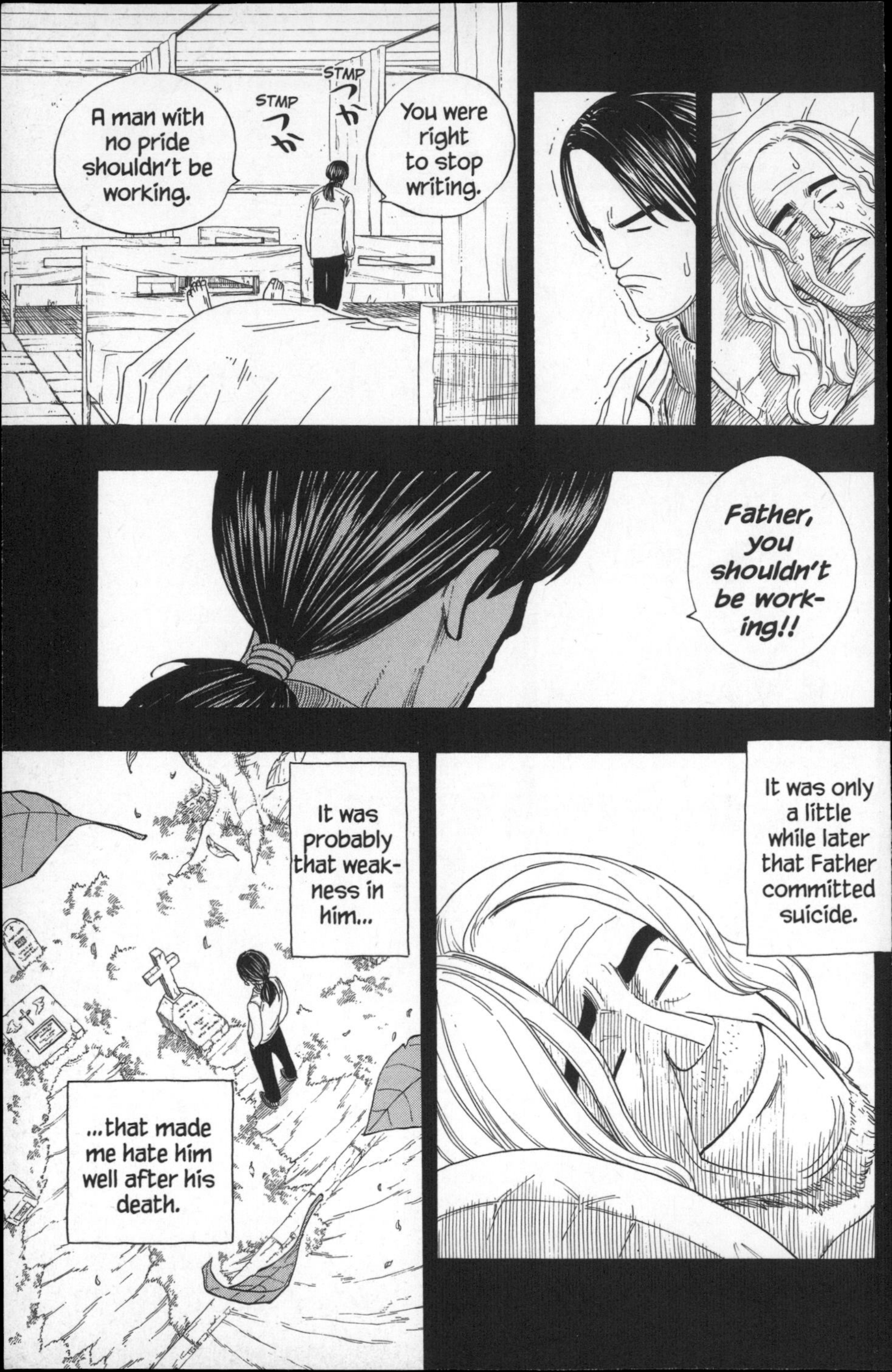
STMP
You were right to stop writing.
STMP
A man with no pride shouldn't be working.
Father, you shouldn't be work-ing!!
It was only a little while later that Father committed suicide.
It was probably that weakness in him...
...that made me hate him well after his death.

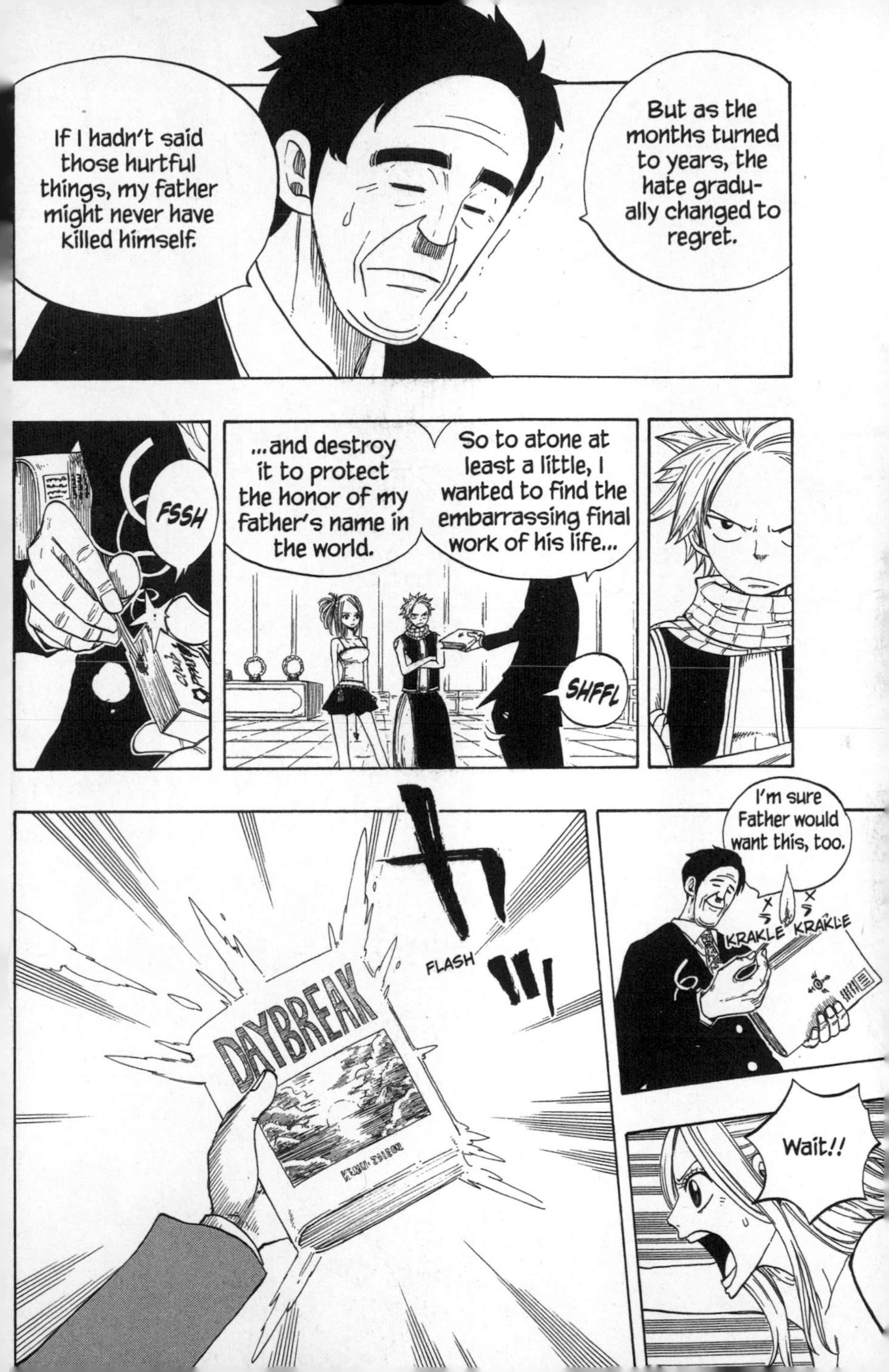
But as the months turned to years, the hate gradually changed to regret.
If I hadn't said those hurtful things, my father might never have killed himself.
So to atone at least a little, I wanted to find the embarrassing final work of his life...
...and destroy it to protect the honor of my father's name in the world.
SHFFL
FSSH
I'm sure Father would want this, too.
KRAKLE KRAKLE
Wait!!
FLASH
DAYBREAK

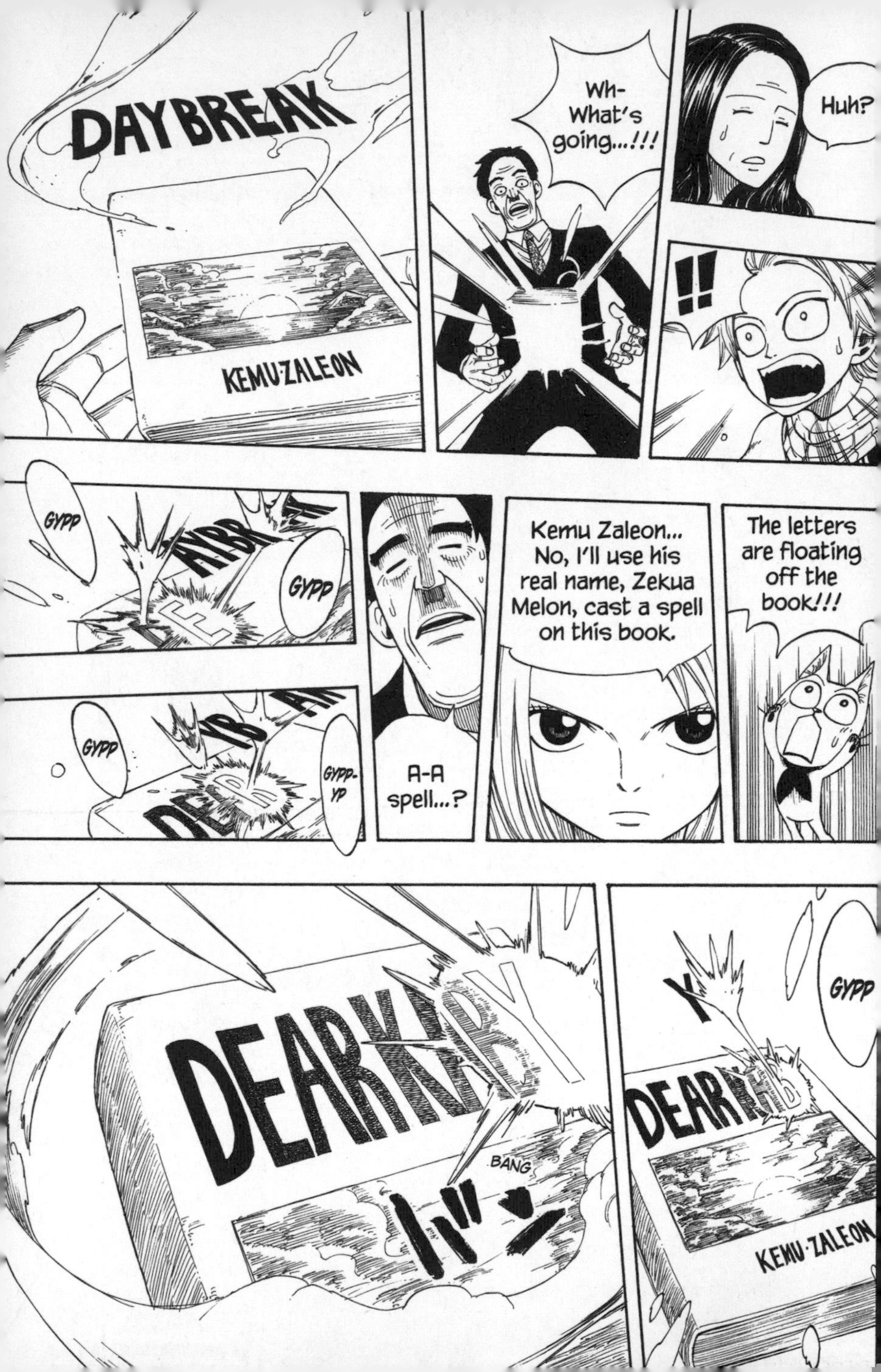
Huh?
!!
Wh- What's going...!!!
DAYBREAK
KEMU·ZALEON
The letters are floating off the book!!!
Kemu Zaleon... No, I'll use his real name, Zekua Melon, cast a spell on this book.
A-A spell...?
GYPP
GYPP
GYPP
GYPP-YP
GYPP
KEMU·ZALEON
BANG

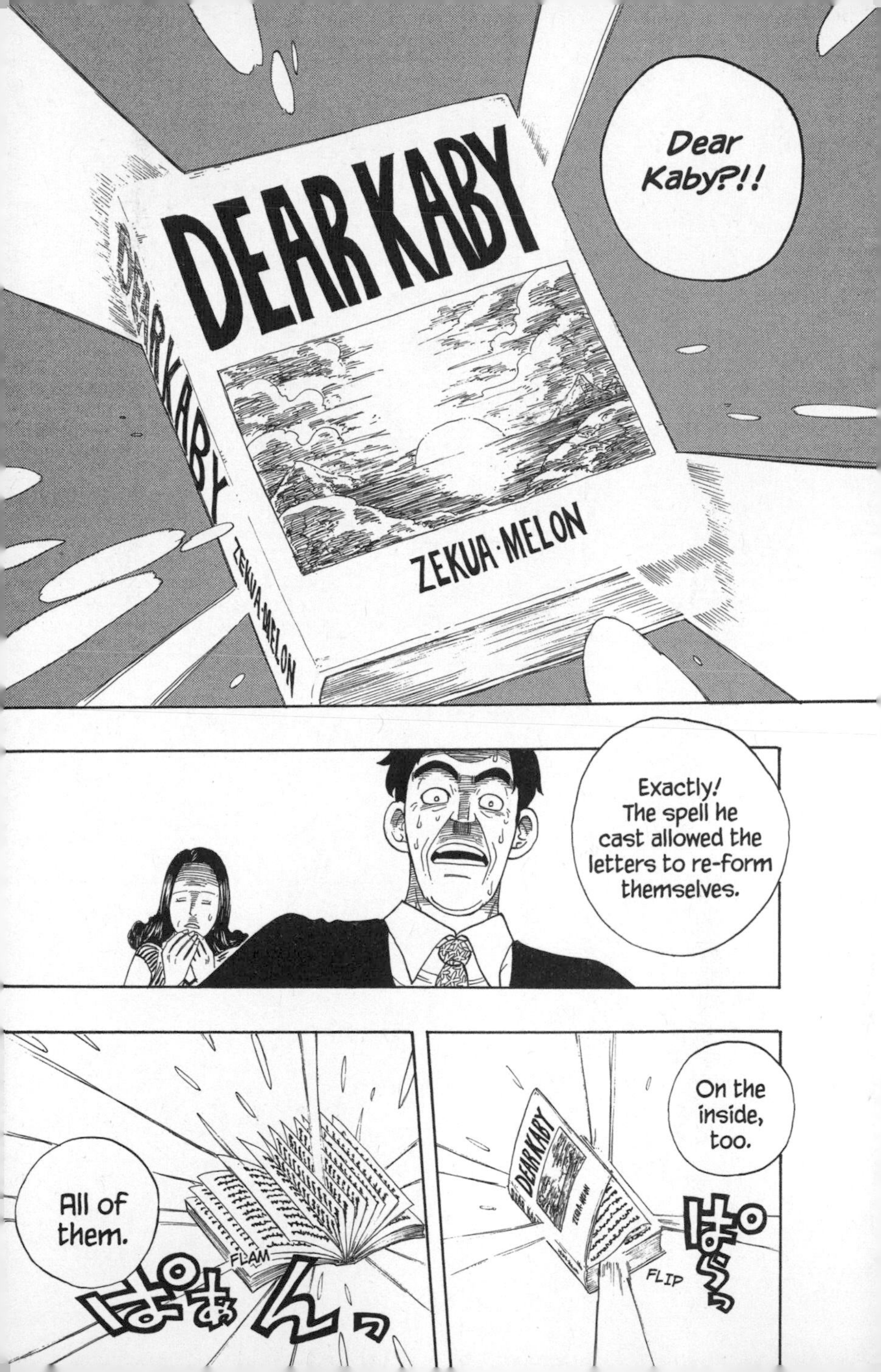
DEAR KABY
ZEKUA·MELON
Dear Kaby?!!
Exactly! The spell he cast allowed the letters to re-form themselves.
On the inside, too.
FLIP
ぱらっ
All of them.
FLAM

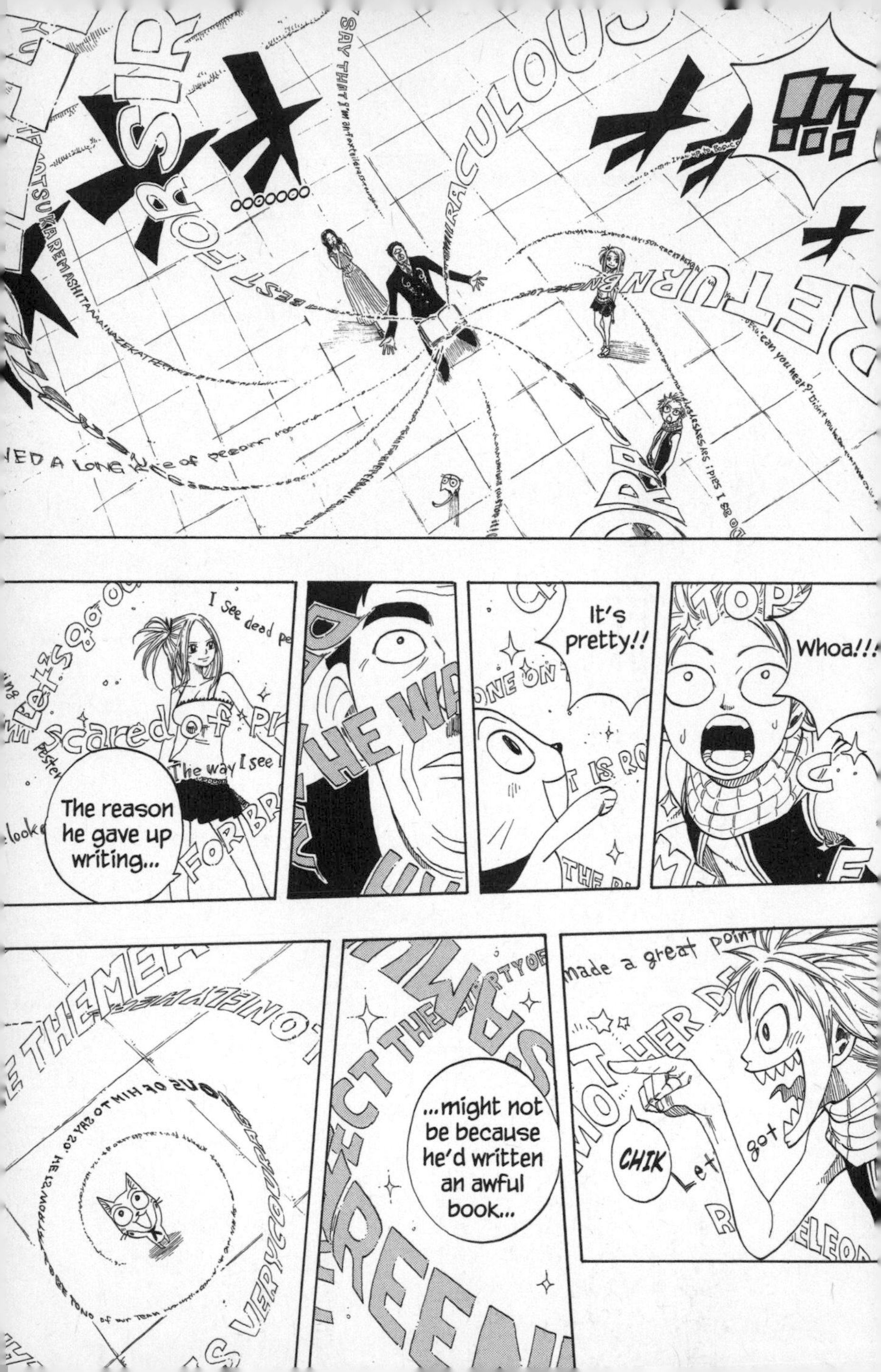
Whoa!!!
It's pretty!!
The reason he gave up writing...
CHIK
...might not be because he'd written an awful book...

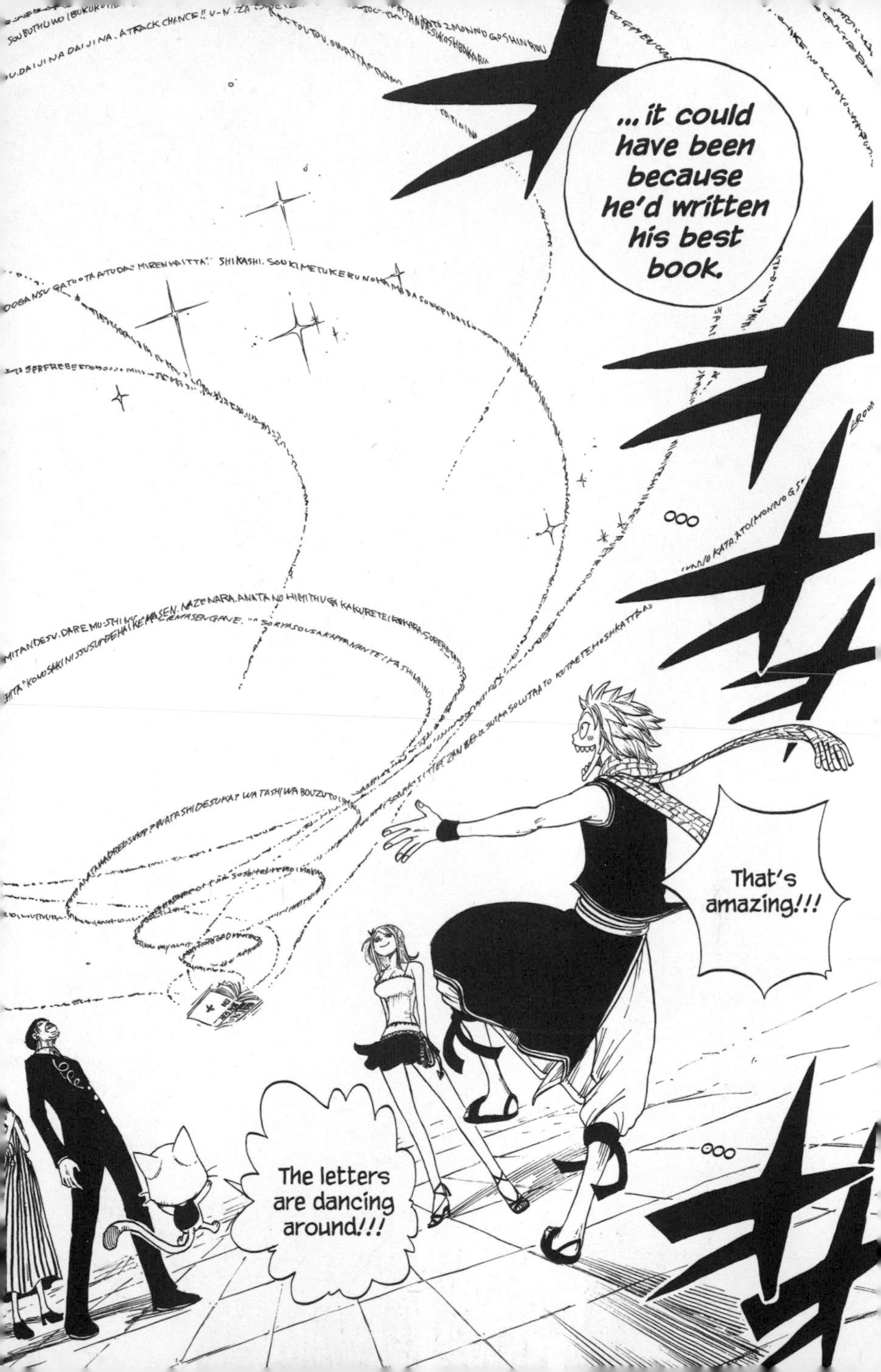
...it could have been because he'd written his best book.
That's amazing!!!
The letters are dancing around!!!

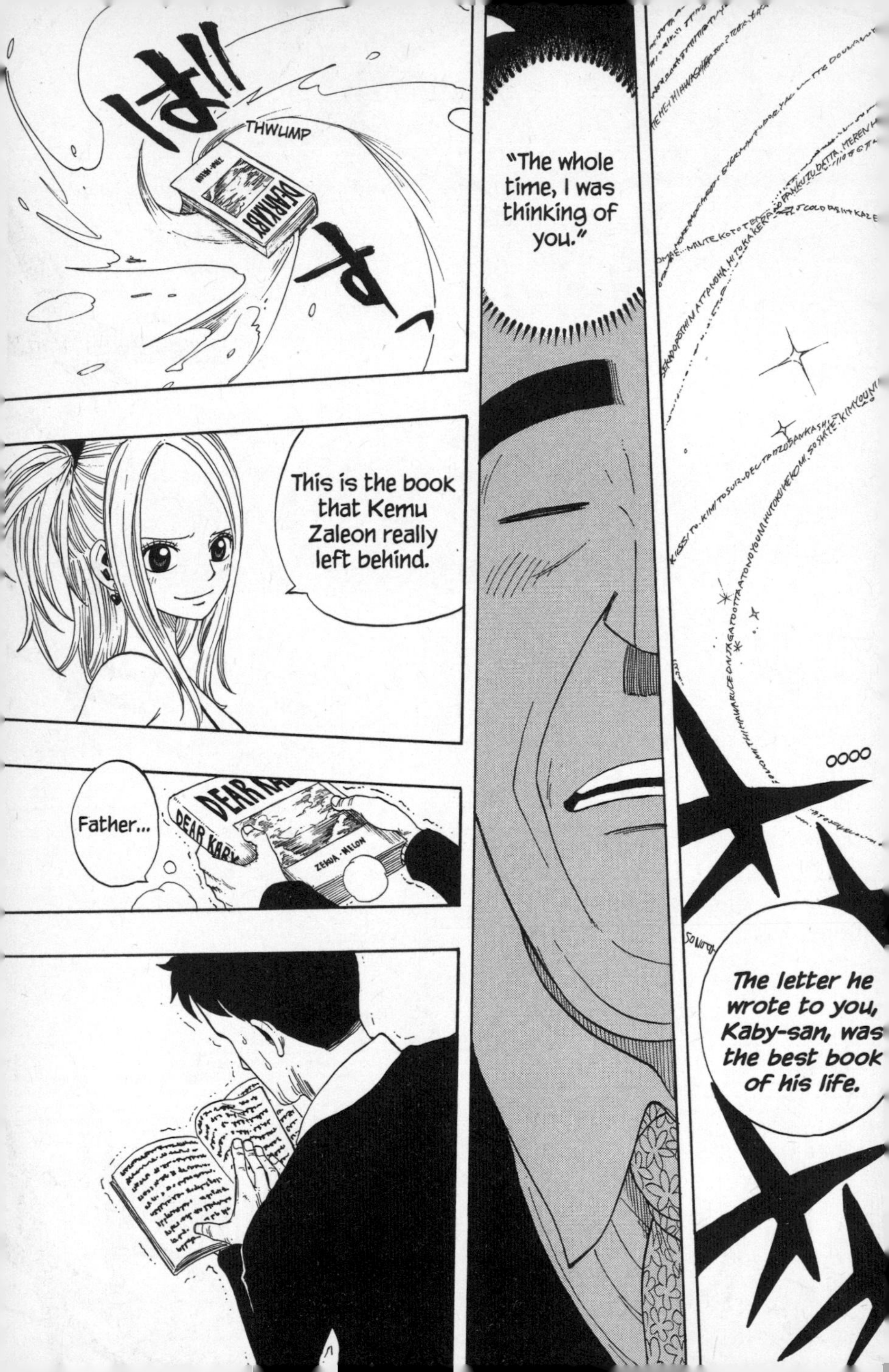

OOOO
The letter he wrote to you, Kaby-san, was the best book of his life.
"The whole time, I was thinking of you."
THWUMP
This is the book that Kemu Zaleon really left behind.
DEAR KARY
Father...

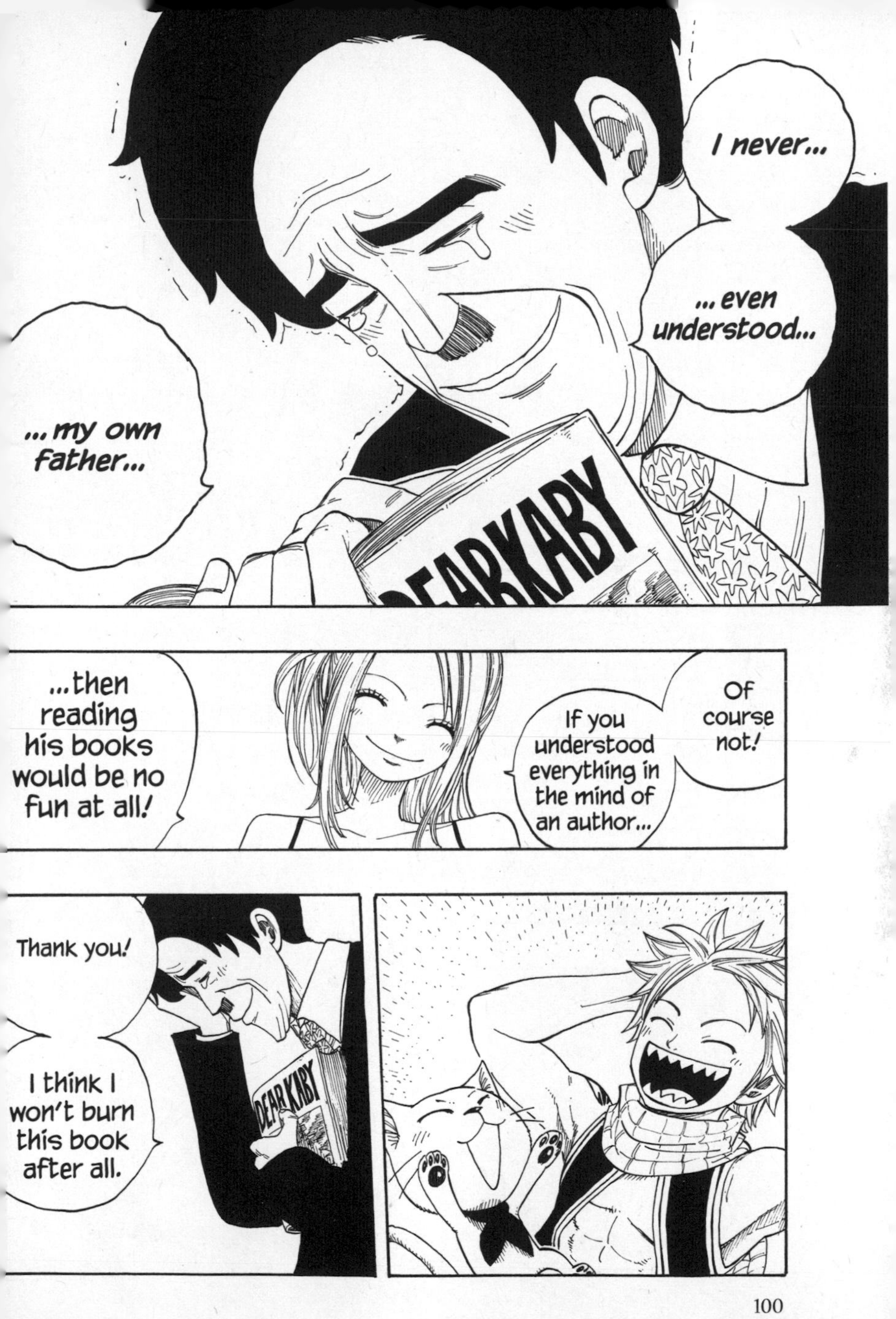
I never...
...even understood...
...my own father...
Of course not!
If you understood everything in the mind of an author...
...then reading his books would be no fun at all!
Thank you!
I think I won't burn this book after all.

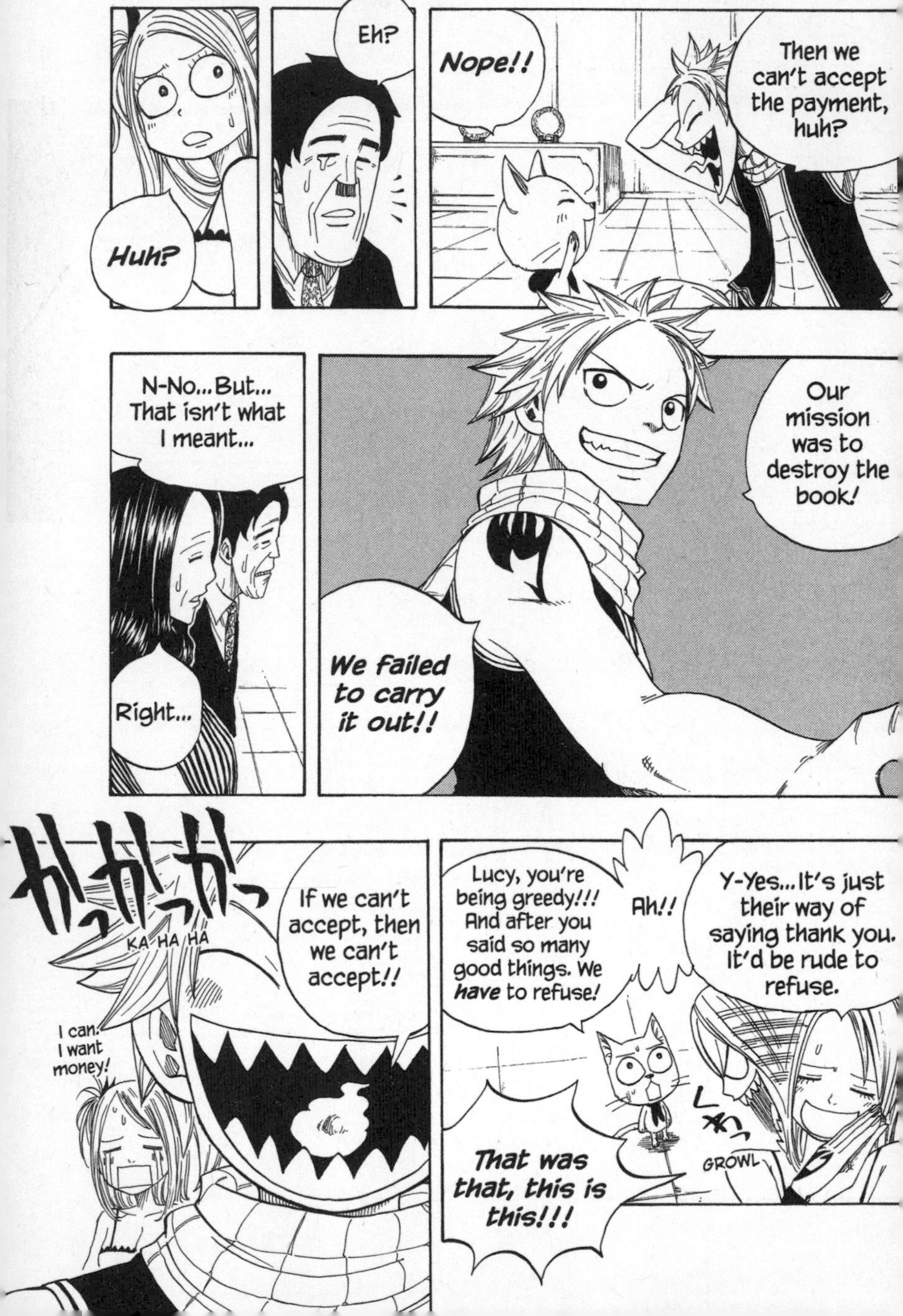
Then we can't accept the payment, huh?
Nope!!
Eh?
Huh?
Our mission was to destroy the book!
We failed to carry it out!!
N-No...But... That isn't what I meant...
Right...
Y-Yes...It's just their way of saying thank you. It'd be rude to refuse.
Ah!!
Lucy, you're being greedy!!! And after you said so many good things. We have to refuse!
GROWL
That was that, this is this!!!
If we can't accept, then we can't accept!!
KA HA HA
I can! I want money!

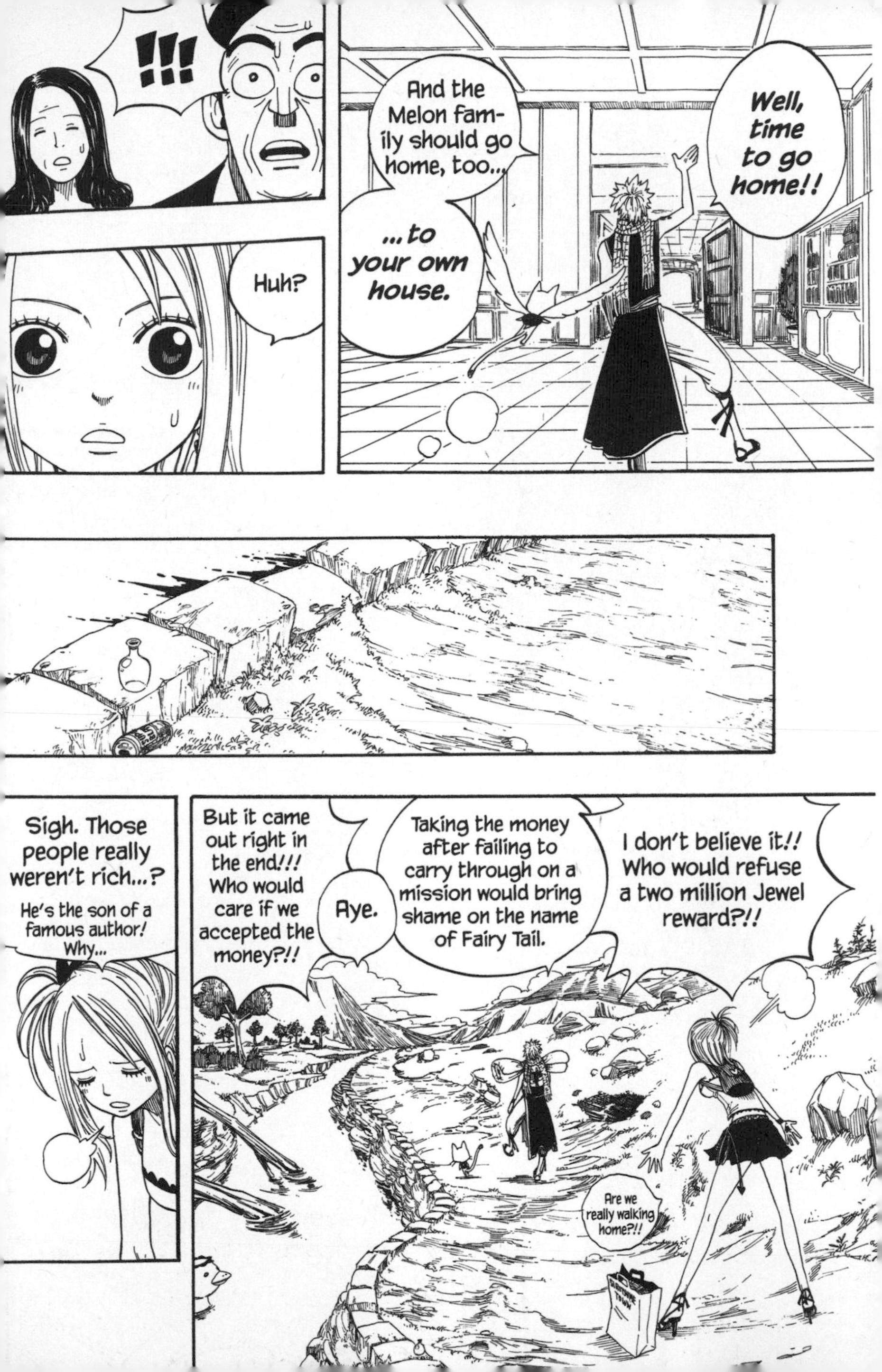
Well, time to go home!!
And the Melon family should go home, too...
...to your own house.
!!!
Huh?
I don't believe it!! Who would refuse a two million Jewel reward?!!
Taking the money after failing to carry through on a mission would bring shame on the name of Fairy Tail.
Aye.
But it came out right in the end!!! Who would care if we accepted the money?!!
Are we really walking home?!!
Sigh. Those people really weren't rich...?
He's the son of a famous author! Why...

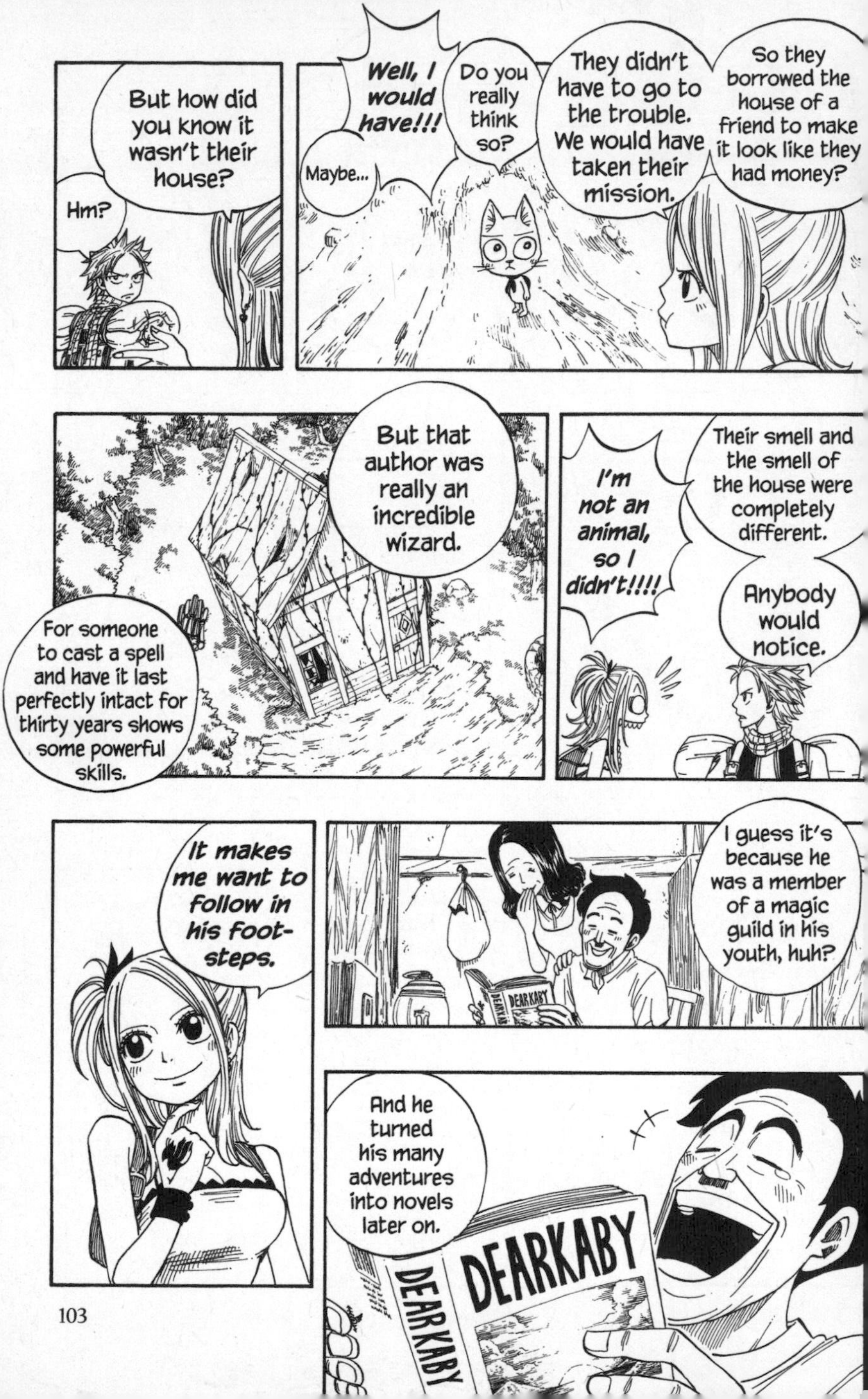
So they borrowed the house of a friend to make it look like they had money?
They didn't have to go to the trouble. We would have taken their mission.
Do you really think so?
Well, I would have!!!
Maybe...
But how did you know it wasn't their house?
Hm?
Their smell and the smell of the house were completely different.
Anybody would notice.
I'm not an animal, so I didn't!!!!
But that author was really an incredible wizard.
For someone to cast a spell and have it last perfectly intact for thirty years shows some powerful skills.
I guess it's because he was a member of a magic guild in his youth, huh?
DEARKABY
And he turned his many adventures into novels later on.
DEARKABY
DEARKABY
It makes me want to follow in his foot-steps.

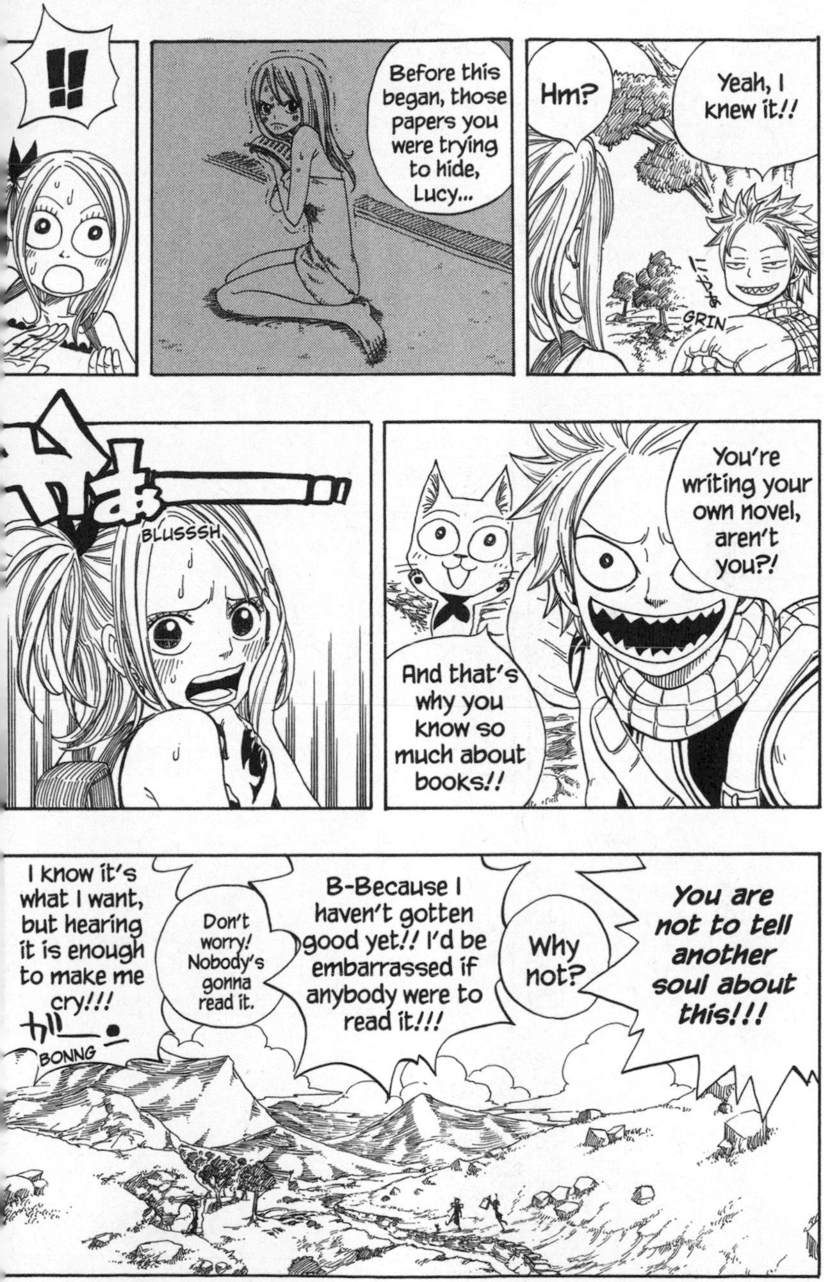
Yeah, I knew it!!
Hm?
GRIN
Before this began, those papers you were trying to hide, Lucy...
!!
You're writing your own novel, aren't you?!
And that's why you know so much about books!!
BLUSSSH
You are not to tell another soul about this!!!
Why not?
B-Because I haven't gotten good yet!! I'd be embarrassed if anybody were to read it!!!
Don't worry! Nobody's gonna read it.
I know it's what I want, but hearing it is enough to make me cry!!!
BONNG

FAIRY TAIL

Chapter 10: The Armored Wizard

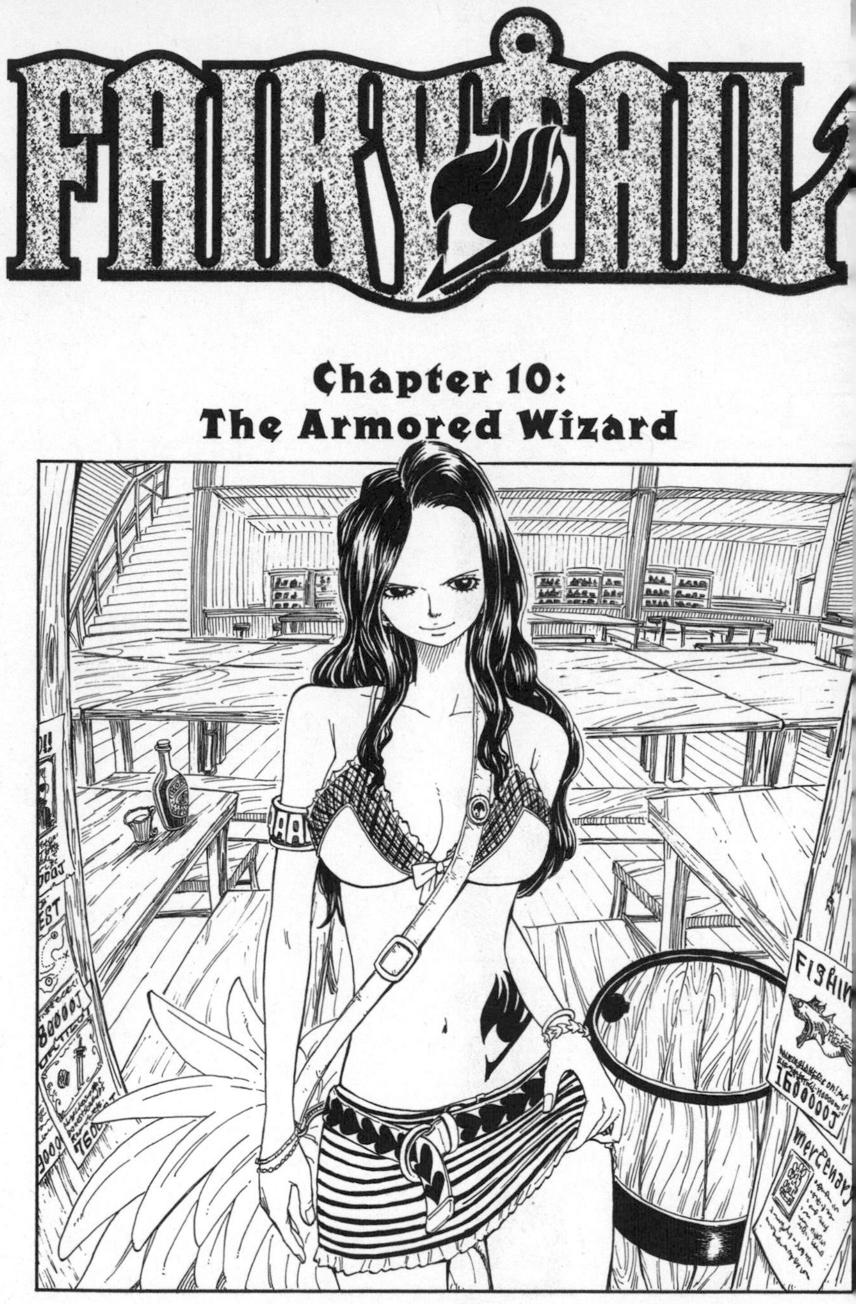

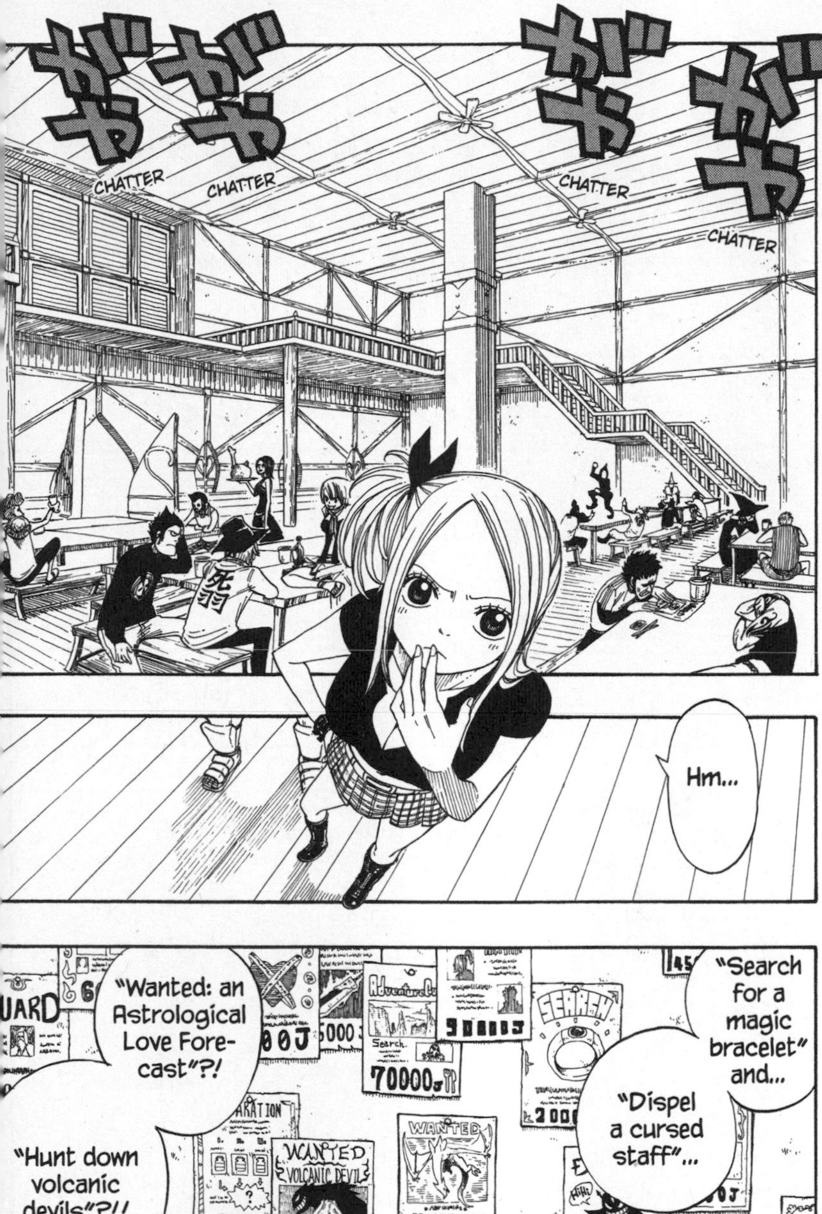
がやがや
CHATTER
CHATTER
がやがや
CHATTER
CHATTER
Hm...
"Search for a magic bracelet" and...
"Dispel a cursed staff"...
"Wanted: an Astrological Love Fore-cast"?!
"Hunt down volcanic devils"?!!
SEARCH
WANTED
140000 J
Search.
70000J
WANTED
VOLCANIC DEVIL

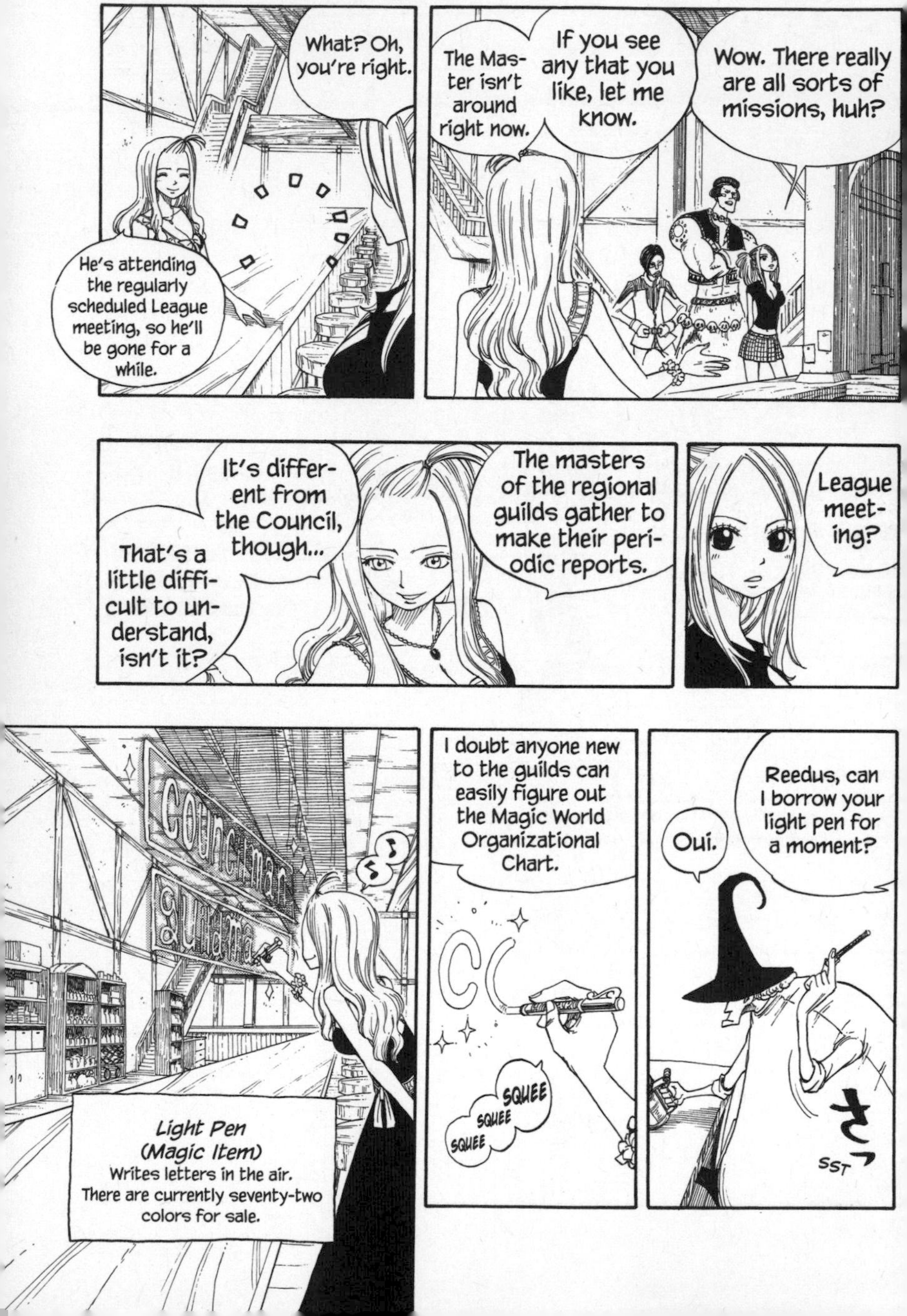
Wow. There really are all sorts of missions, huh?
If you see any that you like, let me know.
The Master isn't around right now.
What? Oh, you're right.
He's attending the regularly scheduled League meeting, so he'll be gone for a while.
League meeting?
The masters of the regional guilds gather to make their periodic reports.
It's different from the Council, though...
That's a little difficult to understand, isn't it?
Reedus, can I borrow your light pen for a moment?
Oui.
SST
I doubt anyone new to the guilds can easily figure out the Magic World Organizational Chart.
SQUEE
SQUEE
SQUEE
Councilman
Light Pen (Magic Item)
Writes letters in the air. There are currently seventy-two colors for sale.

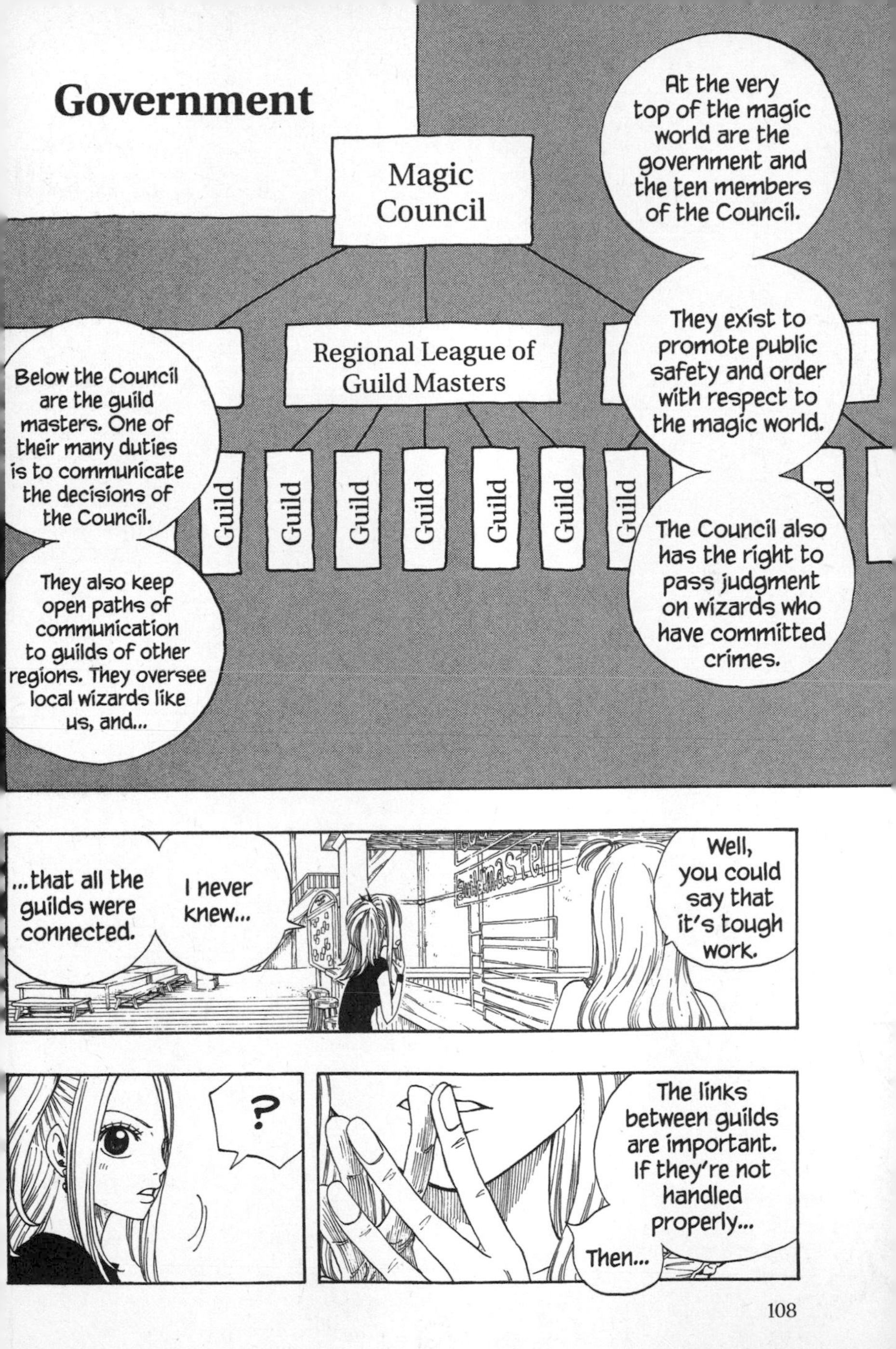
Government
Magic Council
At the very top of the magic world are the government and the ten members of the Council.
They exist to promote public safety and order with respect to the magic world.
The Council also has the right to pass judgment on wizards who have committed crimes.
Regional League of Guild Masters
Guild
Guild
Guild
Guild
Guild
Guild
Guild
Below the Council are the guild masters. One of their many duties is to communicate the decisions of the Council.
They also keep open paths of communication to guilds of other regions. They oversee local wizards like us, and...
Well, you could say that it's tough work.
I never knew...
...that all the guilds were connected.
The links between guilds are important. If they're not handled properly...
Then...
?

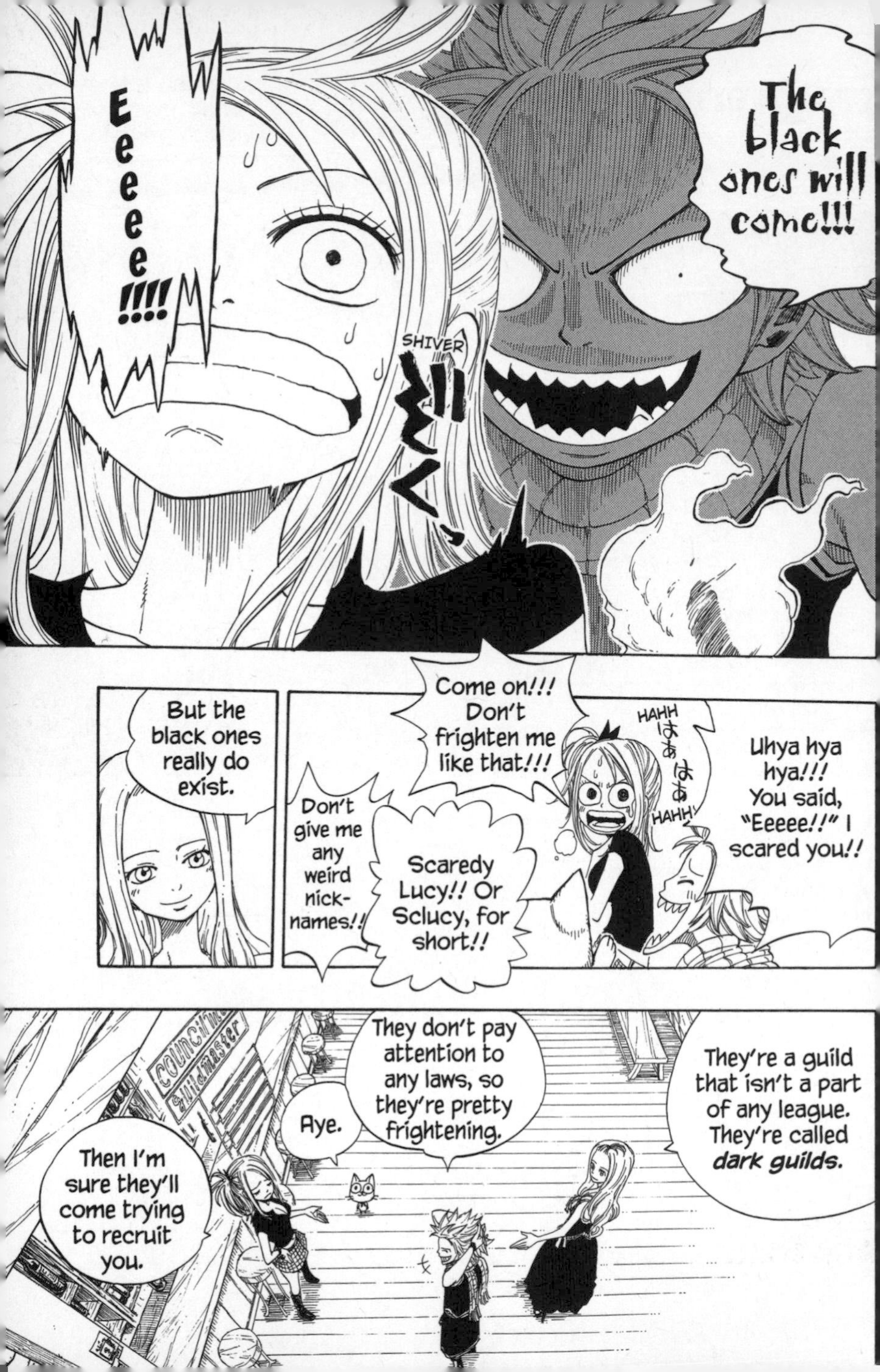
The black ones will come!!!
SHIVER
Eeeee!!!!
Come on!!! Don't frighten me like that!!!
Uhya hya hya!!! You said, "Eeeee!!" I scared you!!
HAHH HAHH
Scaredy Lucy!! Or Sclucy, for short!!
Don't give me any weird nick-names!!
But the black ones really do exist.
They're a guild that isn't a part of any league. They're called *dark guilds.*
They don't pay attention to any laws, so they're pretty frightening.
Aye.
Then I'm sure they'll come trying to recruit you.
Guildmaster

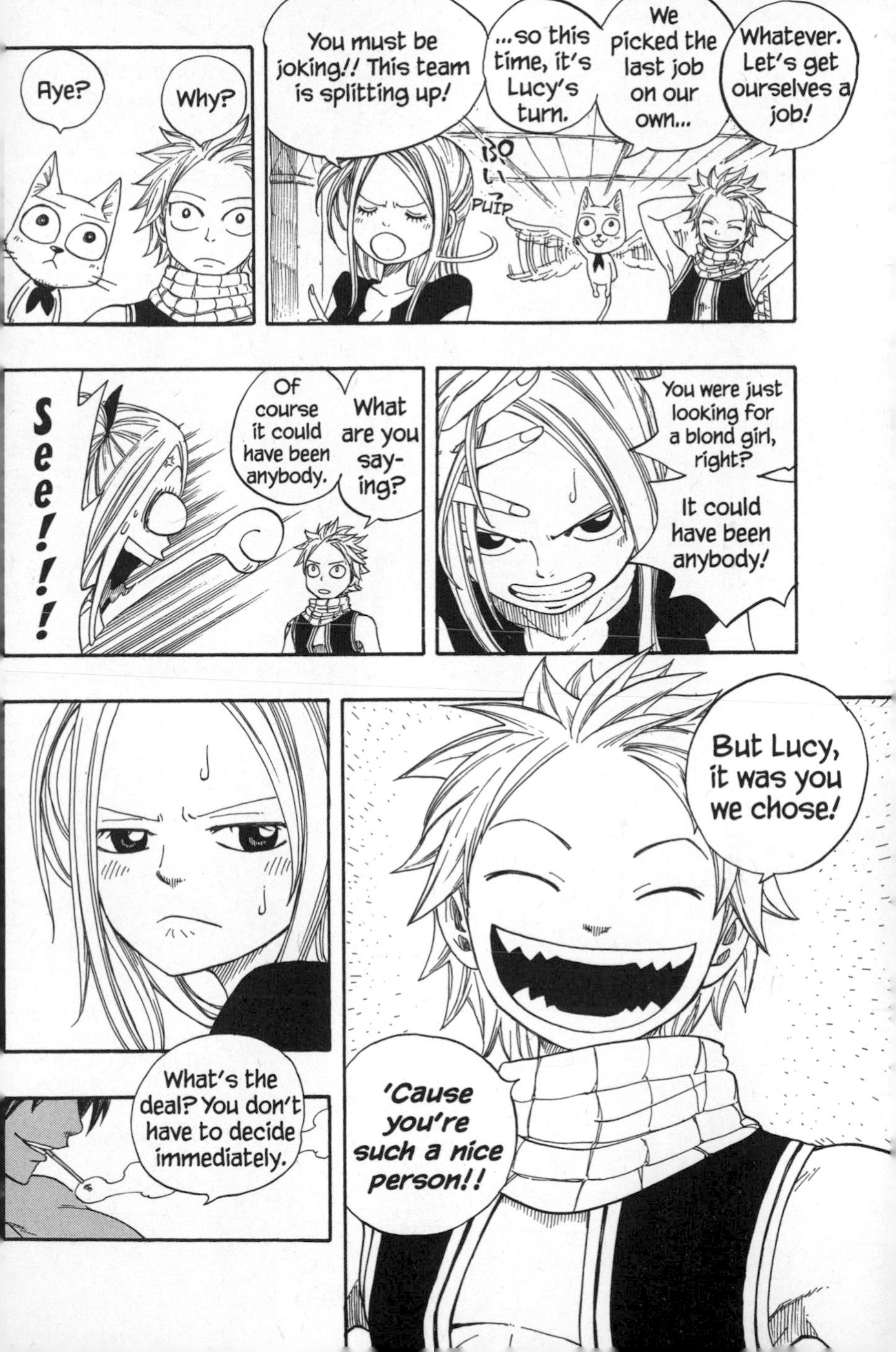
Whatever. Let's get ourselves a job!
We picked the last job on our own...
...so this time, it's Lucy's turn.
You must be joking!! This team is splitting up!
Why?
Aye?
You were just looking for a blond girl, right?
It could have been anybody!
What are you say-ing?
Of course it could have been anybody.
See!!!
But Lucy, it was you we chose!
'Cause you're such a nice person!!
What's the deal? You don't have to decide immediately.

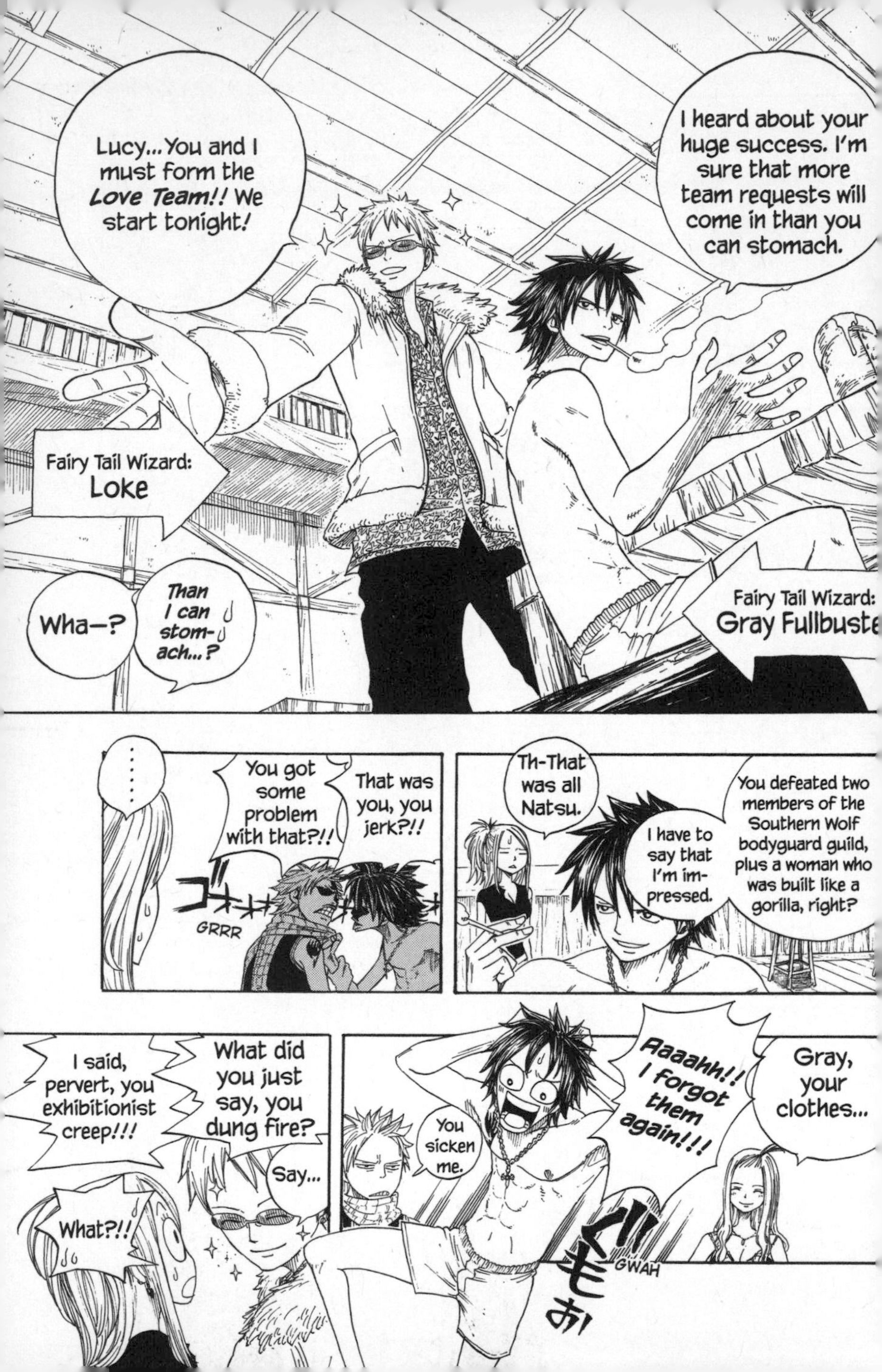
I heard about your huge success. I'm sure that more team requests will come in than you can stomach.
Lucy... You and I must form the *Love Team!!* We start tonight!
Fairy Tail Wizard: Gray Fullbuste
Fairy Tail Wizard: Loke
Than I can stom-ach...?
Wha–?
You defeated two members of the Southern Wolf bodyguard guild, plus a woman who was built like a gorilla, right?
I have to say that I'm im-pressed.
Th-That was all Natsu.
That was you, you jerk?!!
You got some problem with that?!!
GRRR
......
Gray, your clothes...
Aaaahh!! I forgot them again!!!
You sicken me.
GWAH
What did you just say, you dung fire?
I said, pervert, you exhibitionist creep!!!
Say...
What?!!

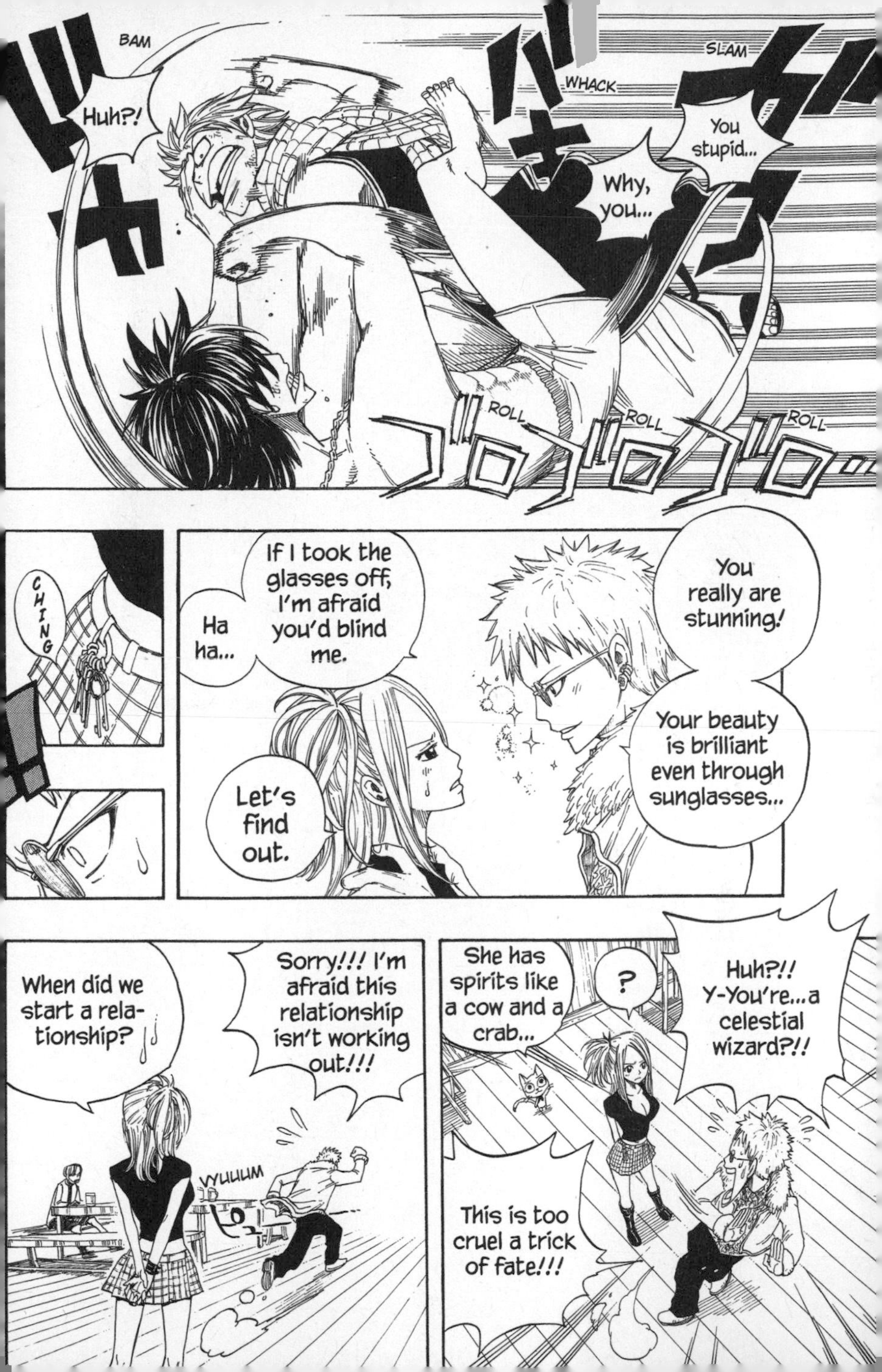
SLAM
You stupid...
WHACK
Why, you...
BAM
Huh?!
ROLL
ROLL
ROLL
You really are stunning!
Your beauty is brilliant even through sunglasses...
If I took the glasses off, I'm afraid you'd blind me.
Ha ha...
Let's find out.
CHING
Huh?!! Y-You're...a celestial wizard?!!
?
She has spirits like a cow and a crab...
This is too cruel a trick of fate!!!
Sorry!!! I'm afraid this relationship isn't working out!!!
When did we start a relationship?
VYUUUM

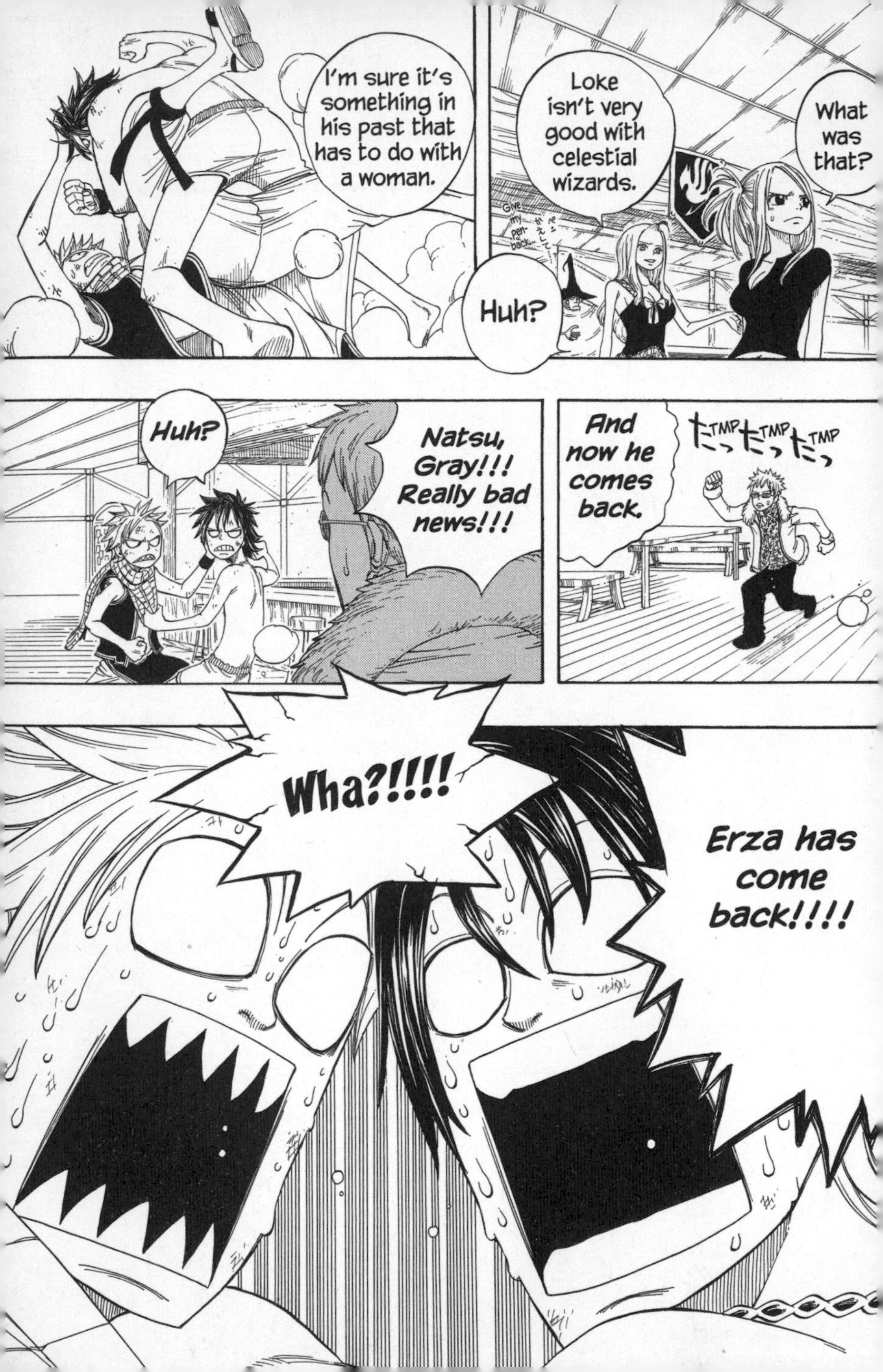
What was that?
Loke isn't very good with celestial wizards.
Give my pen back...
Huh?
I'm sure it's something in his past that has to do with a woman.
TMP TMP TMP
And now he comes back.
Natsu, Gray!!! Really bad news!!!
Huh?
Erza has come back!!!!
Wha?!!!!

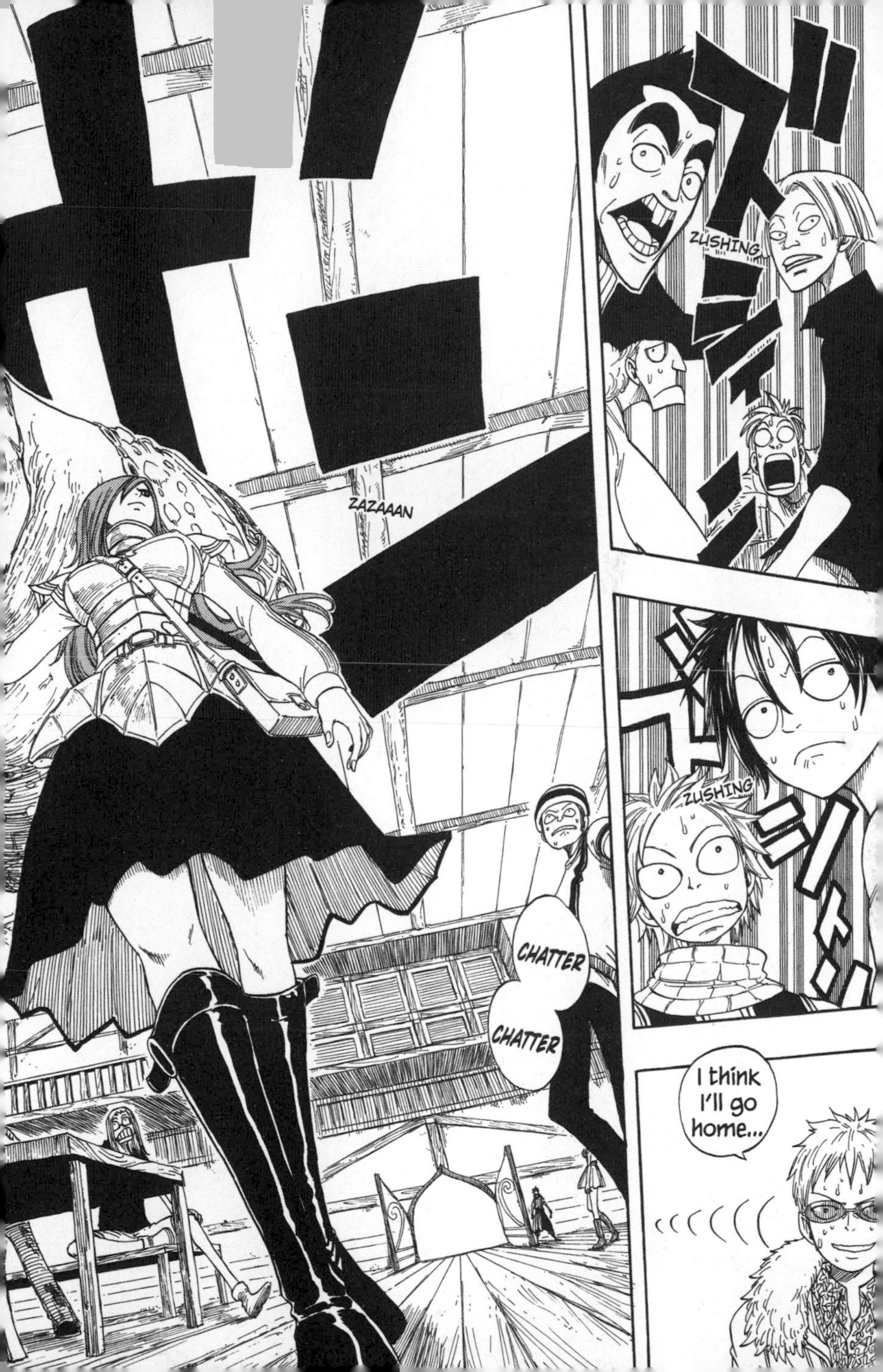
ZUSHING
ZUSHING
I think I'll go home...
ZAZAAAN
CHATTER
CHATTER

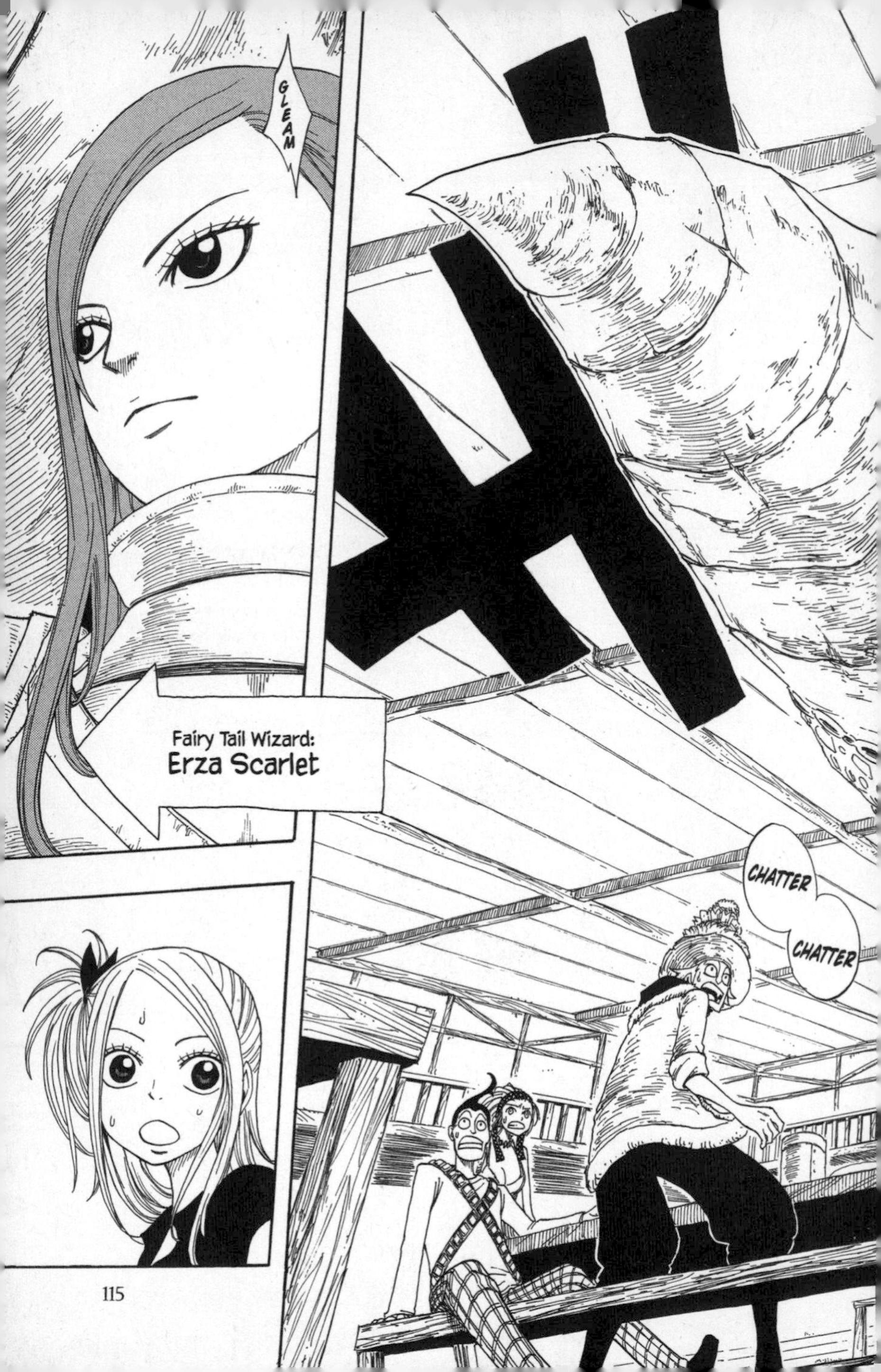
CHATTER
CHATTER
GLEAM
Fairy Tail Wizard:
Erza Scarlet

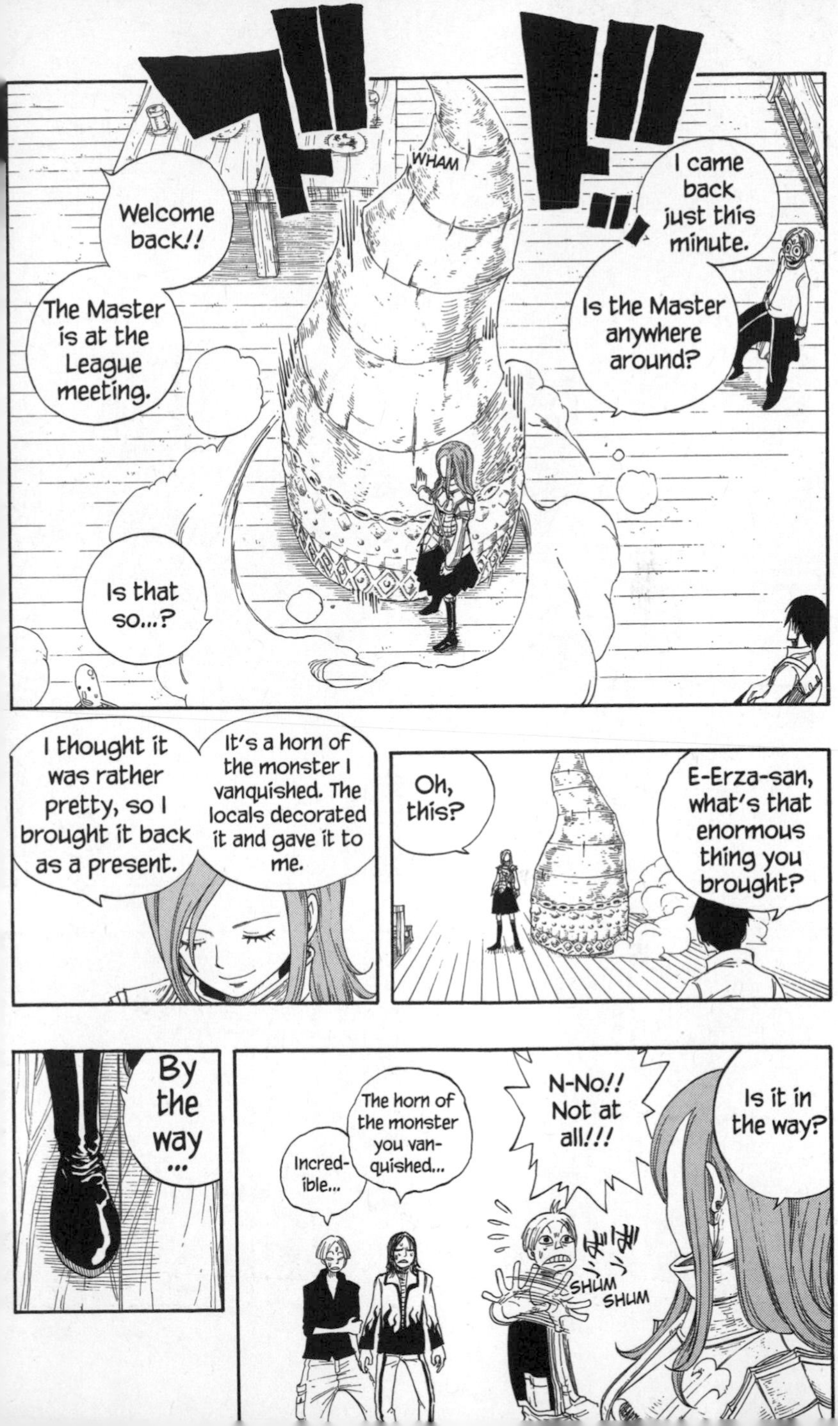
WHAM
I came back just this minute.
Is the Master anywhere around?
Welcome back!!
The Master is at the League meeting.
Is that so...?
E-Erza-san, what's that enormous thing you brought?
Oh, this?
It's a horn of the monster I vanquished. The locals decorated it and gave it to me.
I thought it was rather pretty, so I brought it back as a present.
Is it in the way?
N-No!! Not at all!!!
SHUM SHUM
The horn of the monster you vanquished...
Incredible...
By the way...

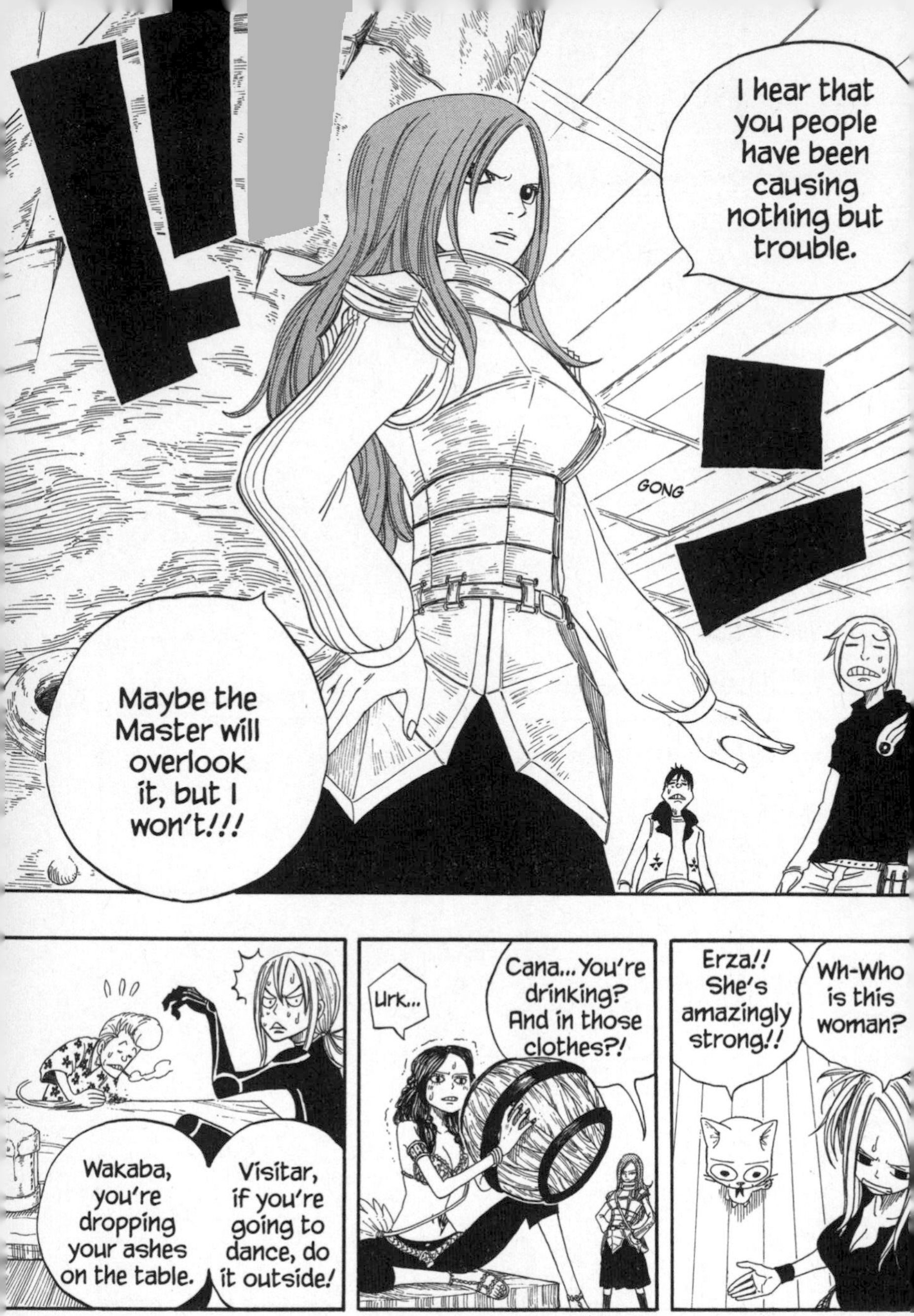
I hear that you people have been causing nothing but trouble.
[redacted]
GONG
Maybe the Master will overlook it, but I won't!!!
Wh-Who is this woman?
Erza!! She's amazingly strong!!
Cana... You're drinking? And in those clothes?!
Urk...
Visitar, if you're going to dance, do it outside!
Wakaba, you're dropping your ashes on the table.

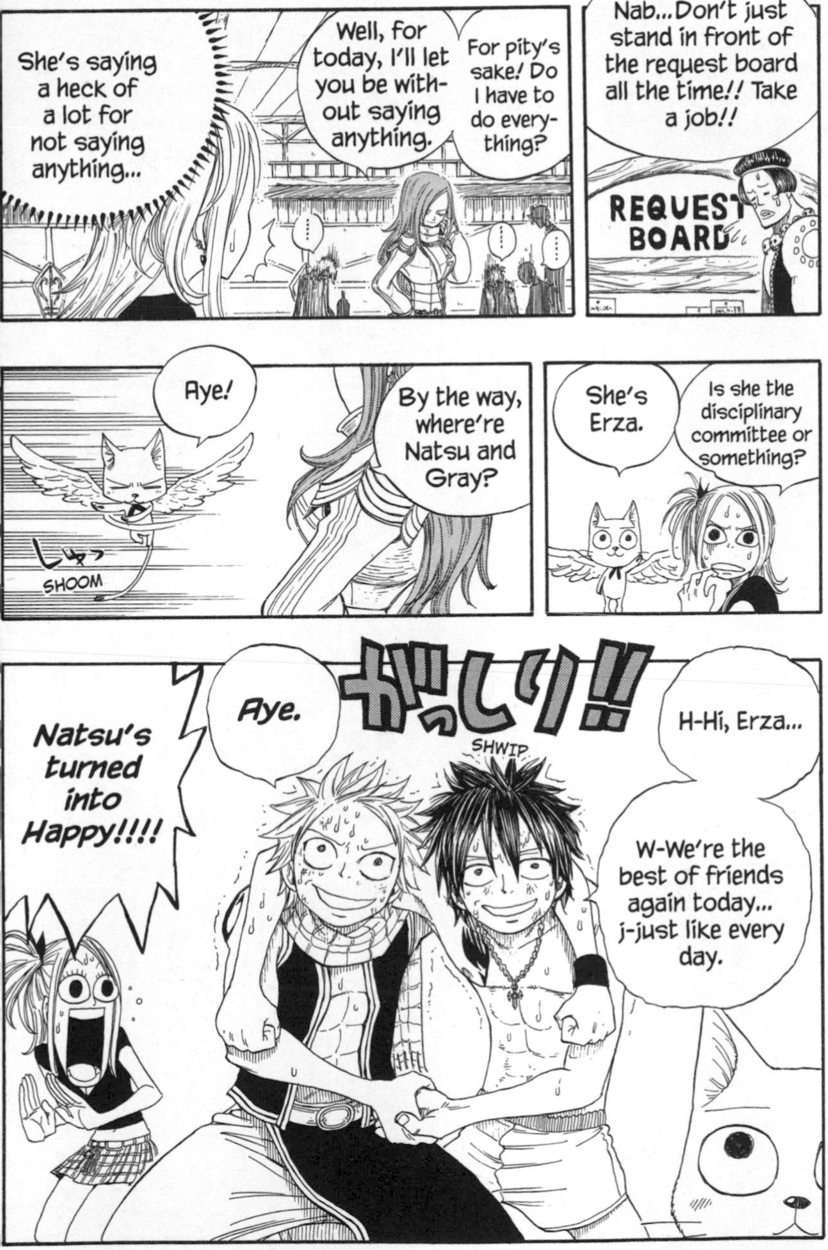

Nab...Don't just stand in front of the request board all the time!! Take a job!!
REQUEST BOARD
For pity's sake! Do I have to do every-thing?
Well, for today, I'll let you be with-out saying anything.
...
...
...
She's saying a heck of a lot for not saying anything...
Is she the disciplinary committee or something?
She's Erza.
By the way, where're Natsu and Gray?
Aye!
しゅっ
SHOOM
H-Hi, Erza...
がっしり!!
SHWIP
Aye.
W-We're the best of friends again today... j-just like every day.
Natsu's turned into Happy!!!!

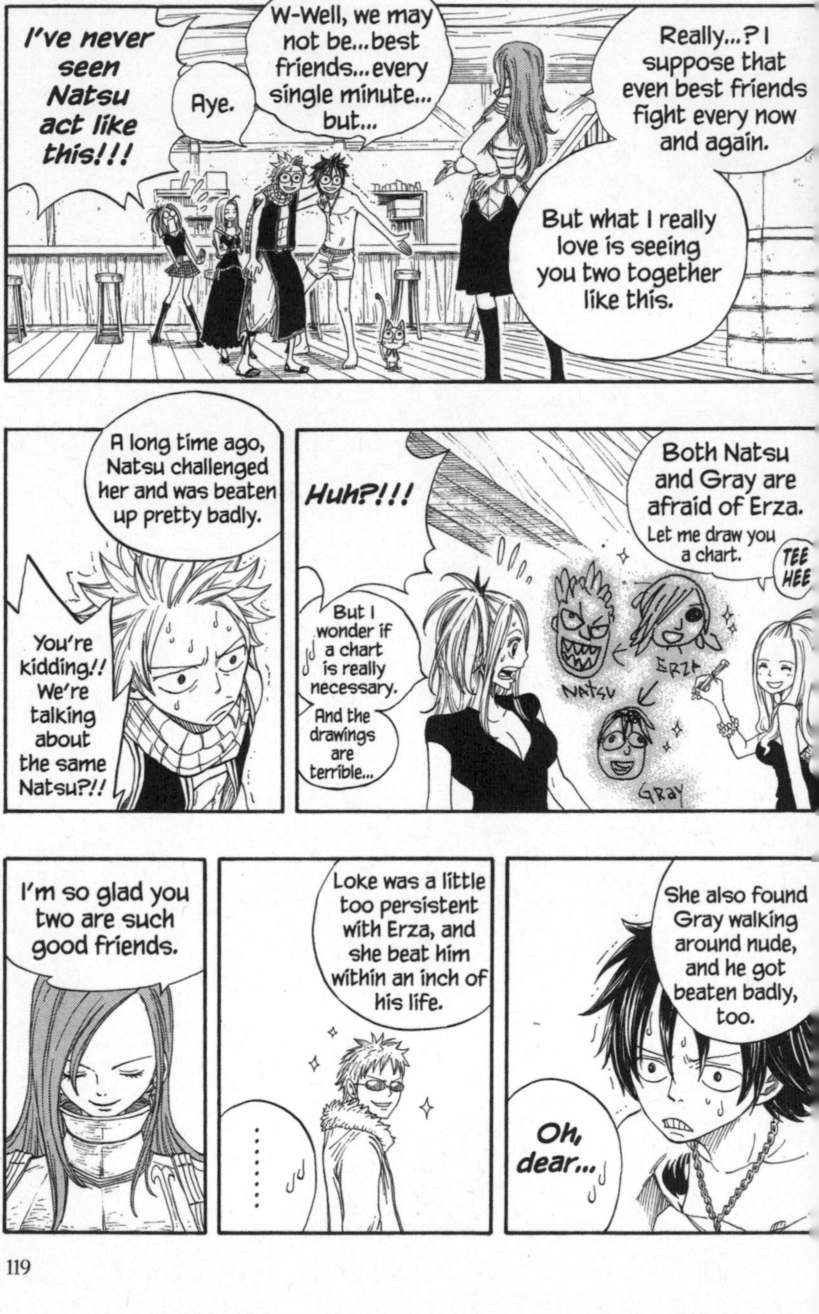
Really...? I suppose that even best friends fight every now and again.
But what I really love is seeing you two together like this.
W-Well, we may not be...best friends...every single minute... but...
Aye.
I've never seen Natsu act like this!!!
Both Natsu and Gray are afraid of Erza.
Let me draw you a chart.
TEE HEE
ERZA
NATSU
GRAY
Huh?!!!
But I wonder if a chart is really necessary.
And the drawings are terrible...
A long time ago, Natsu challenged her and was beaten up pretty badly.
You're kidding!! We're talking about the same Natsu?!!
She also found Gray walking around nude, and he got beaten badly, too.
Oh, dear...
Loke was a little too persistent with Erza, and she beat him within an inch of his life.
....
I'm so glad you two are such good friends.

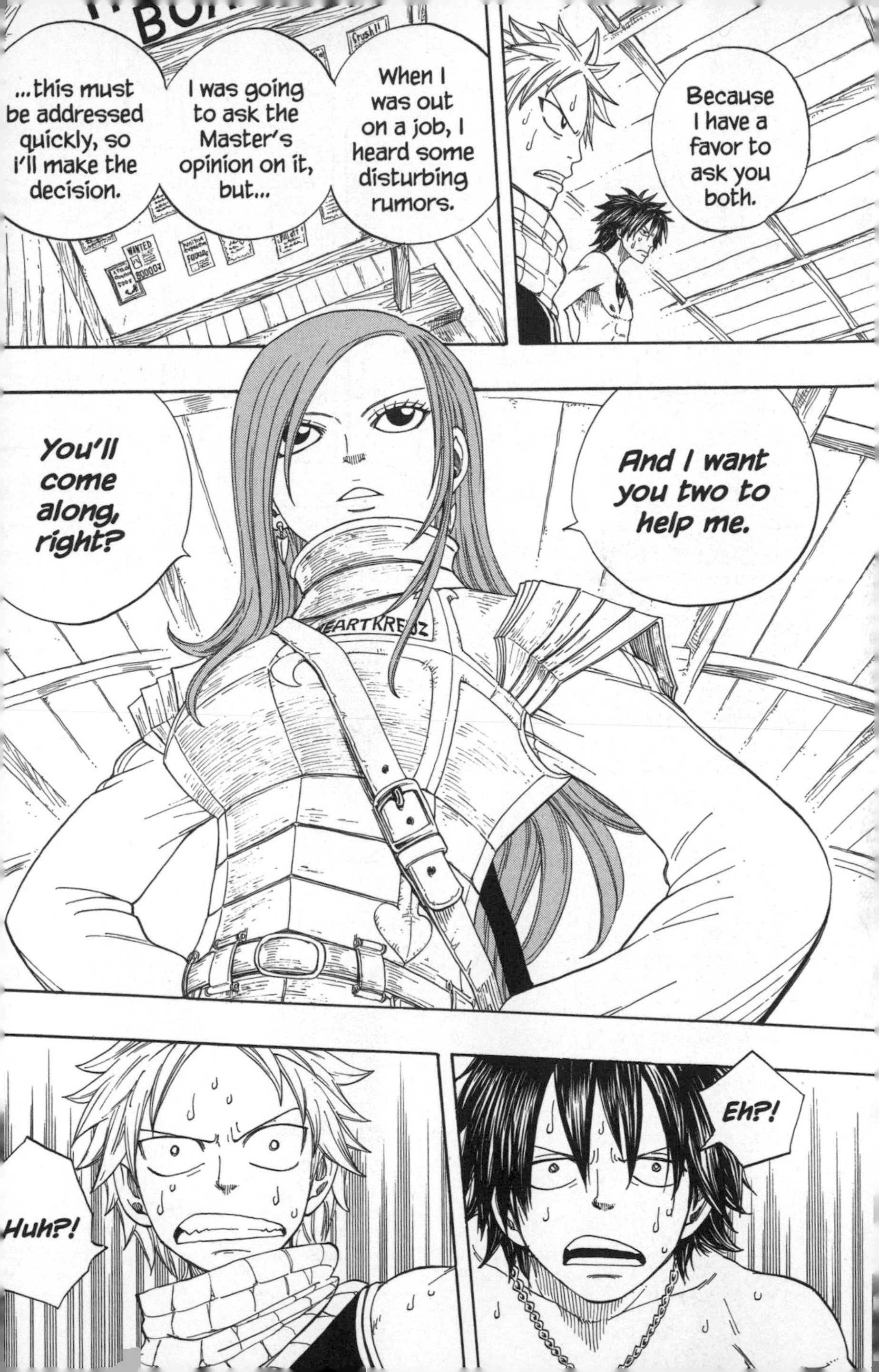
Because I have a favor to ask you both.
When I was out on a job, I heard some disturbing rumors.
I was going to ask the Master's opinion on it, but...
...this must be addressed quickly, so i'll make the decision.
And I want you two to help me.
You'll come along, right?
Eh?!
Huh?!

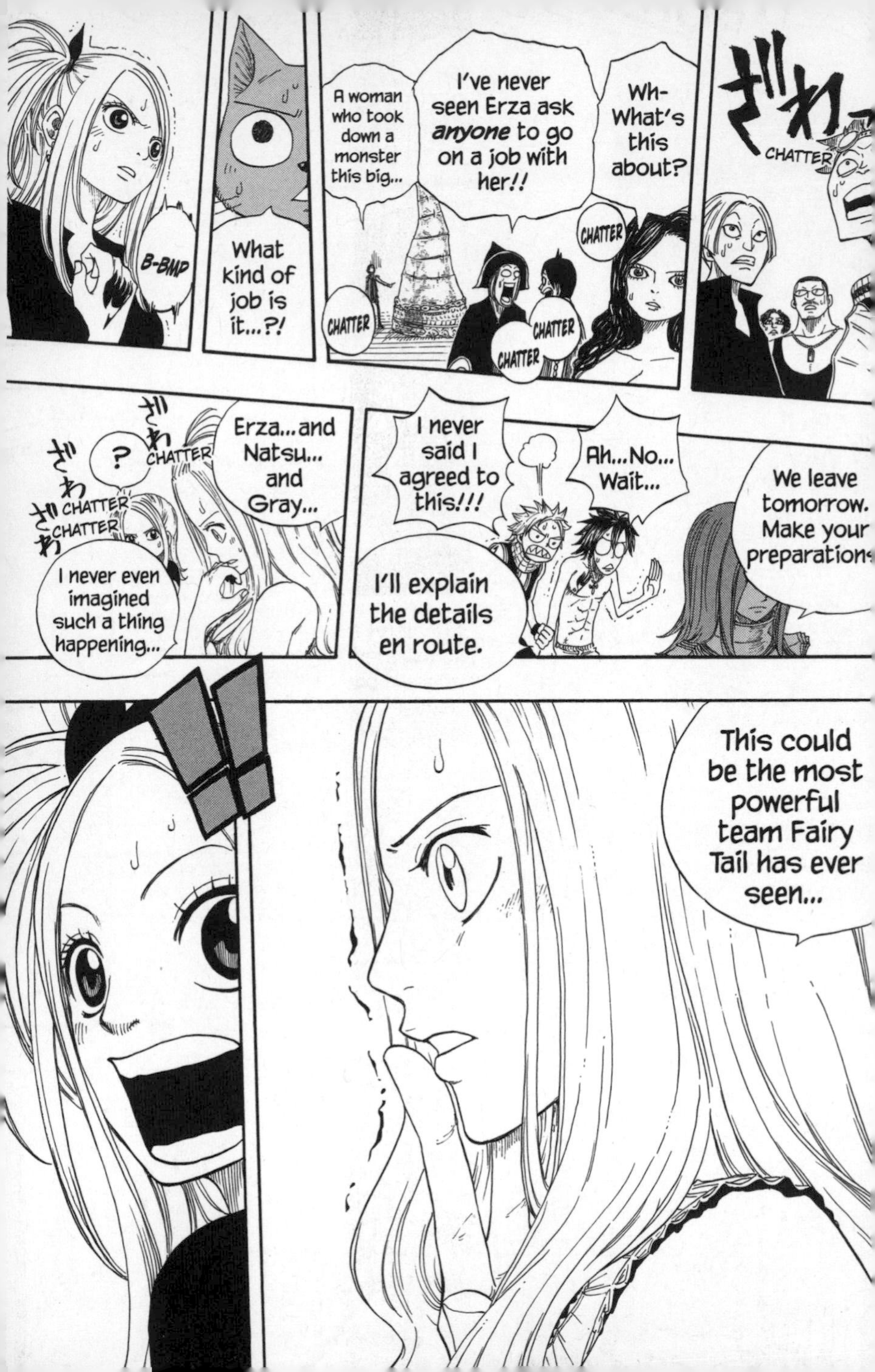

ざわ
CHATTER
Wh- What's this about?
CHATTER
I've never seen Erza ask ***anyone*** to go on a job with her!!
A woman who took down a monster this big...
CHATTER
CHATTER
CHATTER
What kind of job is it...?!
B-BMP
We leave tomorrow. Make your preparations
Ah...No... Wait...
I never said I agreed to this!!!
I'll explain the details en route.
Erza...and Natsu... and Gray...
ざわ
CHATTER
?
ざわ
CHATTER
ざわ
CHATTER
I never even imagined such a thing happening...
This could be the most powerful team Fairy Tail has ever seen...

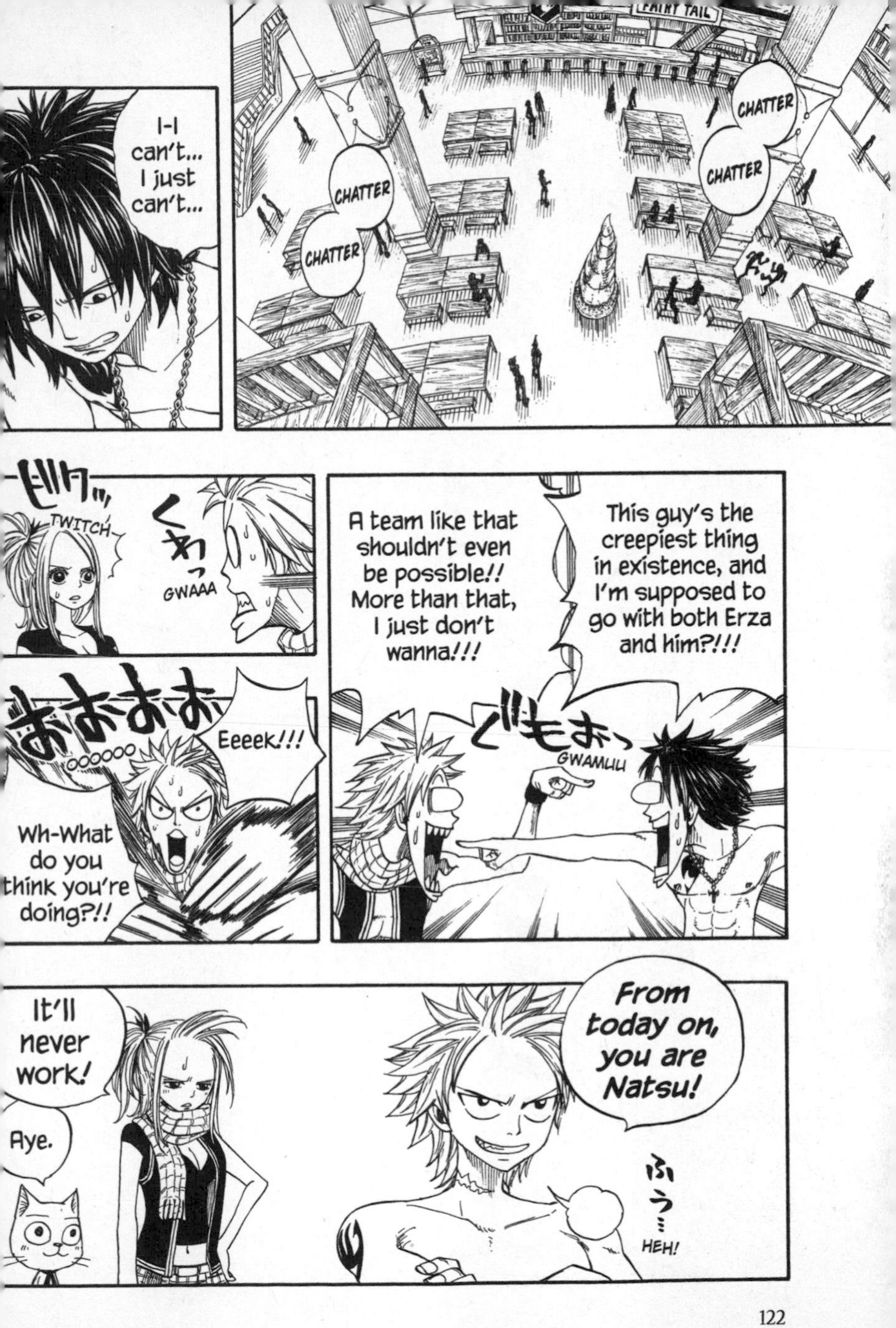
CHATTER
CHATTER
CHATTER
CHATTER
I-I can't... I just can't...
This guy's the creepiest thing in existence, and I'm supposed to go with both Erza and him?!!!
A team like that shouldn't even be possible!! More than that, I just don't wanna!!!
GWAMUU
TWITCH
GWAAA
Eeeek!!!
OOOOOO
Wh-What do you think you're doing?!!
From today on, you are Natsu!
HEH!
It'll never work!
Aye.

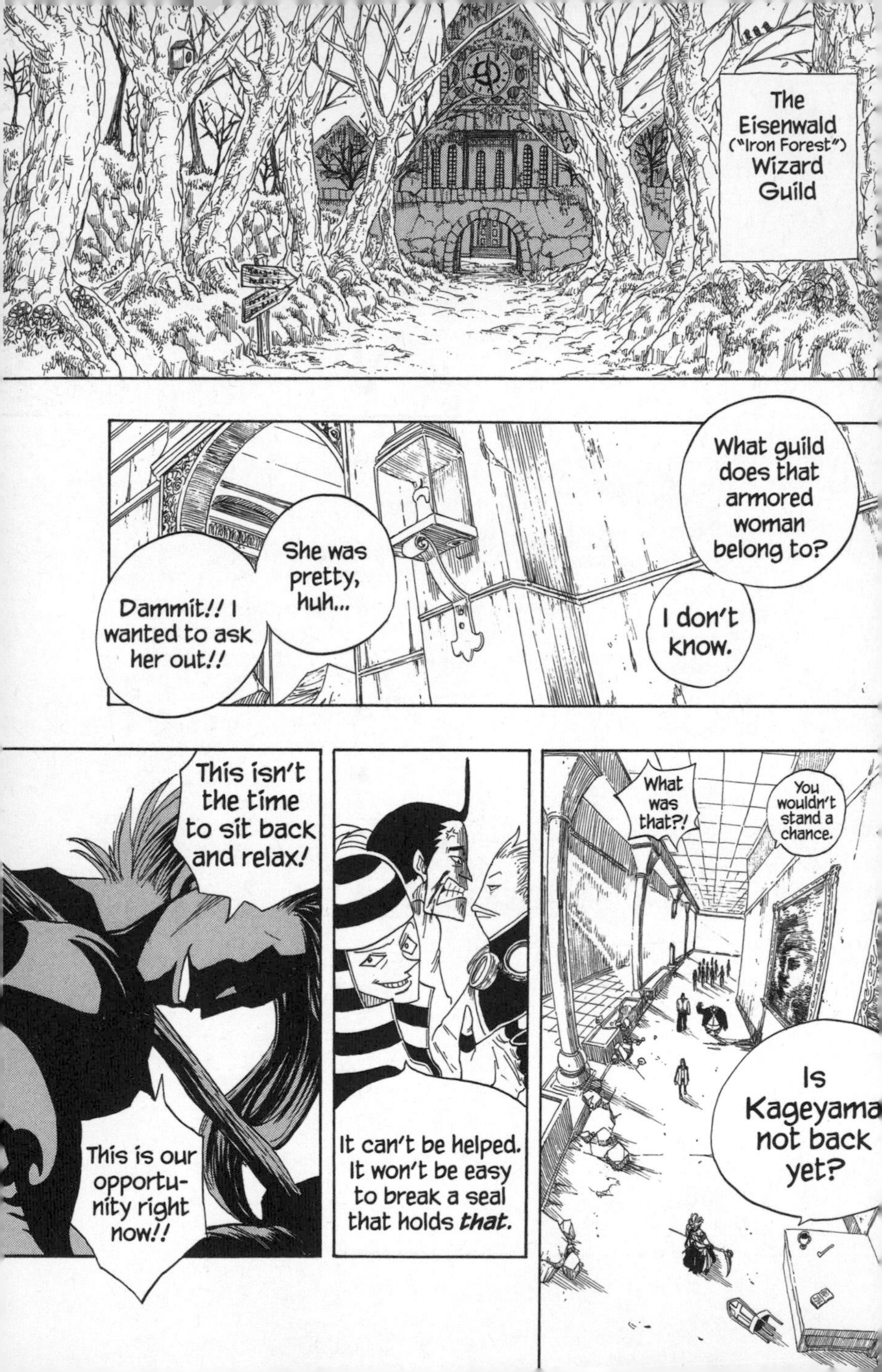
The Eisenwald ("Iron Forest") Wizard Guild
What guild does that armored woman belong to?
I don't know.
She was pretty, huh...
Dammit!! I wanted to ask her out!!
You wouldn't stand a chance.
What was that?!
Is Kageyama not back yet?
It can't be helped. It won't be easy to break a seal that holds *that*.
This isn't the time to sit back and relax!
This is our opportu-nity right now!!

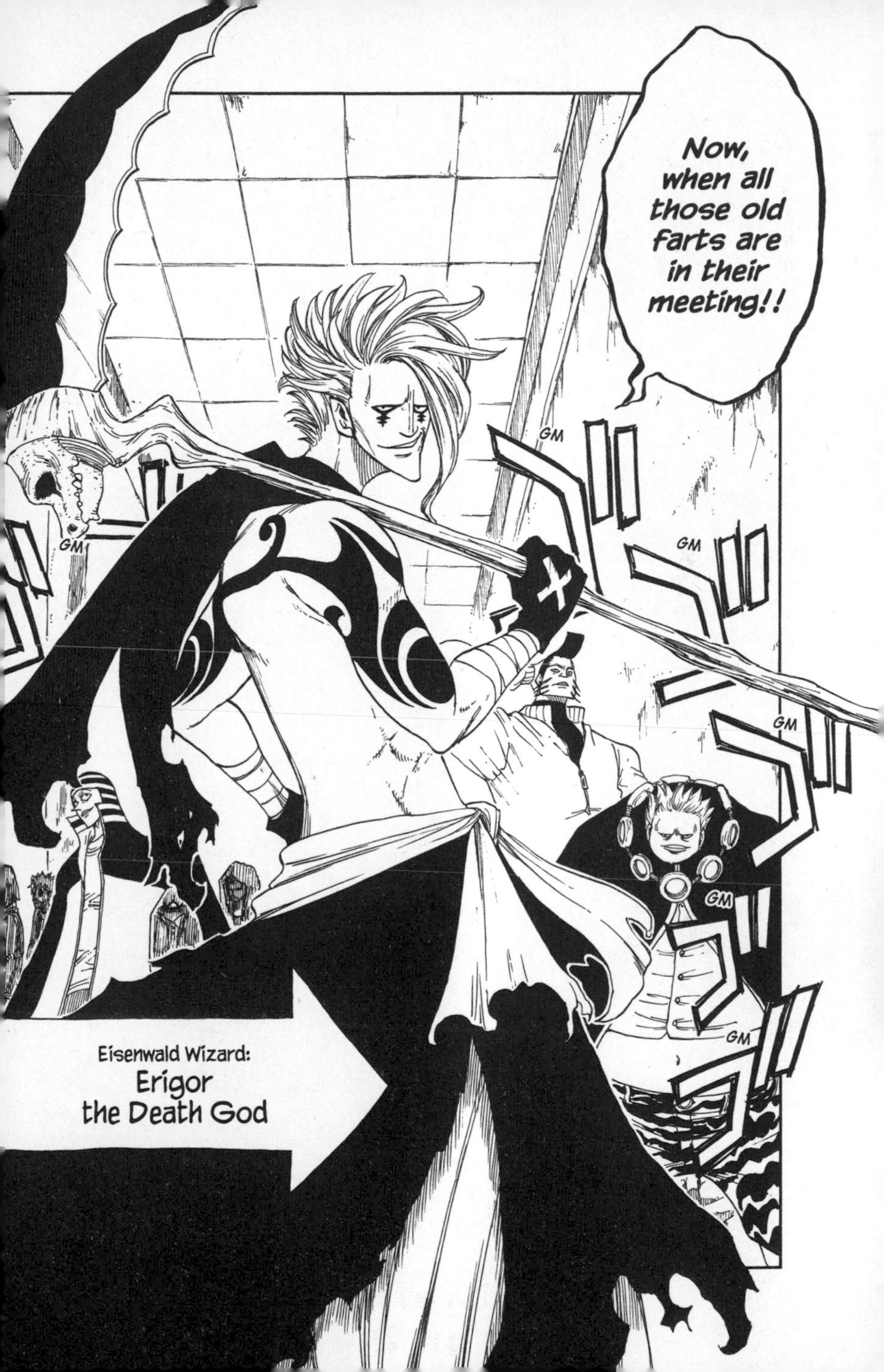
Now, when all those old farts are in their meeting!!
GM
GM
GM
GM
GM
GM
Eisenwald Wizard: Erigor the Death God

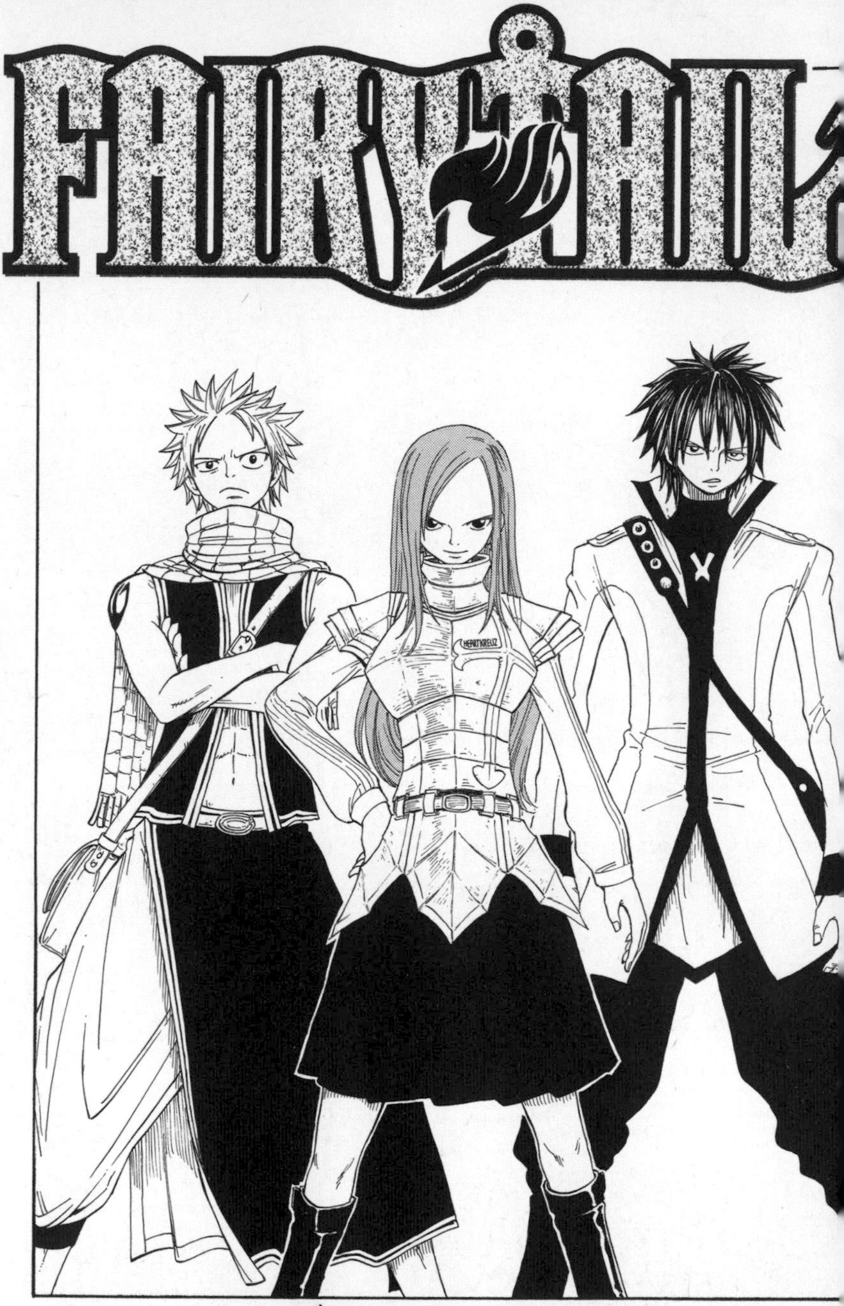

Chapter 11:
Natsu on the Train

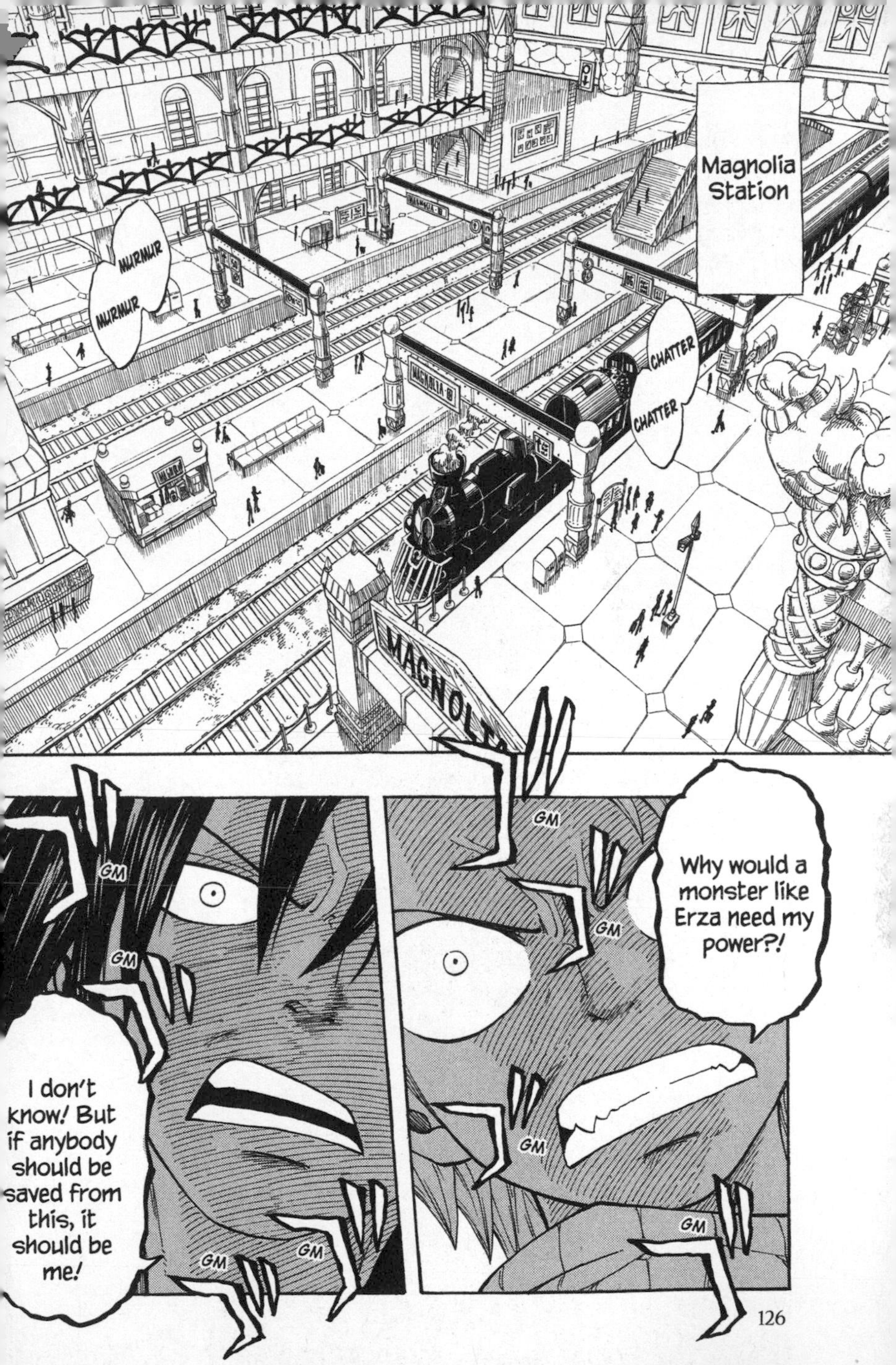
Magnolia Station
CHATTER
CHATTER
MURMUR
MURMUR
MAGNOLIA
GM
GM
Why would a monster like Erza need my power?!
GM
GM
GM
GM
GM
GM
I don't know! But if anybody should be saved from this, it should be me!

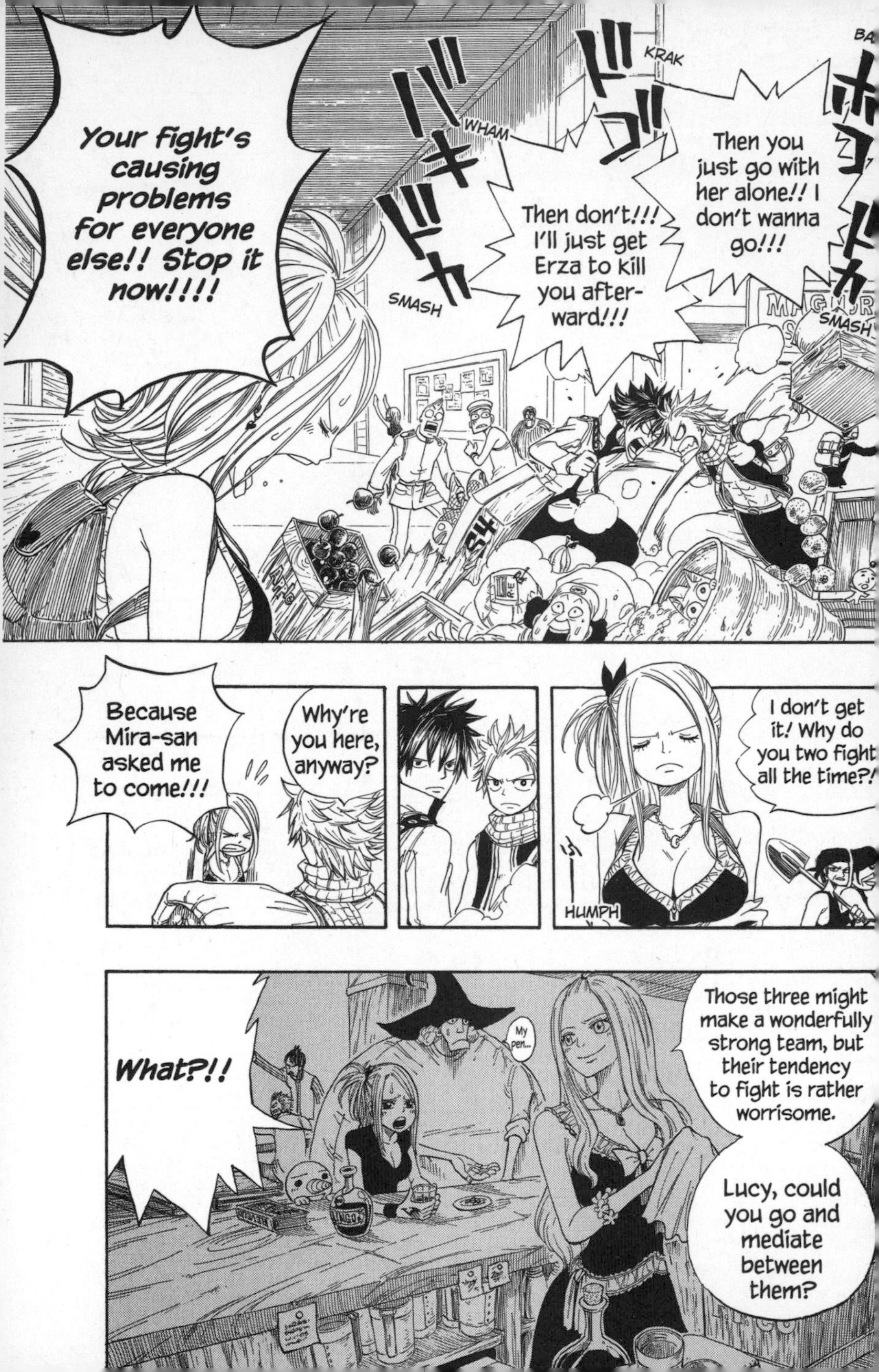
BA
Then you just go with her alone!! I don't wanna go!!!
KRAK
Then don't!!! I'll just get Erza to kill you afterward!!!
WHAM
SMASH
SMASH
Your fight's causing problems for everyone else!! Stop it now!!!!
I don't get it! Why do you two fight all the time?!
HUMPH
Why're you here, anyway?
Because Mira-san asked me to come!!!
Those three might make a wonderfully strong team, but their tendency to fight is rather worrisome.
Lucy, could you go and mediate between them?
My pen...
What?!!

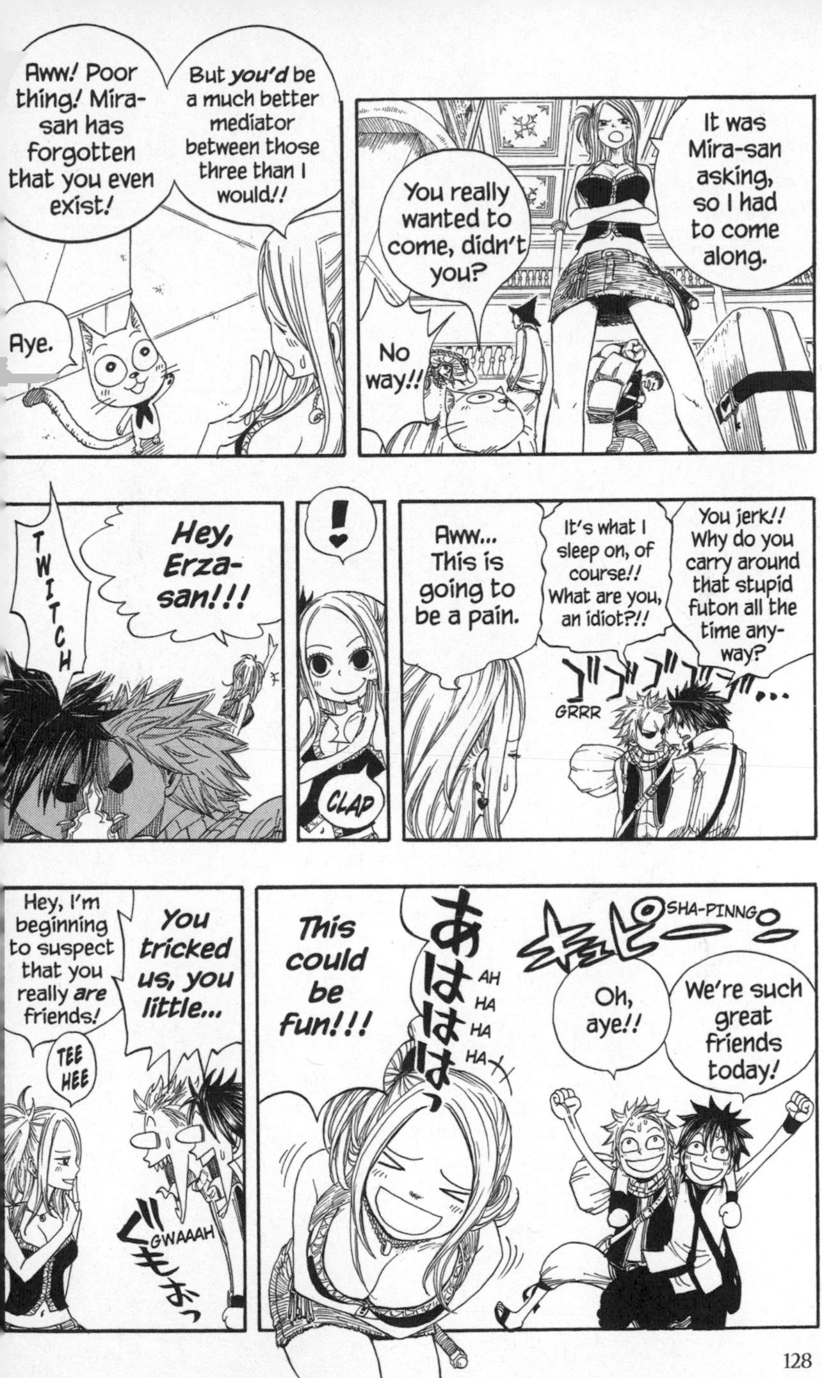
It was Mira-san asking, so I had to come along.
You really wanted to come, didn't you?
No way!!
But *you'd* be a much better mediator between those three than I would!!
Aww! Poor thing! Mira-san has forgotten that you even exist!
Aye.
You jerk!! Why do you carry around that stupid futon all the time anyway?
It's what I sleep on, of course!! What are you, an idiot?!!
GRRR
Aww... This is going to be a pain.
!
CLAP
Hey, Erza-san!!!
TWITCH
We're such great friends today!
Oh, aye!!
SHA-PINNG
This could be fun!!!
あはははっ
AH HA HA HA
You tricked us, you little...
Hey, I'm beginning to suspect that you really *are* friends!
TEE HEE
GWAAAH

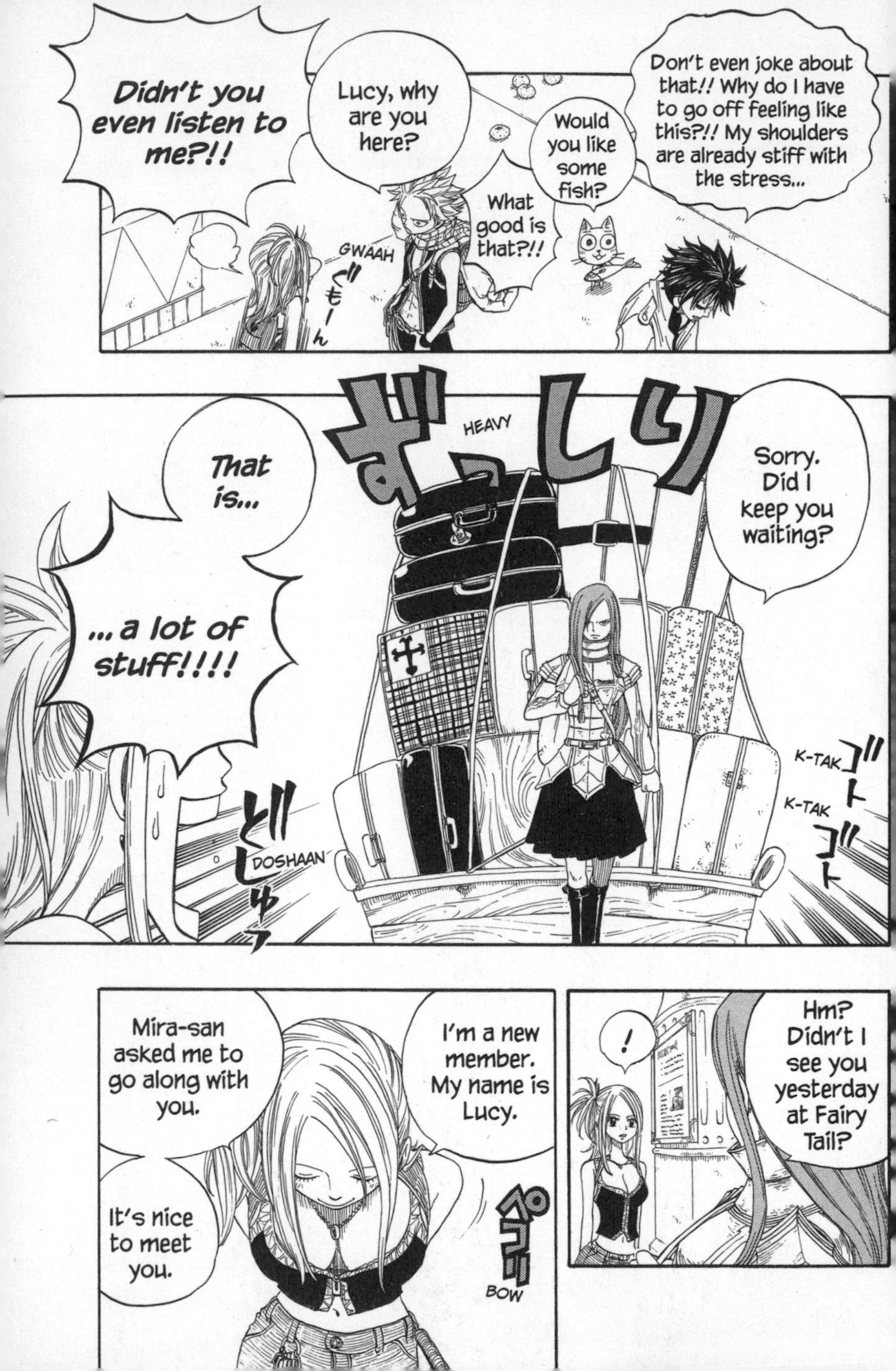

Don't even joke about that!! Why do I have to go off feeling like this?!! My shoulders are already stiff with the stress...
Would you like some fish?
What good is that?!!
Lucy, why are you here?
Didn't you even listen to me?!!
GWAAH
ずっしり
HEAVY
Sorry. Did I keep you waiting?
K-TAK
K-TAK
That is...
...a lot of stuff!!!!
DOSHAAN
!
Hm? Didn't I see you yesterday at Fairy Tail?
I'm a new member. My name is Lucy.
Mira-san asked me to go along with you.
BOW
It's nice to meet you.

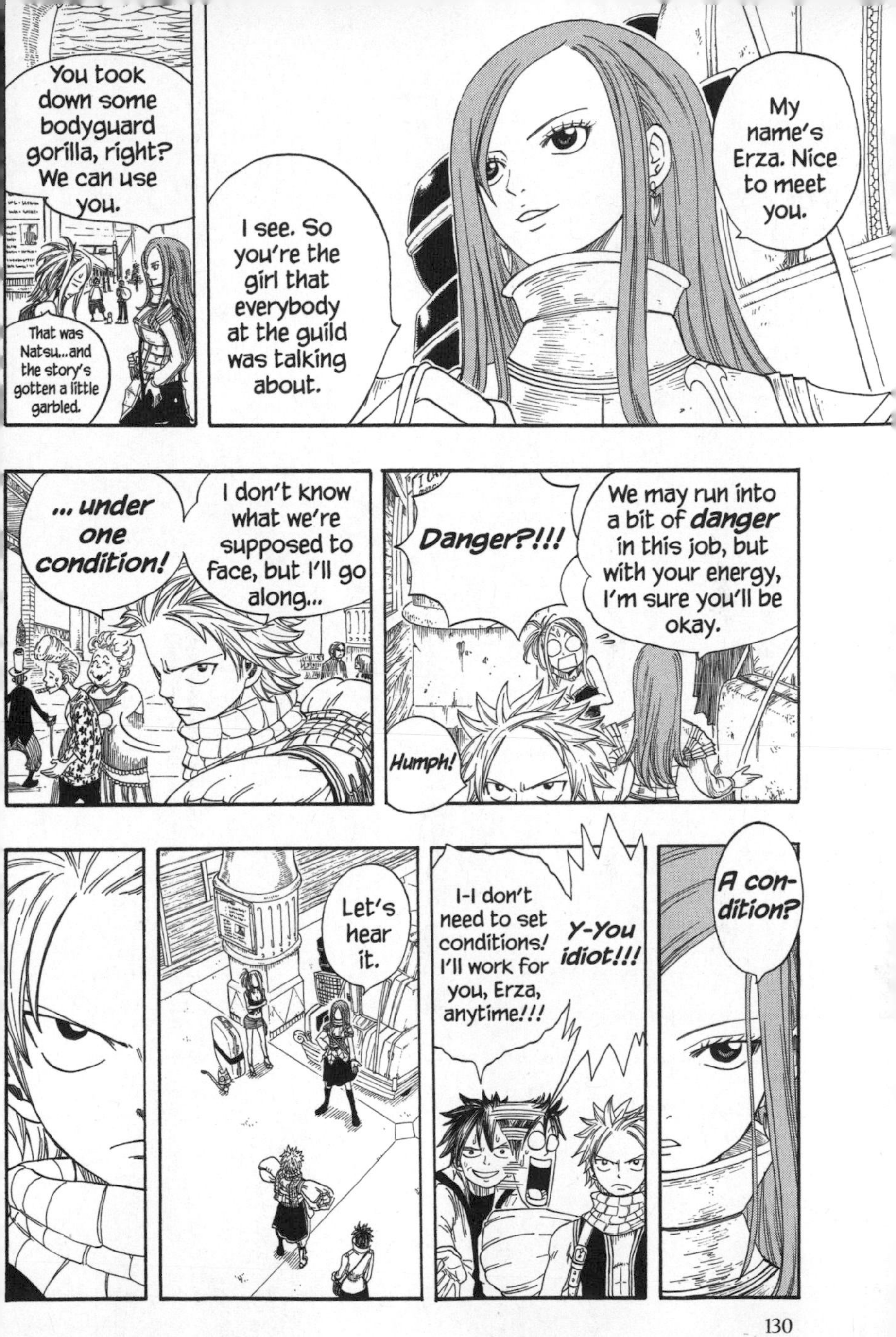
My name's Erza. Nice to meet you.
I see. So you're the girl that everybody at the guild was talking about.
You took down some bodyguard gorilla, right? We can use you.
That was Natsu...and the story's gotten a little garbled.
We may run into a bit of danger in this job, but with your energy, I'm sure you'll be okay.
Danger?!!!
Humph!
I don't know what we're supposed to face, but I'll go along...
...under one condition!
A condition?
I-I don't need to set conditions! I'll work for you, Erza, anytime!!!
Y-You idiot!!!
Let's hear it.

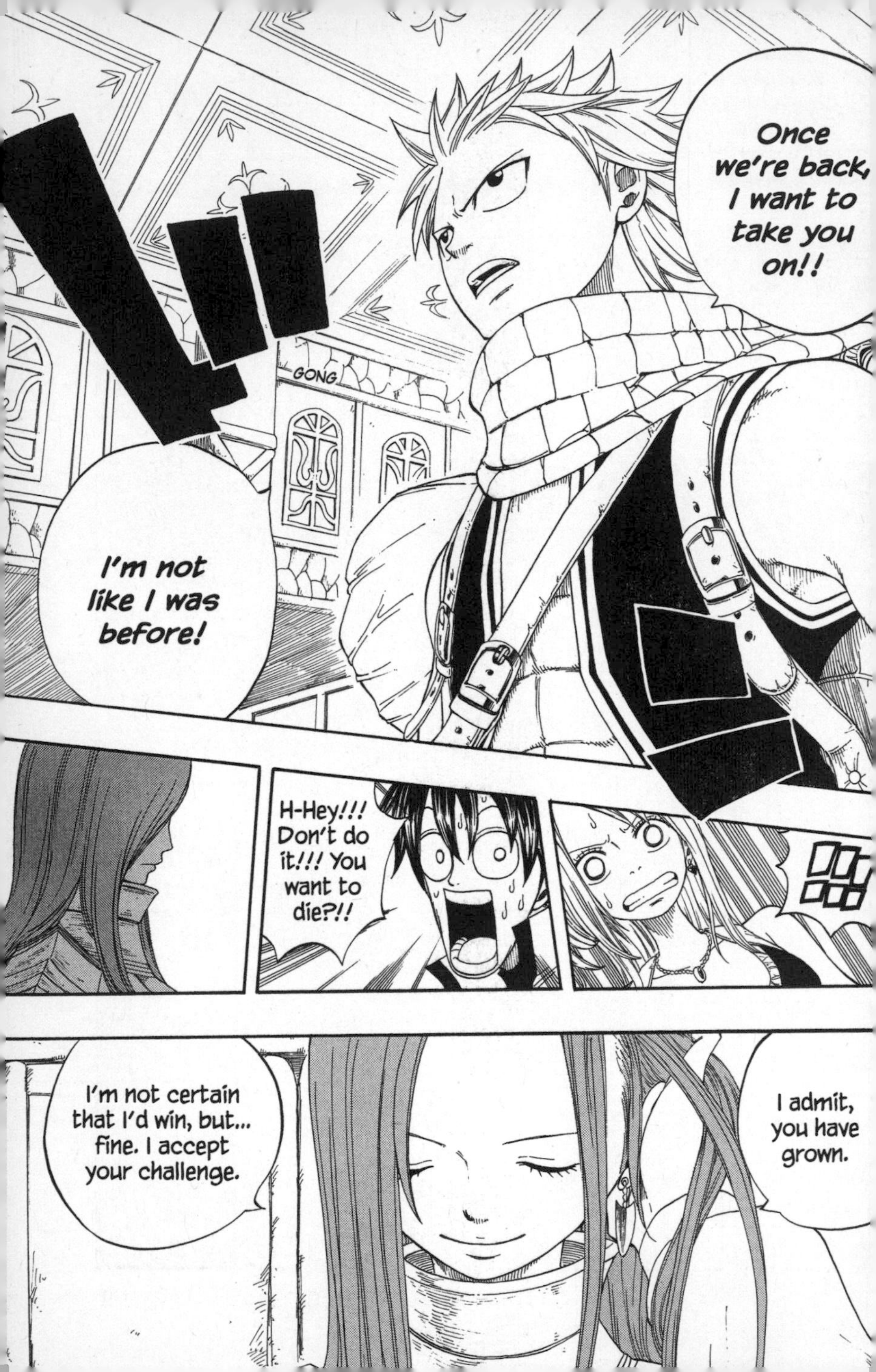
Once we're back, I want to take you on!!
GONG
I'm not like I was before!
H-Hey!!! Don't do it!!! You want to die?!!
I admit, you have grown.
I'm not certain that I'd win, but... fine. I accept your challenge.

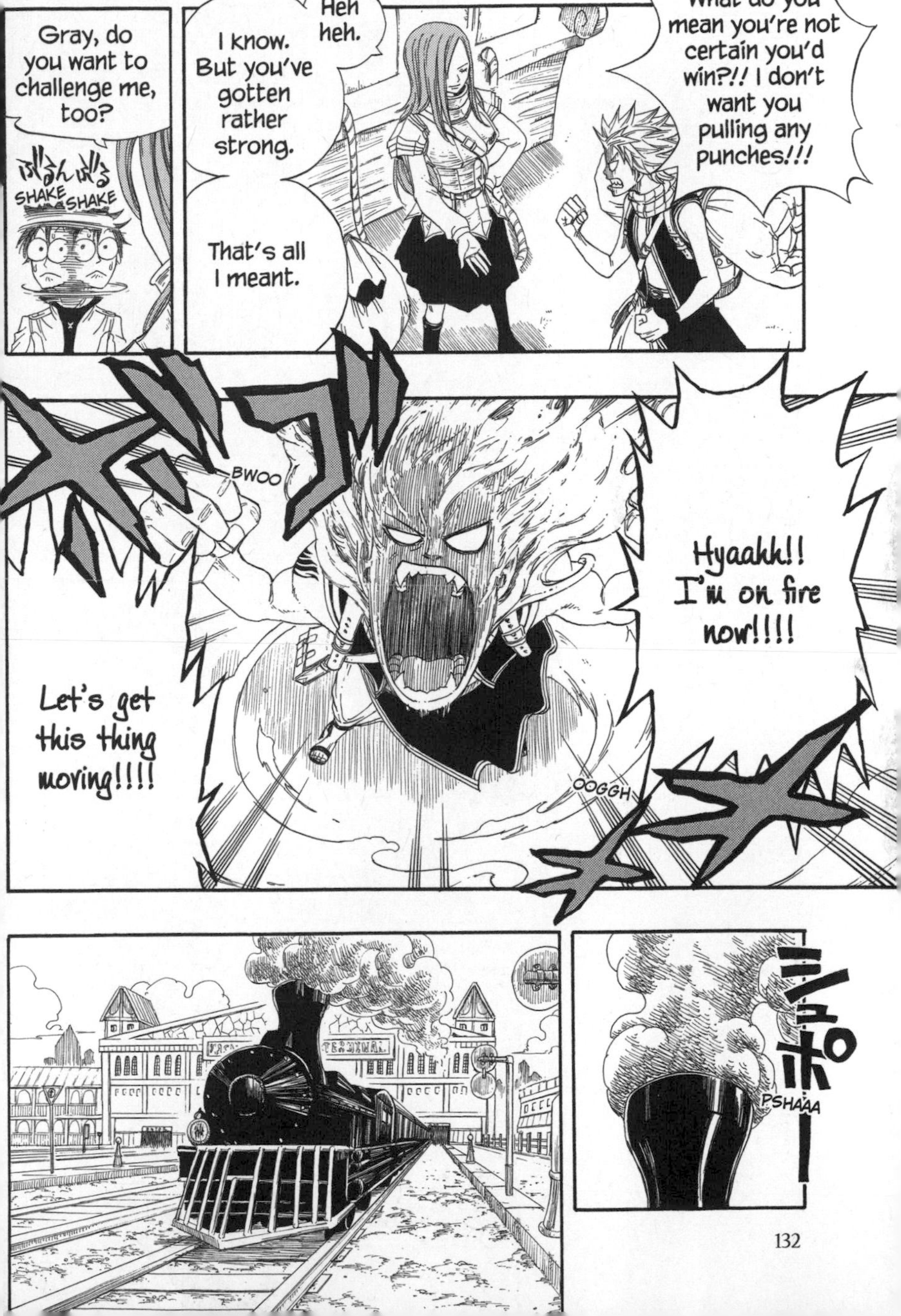
What do you mean you're not certain you'd win?!! I don't want you pulling any punches!!!
Heh heh.
I know. But you've gotten rather strong.
That's all I meant.
Gray, do you want to challenge me, too?
SHAKE SHAKE
Hyaahh!! I'm on fire now!!!!
BWOO
Let's get this thing moving!!!!
OOGGH
PSHAAA

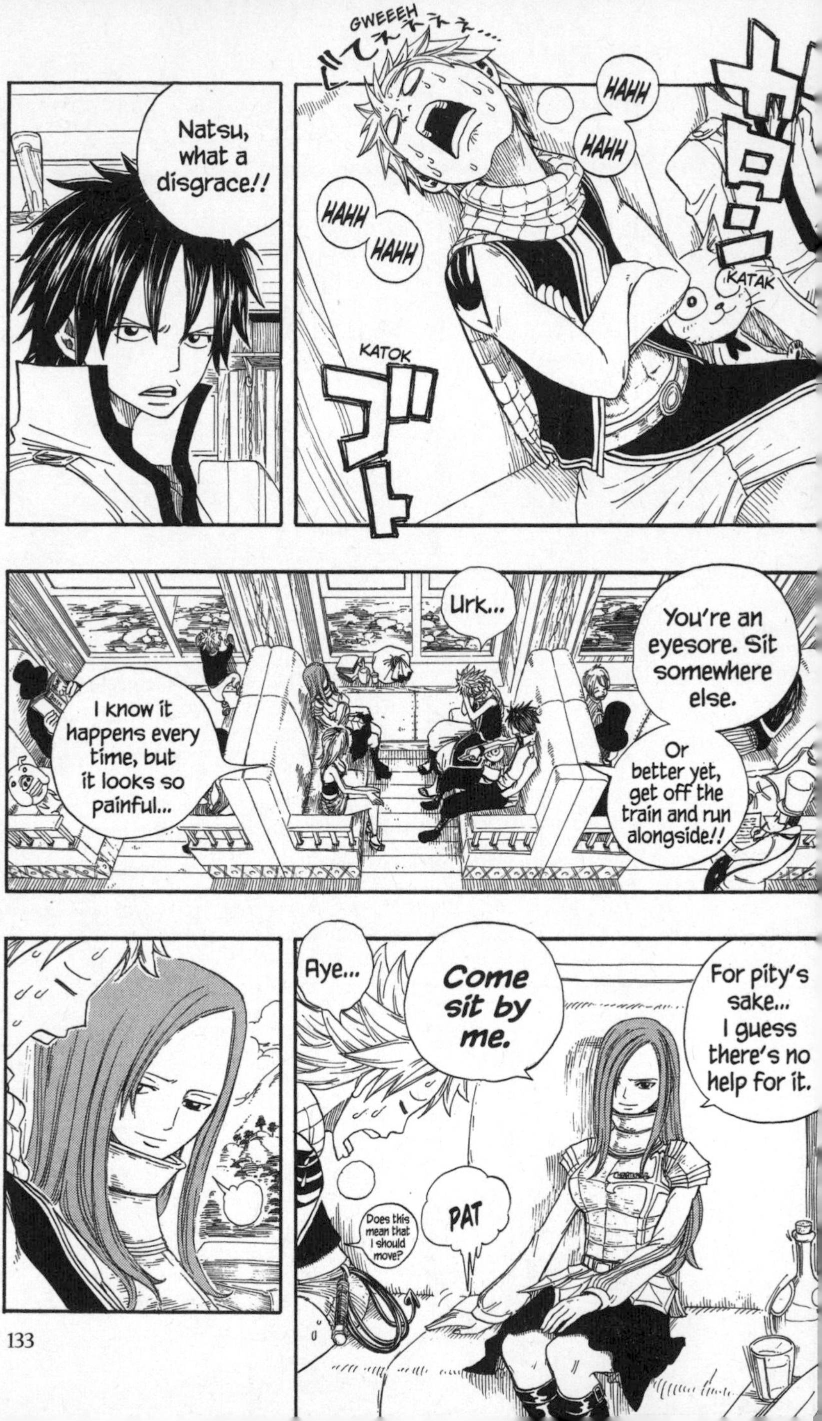
GWEEEH
HAHH
HAHH
HAHH
HAHH
KATAK
KATOK
Natsu, what a disgrace!!
You're an eyesore. Sit somewhere else.
Or better yet, get off the train and run alongside!!
Urk...
I know it happens every time, but it looks so painful...
For pity's sake... I guess there's no help for it.
Come sit by me.
Aye...
PAT
Does this mean that I should move?

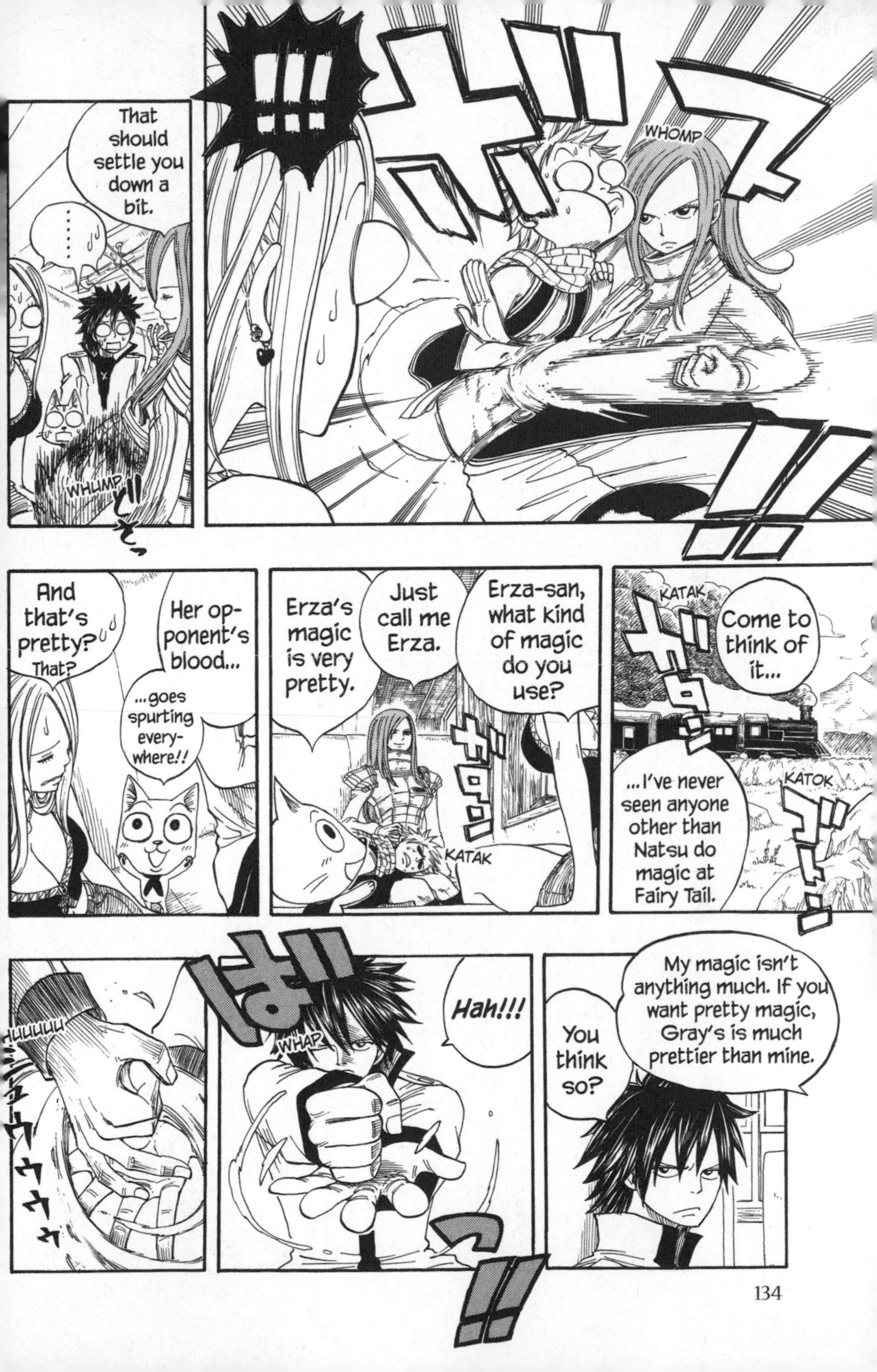
WHOMP
That should settle you down a bit.
......
WHUMP
Come to think of it...
KATAK
...I've never seen anyone other than Natsu do magic at Fairy Tail.
KATOK
Erza-san, what kind of magic do you use?
Just call me Erza.
Erza's magic is very pretty.
KATAK
Her opponent's blood...
...goes spurting everywhere!!
And that's pretty? That?
My magic isn't anything much. If you want pretty magic, Gray's is much prettier than mine.
You think so?
Hah!!!
WHAP

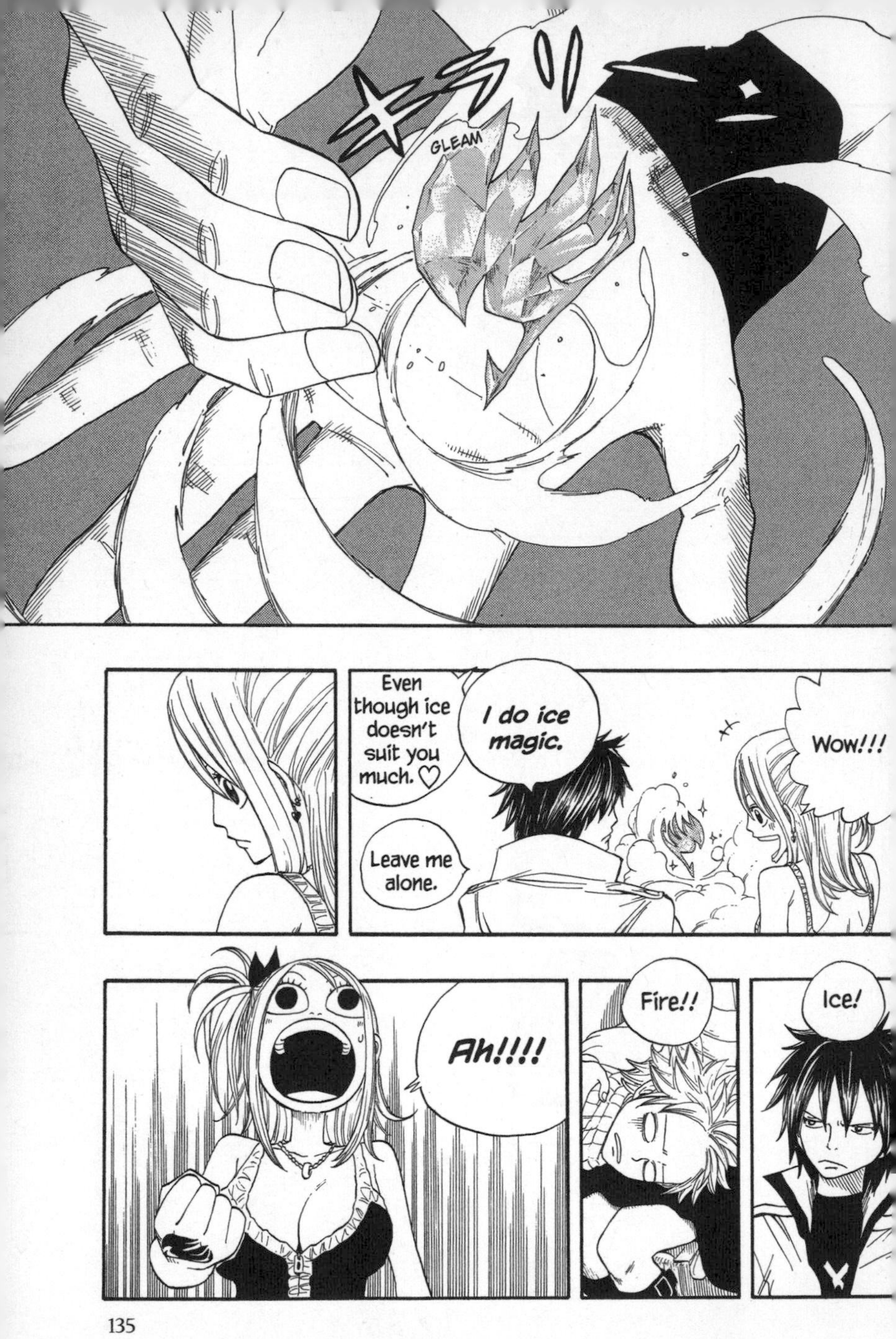
GLEAM
Wow!!!
I do ice magic.
Even though ice doesn't suit you much. ♡
Leave me alone.
Ice!
Fire!!
Ah!!!!

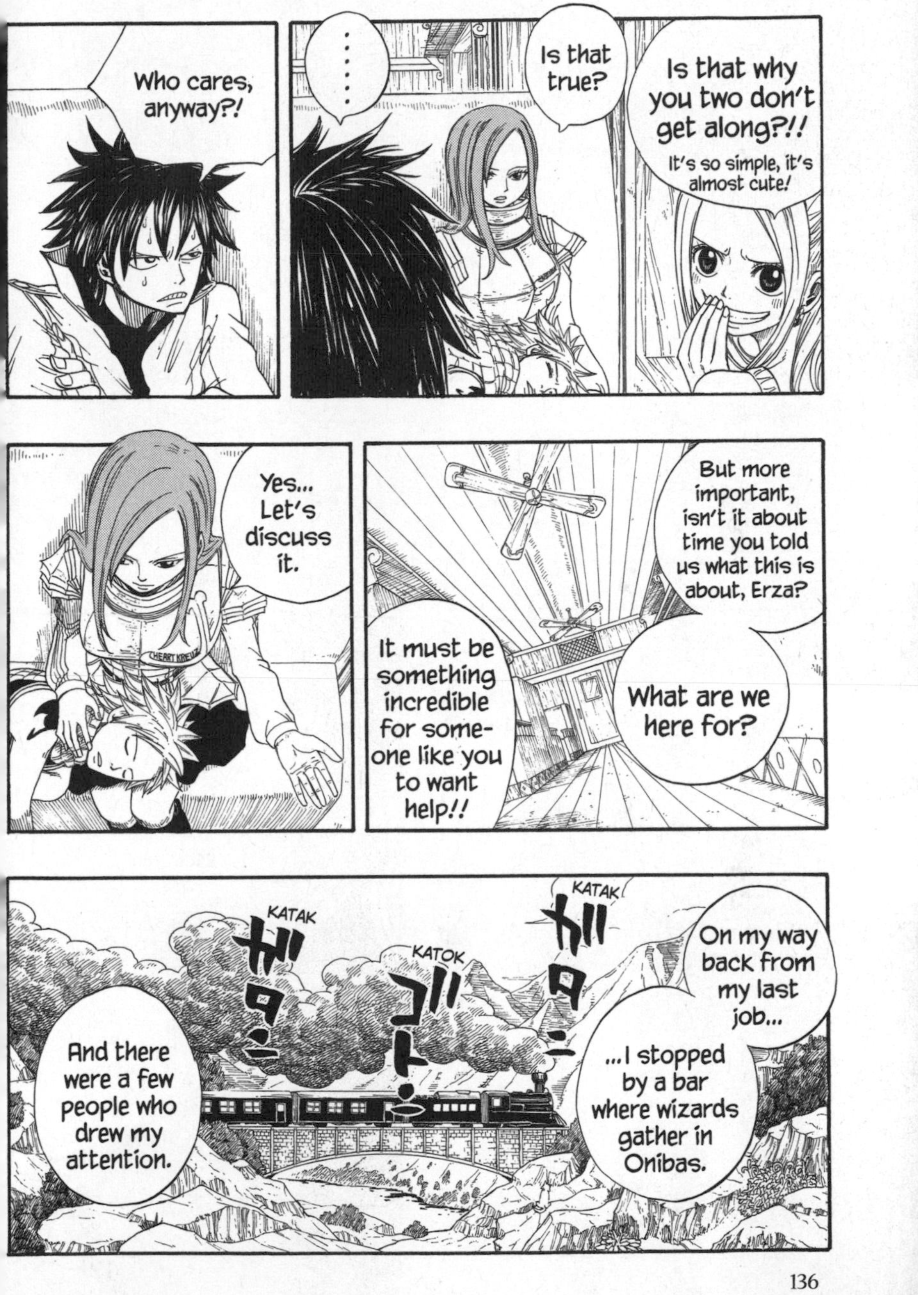

Is that why you two don't get along?!!
It's so simple, it's almost cute!
Is that true?
......
Who cares, anyway?!
But more important, isn't it about time you told us what this is about, Erza?
What are we here for?
It must be something incredible for someone like you to want help!!
Yes... Let's discuss it.
On my way back from my last job...
KATAK
...I stopped by a bar where wizards gather in Onibas.
KATOK
KATAK
And there were a few people who drew my attention.

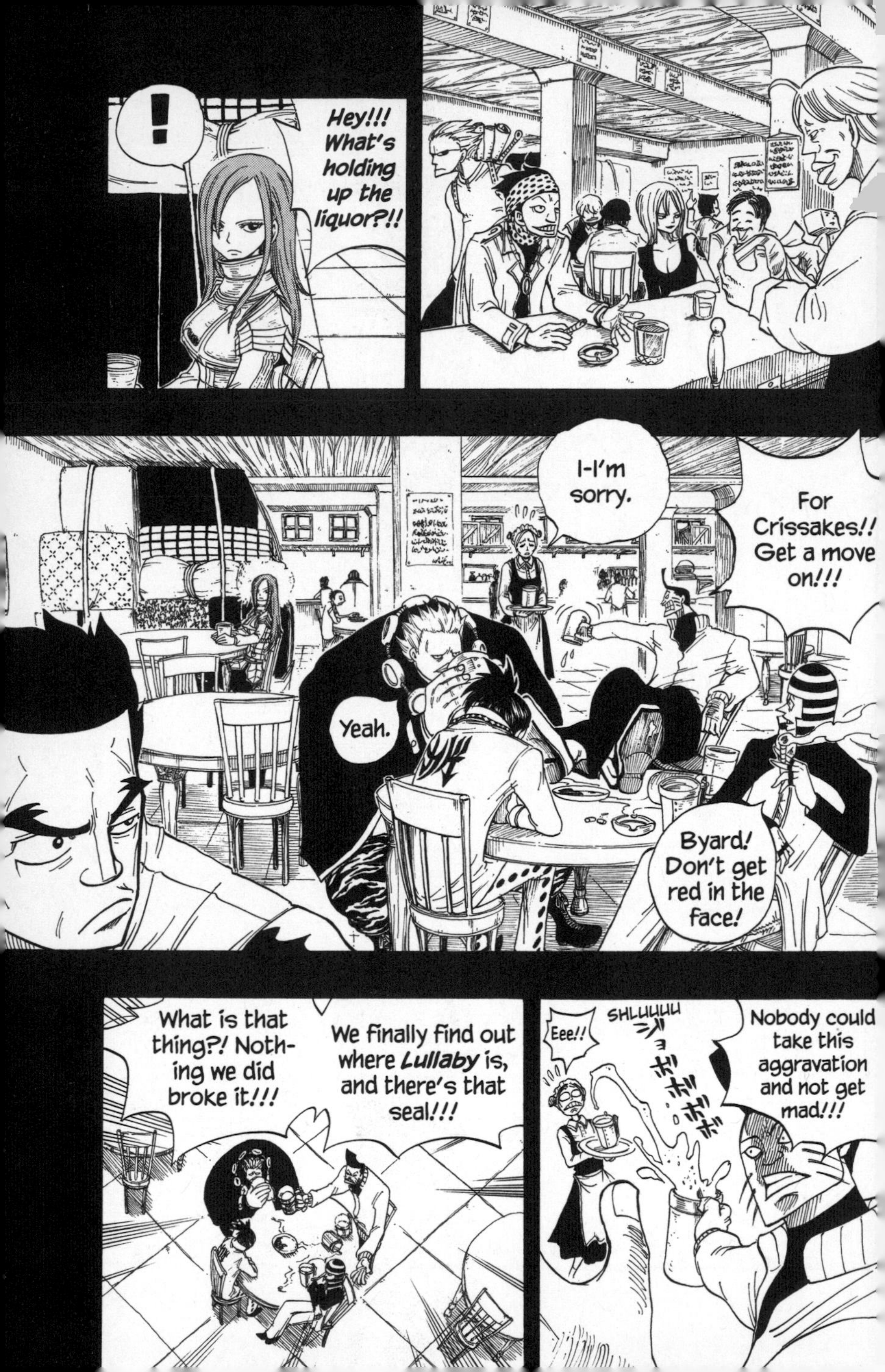
!
Hey!!! What's holding up the liquor?!!
For Crissakes!! Get a move on!!!
I-I'm sorry.
Byard! Don't get red in the face!
Yeah.
Nobody could take this aggravation and not get mad!!!
SHLUUUU
Eee!!
We finally find out where *Lullaby* is, and there's that seal!!!
What is that thing?! Nothing we did broke it!!!

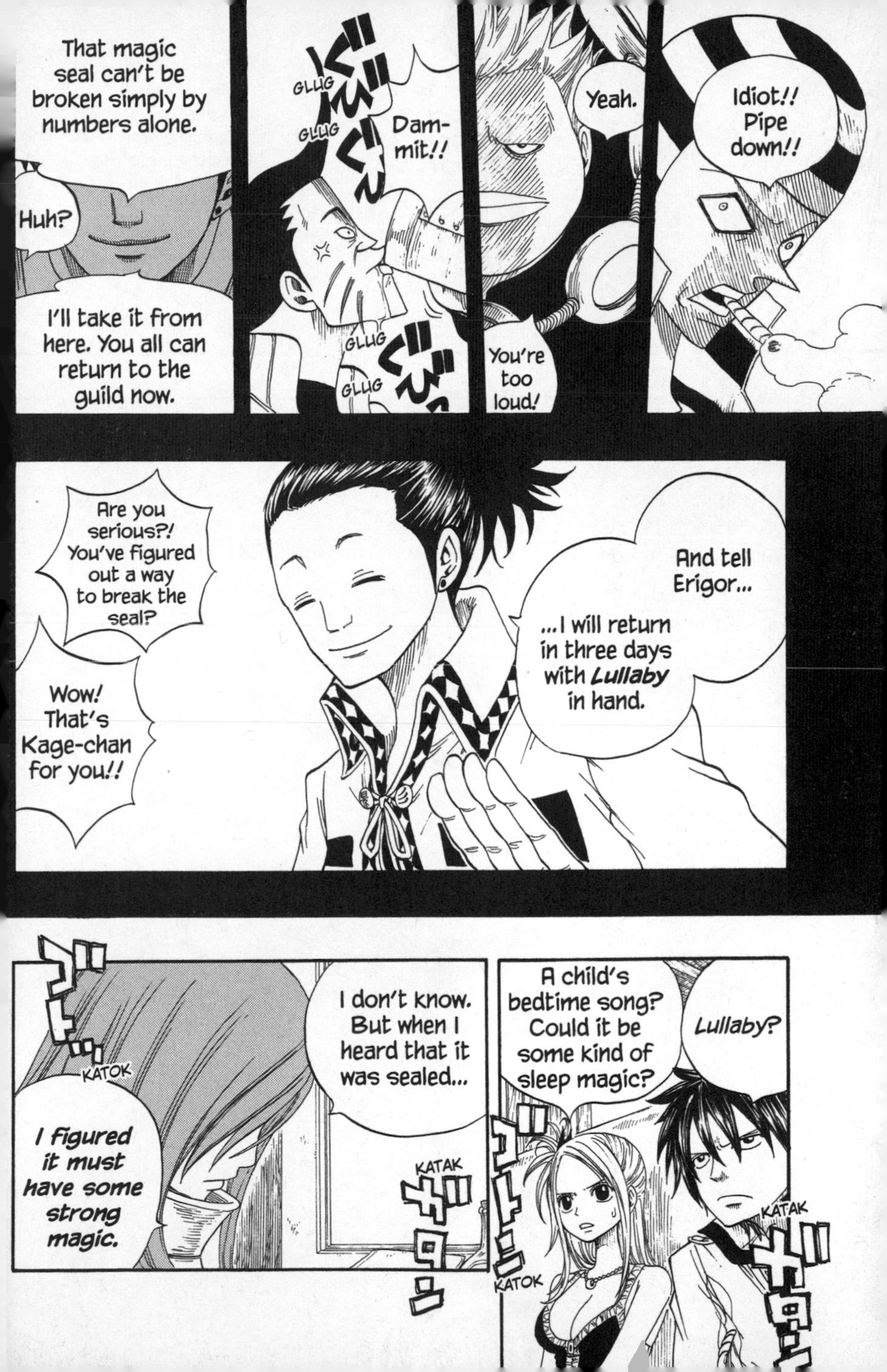
Idiot!! Pipe down!!
Yeah.
You're too loud!
GLUG
GLUG
Dam-mit!!
GLUG
GLUG
That magic seal can't be broken simply by numbers alone.
Huh?
I'll take it from here. You all can return to the guild now.
And tell Erigor...
...I will return in three days with *Lullaby* in hand.
Are you serious?! You've figured out a way to break the seal?
Wow! That's Kage-chan for you!!
Lullaby?
A child's bedtime song? Could it be some kind of sleep magic?
KATAK
KATOK
I don't know. But when I heard that it was sealed...
KATAK
KATOK
I figured it must have some strong magic.

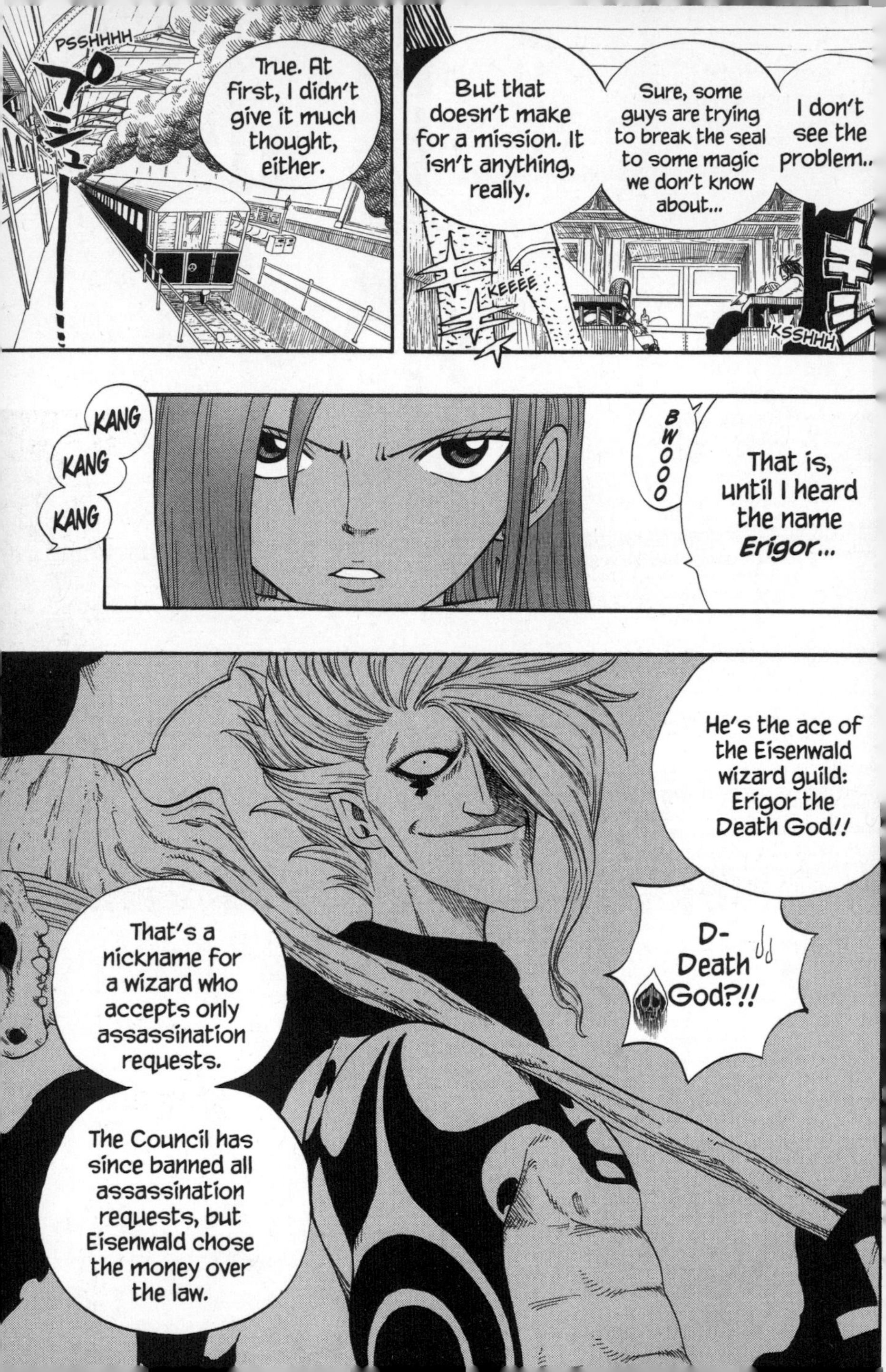
I don't see the problem..
Sure, some guys are trying to break the seal to some magic we don't know about...
But that doesn't make for a mission. It isn't anything, really.
KSSHHH
KEEEE
PSSHHHH
True. At first, I didn't give it much thought, either.
That is, until I heard the name *Erigor*...
BWOOO
KANG
KANG
KANG
He's the ace of the Eisenwald wizard guild: Erigor the Death God!!
D- Death God?!!
That's a nickname for a wizard who accepts only assassination requests.
The Council has since banned all assassination requests, but Eisenwald chose the money over the law.

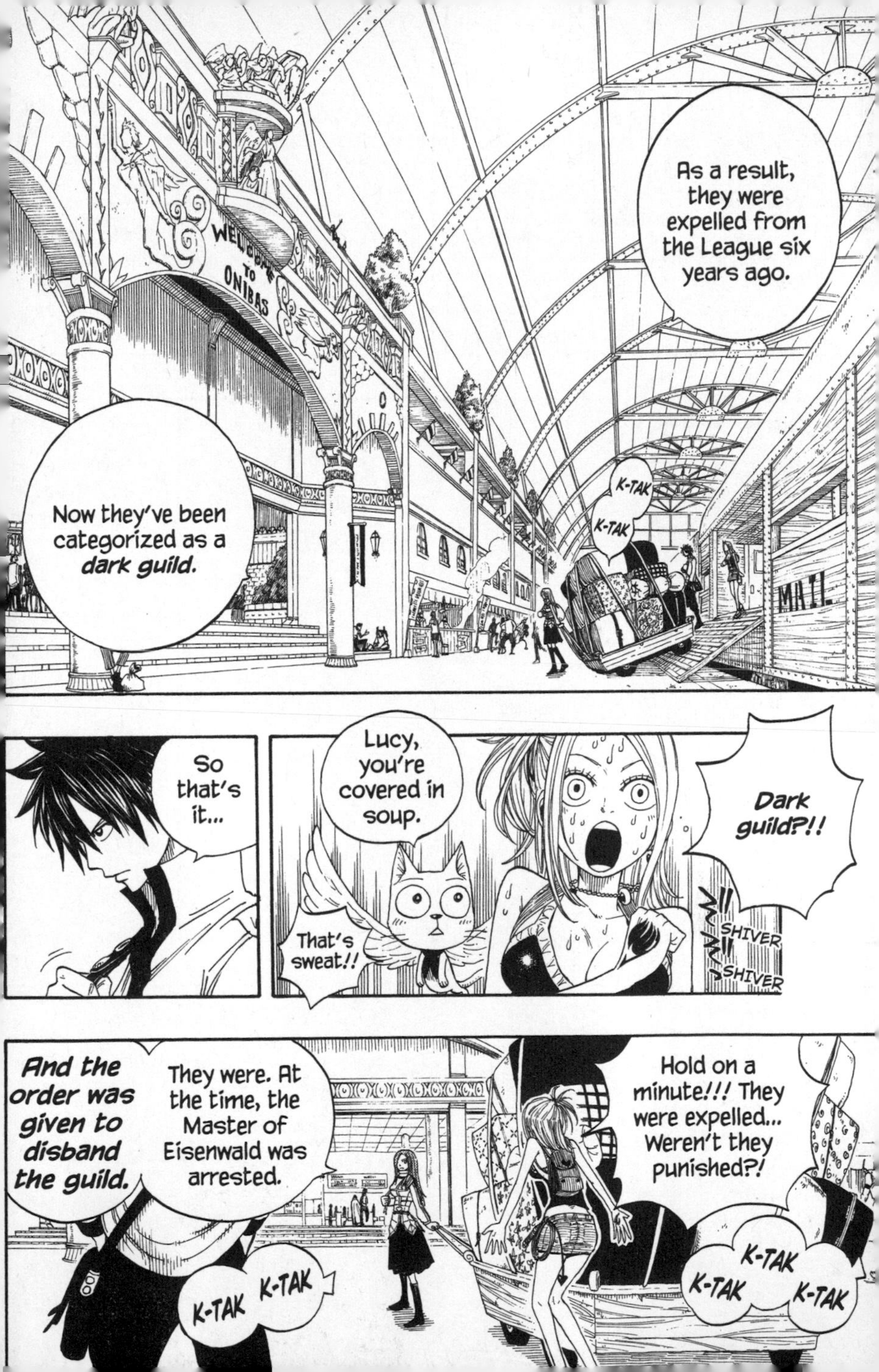
TO ONIBAS
As a result, they were expelled from the League six years ago.
K-TAK
K-TAK
MAIL
Now they've been categorized as a *dark guild.*
Dark guild?!!
SHIVER
SHIVER
Lucy, you're covered in soup.
That's sweat!!
So that's it...
Hold on a minute!!! They were expelled... Weren't they punished?!
K-TAK
K-TAK
K-TAK
They were. At the time, the Master of Eisenwald was arrested.
And the order was given to disband the guild.
K-TAK
K-TAK

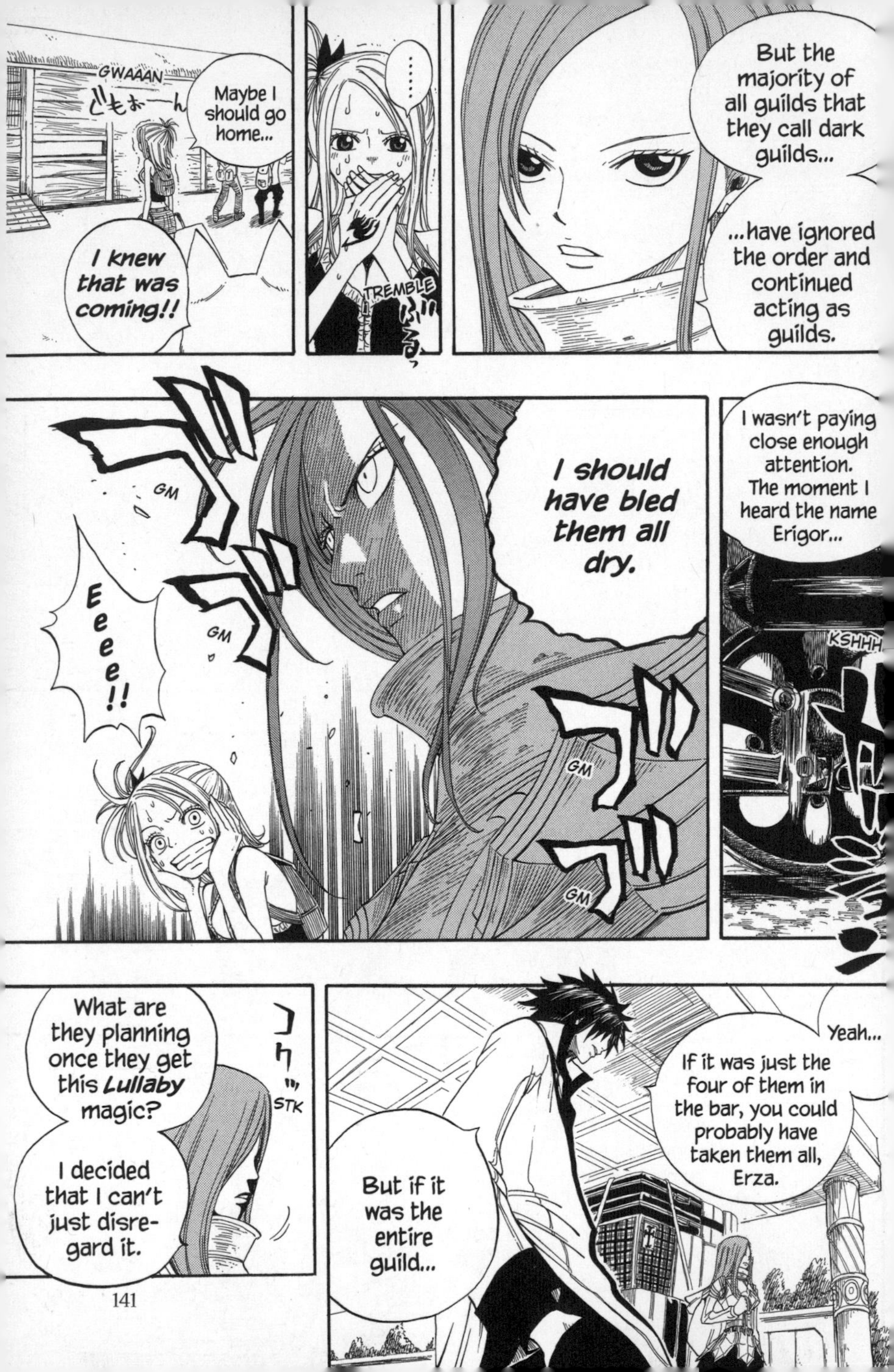
But the majority of all guilds that they call dark guilds...
...have ignored the order and continued acting as guilds.
......
TREMBLE
GWAAAN
Maybe I should go home...
I knew that was coming!!
I wasn't paying close enough attention. The moment I heard the name Erigor...
KSHHH
I should have bled them all dry.
GM
GM
GM
GM
Eeeee!!
Yeah...
If it was just the four of them in the bar, you could probably have taken them all, Erza.
But if it was the entire guild...
What are they planning once they get this *Lullaby* magic?
STK
I decided that I can't just disregard it.

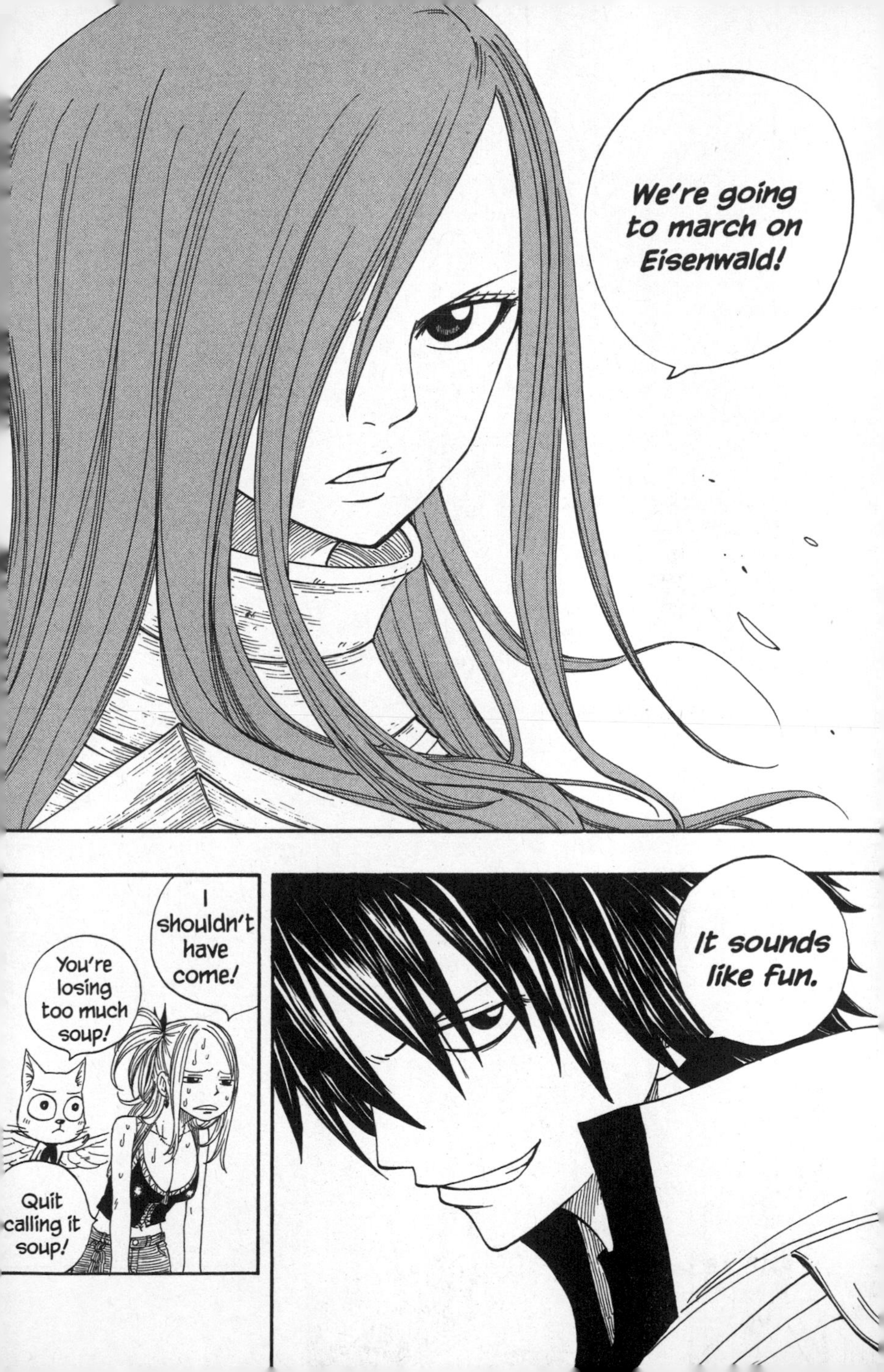
We're going to march on Eisenwald!
It sounds like fun.
I shouldn't have come!
You're losing too much soup!
Quit calling it soup!

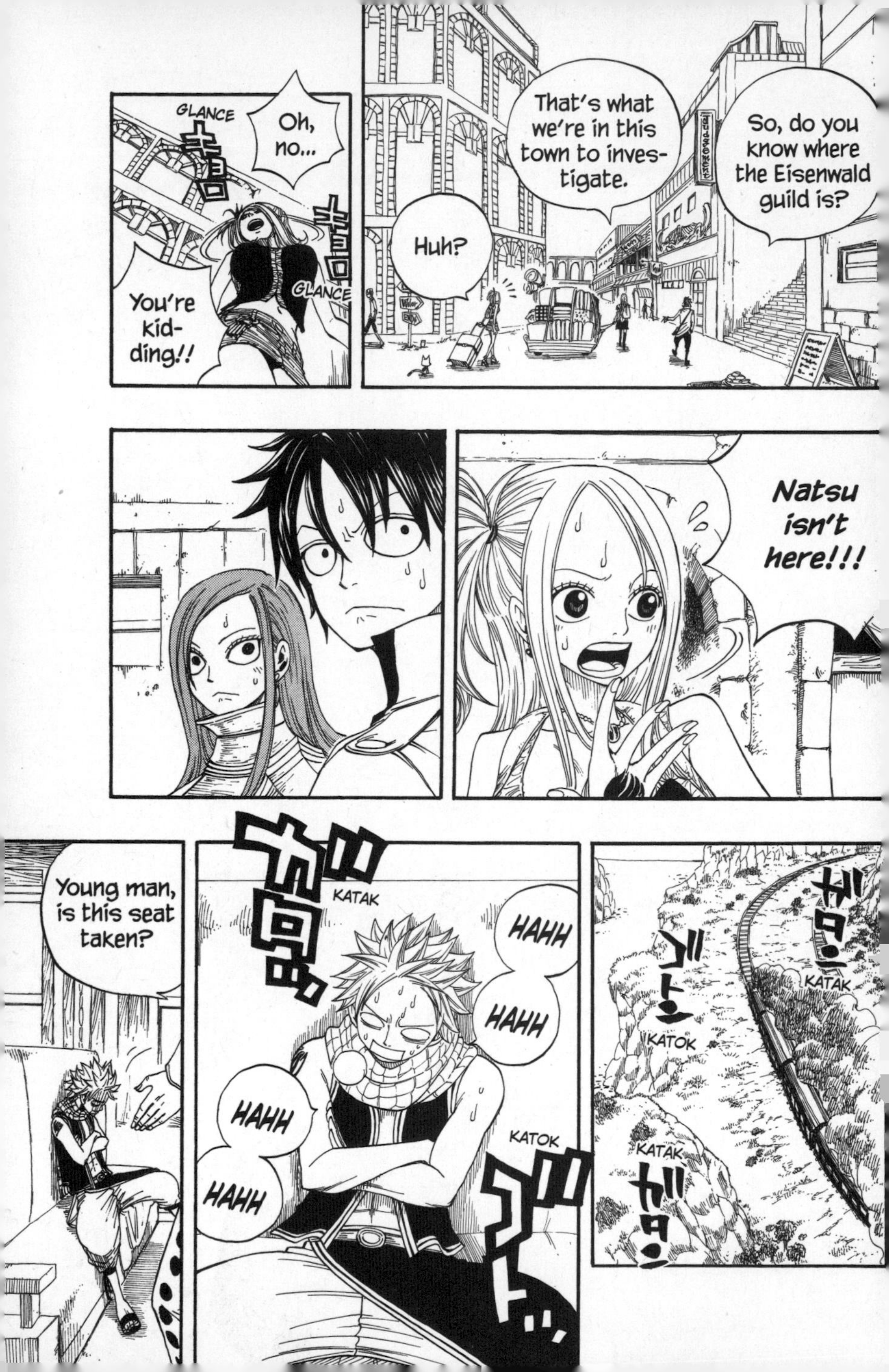
So, do you know where the Eisenwald guild is?
That's what we're in this town to investigate.
Huh?
Oh, no...
GLANCE
GLANCE
You're kid-ding!!
Natsu isn't here!!!
KATAK
KATOK
KATAK
KATAK
HAHH
HAHH
HAHH
HAHH
KATOK
Young man, is this seat taken?

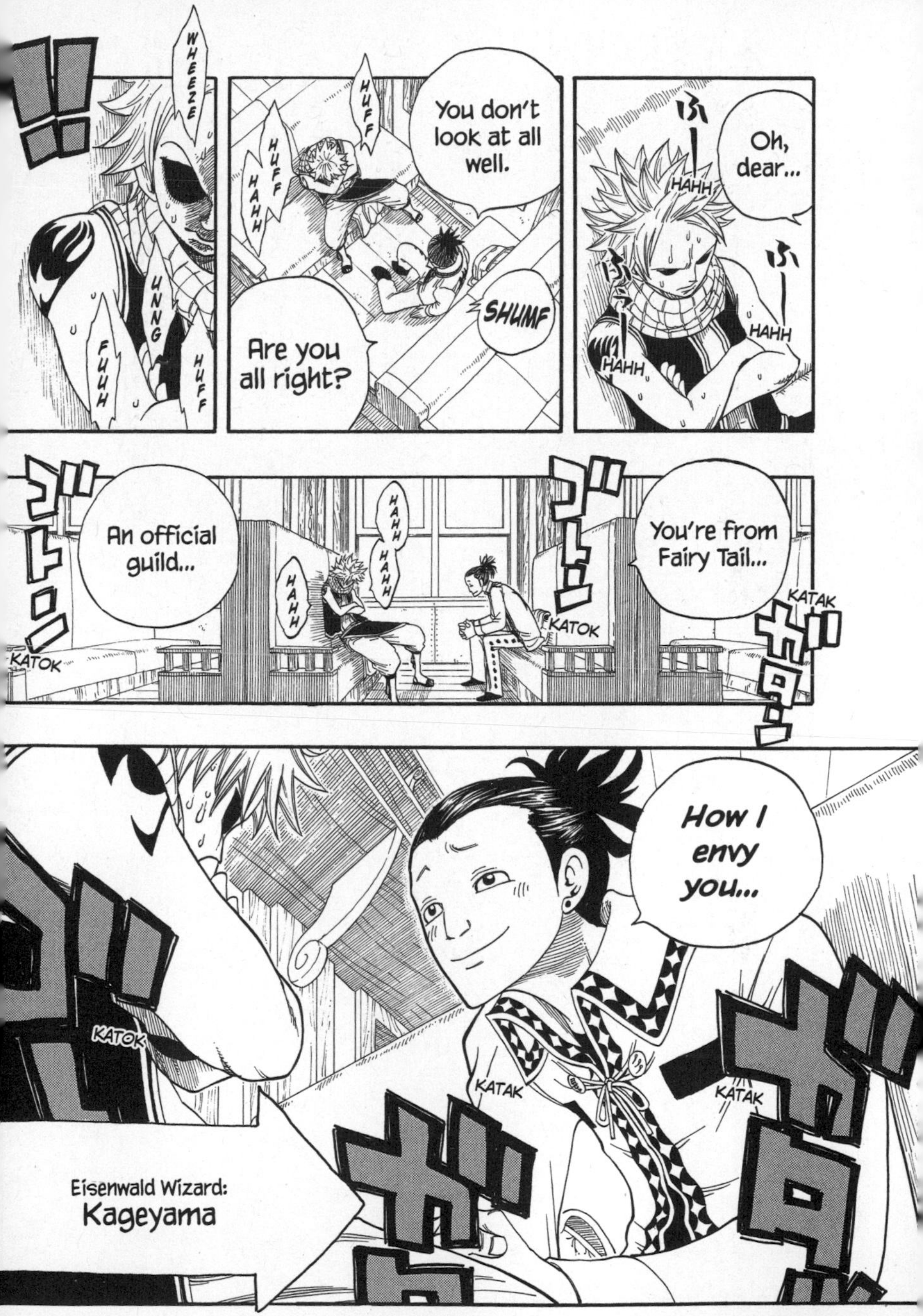
HAHH
Oh, dear...
HAHH
HAHH
You don't look at all well.
HUFF
HUFF
HAHH
SHUMF
Are you all right?
WHEEZE
UNNG
FUUH
HUFF
You're from Fairy Tail...
KATAK
KATOK
HAHH
HAHH
HAHH
An official guild...
KATOK
How I envy you...
KATAK
KATAK
KATOK
Eisenwald Wizard:
Kageyama

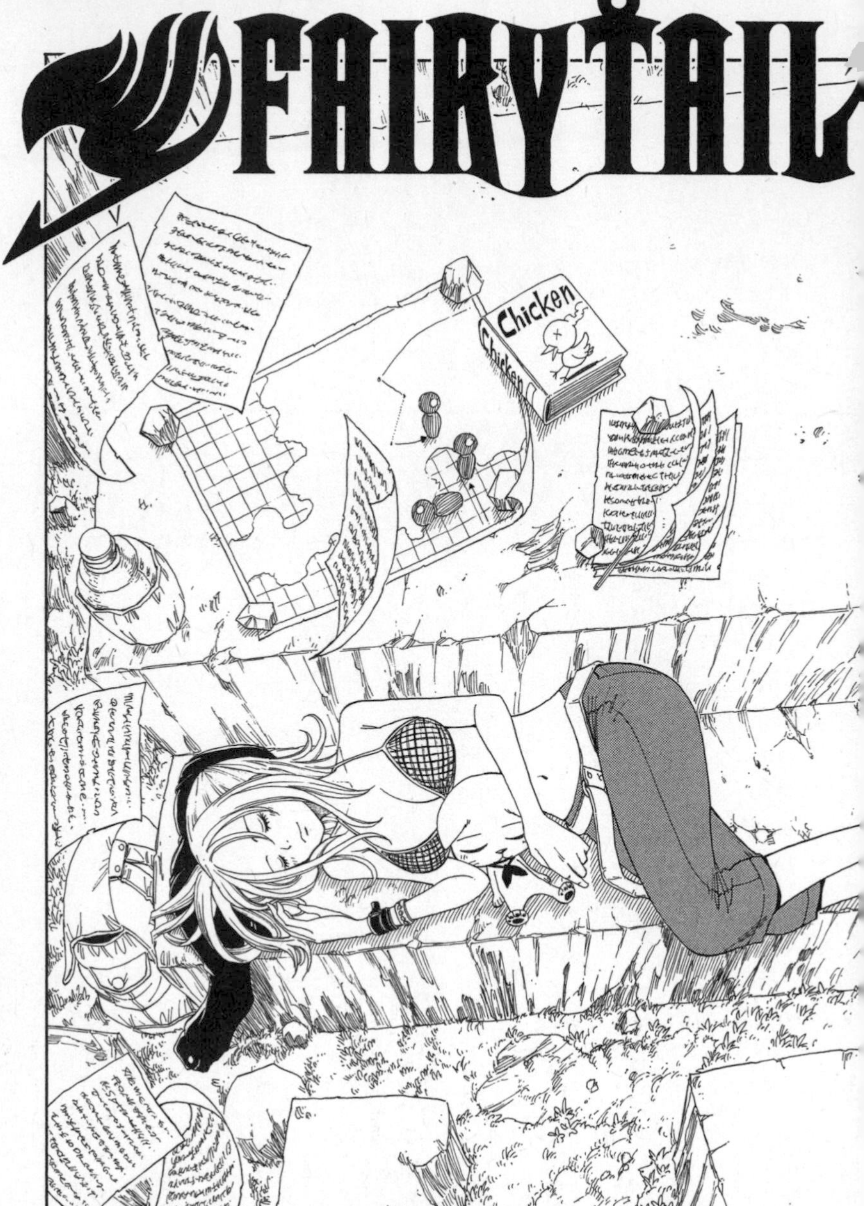
FAIRY TAIL
Chicken
Chicken

Chapter 12:
Spell Song

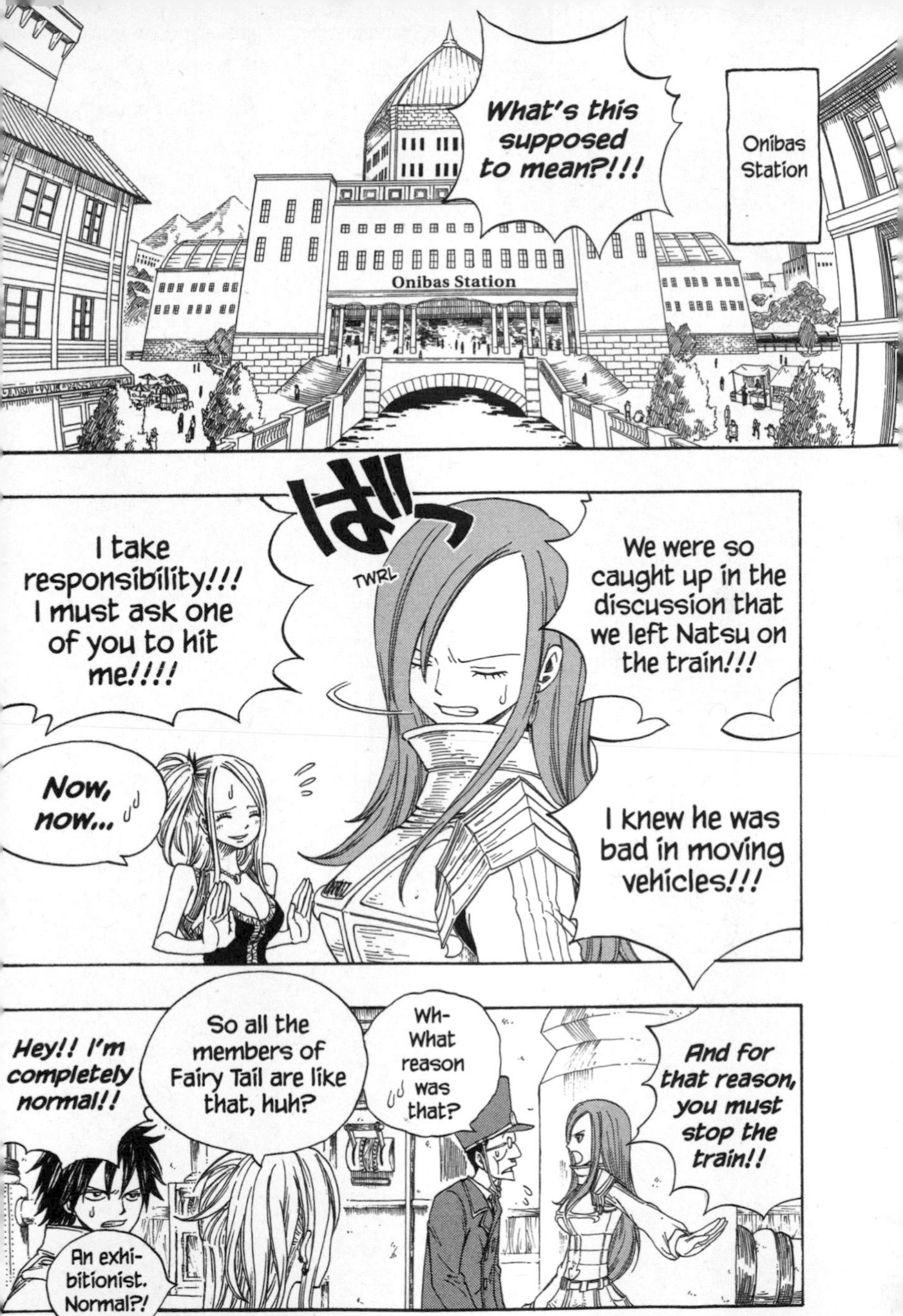
Onibas Station
What's this supposed to mean?!!!
Onibas Station
We were so caught up in the discussion that we left Natsu on the train!!!
I knew he was bad in moving vehicles!!!
はっ
TWRL
I take responsibility!!! I must ask one of you to hit me!!!!
Now, now...
And for that reason, you must stop the train!!
Wh- What reason was that?
So all the members of Fairy Tail are like that, huh?
Hey!! I'm completely normal!!
An exhi-bitionist. Normal?!

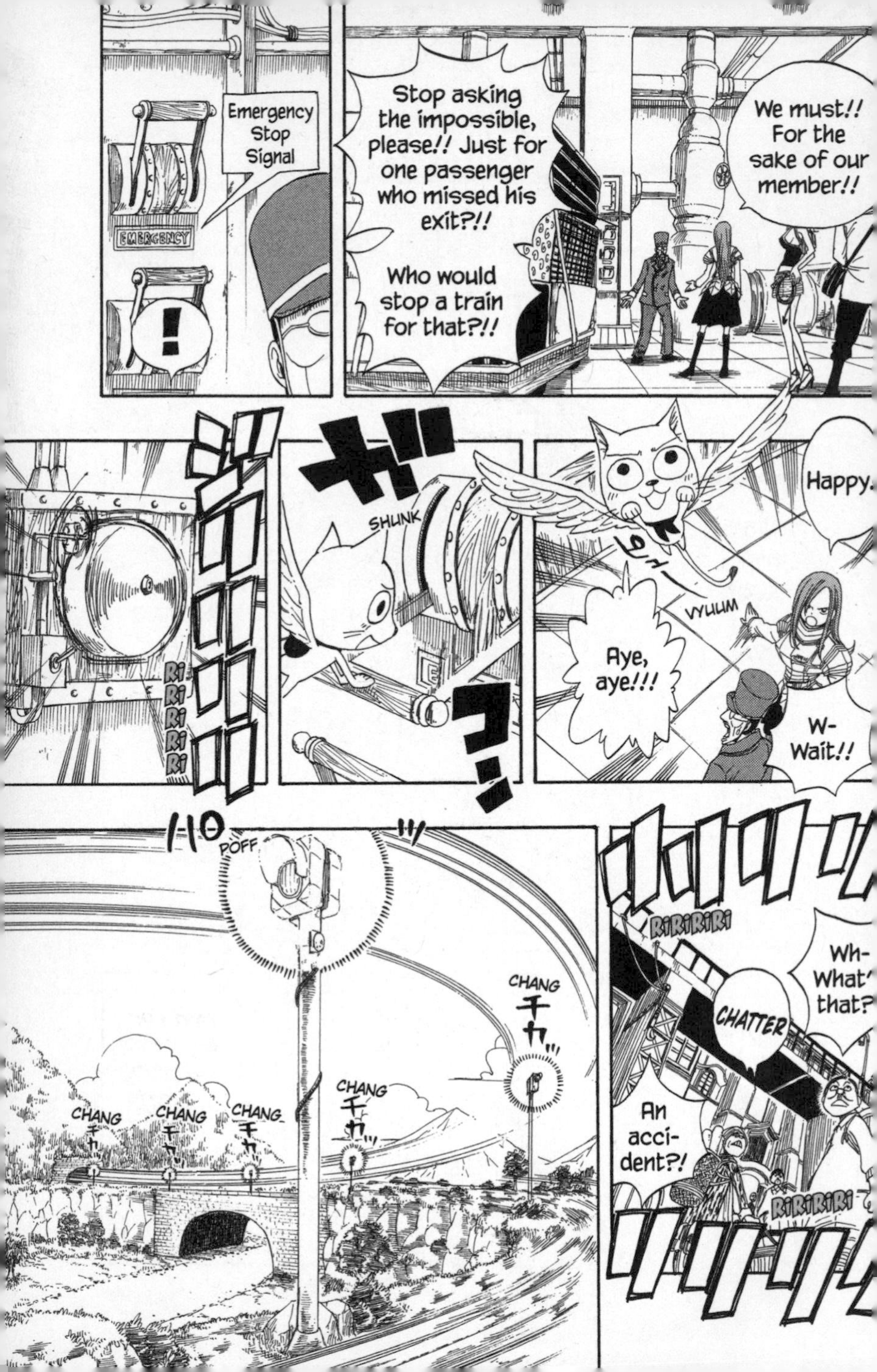
We must!! For the sake of our member!!
Stop asking the impossible, please!! Just for one passenger who missed his exit?!!
Who would stop a train for that?!!
Emergency Stop Signal
EMERGENCY
!
Happy.
Aye, aye!!!
VYUUM
W-Wait!!
SHUNK
RiRiRiRiRi
RiRiRiRi
Wh-What' that?
CHATTER
An accident?!
RiRiRiRi
POFF
CHANG
CHANG
CHANG
CHANG
CHANG

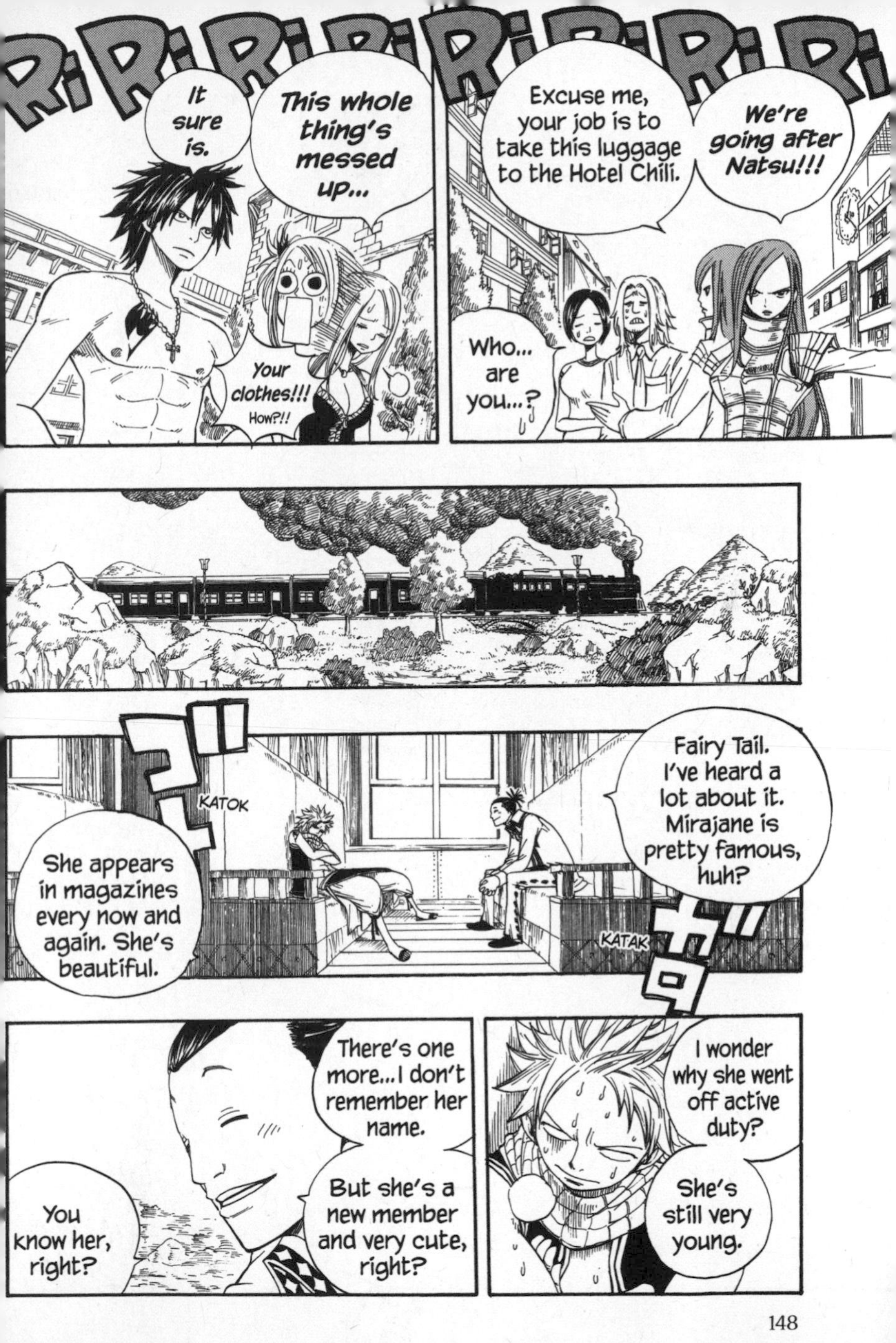
RiRiRiRiRiRiRiRiRiRi
We're going after Natsu!!!
Excuse me, your job is to take this luggage to the Hotel Chili.
Who... are you...?
This whole thing's messed up...
It sure is.
Your clothes!!!
How?!!
Fairy Tail. I've heard a lot about it. Mirajane is pretty famous, huh?
KATAK
KATOK
She appears in magazines every now and again. She's beautiful.
I wonder why she went off active duty?
She's still very young.
There's one more...I don't remember her name.
But she's a new member and very cute, right?
You know her, right?

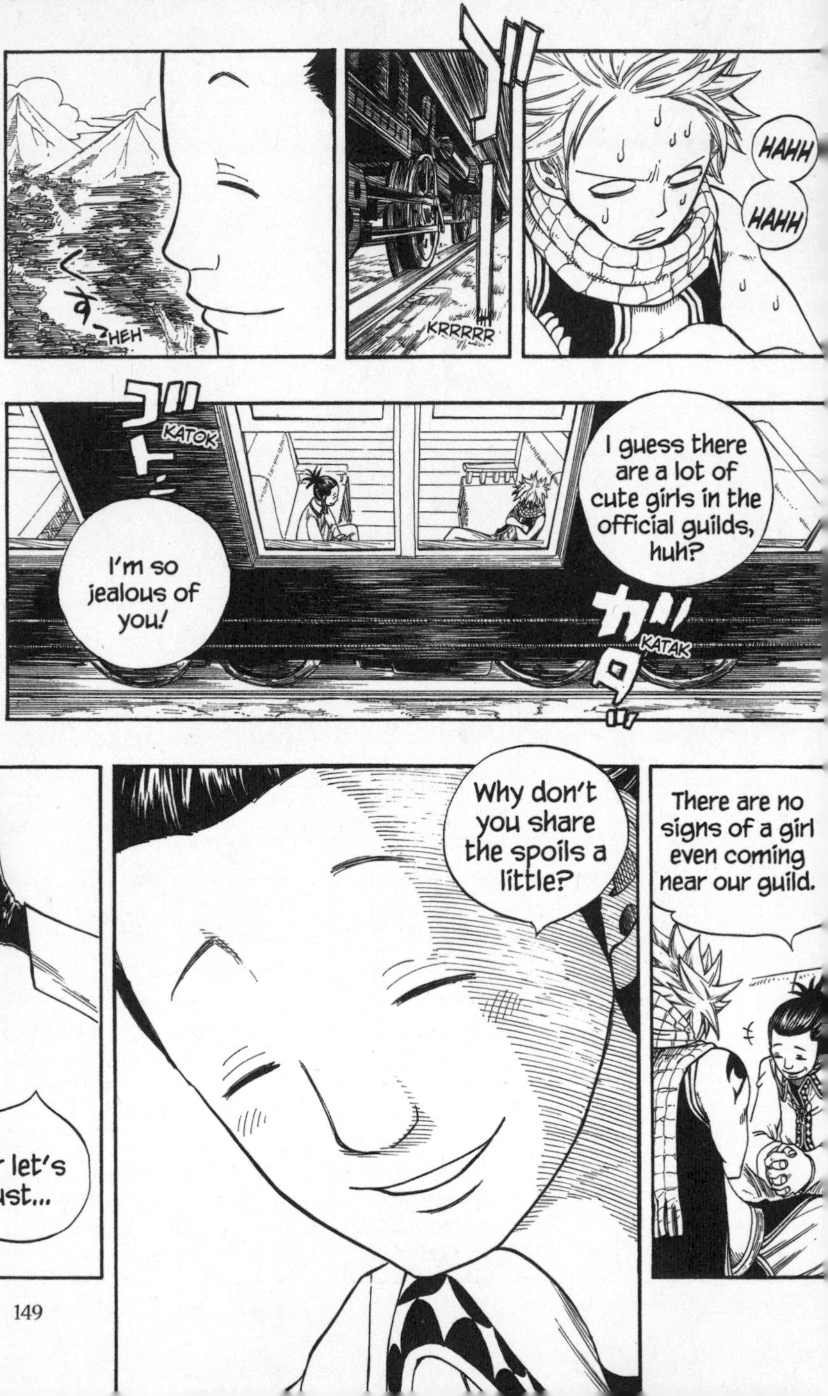
HAHH
HAHH
KRRRRR
HEH
I guess there are a lot of cute girls in the official guilds, huh?
KATOK
I'm so jealous of you!
KATAK
There are no signs of a girl even coming near our guild.
Why don't you share the spoils a little?
Or let's just...

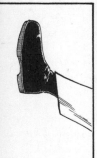

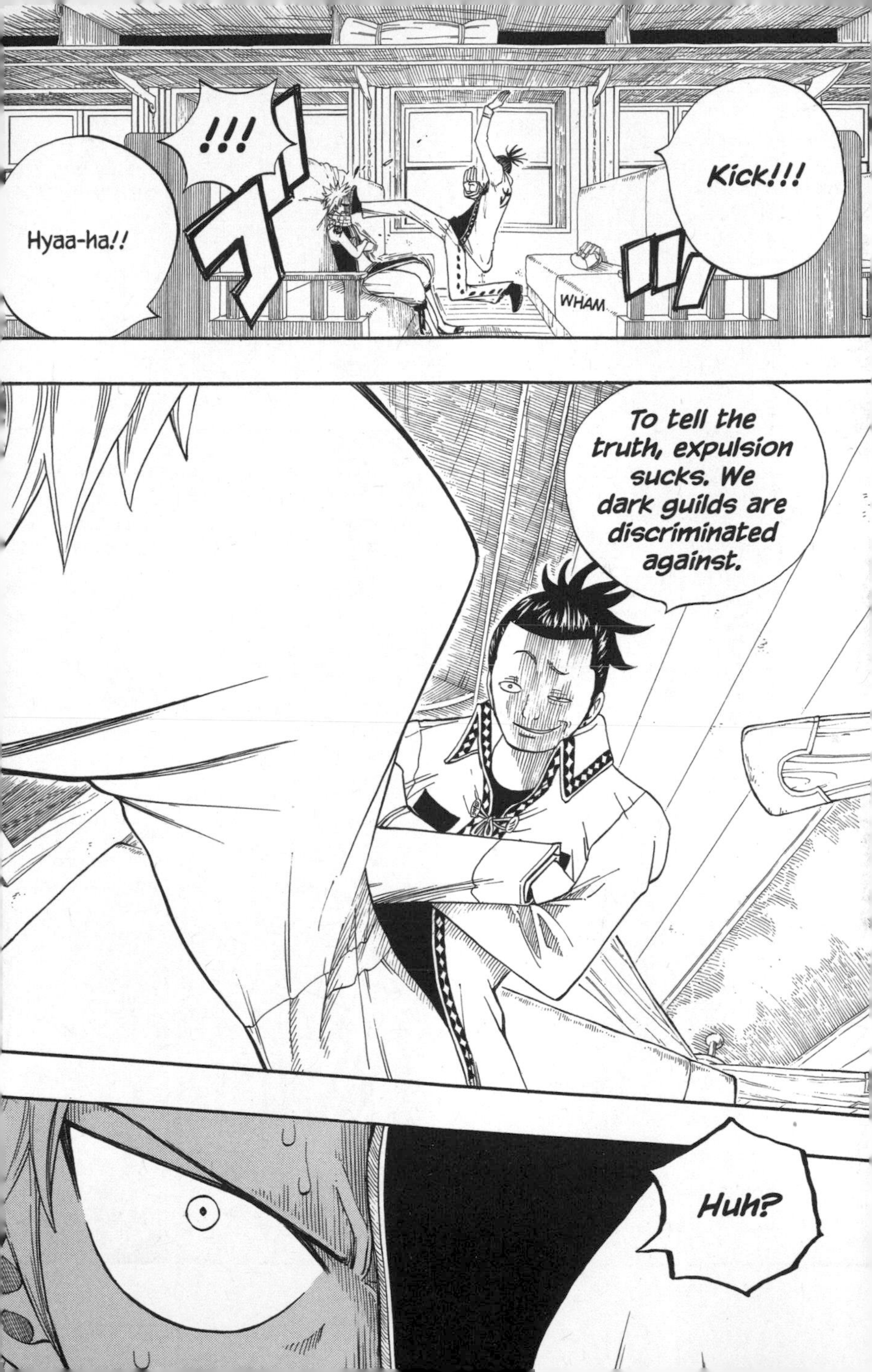
Kick!!!
WHAM
!!!
Hyaa-ha!!
To tell the truth, expulsion sucks. We dark guilds are discriminated against.
Huh?

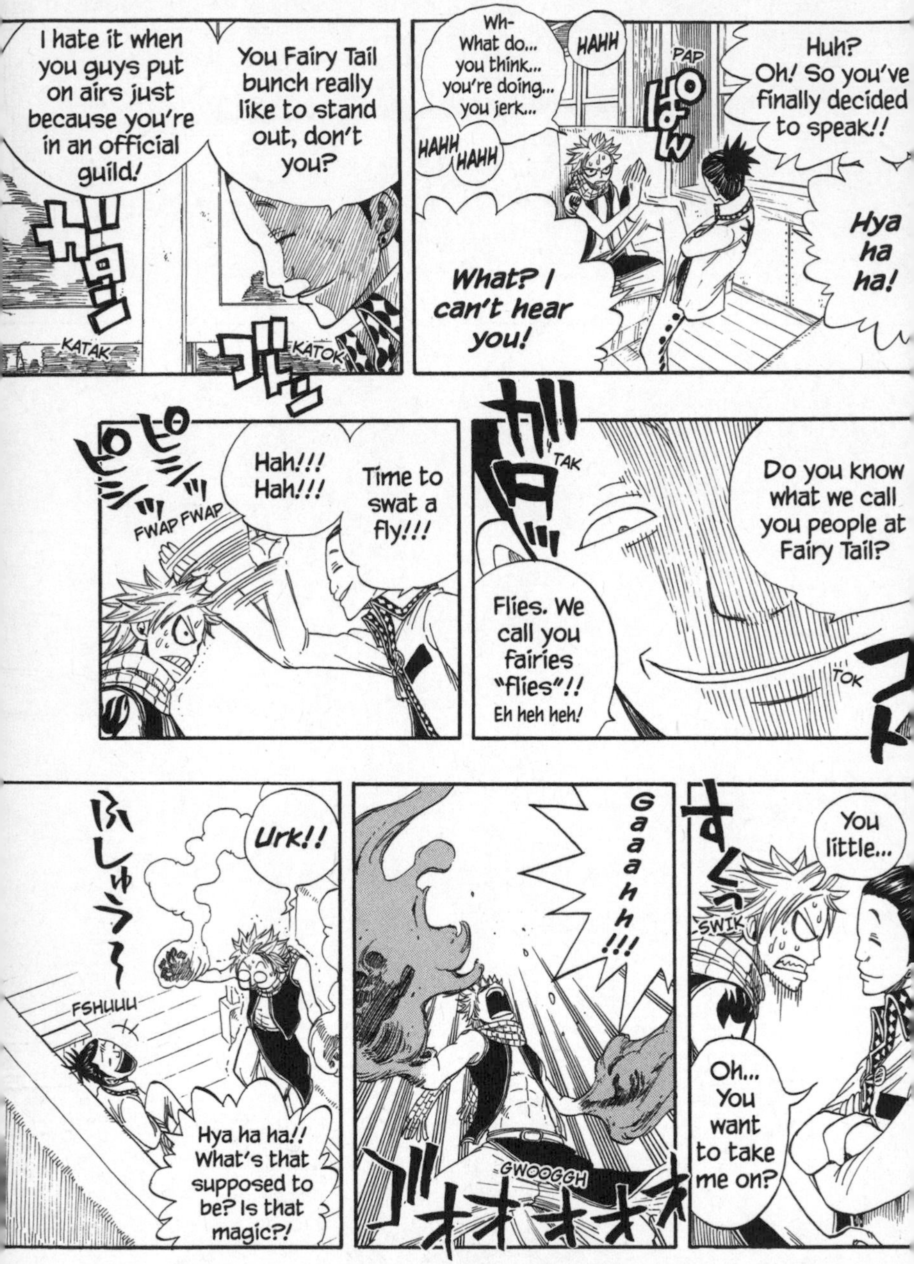
Huh? Oh! So you've finally decided to speak!!
Hya ha ha!
PAP
HAHH
Wh- What do... you think... you're doing... you jerk...
HAHH HAHH
What? I can't hear you!
You Fairy Tail bunch really like to stand out, don't you?
I hate it when you guys put on airs just because you're in an official guild!
KATOK
KATAK
Do you know what we call you people at Fairy Tail?
TOK
TAK
Flies. We call you fairies "flies"!! Eh heh heh!
Time to swat a fly!!!
Hah!!! Hah!!!
FWAP FWAP
You little...
SWIK
Oh... You want to take me on?
Gaaahh!!!
GWOOGGH
Urk!!
FSHUUU
Hya ha ha!! What's that supposed to be? Is that magic?!

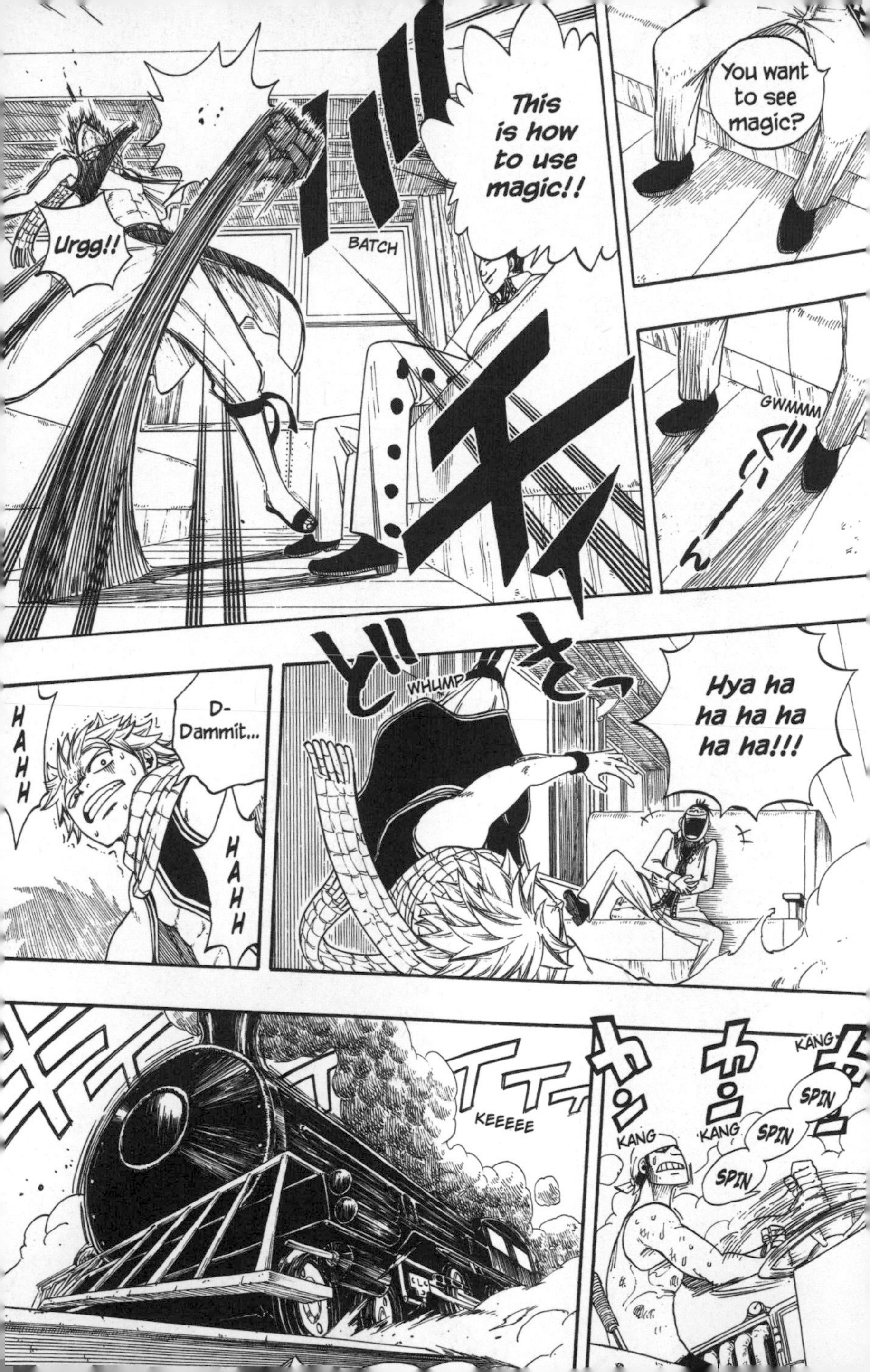
You want to see magic?
GWMMM
This is how to use magic!!
BATCH
Urgg!!
WHUMP
Hya ha ha ha ha ha!!!
D- Dammit...
HAHH
HAHH
KANG
KANG
SPIN
SPIN
SPIN
KANG
KEEEEE

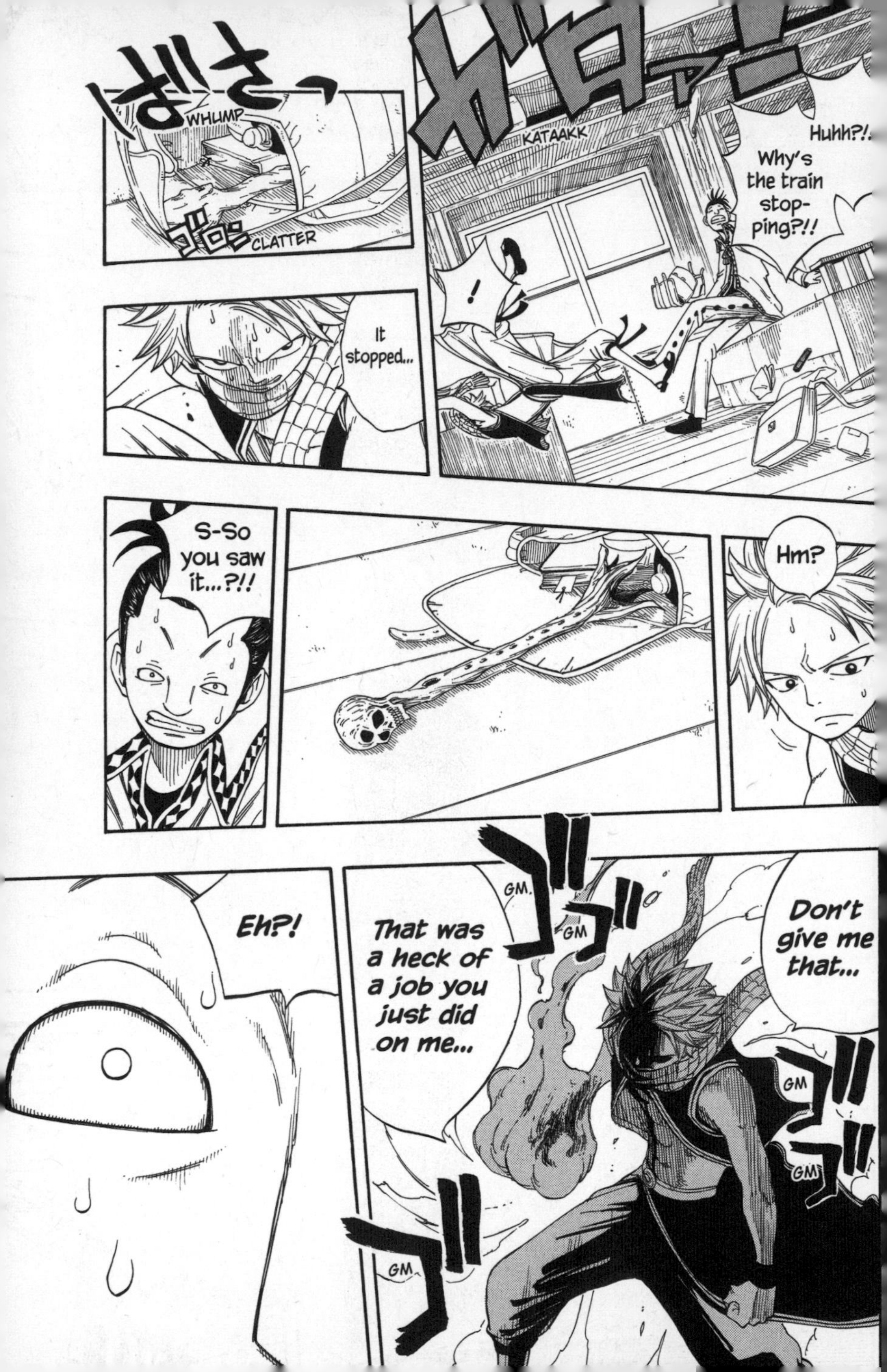
KATAAKK
Huhh?!..
Why's the train stop-ping?!!
!
WHUMP
CLATTER
It stopped...
Hm?
S-So you saw it...?!!
GM
GM
GM
GM
Don't give me that...
That was a heck of a job you just did on me...
Eh?!

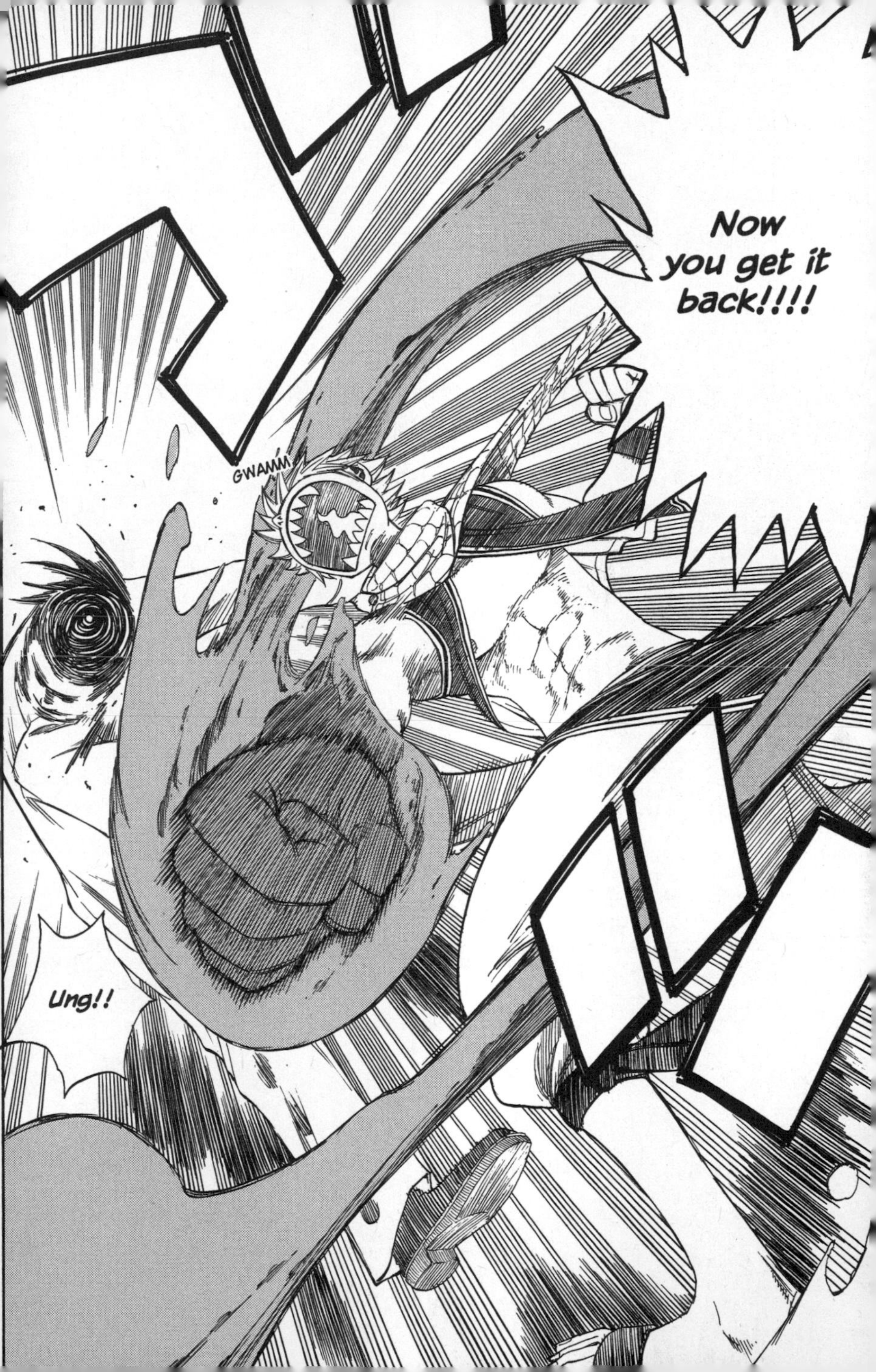
Now you get it back!!!!
GWAMM
Ung!!

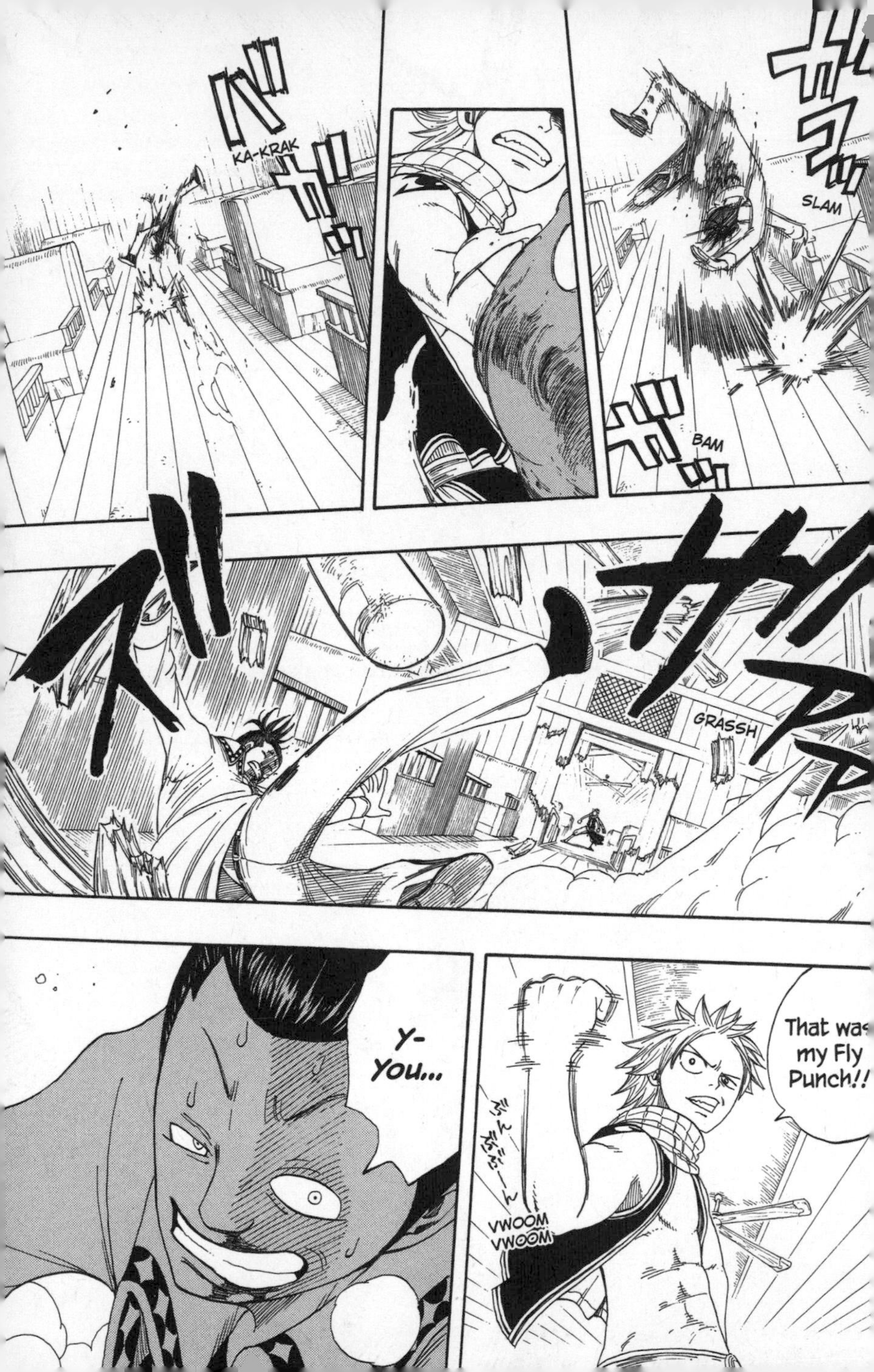
SLAM
BAM
KA-KRAK
GRASSH
That was my Fly Punch!!
VWOOM VWOOM
Y- You...

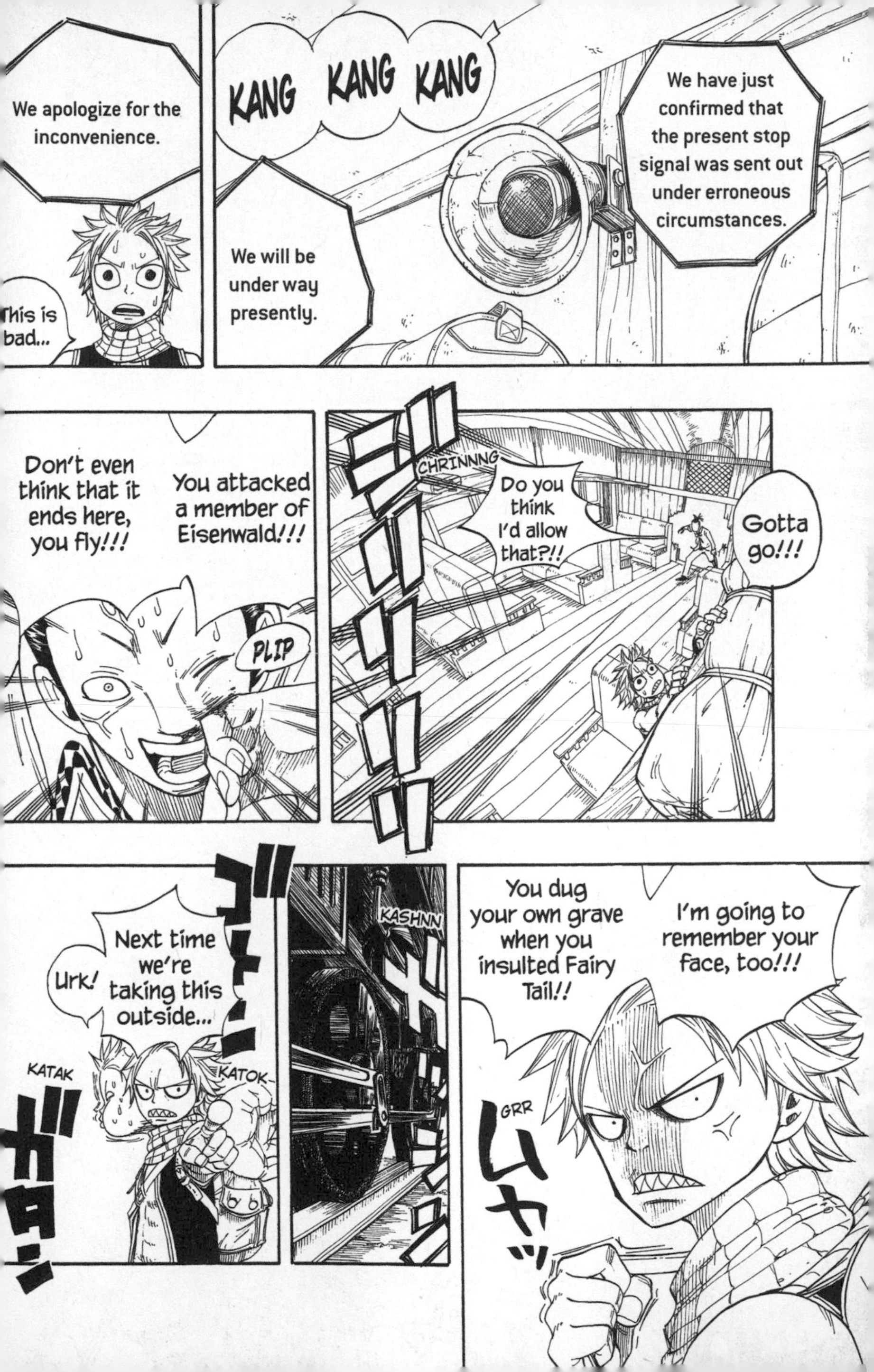
KANG KANG KANG
We have just confirmed that the present stop signal was sent out under erroneous circumstances.
We will be under way presently.
We apologize for the inconvenience.
This is bad...
Gotta go!!!
CHRINNNG
Do you think I'd allow that?!!
You attacked a member of Eisenwald!!!
Don't even think that it ends here, you fly!!!
PLIP
I'm going to remember your face, too!!!
You dug your own grave when you insulted Fairy Tail!!
GRR
KASHNN
Next time we're taking this outside...
Urk!
KATOK-
KATAK

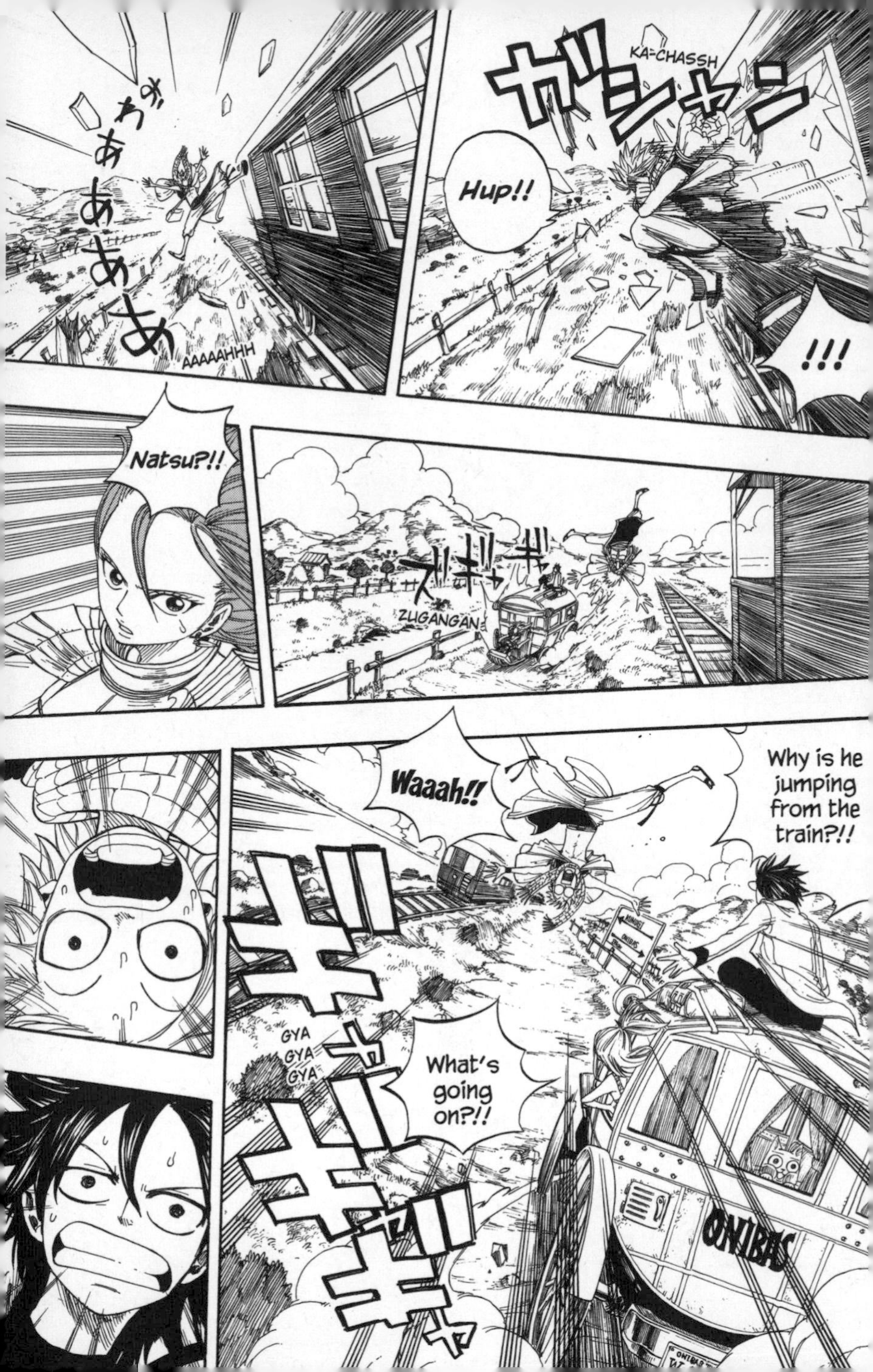
KA-CHASSH
Hup!!
!!!
AAAAAHHH
ZUGANGAN
Natsu?!!
Why is he jumping from the train?!!
Waaah!!
What's going on?!!
GYA GYA GYA
ONIBAS

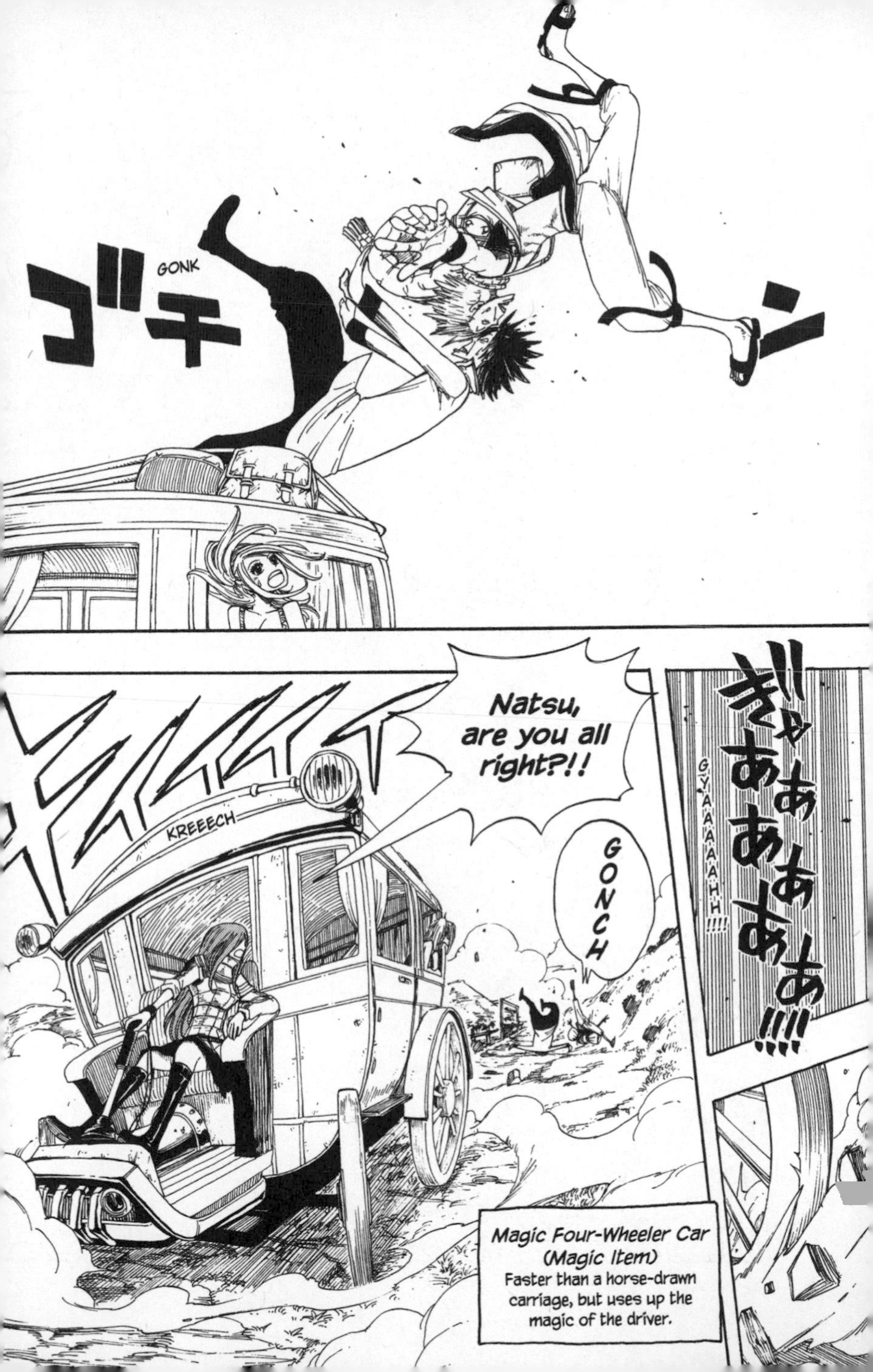
ゴチ
GONK
ン
ぎゃああああ!!!!
GYAAAAAAH!!!!
Natsu, are you all right?!!
GONCH
KREEECH
Magic Four-Wheeler Car
(Magic Item)
Faster than a horse-drawn carriage, but uses up the magic of the driver.

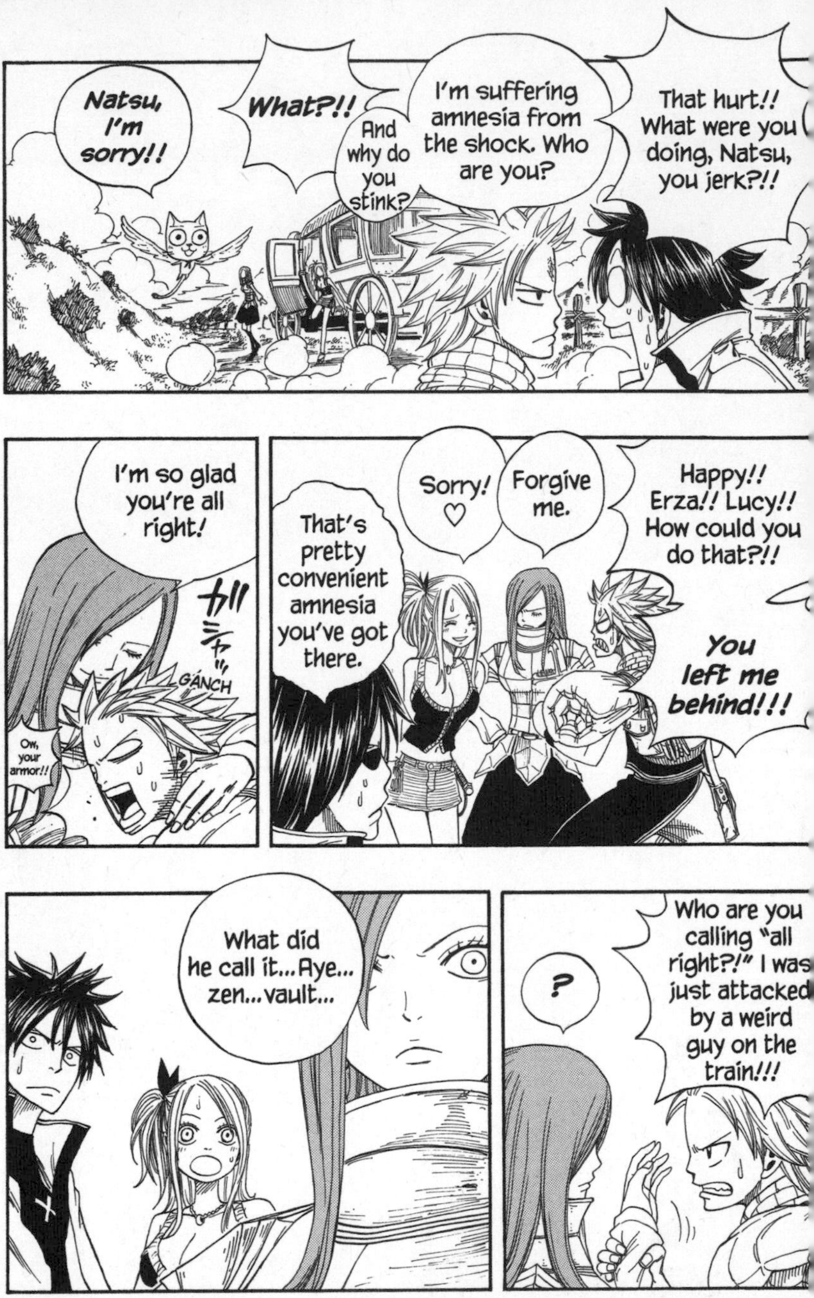
That hurt!! What were you doing, Natsu, you jerk?!!
I'm suffering amnesia from the shock. Who are you?
And why do you stink?
What?!!
Natsu, I'm sorry!!
Happy!! Erza!! Lucy!! How could you do that?!!
You left me behind!!!
Forgive me.
Sorry! ♡
That's pretty convenient amnesia you've got there.
I'm so glad you're all right!
GANCH
Ow, your armor!!
Who are you calling "all right?!" I was just attacked by a weird guy on the train!!!
?
What did he call it...Aye... zen...vault...

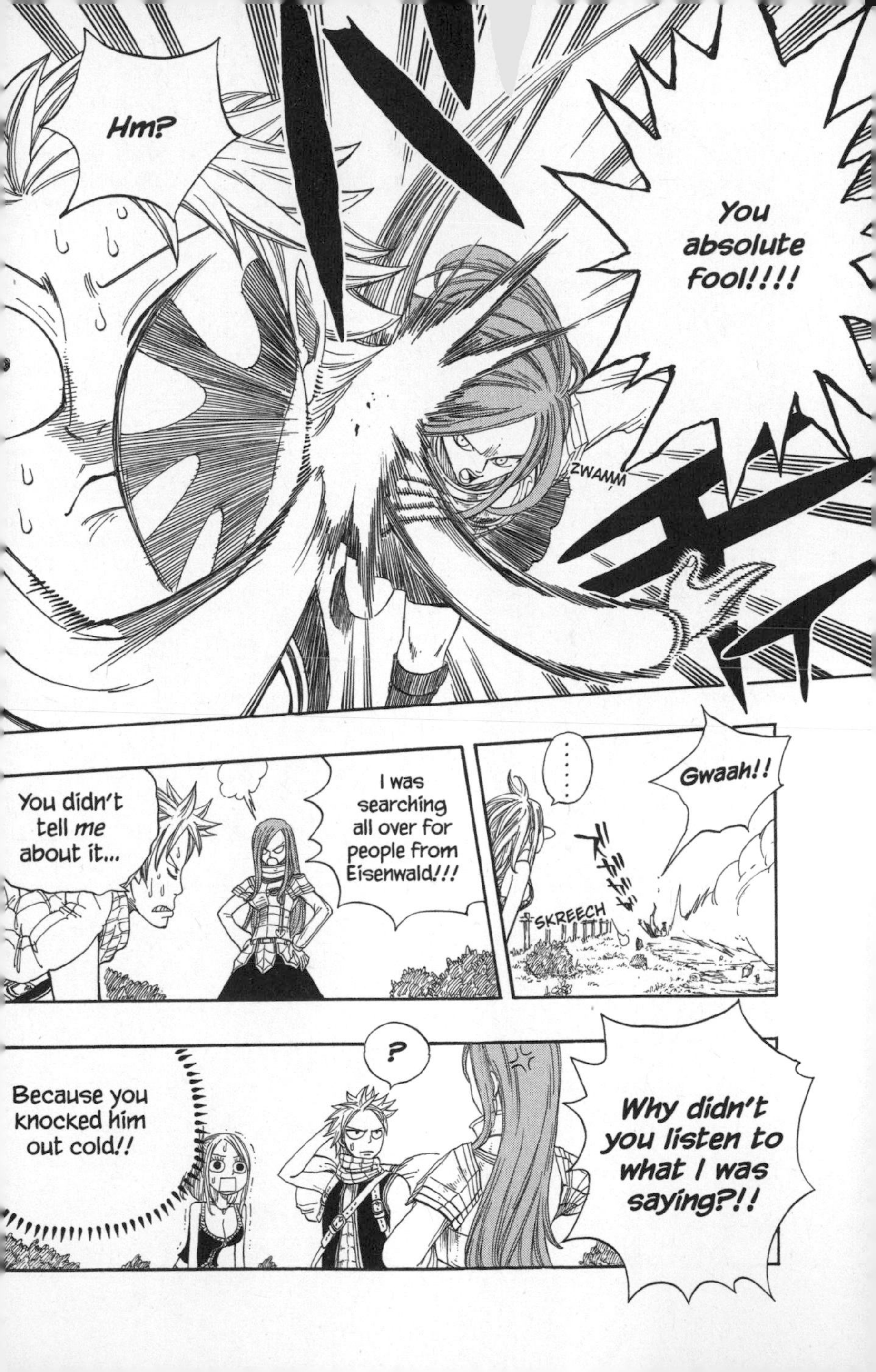
You absolute fool!!!!
Hm?
ZWAMM
......
Gwaah!!
SKREECH
I was searching all over for people from Eisenwald!!!
You didn't tell *me* about it...
Why didn't you listen to what I was saying?!!
?
Because you knocked him out cold!!

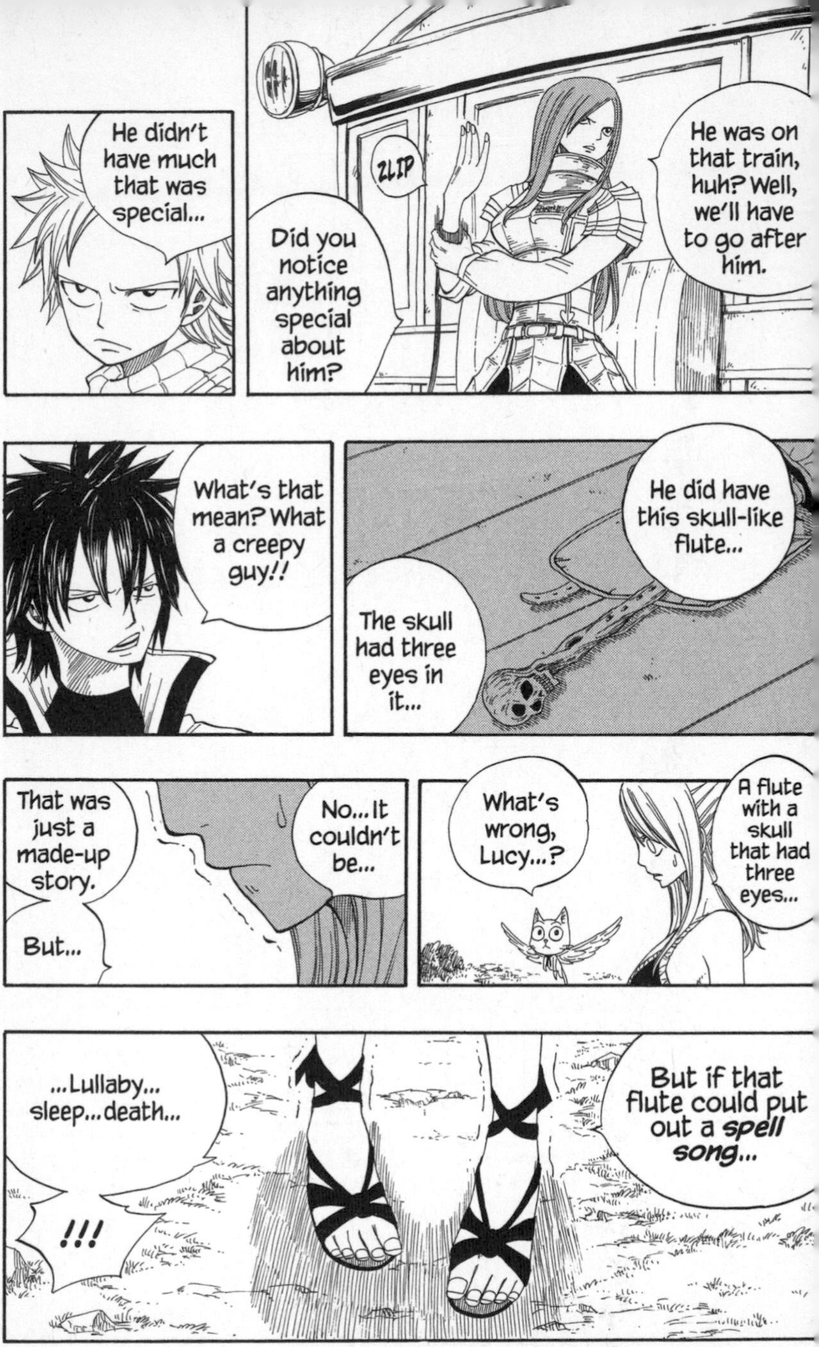
He was on that train, huh? Well, we'll have to go after him.
ZLIP
Did you notice anything special about him?
He didn't have much that was special...
He did have this skull-like flute...
The skull had three eyes in it...
What's that mean? What a creepy guy!!
A flute with a skull that had three eyes...
What's wrong, Lucy...?
No... It couldn't be...
That was just a made-up story.
But...
But if that flute could put out a *spell song*...
...Lullaby... sleep...death...
!!!

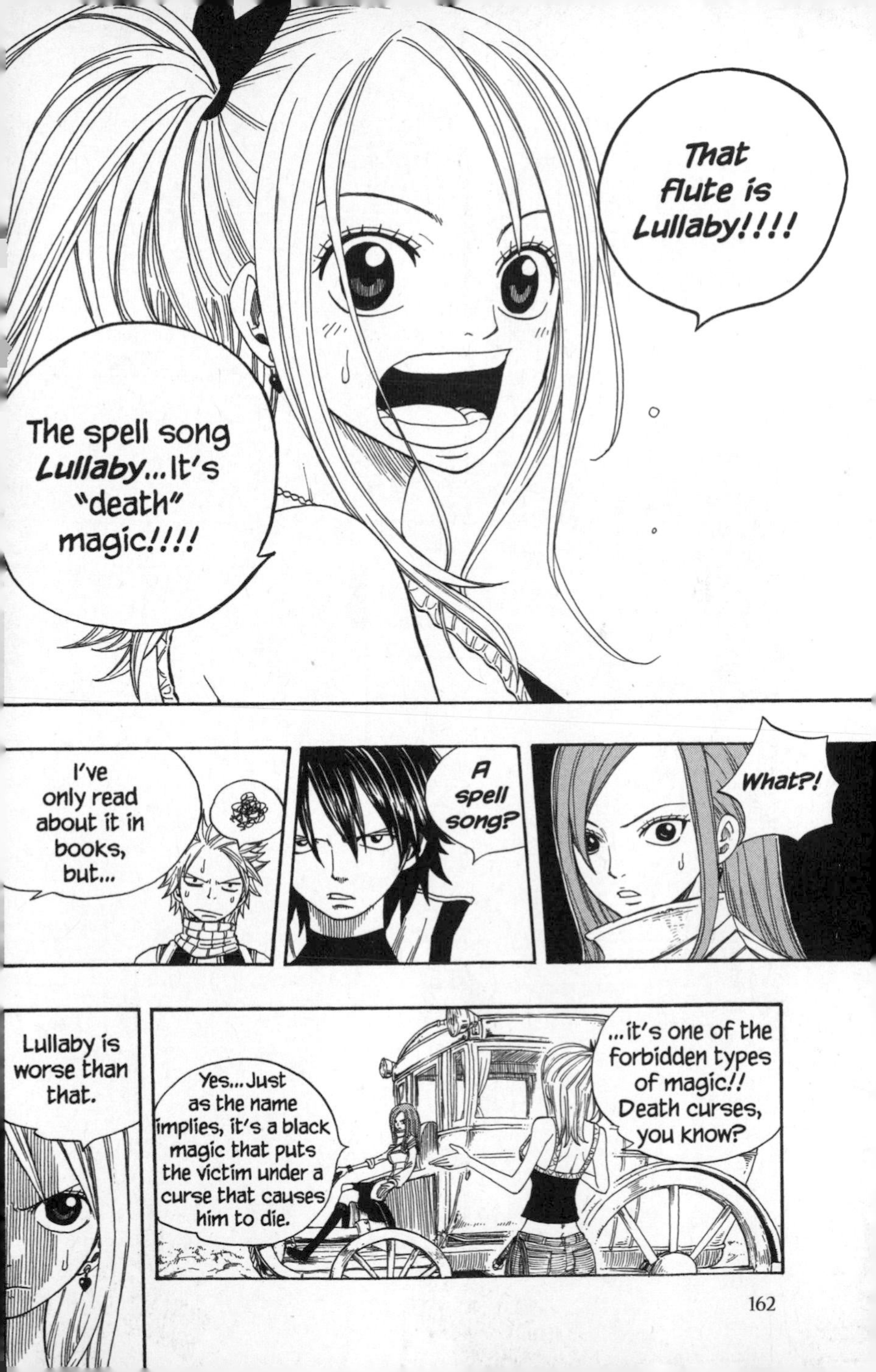
That flute is Lullaby!!!!
The spell song Lullaby... It's "death" magic!!!!
What?!
A spell song?
I've only read about it in books, but...
...it's one of the forbidden types of magic!! Death curses, you know?
Yes... Just as the name implies, it's a black magic that puts the victim under a curse that causes him to die.
Lullaby is worse than that.

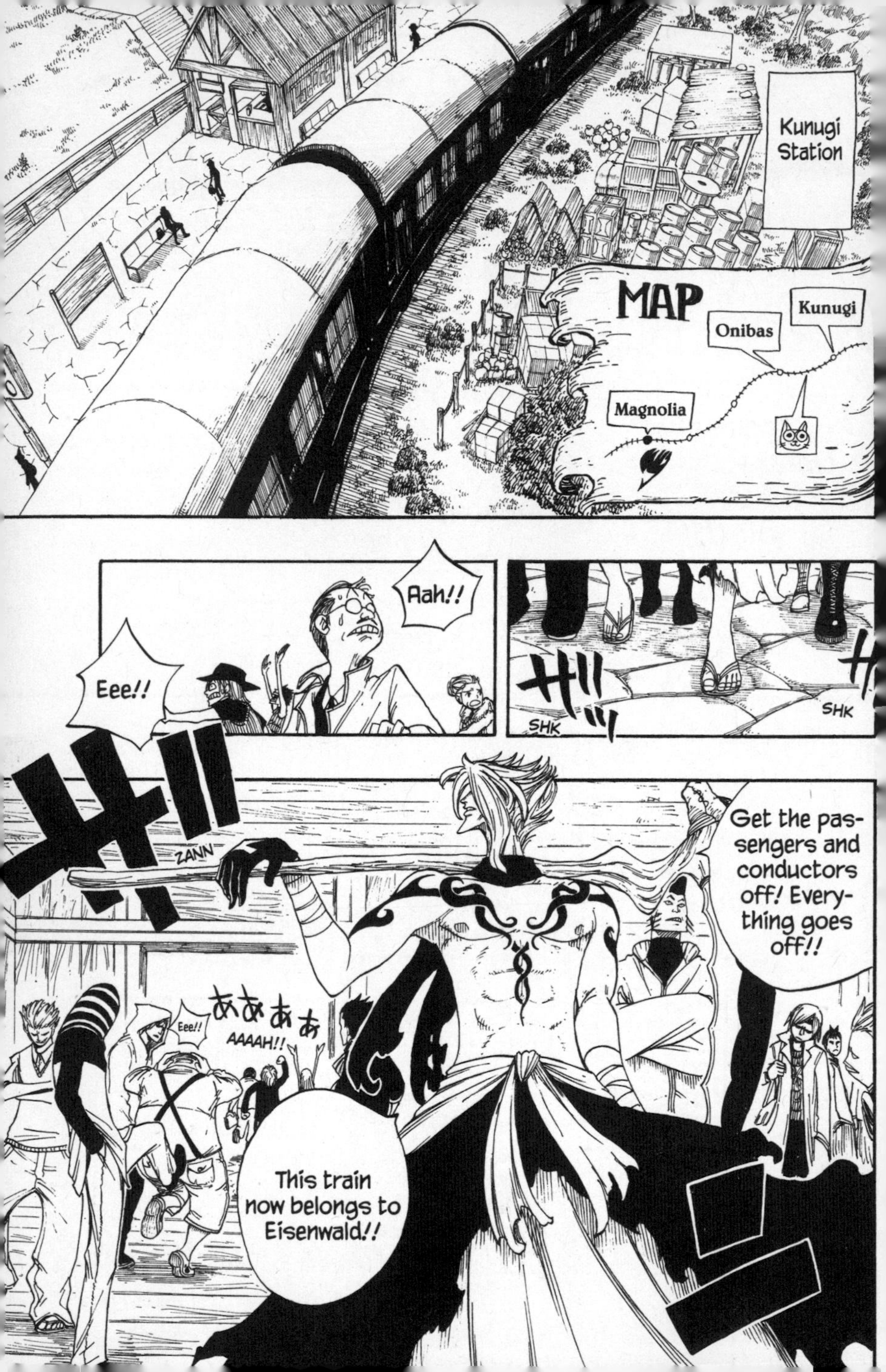
Kunugi Station
MAP
Kunugi
Onibas
Magnolia
SHK
SHK
Aah!!
Eee!!
Get the pas-sengers and conductors off! Every-thing goes off!!
ZANN
ああああ
AAAAH!!
Eee!!
This train now belongs to Eisenwald!!

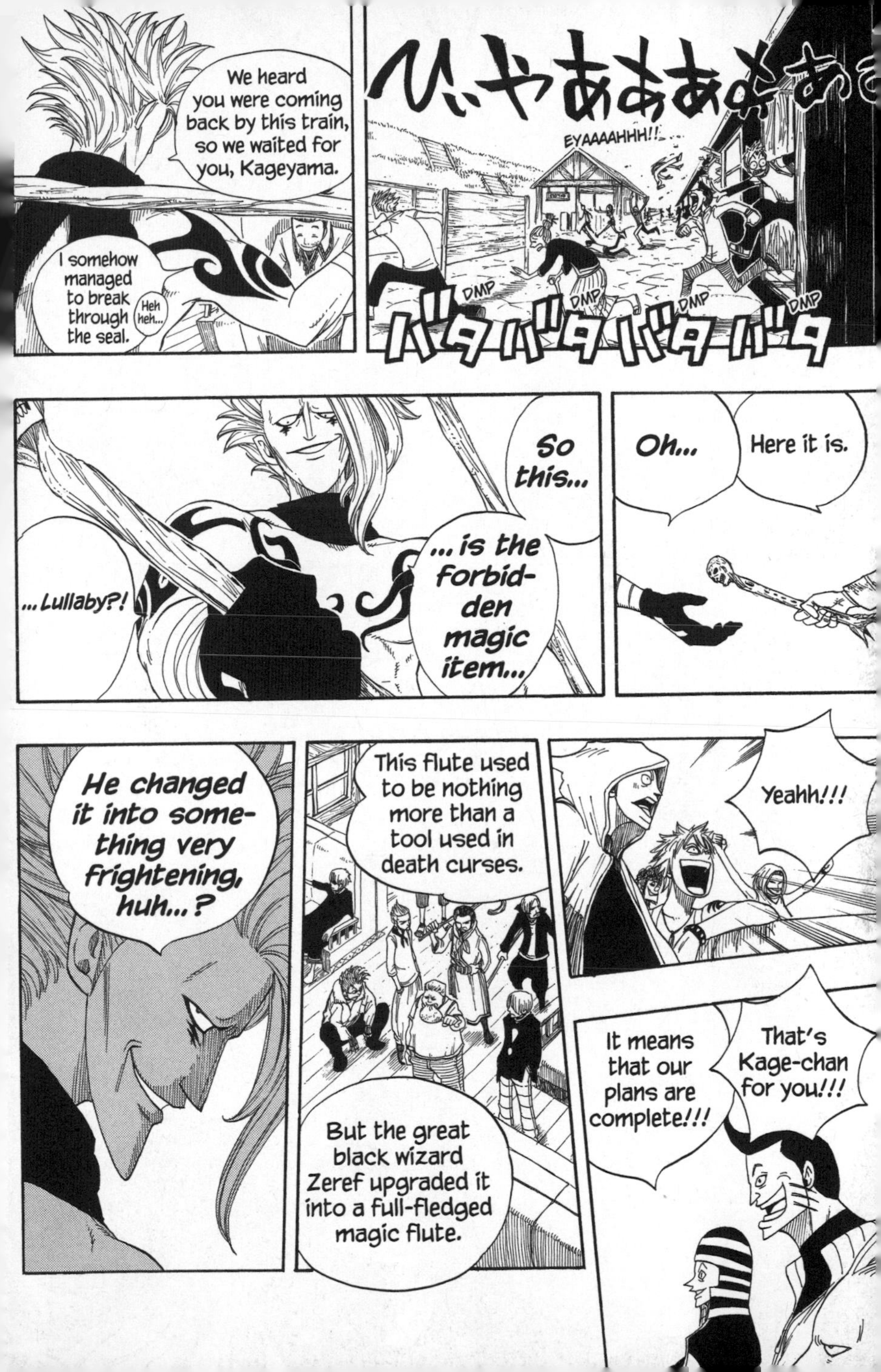
ひぃやあああああ
EYAAAAHHH!!
DMP
DMP
DMP
DMP
バタバタバタバタ
We heard you were coming back by this train, so we waited for you, Kageyama.
I somehow managed to break through the seal.
Heh heh...
Here it is.
Oh...
So this...
...is the forbid-den magic item...
...Lullaby?!
Yeahh!!!
That's Kage-chan for you!!!
It means that our plans are complete!!!
This flute used to be nothing more than a tool used in death curses.
But the great black wizard Zeref upgraded it into a full-fledged magic flute.
He changed it into some-thing very frightening, huh...?

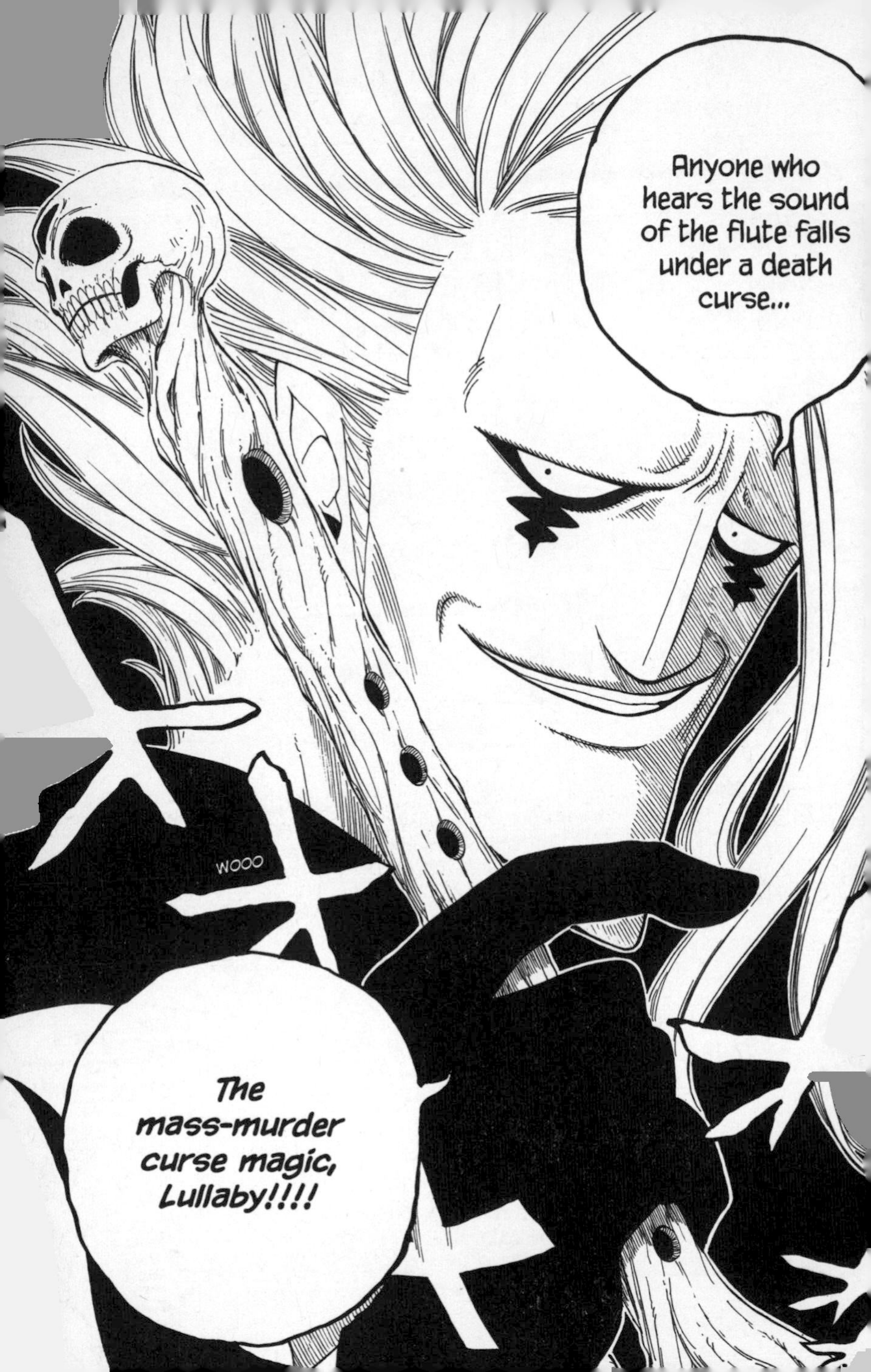
Anyone who hears the sound of the flute falls under a death curse...
WOOO
The mass-murder curse magic, Lullaby!!!!

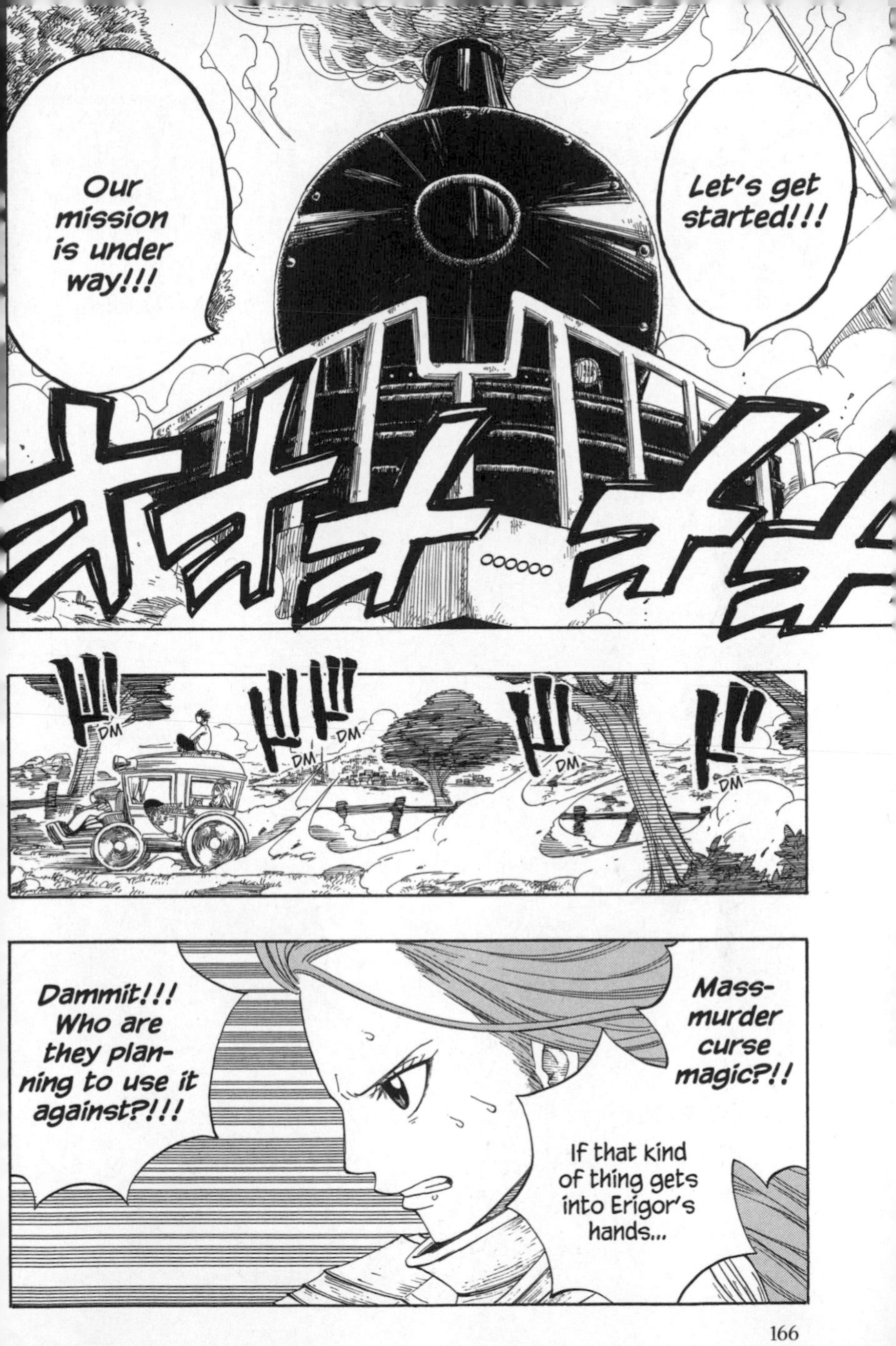
Let's get started!!!
Our mission is under way!!!
oooooo
DM
DM
DM
DM
DM
Mass-murder curse magic?!!
If that kind of thing gets into Erigor's hands...
Dammit!!! Who are they plan-ning to use it against?!!!

Chapter 13: Death Laughs Twice

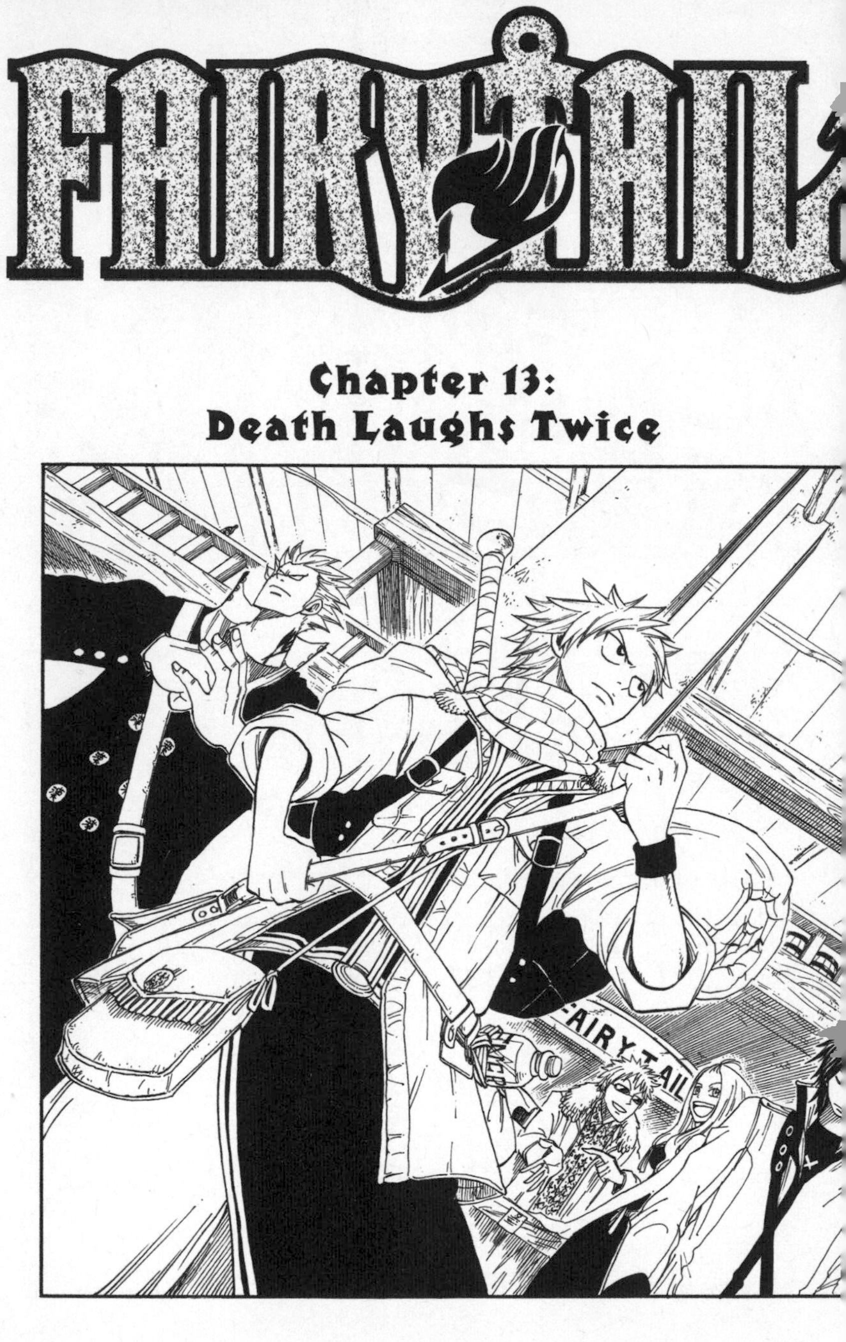
FAIRY TAIL

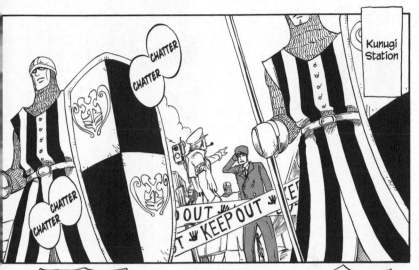

Kunugi Station
CHATTER
CHATTER
CHATTER
CHATTER
KEEP OUT
These men with a cauldron suddenly boarded the train...
I've seen 'em before!! They're from that dark guild that's in these parts!!
I left my work tools on that train!! I'd trade my wife to get them back!!
CHATTER
CHATTER
CHATTER
CHATTER
So those guys stole a train?!!
That's what it sounds like.

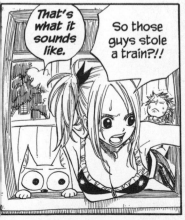

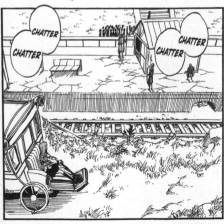

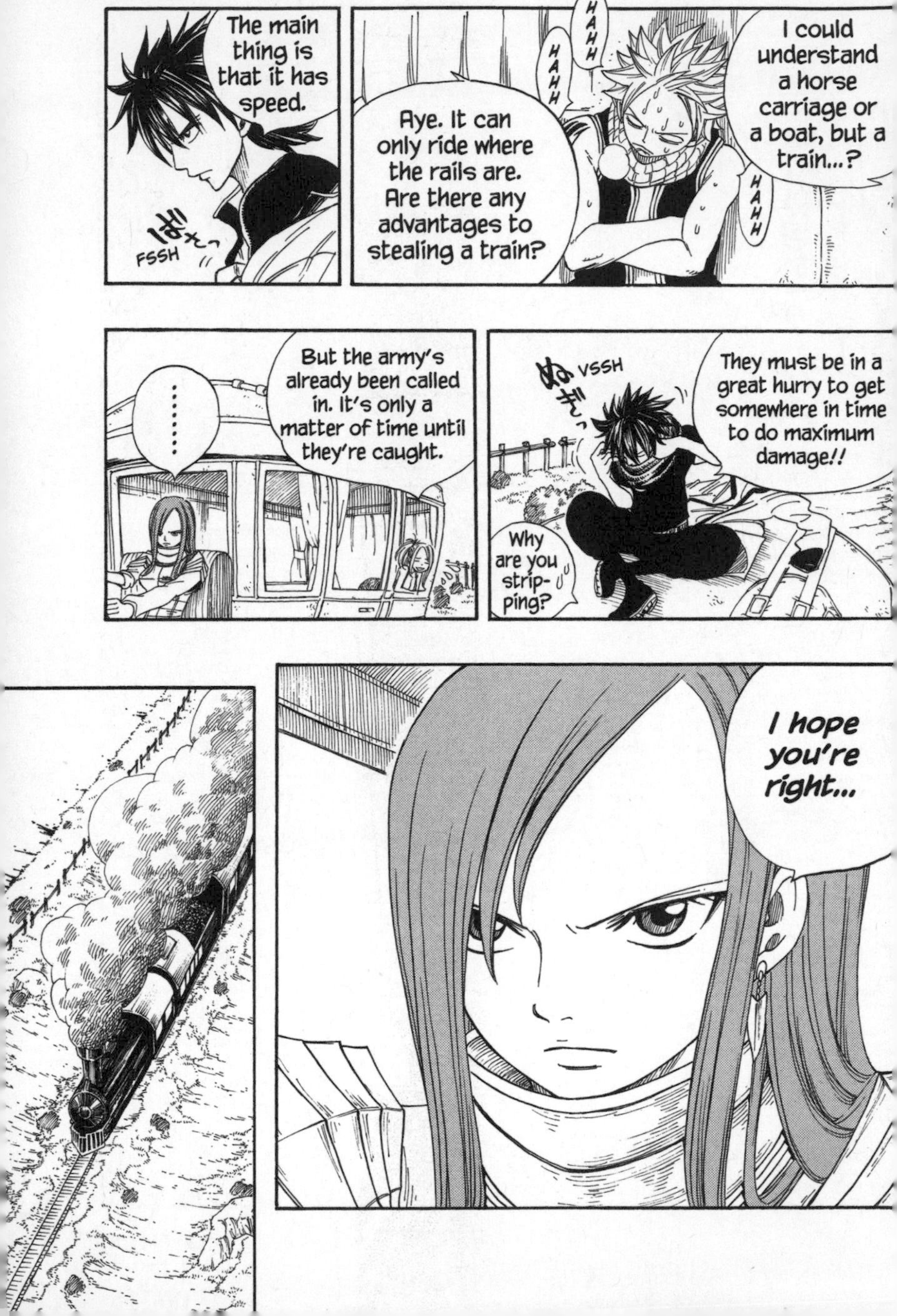
HAHH
HAHH
I could understand a horse carriage or a boat, but a train...?
HAHH
Aye. It can only ride where the rails are. Are there any advantages to stealing a train?
The main thing is that it has speed.
ぼそっ
FSSH
They must be in a great hurry to get somewhere in time to do maximum damage!!
ぬぎっ
VSSH
Why are you strip-ping?
But the army's already been called in. It's only a matter of time until they're caught.
......
I hope you're right...

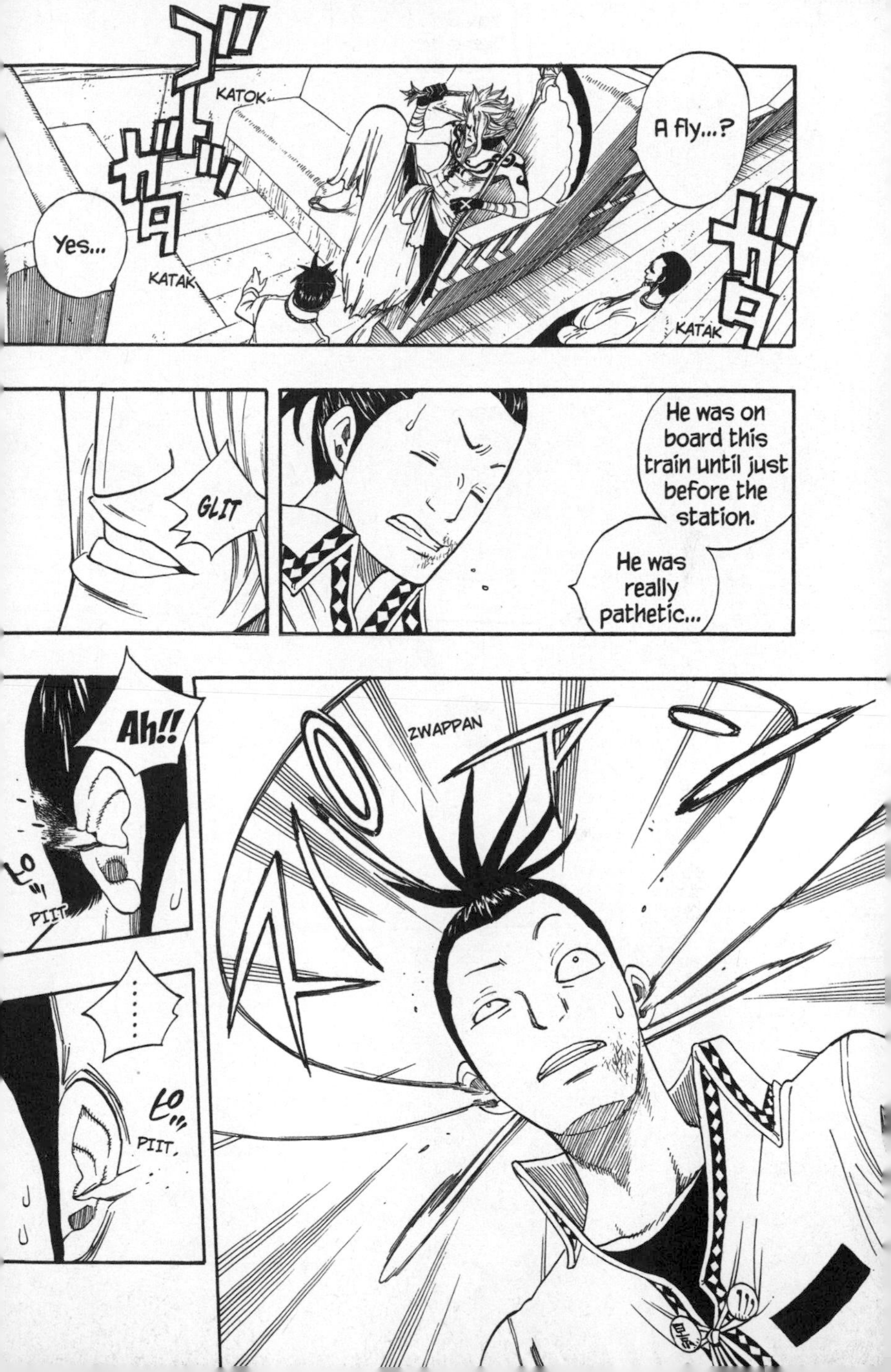
A fly...?
KATAK
KATOK
Yes...
KATAK
He was on board this train until just before the station.
He was really pathetic...
GLIT
ZWAPPAN
Ah!!
PIIT
......
PIIT.

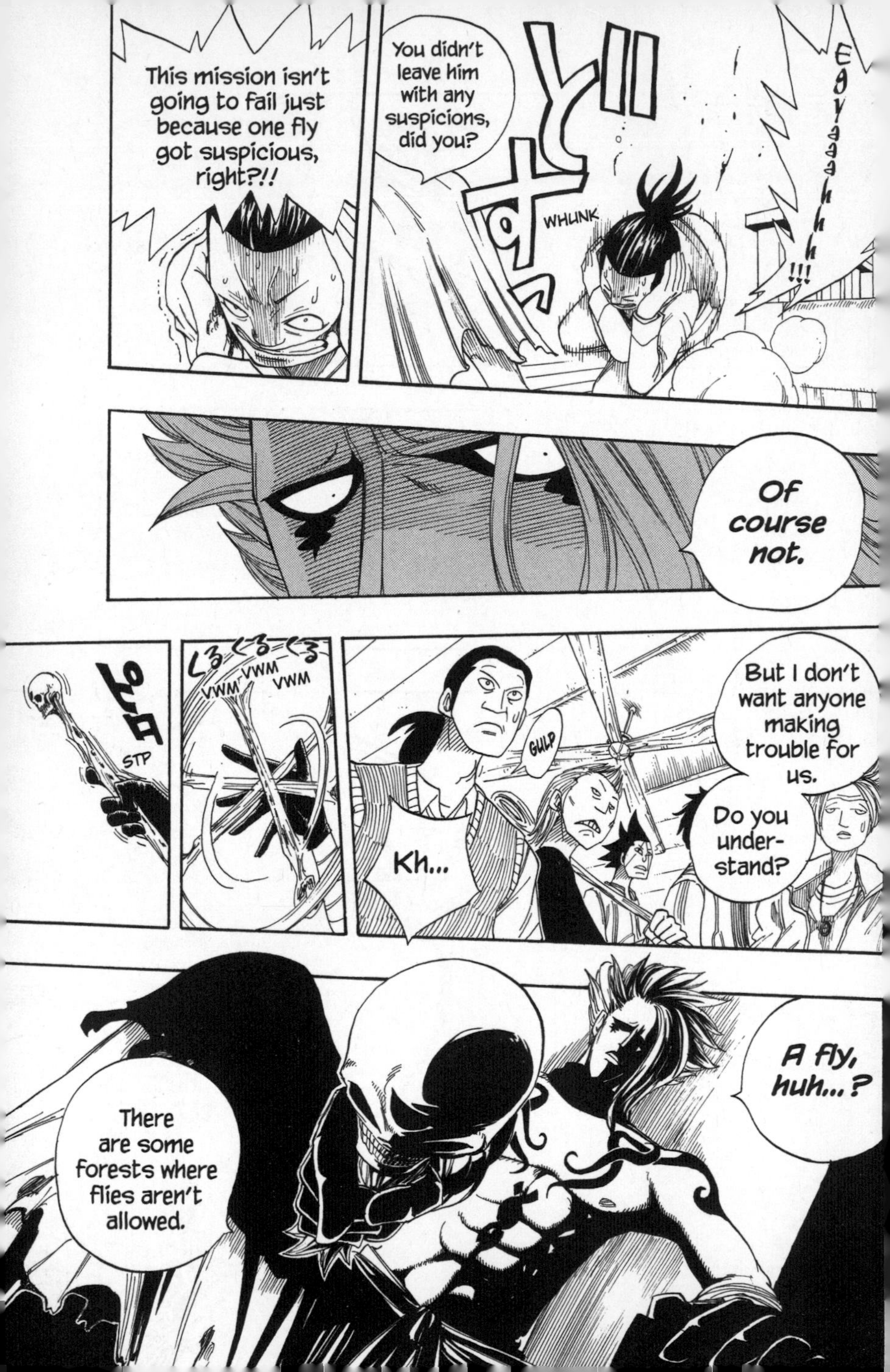
Egyaaahhh!!!
WHUNK
You didn't leave him with any suspicions, did you?
This mission isn't going to fail just because one fly got suspicious, right?!!
Of course not.
But I don't want anyone making trouble for us.
Do you understand?
GULP
Kh...
くるくるくる
VWM VWM VWM
STP
A fly, huh...?
There are some forests where flies aren't allowed.

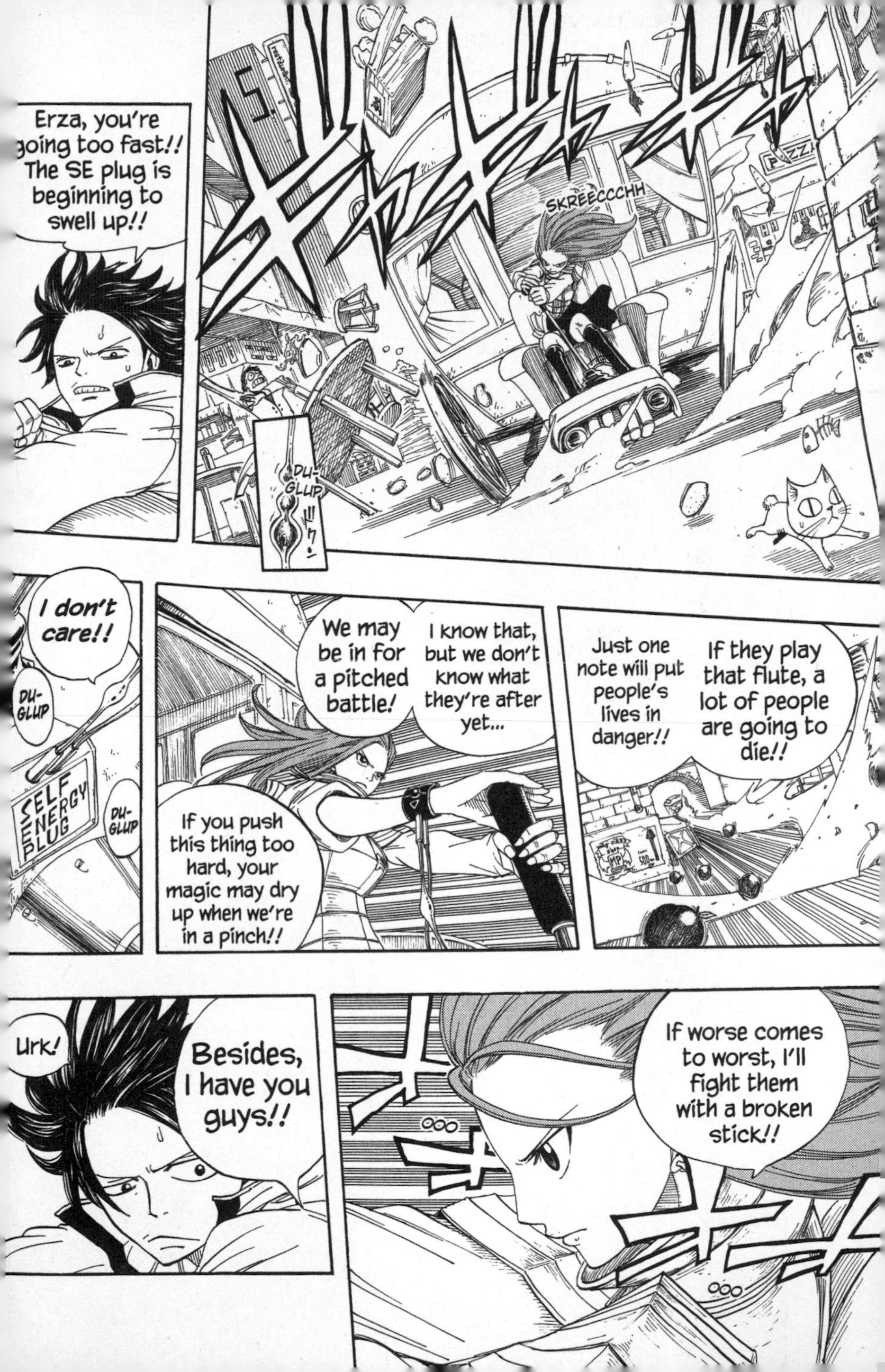

SKREECCCHH
DU-GLUP
Erza, you're going too fast!! The SE plug is beginning to swell up!!
If they play that flute, a lot of people are going to die!!
Just one note will put people's lives in danger!!
I know that, but we don't know what they're after yet...
We may be in for a pitched battle!
If you push this thing too hard, your magic may dry up when we're in a pinch!!
I don't care!!
DU-GLUP
SELF ENERGY PLUG
DU-GLUP
If worse comes to worst, I'll fight them with a broken stick!!
Besides, I have you guys!!
Urk!

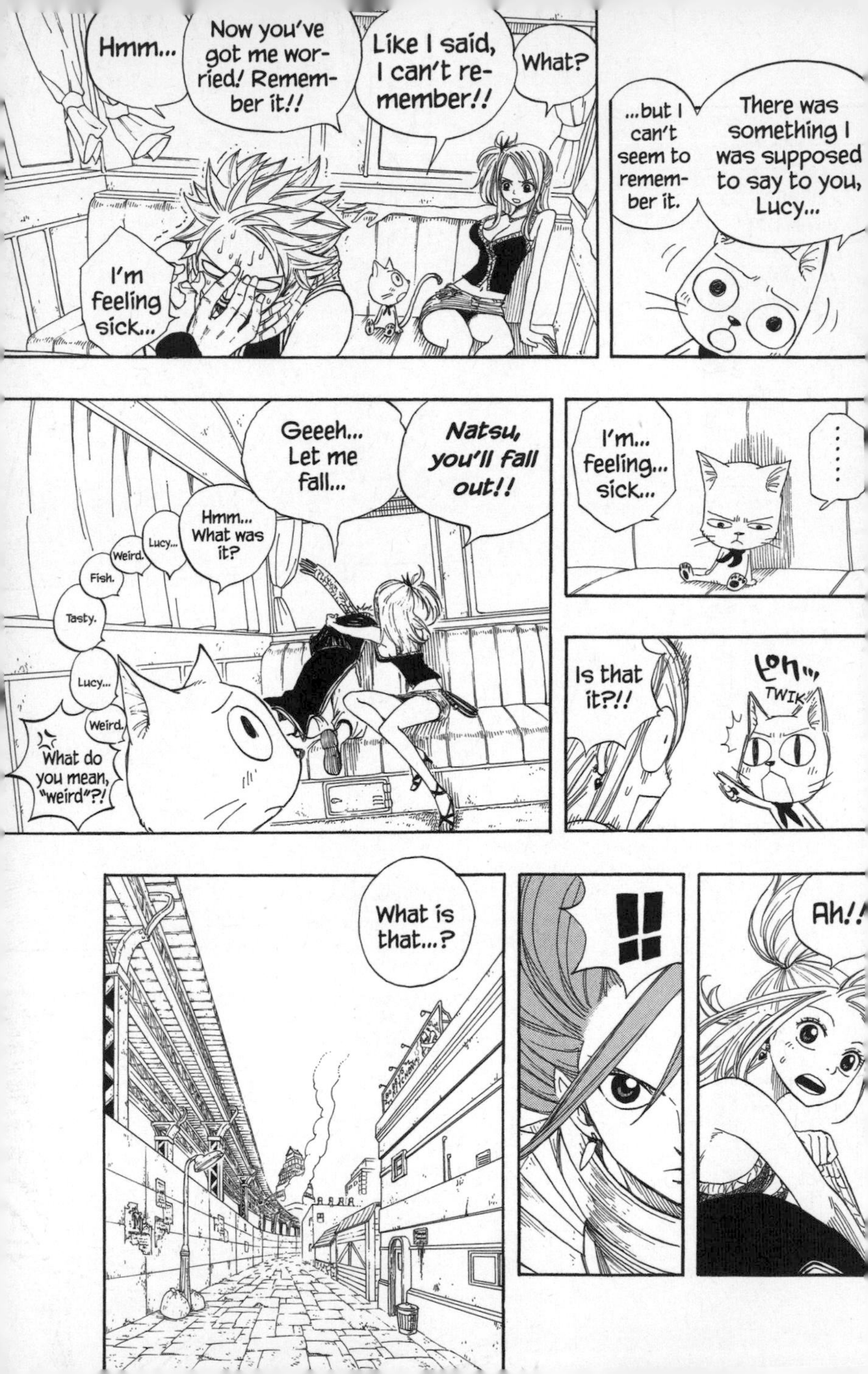
There was something I was supposed to say to you, Lucy...
...but I can't seem to remember it.
What?
Like I said, I can't remember!!
Now you've got me worried! Remember it!!
Hmm...
I'm feeling sick...
......
I'm... feeling... sick...
TWIK
Is that it?!!
Natsu, you'll fall out!!
Geeeh... Let me fall...
Hmm... What was it?
Lucy...
Weird.
Fish.
Tasty.
Lucy...
Weird.
What do you mean, "weird"?!
Ah!!
!!
What is that...?

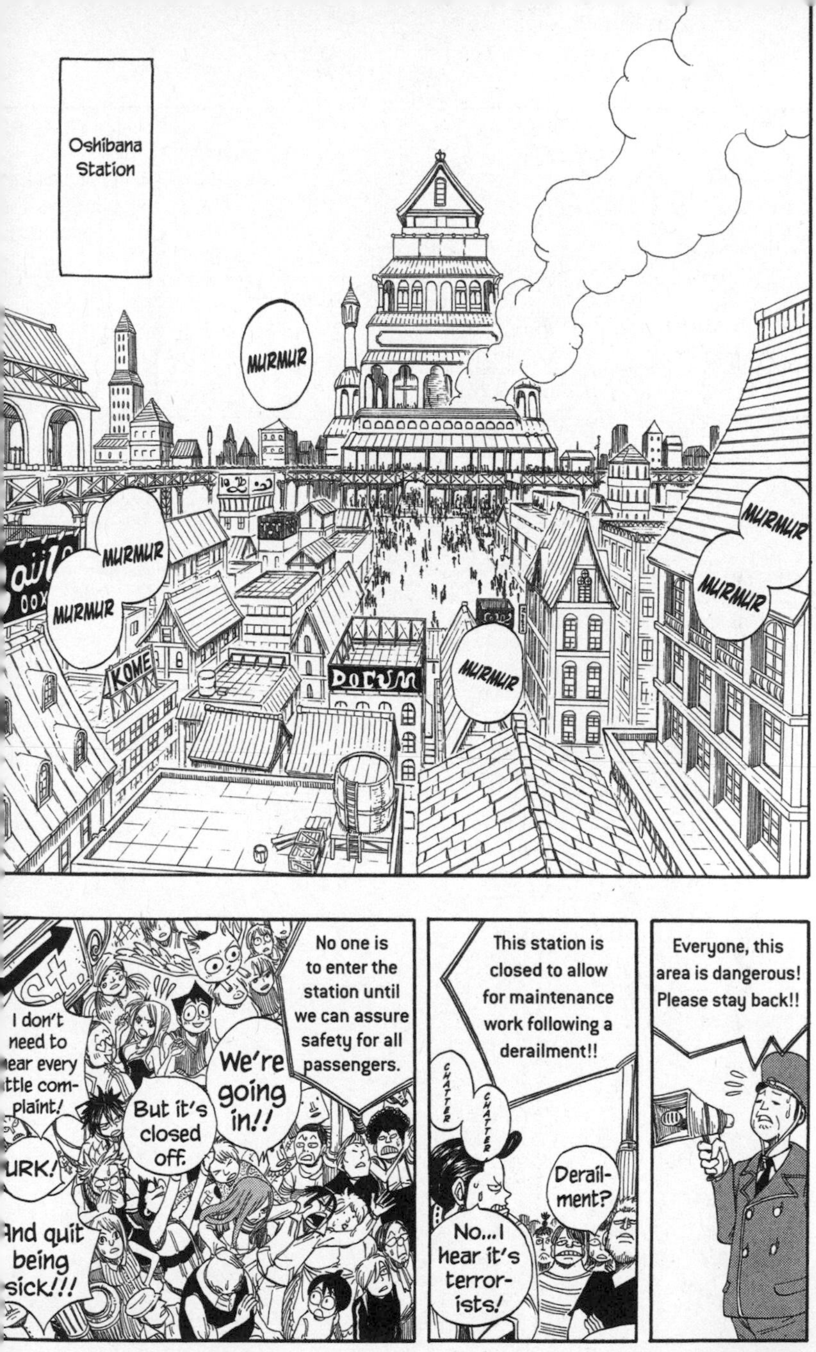
Oshibana Station
MURMUR
MURMUR
MURMUR
MURMUR
MURMUR
MURMUR
Everyone, this area is dangerous! Please stay back!!
This station is closed to allow for maintenance work following a derailment!!
CHATTER
CHATTER
Derail-ment?
No...I hear it's terror-ists!
No one is to enter the station until we can assure safety for all passengers.
We're going in!!
But it's closed off.
I don't need to ear every ttle com-plaint!
RK!
nd quit being sick!!!

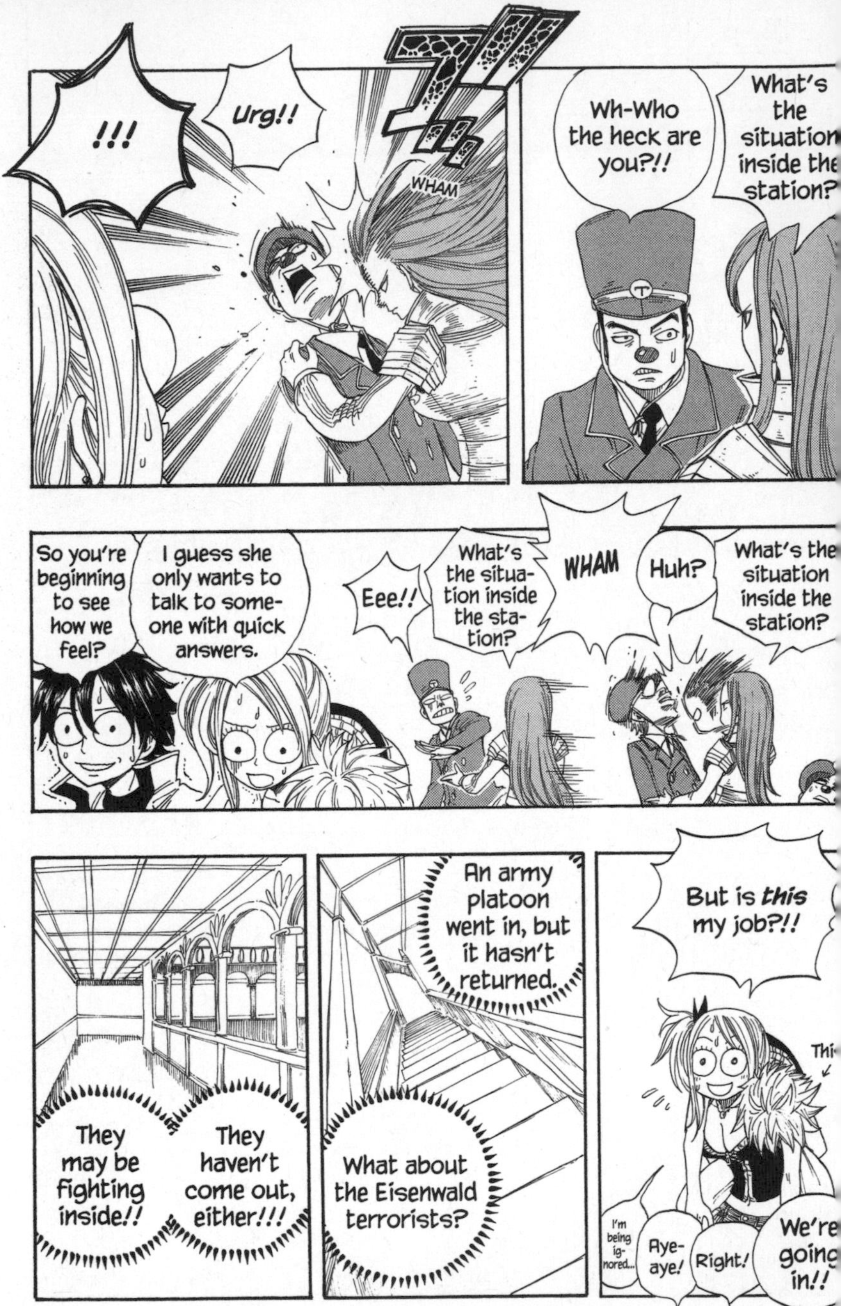
What's the situation inside the station?
Wh-Who the heck are you?!!
WHAM
Urg!!
!!!
What's the situation inside the station?
Huh?
WHAM
What's the situation inside the station?
Eee!!
I guess she only wants to talk to someone with quick answers.
So you're beginning to see how we feel?
But is *this* my job?!!
We're going in!!
Right!
Aye-aye!
I'm being ignored...
An army platoon went in, but it hasn't returned.
What about the Eisenwald terrorists?
They haven't come out, either!!!
They may be fighting inside!!

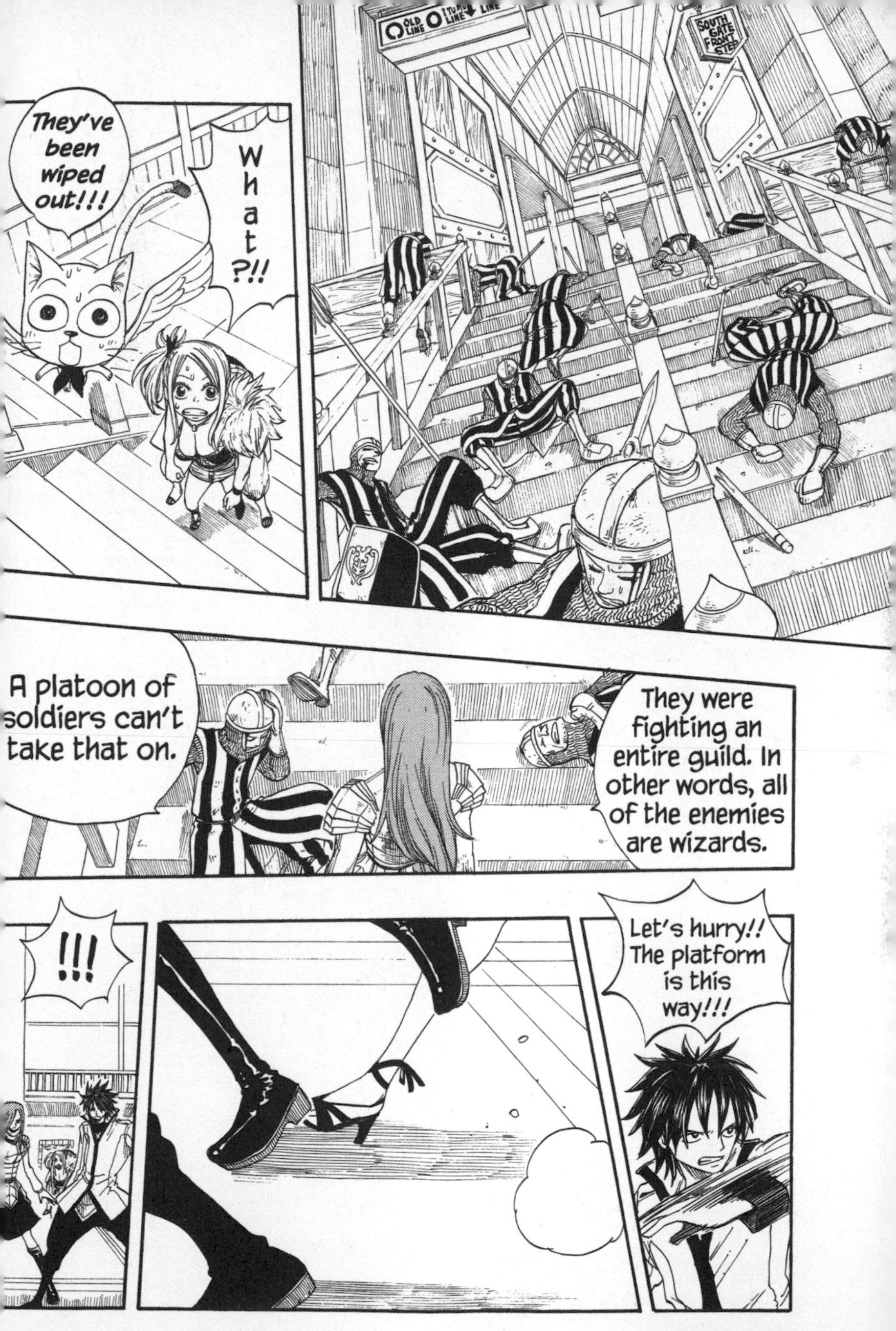
SOUTH GATE FRONT STEP
OLD LINE
What?!!
They've been wiped out!!!
They were fighting an entire guild. In other words, all of the enemies are wizards.
A platoon of soldiers can't take that on.
Let's hurry!! The platform is this way!!!
!!!

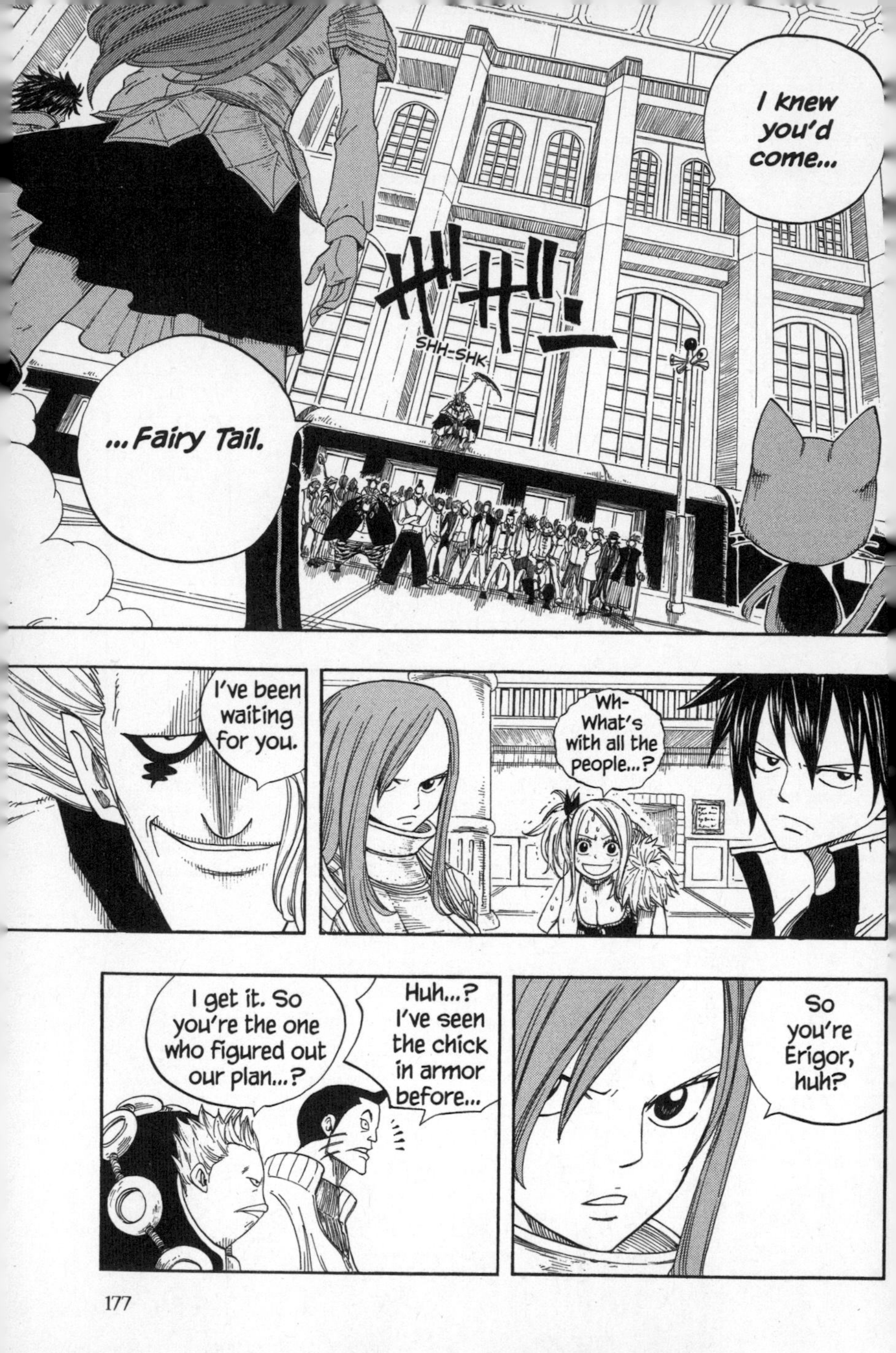
I knew you'd come...
SHH-SHK
...Fairy Tail.
Wh- What's with all the people...?
I've been waiting for you.
So you're Erigor, huh?
Huh...? I've seen the chick in armor before...
I get it. So you're the one who figured out our plan...?

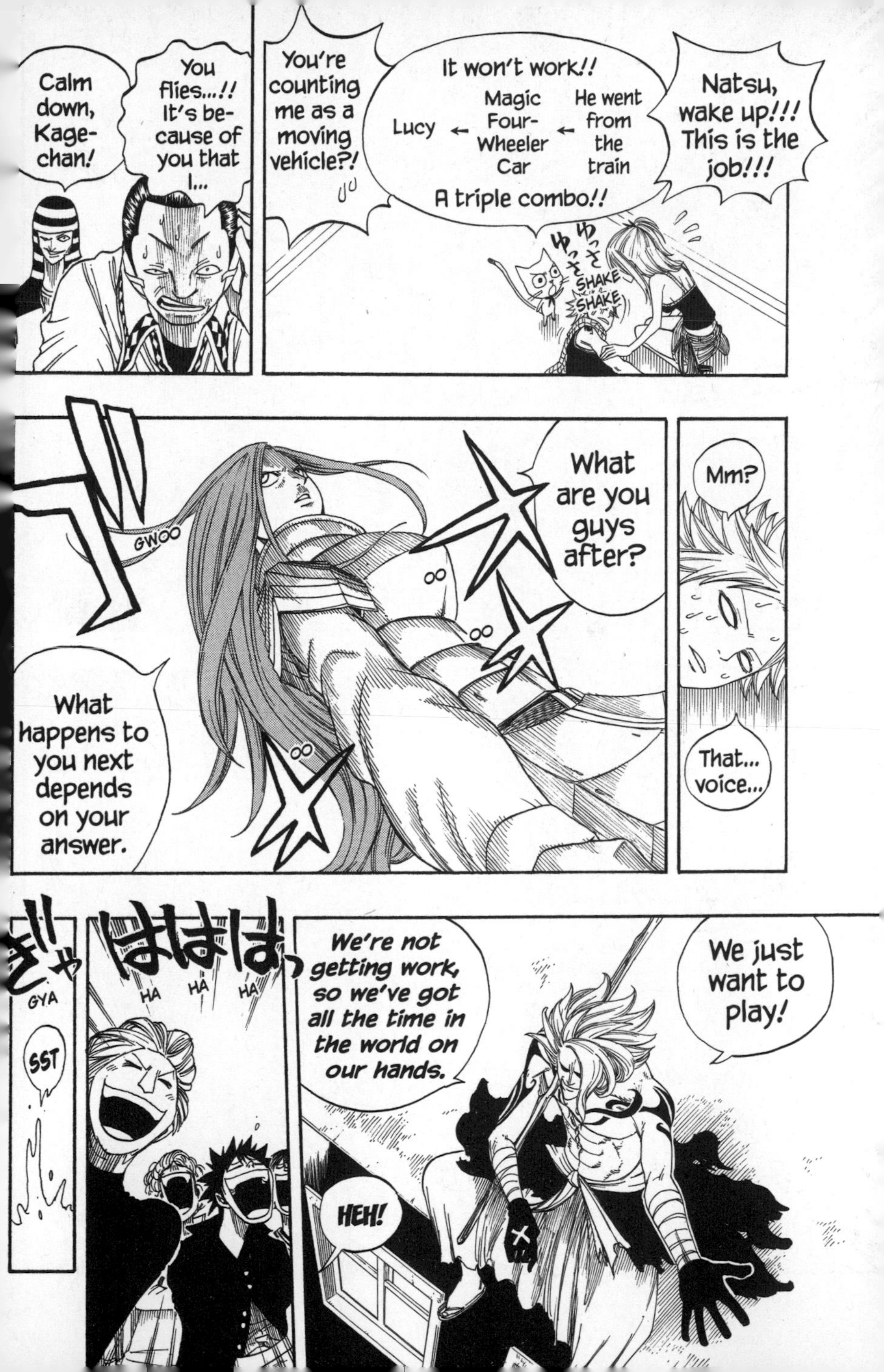

Natsu, wake up!!! This is the job!!!
It won't work!!
Lucy ← Magic Four-Wheeler Car ← He went from the train
A triple combo!!
You're counting me as a moving vehicle?!
ゆっさ ゆっさ
SHAKE SHAKE
You flies...!! It's be-cause of you that I...
Calm down, Kage-chan!
Mm?
That... voice...
What are you guys after?
GWOO
What happens to you next depends on your answer.
We just want to play!
We're not getting work, so we've got all the time in the world on our hands.
HEH!
ははは
HA HA HA
ぎゃ
GYA
SST

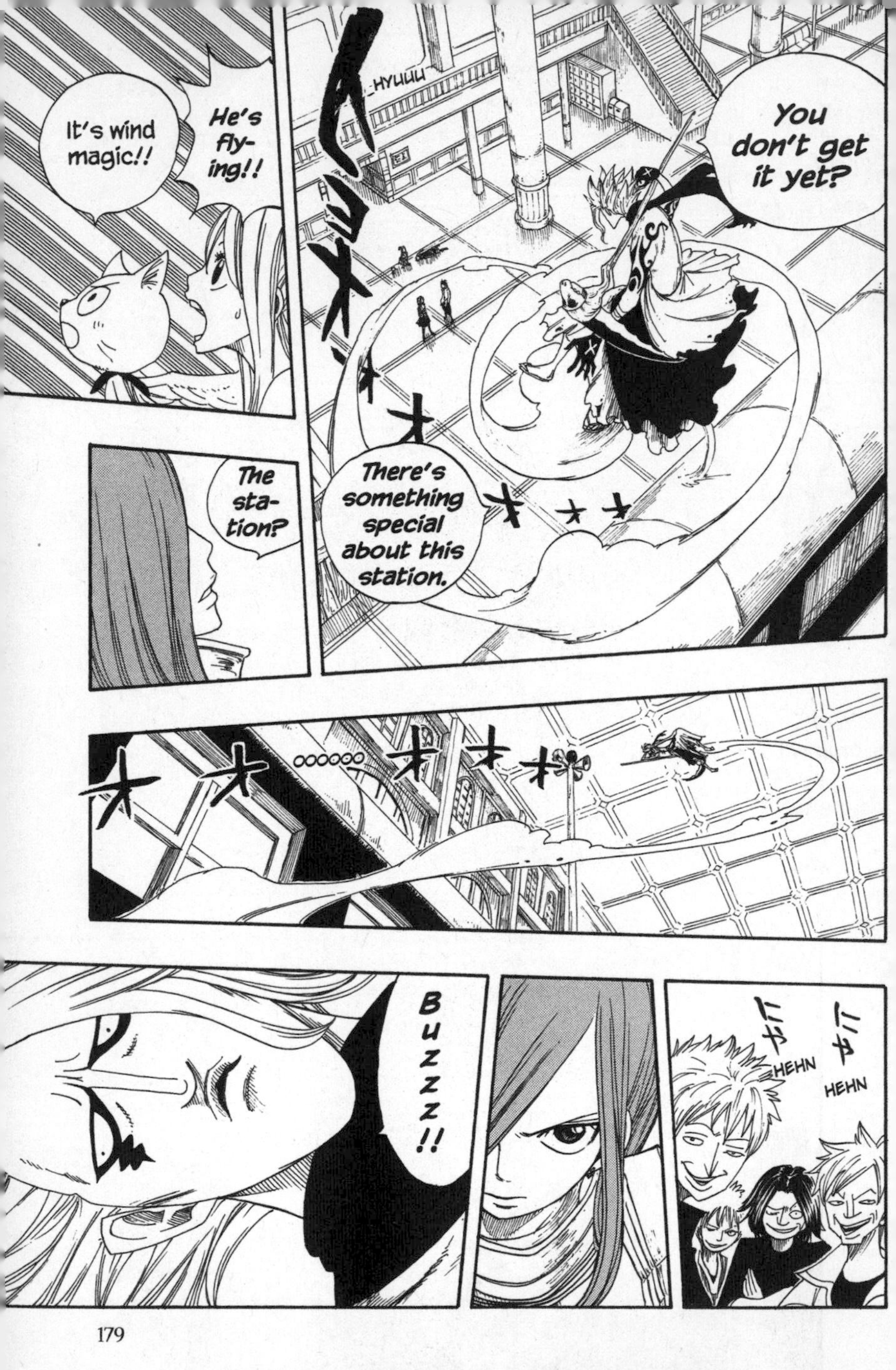
HYUUU
You don't get it yet?
There's something special about this station.
He's flying!!
It's wind magic!!
The station?
oooooo
HEHN
HEHN
Buzzz!!

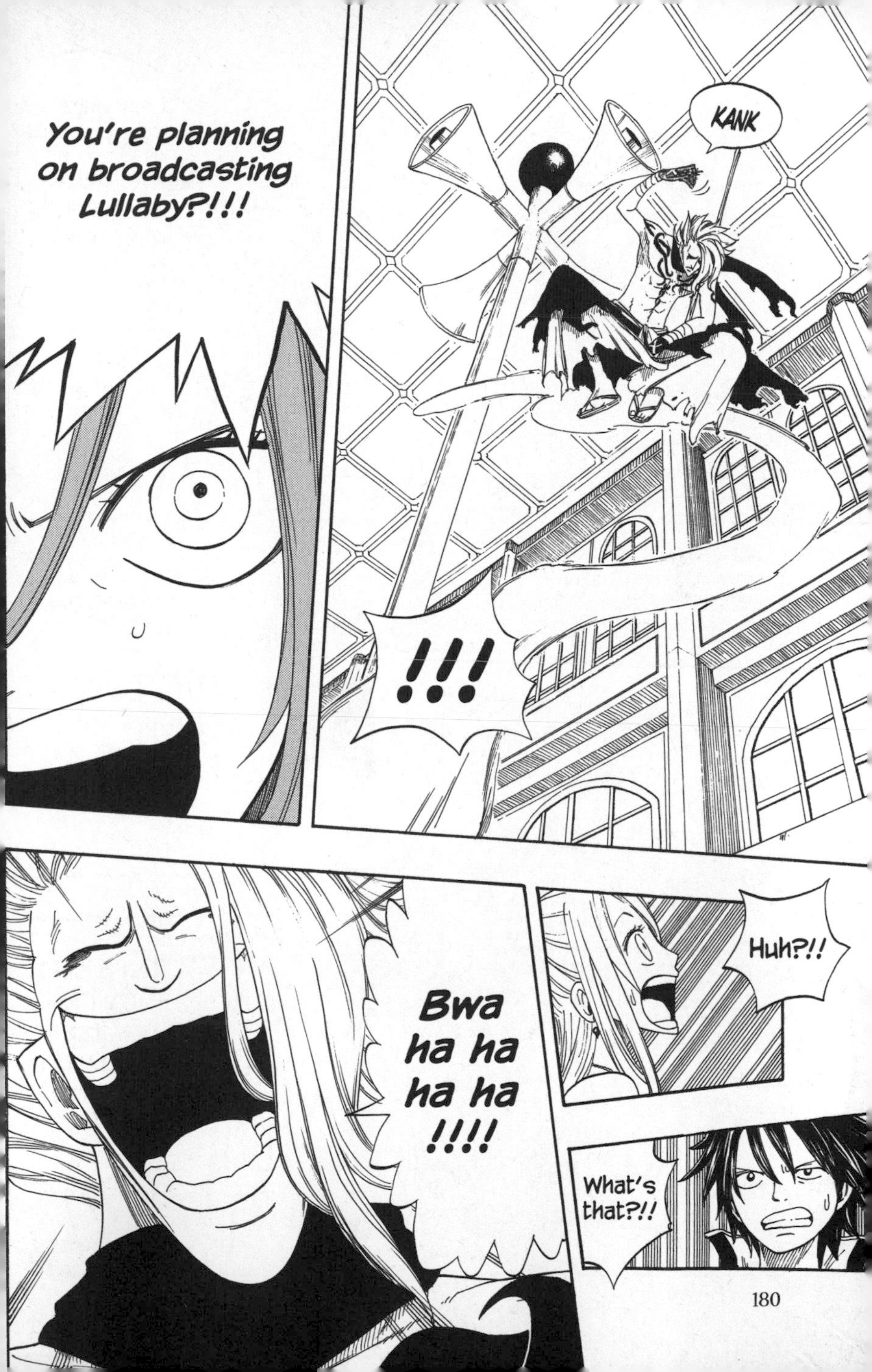
KANK
!!!
You're planning on broadcasting Lullaby?!!!
Huh?!!
What's that?!!
Bwa ha ha ha ha !!!!

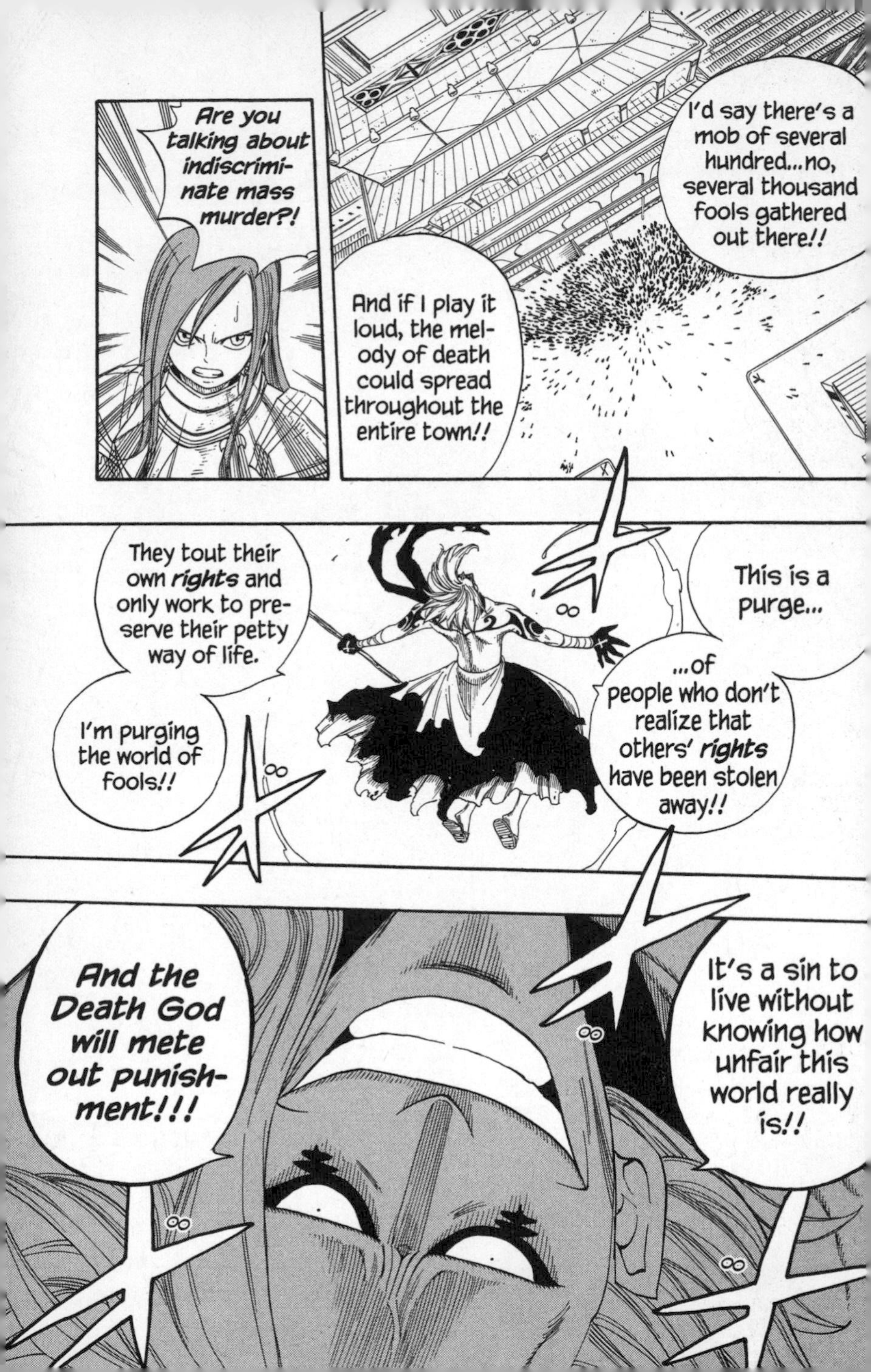
I'd say there's a mob of several hundred...no, several thousand fools gathered out there!!
And if I play it loud, the melody of death could spread throughout the entire town!!
Are you talking about indiscriminate mass murder?!
This is a purge...
...of people who don't realize that others' *rights* have been stolen away!!
They tout their own *rights* and only work to preserve their petty way of life.
I'm purging the world of fools!!
It's a sin to live without knowing how unfair this world really is!!
And the Death God will mete out punishment!!!

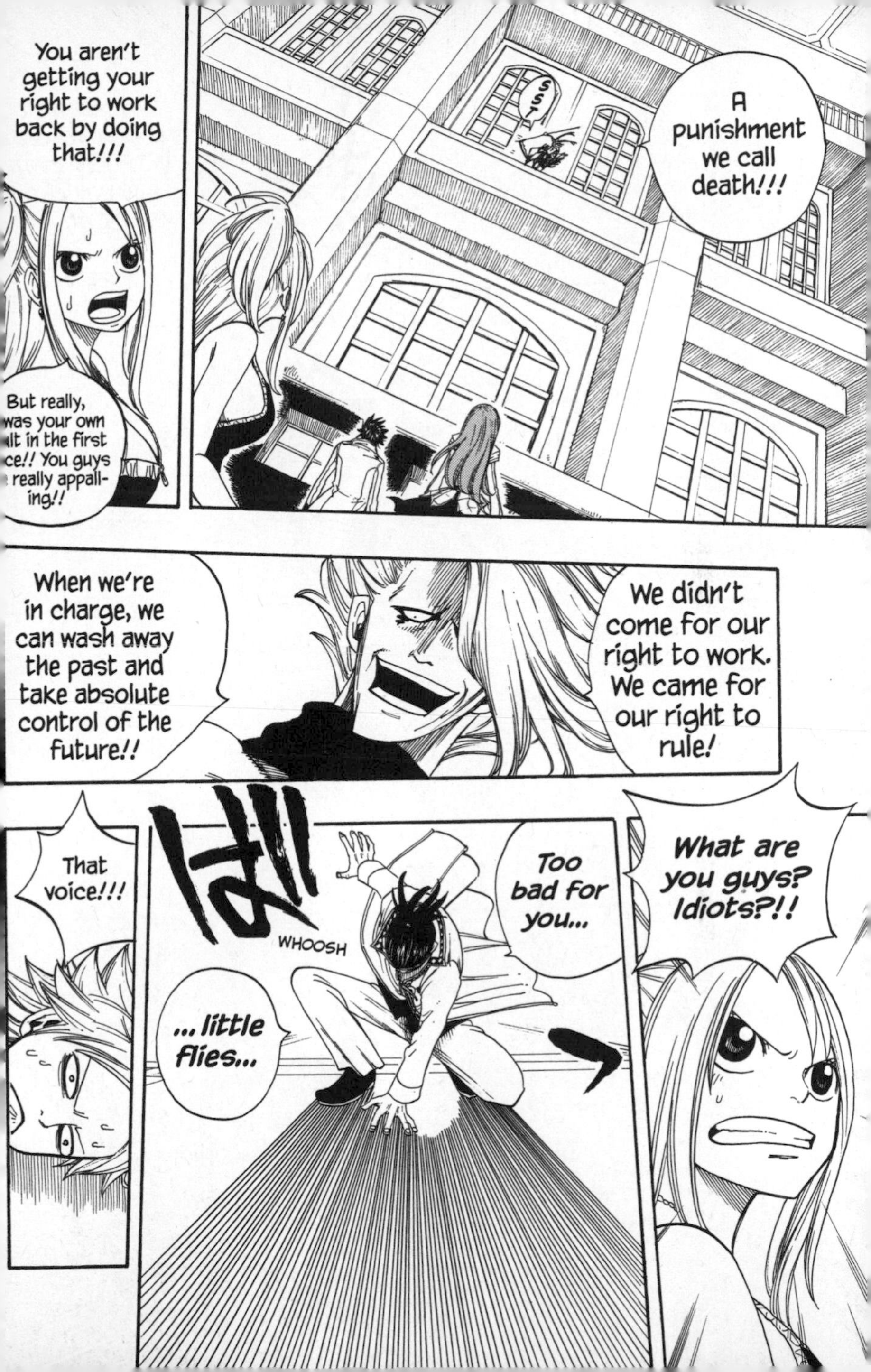
A punishment we call death!!!
You aren't getting your right to work back by doing that!!!
But really, was your own lt in the first ce!! You guys really appall-ing!!
We didn't come for our right to work. We came for our right to rule!
When we're in charge, we can wash away the past and take absolute control of the future!!
What are you guys? Idiots?!!
Too bad for you...
...little flies...
WHOOSH
That voice!!!

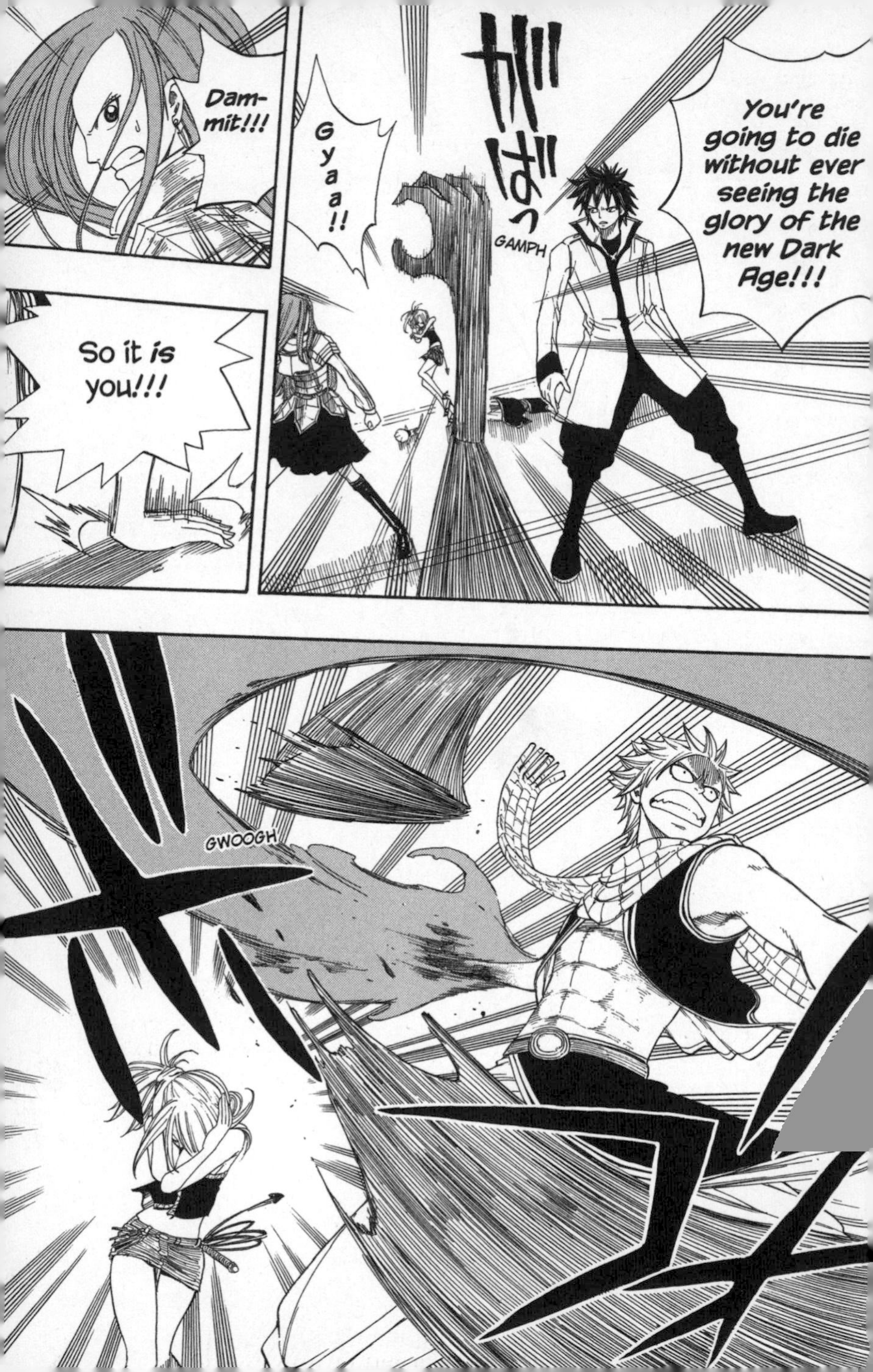
You're going to die without ever seeing the glory of the new Dark Age!!!
がばっ
GAMPH
Gyaa!!
Dam-mit!!!
So it is you!!!
GWOOGH

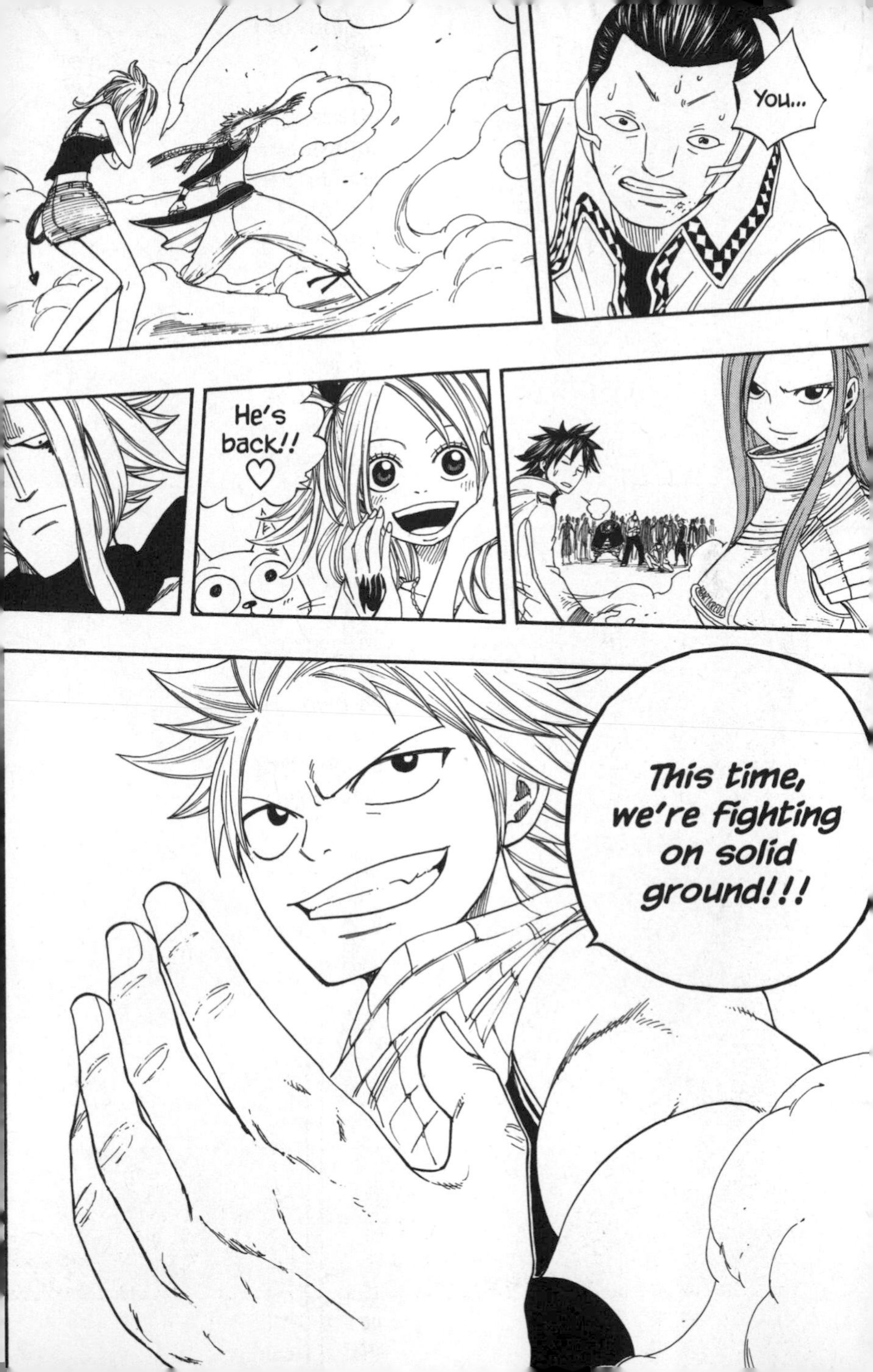
You...
He's back!! ♡
This time, we're fighting on solid ground!!!

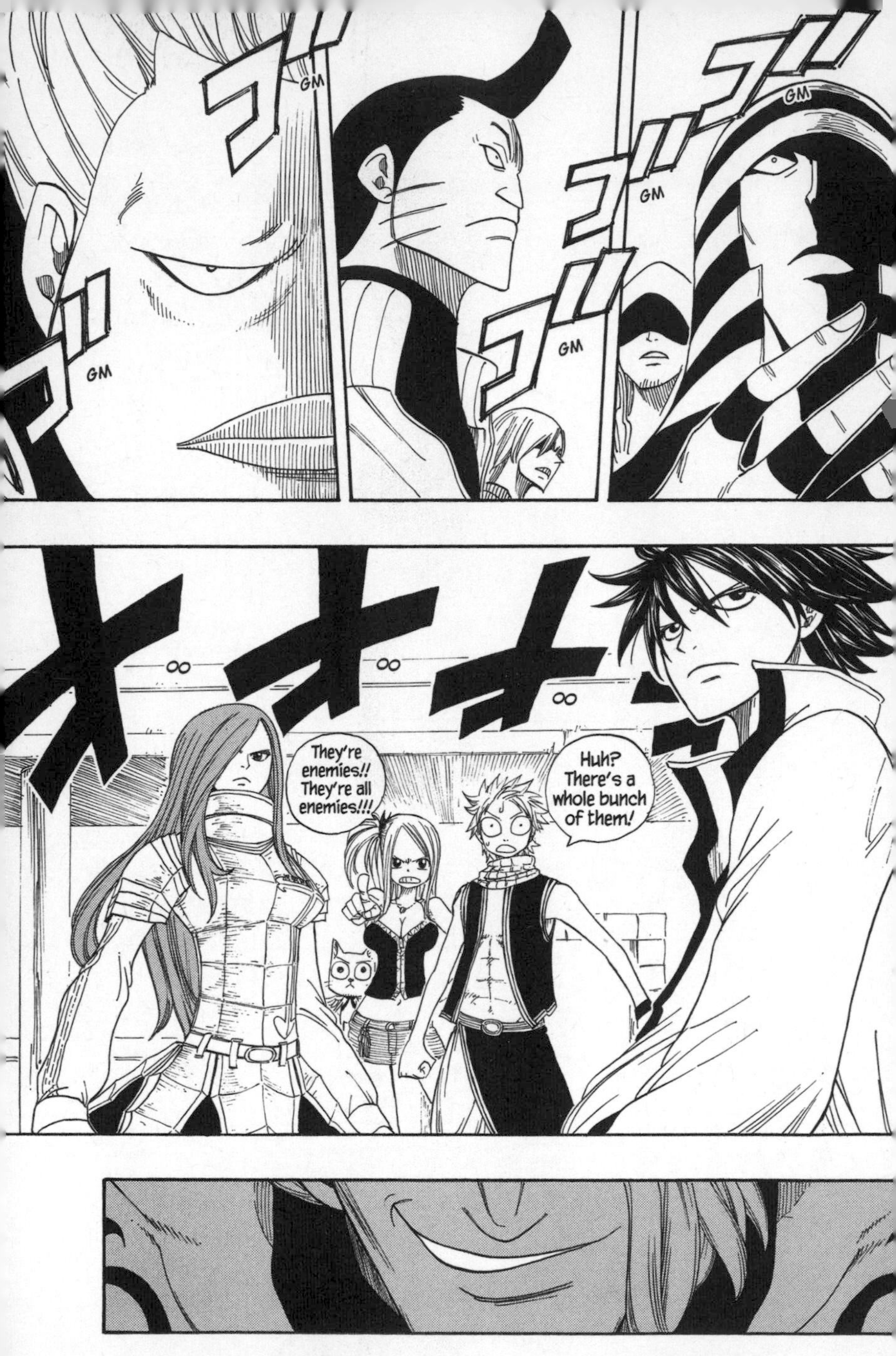
GM
GM
GM
GM
GM
Huh? There's a whole bunch of them!
They're enemies!! They're all enemies!!!

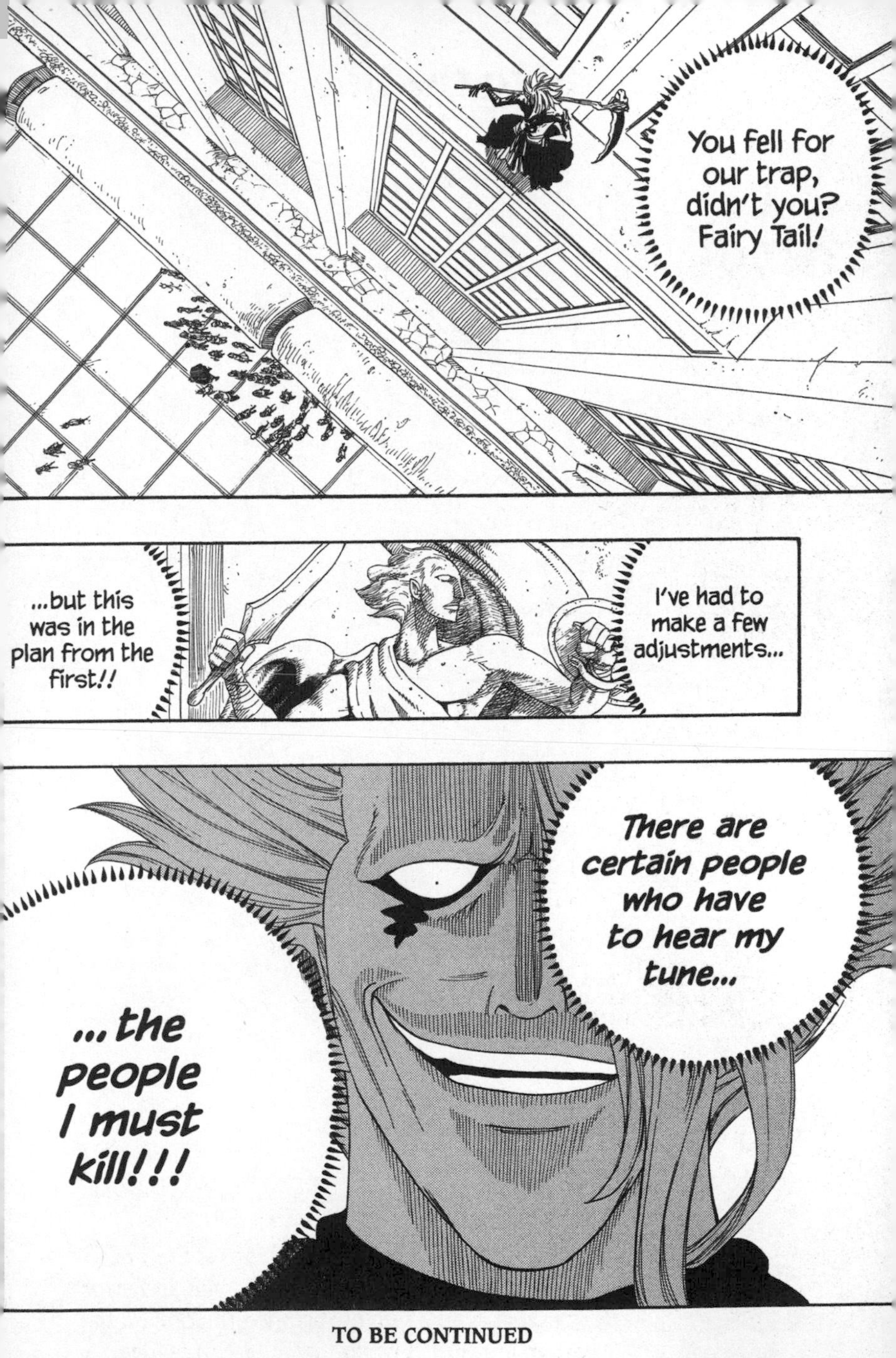
You fell for our trap, didn't you? Fairy Tail!
I've had to make a few adjustments...
...but this was in the plan from the first!!
There are certain people who have to hear my tune...
...the people I must kill!!!

TO BE CONTINUED

The Road to the Fairy Tail Mark

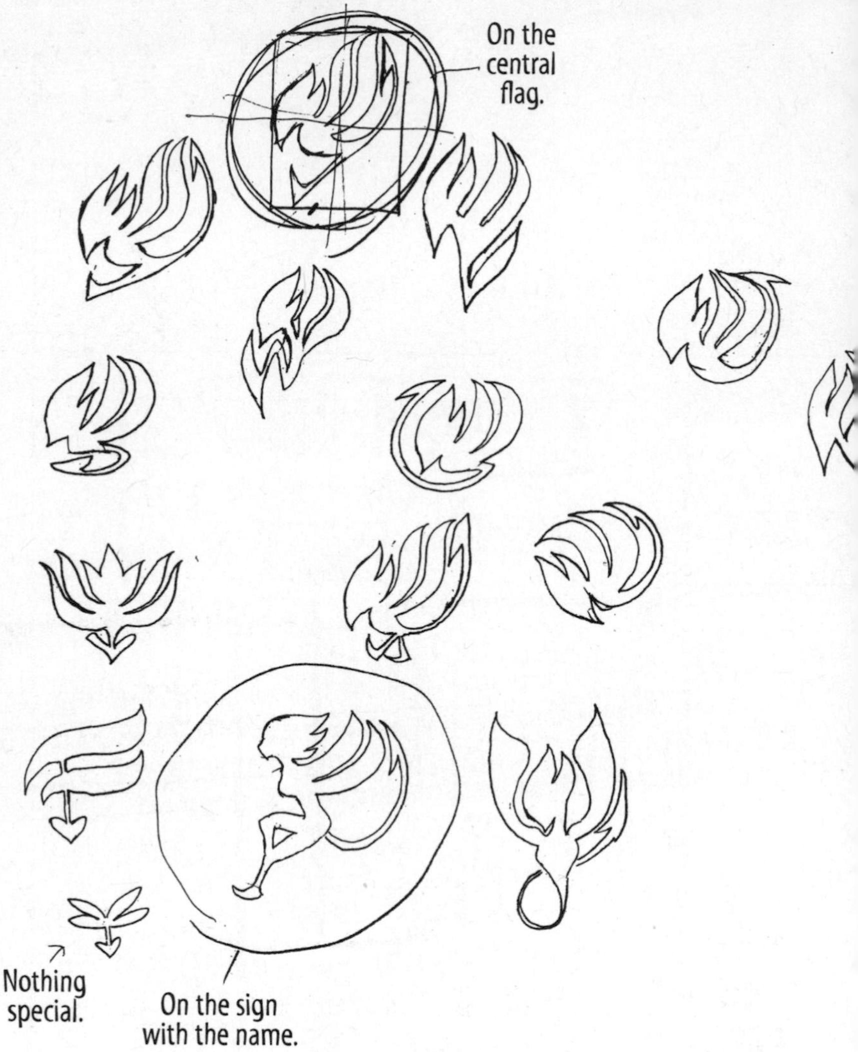
On the central flag.
Nothing special.
On the sign with the name.

The one in the circle at the very top is the final approved design. There was a lot of trial and error to get to that point, huh? I included the one on the bottom left, but it wasn't ever a serious idea.

This Is the Place Where Fairy Tail Is Made!!!

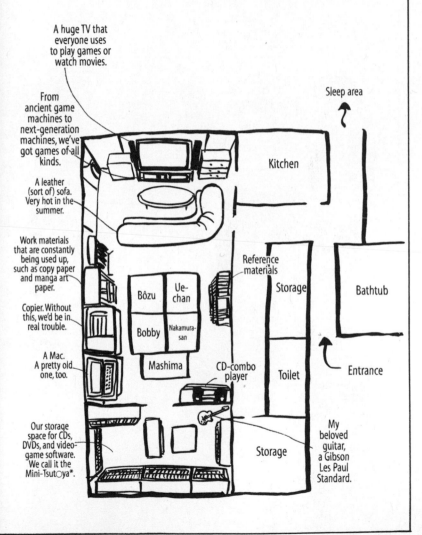

A huge TV that everyone uses to play games or watch movies.

From ancient game machines to next-generation machines, we've got games of all kinds.

A leather (sort of) sofa. Very hot in the summer.

Work materials that are constantly being used up, such as copy paper and manga art paper.

Copier. Without this, we'd be in real trouble.

A Mac. A pretty old one, too.

Our storage space for CDs, DVDs, and video-game software. We call it the Mini-Tsut○ya*.

Sleep area

Kitchen

Reference materials

Storage

Bathtub

Bôzu

Ue-chan

Bobby

Nakamura-san

Mashima

CD-combo player

Storage

Toilet

Entrance

My beloved guitar, a Gibson Les Paul Standard.

*Tsutaya is a large Japanese music and video rental chain.

This Is the Fairy Tail Staff!!!

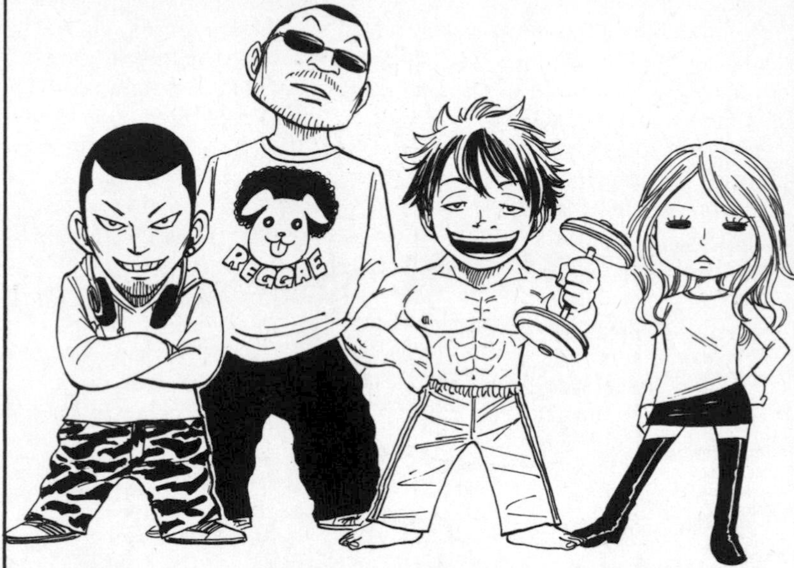
REGGAE

Bôzu
(At first glance, he looks like a bad guy.)

Bobby
(At first glance, low-ranking Yakuza punk.)

Ue-chan
(At first glance, muscles.)

Nakamura-san
(At first glance, you'd think she parties late into the night.)

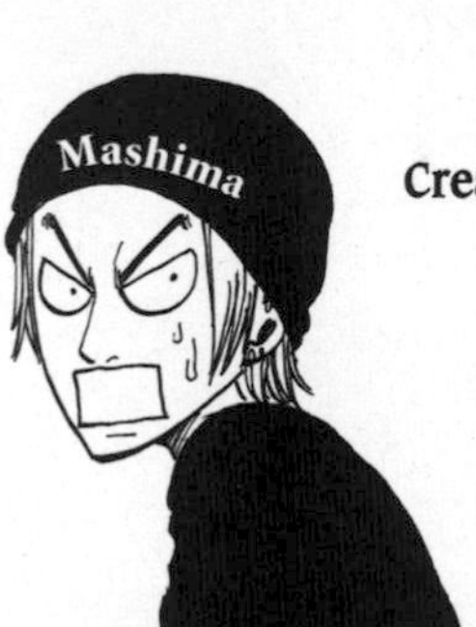
Mashima

Creator (Originally a street punk.)

When people talk about this work, they always seem to say that it's a punk fantasy, but...Maybe it's because the people making it are punks and the work itself is fantasy...? Could that be it? But really, we're all great people!

About the Naming of the Characters

The main character is named Natsu. This is the truth. The name of my last main character was Haru (Japanese for "spring"), and after Haru comes Natsu (Japanese for "summer"). Sorry. Happy was originally named Freyr. It's the name of a Norse god. That was too much for him, so I changed it to something more appropriate. Lucy is from a Beatles song. At the time I decided to name her, the song was running through my mind. I don't remember exactly what I was thinking when I named Makarov, but I recall wanting something that sounded vaguely Russian. Mirajane is the name of a character I came to know in an online game. I don't remember where I got Gray. (Ha ha!) The name of Erza came from the heroine of my ancient short story "Fairy Tale," Eru. Loke is named after the Norse god. I wanted a somewhat cute name for the Elfman character, so I came up with that name. Cana comes from the arcana of tarot cards. Hmm. Looking this over, I get the feeling that there are a lot of names I didn't think too hard about. By the way, this image of Lucy was a rejected idea from before the series was launched. I don't remember why I drew it, but it came out of a drawer of old drawings, and I thought I'd include it as a bonus.

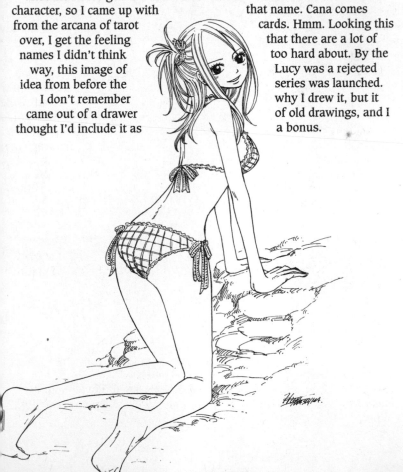

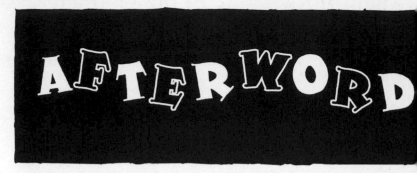

AFTERWORD

The second volume. In what seems like no time at all, we have the second volume. Boy, that was fast! What with one thing and another, I' been pretty busy lately, and the time just seems to be flying by. It only seems like a little while back that I started this series, and we're already publishing the second volume! At this pace, I'll be releasing the tenth volume in no time flat.... Naw, just kidding. I don't know if it'll even be popular enough to last that long, and I decided a while ago to stop stressing over the future. That's right, speaking of the future, I haven't given any thought to how this series is going to turn out! (Ha ha!) Othe artists and editors have commented, "Your universe looks like it's going to expand to an amazing size, huh?" But to tell the truth, I haven't real thought about it. What should I do...? Series currently in planning stag I've been simply enjoying myself for such a long time, I really should ge serious!! But once I say that, I forget about the future and get absorbed in drawing pages again. Because of that, I wonder myself what's going happen next, and without quite knowing, I just keep on going. But... that's all right for now.

And for that reason, I'm looking for letters from you fans. You can say, "I want Natsu to take on this kind of job!" Or, "I'd like to see this kind of stuff in the bonus pages of the graphic novel!" Now accepting suggestions.

Kodansha Comics
451 Park Ave. South, 7th Floor
New York, NY 10016
publicity@kodanshacomics.com

Any letters sent to this address will definitely get to me personally. Please write! And so... On to the third volume!! It will come out, right? Volume 3...

About the Creator

HIRO MASHIMA was born May 3, 1977, in Nagano Prefecture. His series *Rave Master* has made him one of the most popular manga artists in America. *Fairy Tail*, currently being serialized in *Weekly Shônen Magazine*, is his latest creation.

Translation Notes

Japanese is a tricky language for most Westerners, and translation is often more art than science. For your edification and reading pleasure, here are notes on some of the places where we could have gone in a different direction in our translation of the work, or where a Japanese cultural reference is used.

General Notes:
Wizard

In the original Japanese version of *Fairy Tail*, you'll find panels in which the English word "wizard" is part of the original illustration. So this translation has taken that as its inspiration and translated the word *madōshi* as "wizard." But *madōshi*'s meaning is similar to certain Japanese words that have been borrowed by the English language, such as *judo* (the soft way) and *kendo* (the way of the sword). *Madō* is the way of magic, and *madōshi* are those who follow the way of magic. So although the word "wizard" is used in the original dialogue, a Japanese reader would be likely to think not of traditional Western wizards such as Merlin or Gandalf, but of martial artists.

Names

Hiro Mashima has graciously agreed to provide official English spellings for just about all the characters in *Fairy Tail*. Because this version of *Fairy Tail* is the first publication of most of these spellings, there will inevitably be differences between these spellings and some of the fan interpretations that may have spread throughout the Web or in other fan circles. Rest assured that the spellings contained in this book are the spellings that Mashima-sensei wanted for *Fairy Tail*.

Greasy foods, page 7

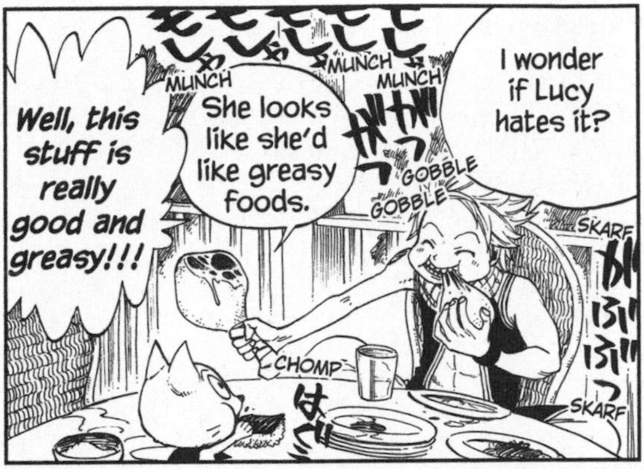
I wonder if Lucy hates it?
MUNCH
MUNCH
She looks like she'd like greasy foods.
MUNCH
Well, this stuff is really good and greasy!!!
GOBBLE
GOBBLE
SKARF
SKARF
CHOMP

The Japanese diet is famous for its low fat content, but there are many native Japanese foods that are just as artery-clogging and delicious as any famously fatty Western dish. Meats, fried foods, and other foods with high fat and oil content are called *aburakkoi*. Aside from the standard "greasy" foods like fatty pork or beef, or the cooked-in-oil foods such as tempura, the entire class of "rich" foods with a high fat or butter content are also described as *aburakkoi*. Because of its fattening reputation, women are supposed to avoid *aburakkoi* food, but the sweet taste of rich foods is hard for anybody to avoid.

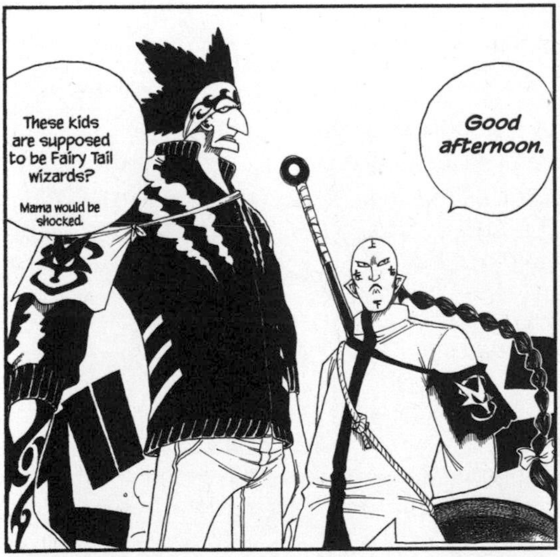
Good afternoon.
These kids are supposed to be Fairy Tail wizards?
Mama would be shocked.

Face markings, page 36

The smaller of the two Vanish Brothers is dressed in the classic style of a Chinese Buddhist monk. The markings on his face, while seeming to hold deep meanings, actually only say "up" on his forehead, "down" on his chin, and "right" and "left" for his right and left cheeks, respectively.

Good afternoon, page 36

The monk-style Vanish Brother actually used the English, "Good afternoon," in his greeting to Natsu and the team. A peculiar aspect of his speech is that he often peppers it with English words (despite his distinct Chinese appearance). Since only a small minority of readers of this translation would be able to understand the Japanese equivalents of these words (let alone any other language), I decided to leave the English in English and use other ways to put across the pretentiousness of his character.

Mama, page 36

Who is the spiky-haired Vanish Brother talking about when he constantly refers to "Mama"? We don't know yet. Hopefully that question will be answered during the course of *Fairy Tail's* development as a series.

Bodybuilding, page 48

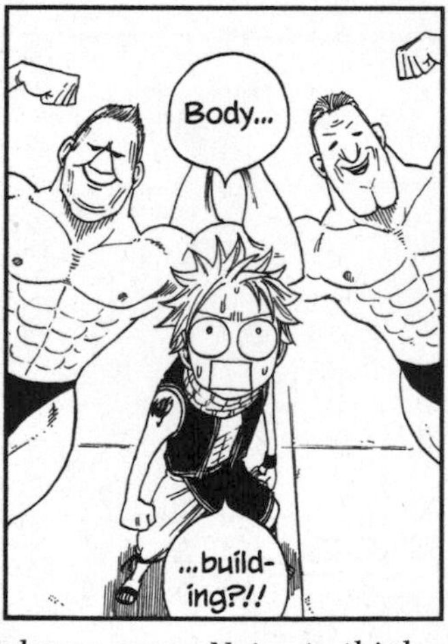
Body...
...build-ing?!!

When describing what he considered to be the main weakness of wizards, the monk-style Vanish Brother used the Japanese word *nikutai*. When taken as a whole, *nikutai* simply means "body" in the sense of a flesh-and-blood body. But the Japanese word is made up of two kanji, one that means "muscles" and another kanji which alone also means "body." Natsu, glomming on to the "muscle" meaning, thought of bodybuilders; however, just hearing the word "body" in English wouldn't give the impression of bodybuilding. So I arranged the translation so that the Vanish Brothers' dialogue causes Natsu to think of "bodybuilders" without changing the meaning of either the Vanish Brothers' lines or Natsu's.

Didn't croak, page 54

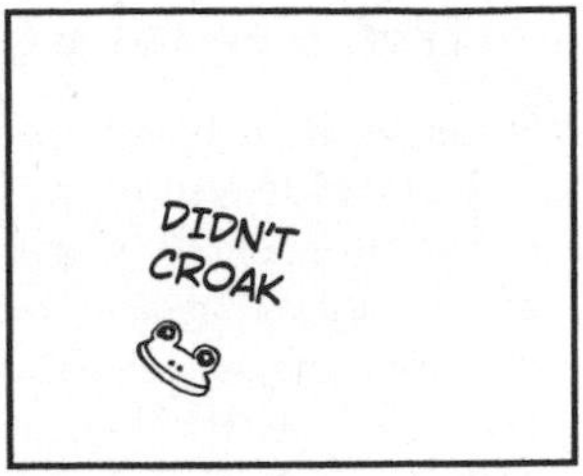
DIDN'T CROAK

The actual sound effect, *kero*, is the sound of someone bouncing back from what one would think of as a severe blow. However, it is very close in sound to *gero*, which is, to the Japanese, the sound that a frog makes. Unfortunately, "ribbit" does not have a "bouncing back" meaning in English, but since "to croak" means both "to make a sound like a frog" and "to die," that became the basis for the translation of the pun on this page.

End a sentence with "-*kani*," page 74

Many manga and anime fans are familiar with characters who end their sentences with odd syllables. The eternally popular Lum of Rumiko Takahashi's *Urusei Yatsura* manga always ended her sentences with "-*cha*." And most depictions of crabs on TV, picture books, or other media will have the crab end its sentences with "-*kani*" (a sound considered especially cute). It is so much a Japanese custom, that it's almost expected for any crab characters to end their sentences that way. So when Cancer ends his sentences with "-*ebi*" ("shrimp"), it comes as a great shock to Happy.

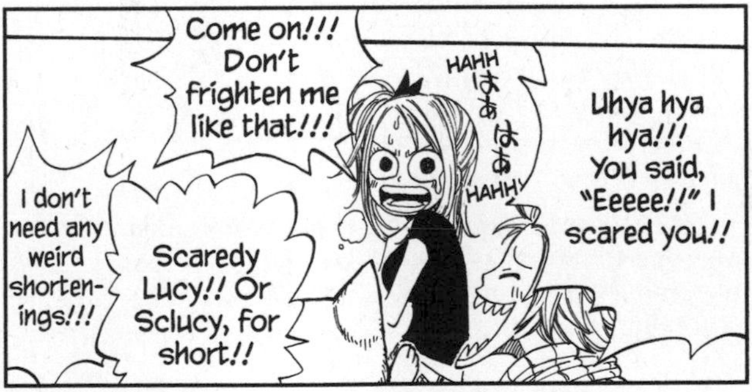
Uhya hya hya!!! You said, "Eeeee!!" I scared you!!
HAHH はあ はあ HAHH
Come on!!! Don't frighten me like that!!!
Scaredy Lucy!! Or Sclucy, for short!!
I don't need any weird shortenings!!!

Sclucy, page 109

In the Japanese version, Natsu's nickname for Lucy was a combination of the Japanese word for "scaredy cat" (*bibiri*), and the Japanese pronunciation of Lucy's name (*Rushii*), shortening it to *Birii*. The Japanese nickname wouldn't work very well with English-language readers, so it was changed to Sclucy, which would be a little more familiar.

Just call me Erza, page 134

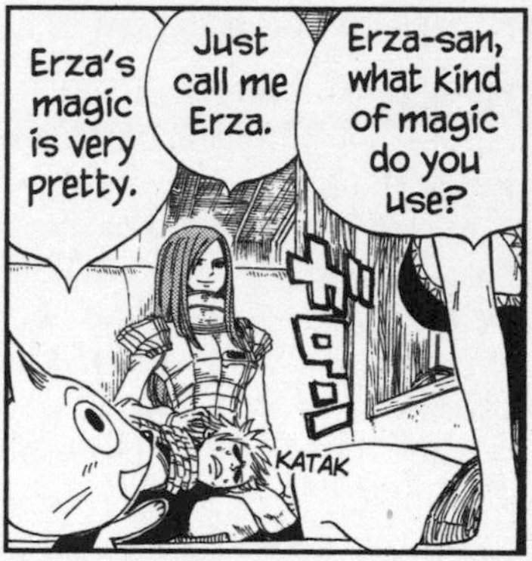
Erza-san, what kind of magic do you use?
Just call me Erza.
Erza's magic is very pretty.
KATAK

In this panel we have some of the workings of Japanese honorifics (see the list at the end of the book) in action. Erza is forgoing some of the niceties of the Japanese language, and telling Lucy that she doesn't need to add the *-san* honorific to Erza's name. There is a very similar English language situation. If you were to meet someone named Jonathan Smith, and you called him Mr. Smith, he might ask you to instead call him Jon. The feeling implied in "Call me Jon," in this situation is almost exactly the same as Erza's "Just call me Erza," in the manga.

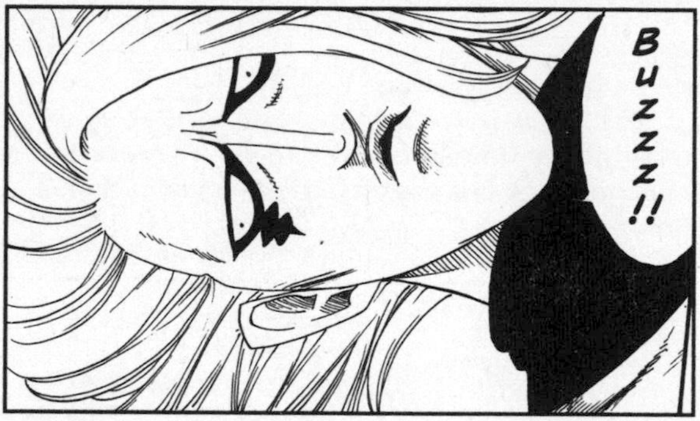
BUZZZ!!

Buzzz, page 179

As in America, TV game shows are very popular in Japan. And the ever-popular buzzer, to tell when time is up or when an answer is wrong, is also found on both sides of the Pacific. The buzz on this page is Erigor's way of saying that time is up for the members of Fairy Tail to make their guesses.

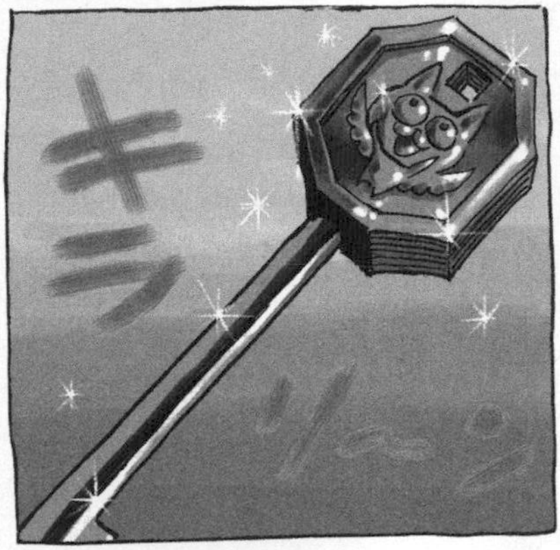
キラ

It's so much fun to come up with all the different kinds of magic...or at least it *should* be!! But aside from Natsu and Lucy, there are so many characters, and I have to think up different types of magic and abilities for each of them! That's what it means to build a world, and it's pretty rough work! Still, there are some very intricate backgrounds for the supporting characters, and someday I'd like to go into these in detail.

—Hiro Mashima

Honorifics Explained

Throughout the Kodansha Comics books, you will find Japanese honorifics left intact in the translations. For those not familiar with how the Japanese use honorifics and, more important, how they differ from honorifics in American English, we present this brief overview.

Politeness has always been a critical facet of Japanese culture. Ever since the feudal era, when Japan was a highly stratified society, use of honorifics—which can be defined as polite speech that indicates relationship or status—has played an essential role in the Japanese language. When addressing someone in Japanese, an honorific usually takes the form of a suffix attached to one's name (example: "Asuna-san"), is used as a title at the end of one's name, or appears in place of the name itself (example: "Negi-sensei," or simply "Sensei!").

Honorifics can be expressions of respect or endearment. In the context of manga and anime, honorifics give insight into the nature of the relationship between characters. Many English translations leave out these important honorifics and therefore distort the feel of the original Japanese. Because Japanese honorifics contain nuances that English honorifics lack, it is our policy at Kodansha not to translate them. Here, instead, is a guide to some of the honorifics you may encounter in Kodansha Comics.

-san: This is the most common honorific and is equivalent to Mr., Miss, Ms., or Mrs. It is the all-purpose honorific and can be used in any situation where politeness is required.

-sama: This is one level higher than "-san" and is used to confer great respect.

-dono: This comes from the word "tono," which means "lord." It is an even higher level than "-sama" and confers utmost respect.

-kun: This suffix is used at the end of boys' names to express familiarity or endearment. It is also sometimes used by men among friends, or when addressing someone younger or of a lower station.

-chan: This is used to express endearment, mostly toward girls. It is also used for little boys, pets, and even among lovers. It gives a sense of childish cuteness.

Bozu: This is an informal way to refer to a boy, similar to the English terms "kid" and "squirt."

Sempai/
Senpai: This title suggests that the addressee is one's senior in a group or organization. It is most often used in a school setting, where underclassmen refer to their upperclassmen as "sempai." It can also be used in the workplace, such as when a newer employee addresses an employee who has seniority in the company.

Kohai: This is the opposite of "sempai" and is used toward underclassmen in school or newcomers in the workplace. It connotes that the addressee is of a lower station.

Sensei: Literally meaning "one who has come before," this title is used for teachers, doctors, or masters of any profession or art.

-[blank]: This is usually forgotten in these lists, but it is perhaps the most significant difference between Japanese and English. The lack of honorific means that the speaker has permission to address the person in a very intimate way. Usually, only family, spouses, or very close friends have this kind of permission. Known as *yobisute*, it can be gratifying when someone who has earned the intimacy starts to call one by one's name without an honorific. But when that intimacy hasn't been earned, it can be very insulting.

Preview of Volume 3

We're pleased to present you with a preview from volume 3, now available from Kodansha Comics. Check out our Web site (www.kodanshacomics.com) for more details!

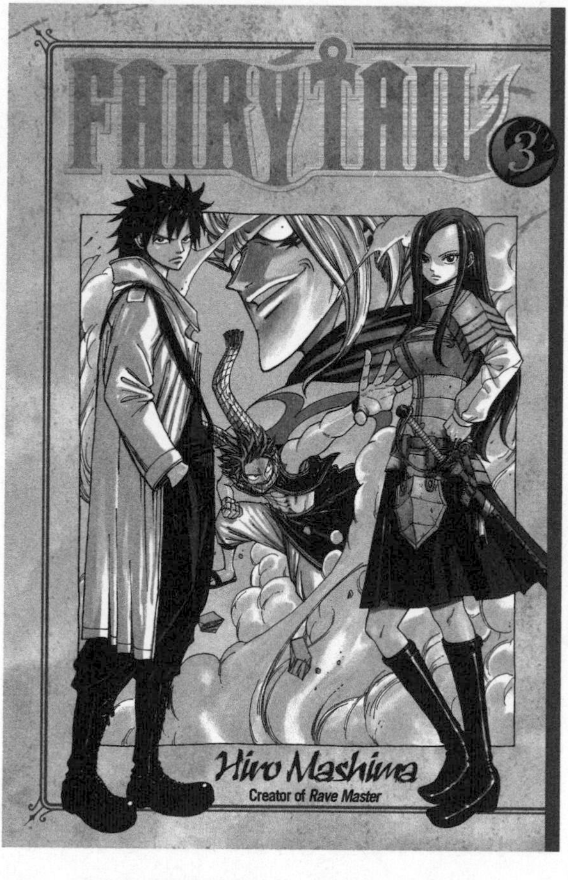
FAIRY TAIL
3
Hiro Mashima
Creator of Rave Master

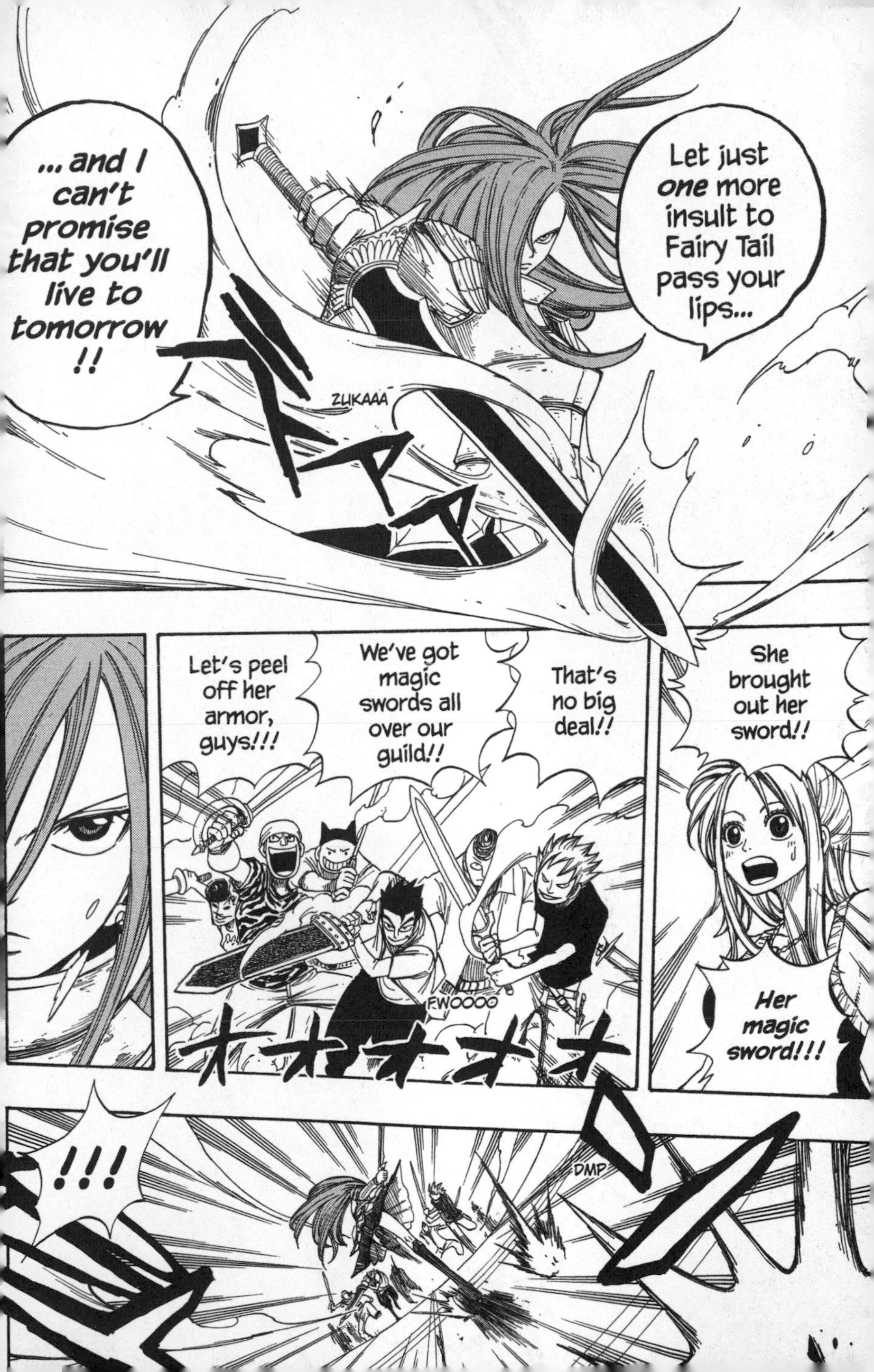
Let just *one* more insult to Fairy Tail pass your lips...
...and I can't promise that you'll live to tomorrow!!
ZUKAAA
She brought out her sword!!
Her magic sword!!!
That's no big deal!!
We've got magic swords all over our guild!!
Let's peel off her armor, guys!!!
FWOOOO
DMP
!!!

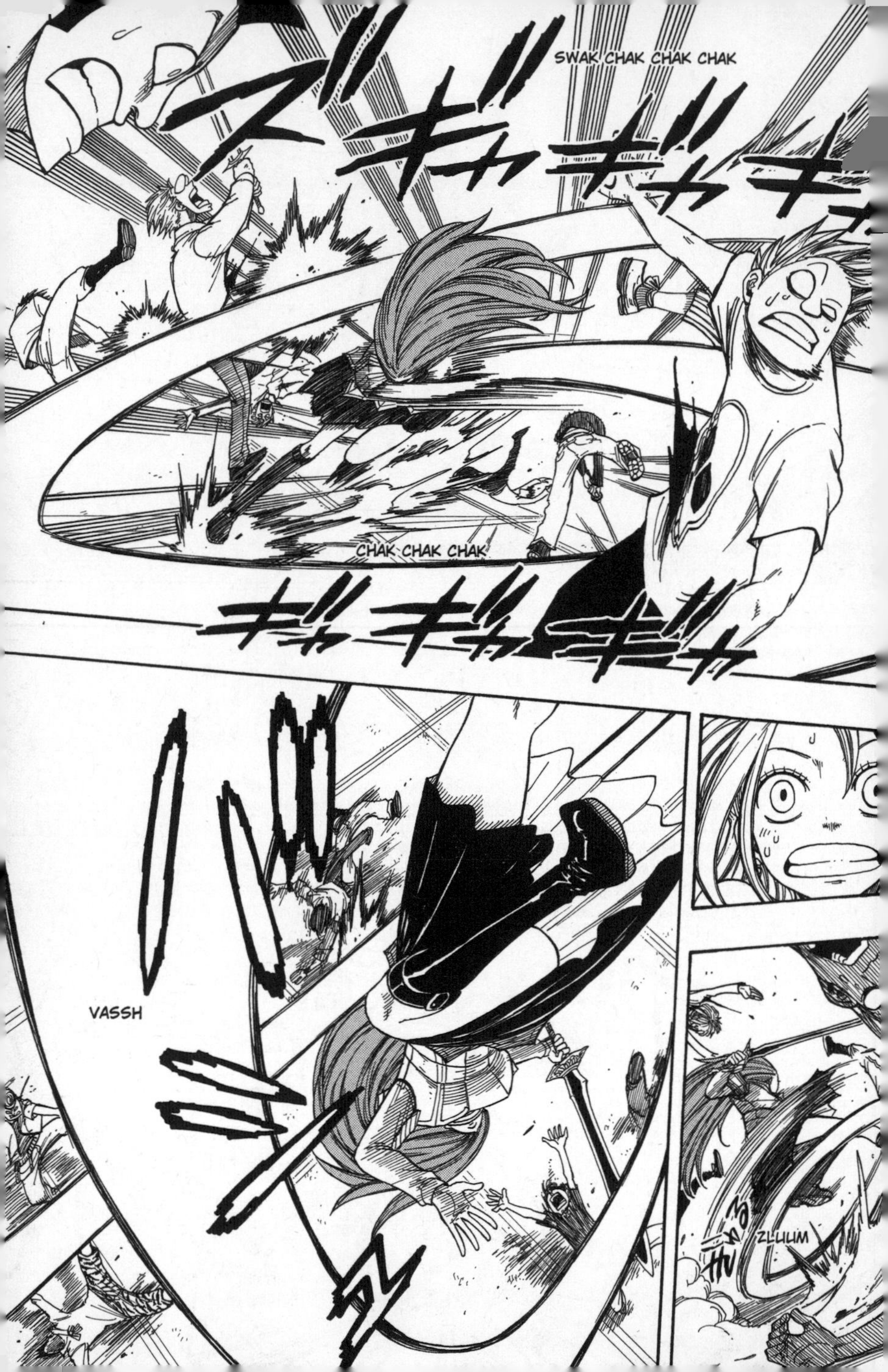
SWAK CHAK CHAK CHAK
CHAK CHAK CHAK
ZLLULM
VASSH

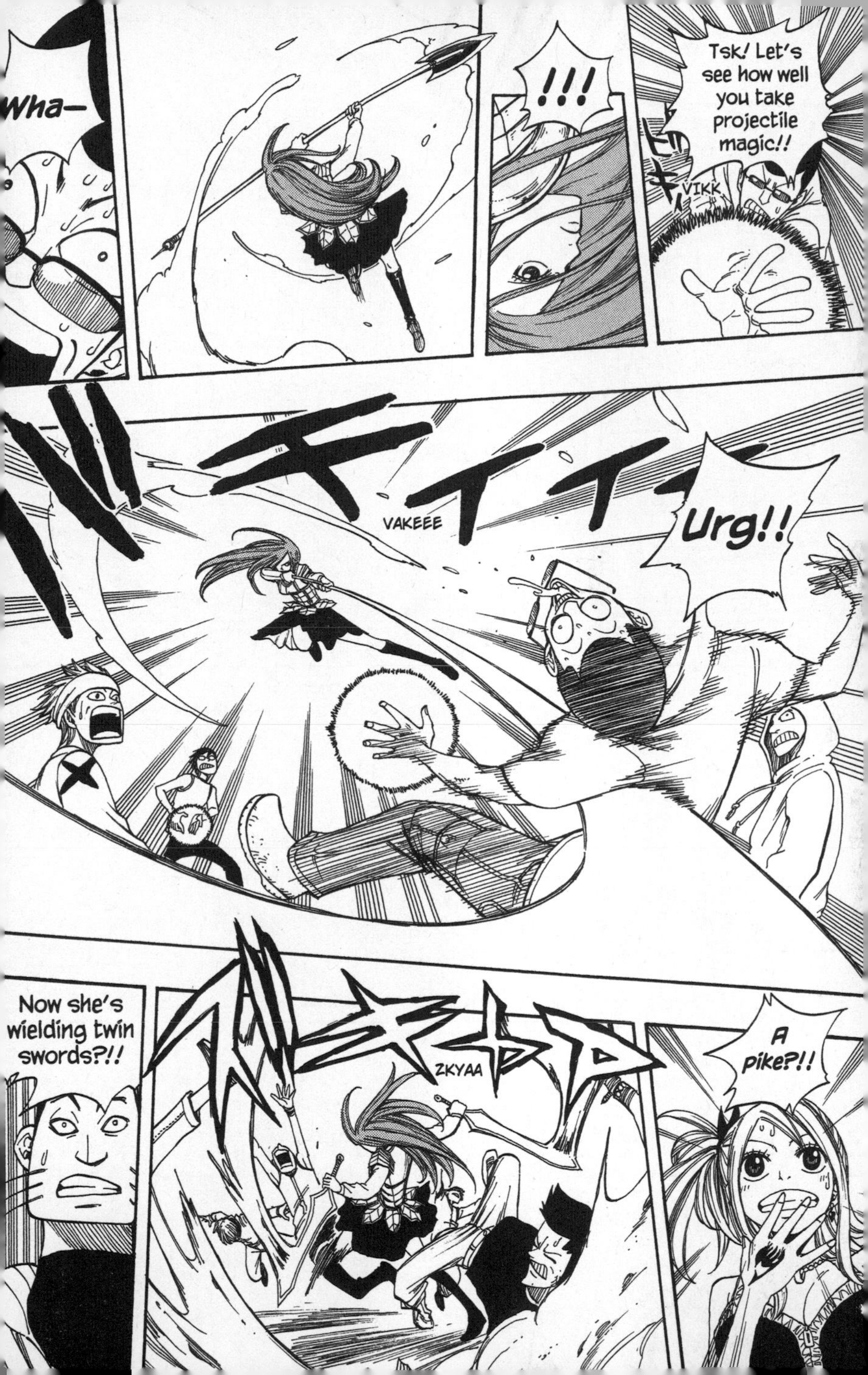
Tsk! Let's see how well you take projectile magic!!
VIKK
!!!
Wha—
Urg!!
VAKEEE
A pike?!!
ZKYAA
Now she's wielding twin swords?!!

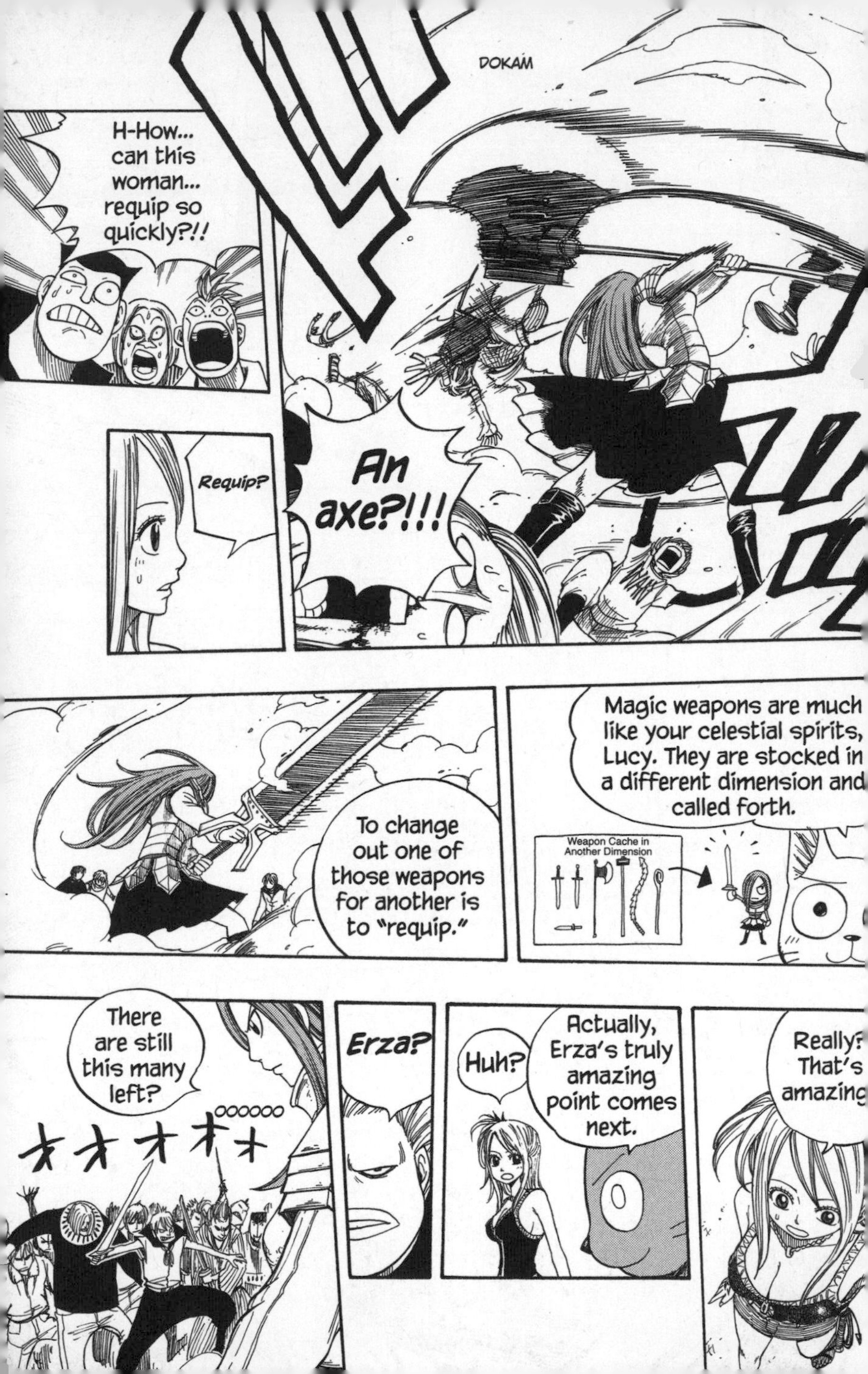

DOKAM
An axe?!!!
H-How... can this woman... requip so quickly?!!
Requip?
Magic weapons are much like your celestial spirits, Lucy. They are stocked in a different dimension and called forth.
Weapon Cache in Another Dimension
To change out one of those weapons for another is to "requip."
Really? That's amazing
Actually, Erza's truly amazing point comes next.
Huh?
Erza?
There are still this many left?
OOOOOO
オオオオオ

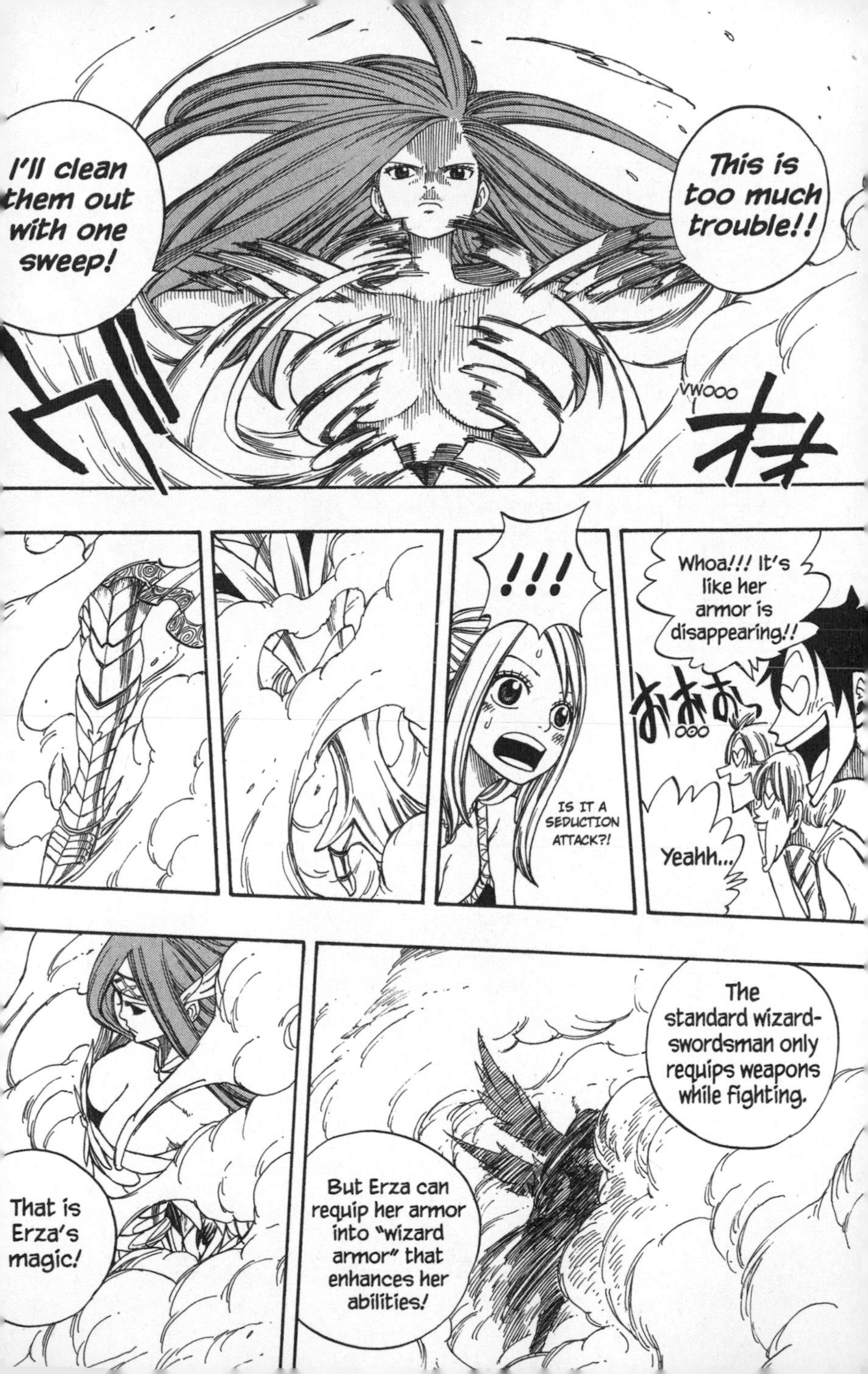
This is too much trouble!!
I'll clean them out with one sweep!
VWOOO
Whoa!!! It's like her armor is disappearing!!
Yeahh...
!!!
IS IT A SEDUCTION ATTACK?!
The standard wizard-swordsman only requips weapons while fighting.
But Erza can requip her armor into "wizard armor" that enhances her abilities!
That is Erza's magic!

A Kodansha Comics trade Paperback Original

Fairy Tail volume 2 copyright © 2007 by Hiro Mashima
English translation copyright © 2008 by Hiro Mashima

Published in the United States by Kodansha Comics, an imprint of Kodansha USA Publishing, LLC., New York.

Publication rights for this English edition arranged through Kodansha Ltd., Tokyo.

First published in Japan in 2007 by Kodansha Ltd., Tokyo

ISBN 978-1-612-62277-4

Printed in the United States of America

www.kodanshacomics.com

9   8   7

Translator/Adapter—William Flanagan
Lettering—North Market Street Graphics

TOMARE!

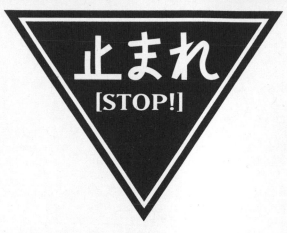

[STOP!]

You're going the wrong way!

Manga is a completely different type of reading experience.

To start at the *beginning*, go to the *end*!

That's right! Authentic manga is read the traditional Japanese way—from right to left, exactly the opposite of how American books are read. It's easy to follow: Just go to the other end of the book and read each page—and each panel—from right side to left side, starting at the top right. Now you're experiencing manga as it was meant to be!